Five Star Music Makeover

Five Star Music Makeover

The Independent Artist's Guide for Singers, Songwriters, Bands, Producers, and Self-Publishers

Coreen Sheehan
Anika Paris
Eric Corne
Michael Eames
Bobby Borg

Hal Leonard Books
An Imprint of Hal Leonard Corporation

Published in 2016 by Hal Leonard Books
An Imprint of Hal Leonard Corporation
7777 West Bluemound Road
Milwaukee, WI 53213

Trade Book Division Editorial Offices
33 Plymouth St., Montclair, NJ 07042

Lyrics from "Box You Up" used by permission of Natania Lalwani. Lyrics from "So So Bad" used by permission of Everett Coast (Danny Byrnes and Josh Misko). Lyrics from "Dark Night" used by permission of GSavage.

Printed in the United States of America

Book design by Kristina Rolander

Library of Congress Cataloging-in-Publication Data
Names: Sheehan, Coreen. | Paris, Anika. | Corne, Eric, 1970- | Eames, Michael, 1967- | Borg, Bobby.
Title: Five star music makeover : an independent artist's guide for singers, songwriters, bands, producers, and self-publishers / Coreen Sheehan, Anika Paris, Eric Corne, Michael Eames, Bobby Borg.
Description: Montclair, NJ : Hal Leonard Books, 2016. | Includes index.
Identifiers: LCCN 2016002864 | ISBN 9781495021756
Subjects: LCSH: Popular music--Vocational guidance. | Popular music--Writing and publishing--Vocational guidance | Singing--Vocational guidance.
Classification: LCC ML3795 .F5465 2016 | DDC 780.23--dc23
LC record available at http://lccn.loc.gov/2016002864

ISBN 978-1-4950-2175-6

www.halleonardbooks.com

Contents

Preface

Welcome, Singers, Songwriters, Producers, Artists, and Bands

Music is your life. You hear it streaming over the Web, thumping from car stereos, blasting at music festivals, and playing in stores and restaurants, and on television shows and films. You watch your favorite artists performing on video channels and you read about them winning awards. You feel that you have the raw talent to make it, and now it's your time to be seen and heard! But with the overwhelming amount of information and services available to you in an oversaturated marketplace, where and how should you get started with your music career? You've come to the right place!

How This Book Can Help You

Five Star Music Makeover is the collaboration of five industry professionals who have over 100 years of collective experience. The book cuts to the chase and provides aspiring artists with practical advice that would otherwise cost several years of personal experience and/or thousands of dollars in coaching and producer fees. In a digital age that allows musicians to act as their own record companies, create their own buzz, and create favorable industry alliances, there has never been a better time for an all-in-one book that tackles the important skills that musicians need to succeed.

What This Book Covers

While there are numerous factors that contribute to the success of an artist's career, *Five Star Music Makeover* focuses on five important concepts:

- **Singing:** A key element to the success of any artist or band is the unique and quality performance of the vocalist. Being a great vocalist requires countless hours of training and an understanding of how to build muscle memory for a controlled vocal production, increase vocal stamina, consistently deliver a stellar performance, maintain physical health while touring, and much more.
- **Songwriting:** We all want to write that song millions will soon know by heart. But how do we take our musical inspirations and turn them into something memorable? To achieve longevity in the music industry, your original songs need to stand out above the rest. As a creative artist, your signature sound and style are imperative for survival. And, if you are part of a writing/production team, you have to be ahead of the curve to get noticed in the flooded marketplace. This section will delve into the intricacies of songwriting and help you discover ways to continually tap into your creative muse.

- **Recording:** To succeed in the music industry today, independent artists require a combination of artistic and technical skills. So, whether you utilize new technologies or vintage equipment, capture your music on home recording gear or collaborate with a professional producer, always strive to produce music that showcases your strengths as an artist, at a professional level.
- **Publishing:** Music publishing is the business of songs—and your songs (a.k.a. your copyrights) are perhaps one of the most valuable assets that you'll ever own. A song can go on to live and generate money long after your career is over, and even long past your time on the face of this earth. Music publishing is an area where fortunes have been both lost and found. In this section, you'll learn how to make it a cornerstone of your career.
- **Promoting:** Promotion, or, as some say, "getting your music out there," involves much more than just building a website and updating the latest social networking sites. It requires a deeper understanding of your target audience, your unique selling points, and your competitive advantage in the music marketplace. Make no mistake, promotion is not just about *doing things right*; it is about *doing the right things* and getting measurable results that take you to that next level of your career.

How This Book Is Unique

No other book in the marketplace today provides the collective wisdom of five music industry professionals discussing five key skills needed to succeed. Additionally, this book provides insiders' stories and anecdotes, helpful tips, creative exercises, celebrity interviews, links to online media and author interviews, and all the practical expertise necessary to advance your music career. In a digital age where the web is overflowing with free and often misleading advice, *Five Star Music Makeover* is a complete and practical career guide, a resource that transforms artists from good to great.

Who Are the Authors?

Five Star Music Makeover features five authors on five specific areas of the music business:

- **Coreen Sheehan** (Part 1: Singing) is a three-time winner of LA's Best Rock Vocalist Award, a music consultant for the series *You Rock* (VH1), and a nominee for the Grammy Music Educator Award in 2013 and 2014. She has toured and recorded with artists worldwide, sharing the stage with David Lee Roth and the Foo Fighters. Her work can also be seen (and heard) in TV commercials in the U.S., Germany, Japan (MTV), and South Korea. Coreen is the author of *Rock Vocals* and has written curricula for several music schools in Japan and for Musicians Institute, where she has won the Vocal Instructor of the Year Award and Curricular Appreciation Award. With more than twenty years of industry experience, she instructs and guest lectures at M.I., M.I. Japan, the Grammy Museum, UCLA and UCLA Extension, and more. Coreen resides in Los Angeles, California. For more information, please visit her website at www.coreensheehan.net.

- **Anika Paris** (Part 2: Songwriting) is a CRIA (Canadian Recording Industry Association) double platinum award-winning singer/songwriter, recipient of ASCAP's Abe Oleman Scholarship, and an HOLA Award Winner for outstanding music in a musical. As a poet, she was nominated for the International Latin Poetry Award for her book *Woven Voices* (Scapegoat Press), and is the author of *Making Your Mark in Music: Stage Performance Secrets* (Hal Leonard). Her songs can be heard in major motion pictures with Miramax, Lionsgate, and Universal. A classically trained pianist, she composes for Warner Bros Telepictures, Multistages, and the League of Professional Theatre Women. She has recorded three solo CDs and toured the world performing with Stevie Wonder, John Legend, and John Mayer. With over twenty-five years of experience on and off the stage, she is an adjunct professor at Musicians Institute and UCLA Extension and guest lectures at the Grammy Museum and USC. She splits her time between New York and California and resides in Los Angeles. For more information visit www.anikaparismusic.com.
- **Eric Corne** (Part 3: Producing) is a Canadian producer, engineer, and singer/songwriter currently based in Los Angeles. Eric's recording credits include John Mayall, Glen Campbell, Lucinda Williams, Walter Trout, Joe Bonamassa, Jeff Healy, Michelle Shocked, DeVotchKa, Airto Moreira (Joni Mitchell), Clem Burke (Blondie), Nancy Wilson (Heart), John Doe (X), Joanna Wang and Kim Deal (the Pixies). In addition, Eric has written or recorded music for film, television, and video games, including HBO's *True Blood, Crazy Stupid Love*, and trailers for Sony's *Resistance 2*, and *Underworld 2*. Eric was head engineer at Dusty Wakeman's iconic Mad Dog Studios for years, before striking out on his own and founding Forty Below Records. The label is distributed by SONY/RED in North America and Proper Music Group in the UK and Europe. For more information, please see ericcornemusic.com and fortybelowrecords.com.
- **Michael Eames** (Part 4: Publishing) is a trained composer, songwriter, and pianist with experience in film scoring who studied at Cornell University and UCLA Extension. As president of PEN Music Group, Inc. (www.penmusic.com), Michael oversees all aspects of the operation, with a focus on pitching the catalogue to all media and business development. PEN currently represents Don Felder (formerly of the Eagles), John Farrar (Olivia Newton-John's longtime producer), Olivia Newton-John herself, Brian Eno, and Donny Markowitz (Oscar-winner for "(I've Had) The Time of My Life" from *Dirty Dancing*), among numerous others. Prior to starting PEN, Michael oversaw the international activities and Film/TV department of Don Williams Music Group, where he was responsible for song catalogues such as Jimi Hendrix, Chicago, and Roy Orbison. He has also worked with the catalogue of Brian Wilson of the Beach Boys and the management and music supervision firm The Derek Power Company. As of January 2015 Michael is the president of the nationwide Association of Independent Music Publishers (AIMP) and is also a member of the California Copyright Conference (CCC) and the National Academy of Recording Arts and Sciences (NARAS).
- **Bobby Borg** (Part 5: Promoting) is a former major label, independent, and DIY recording/touring artist with over twenty-five years' experience working alongside the most respected managers, producers, and A&R executives in the music industry. He served as the vice president of special events for the Los Angeles chapter of the American Marketing Association

and as chairman of music business at Musicians Institute in Hollywood, California. A recipient of UCLA Extension's Distinguished Instructor of the Year Award, Borg teaches DIY music marketing, music publishing, and general music business classes both online and on campus, and speaks regularly at Berklee College of Music and other distinguished schools worldwide. Borg is the author of *Music Marketing for the DIY Musician*, *Business Basics for Musicians*, and over 1,000 magazine and blog articles for Billboard.com, Hypebot, SonicBids, Music Connection, Disc Makers, Band Zoogle, and more. He is the founder of Bobby Borg Consulting, where he assists an international client base of rising music professionals. He lives in Los Angeles. For more information, please see www.bobbyborg.com.

How Should You Use This Book?

The best way to read this book is from cover to cover. However, *Five Star Music Makeover* is designed so that each of the five sections stands alone, allowing you to quickly find the specific advice you need.

Want to Stay Connected?

To read more about the authors and the topics covered in this book:

www.coreensheehan.net
www.anikaparismusic.com
www.ericcornemusic.com
www.penmusic.com
www.bobbyborg.com
www.fivestarmusicmakeover.com

That's about all. Good luck and let's get started.

Acknowledgments

Coreen Sheehan: I would like to thank my husband, Ben Avesani, for his love and support and for always giving me the inspiration to be my best. I would also like to thank my father, Grant Sheehan, whose influence and guidance helped me to become the vocalist, musician, and performer I am today. Special thanks go out to those who graciously offered their testimonials and to those directly involved in Part 1 of this book, including Marianne Sheehan, Grant Sheehan Jr., Natalie Bopp and Bopp Photography, Christian (Vixen) Klikovits, Doug Woods, Lorca Peress, Dan Kimpel, Debra Byrd, Donny Greundler, Beth Marlis, Whole Lotta Rosies, Trudi Keck, Osaka School of Music, Musicians Institute, clients, students, and other music institutions around the world. My mentors Terry Carter and Brad Divens from Wrathchild America. Thanks for showing me the ropes! Many thanks to John Cerullo for believing in this project, to Bernadette Malavarca, Jessica Burr, and the entire Hal Leonard Performing Artists Publishing Group family, and to my fellow authors of this book, Anika Paris, Bobby Borg, Eric Corne, and Michael Eames, who have dedicated their time and expertise to make my vision of this project become a reality.

Anika Paris: I would like to thank all of you who helped me with the making of this book. I would like thank Dean Landon, my songwriting partner in life, for your love and support and for giving me the inspiration to be a better person each and every day. My heartfelt thanks to Gloria Vando and Maurice Peress for your educational wisdom, guidance, and continued support. Thanks especially to John Cerullo for your belief in this book, to editors Bernadette Malavarca and Zahra Brown for their hard work, and to Jessica Burr and everyone at Hal Leonard Performing Arts Publishing Group. To the songwriting contributors, Danny Byrne, Josh Misko, Natania Lalwani, and Dionte Flemonz, for your participation and lyrical contributions. To Allan Rich and Lindy Robbins, for your interviews about the world of songwriting. Thanks to all of my music industry colleagues, students, and artists, and to UCLA Extension, Musicians Institute, and the Grammy Museum for their continued support. I would like to thank Beth Marlis, Donny Gruendler, Don Grierson, Ron Dziubla, and Dan Kimpel for championing me. Special thanks to Coreen Sheehan for asking me to be part of this project, and to all the other Five Star authors, Bobby Borg, Eric Corne, and Michael Eames, for your insight, knowledge, and collaborative spirit. Lastly to my late grandmother Anita Velez-Mitchell, whose song will never end.

Eric Corne: I would like to thank my beautiful wife, Aimee, and wonderful children, Ira and Lilly, for all of their love, support and inspiration; my fantastic parents and siblings; my right-hand man, Ben Loshin, for the great work on this book, with the label, and in the studio; Dusty Wakeman, for giving me the opportunity to be his engineer at Mad Dog Studios; Greg Panciera, for recruiting me to teach at the Musicians Institute; the great engineers I learned from—Eddie Kramer, David Bianco, Krisjan Leslie, Dusty; blues legends John Mayall and Walter Trout—it continues to be an honor and a thrill; Marie Trout; Mark Chalecki; Kenny Aronoff; Taras Prodaniuk; Jeffrey Wolman; Anthony Wolch at Engagement Labs; all my musician and artist mates—I love you guys and couldn't do it without you; everyone at Hal Leonard, especially John Cerullo, Bernadette Malavarca, and Jessica Burr; Samur Khouja, Brian Arbuckle, David Wykoff, Universal Audio,

Apple Logic, Avid, and The Musician's Institute; as well as my exceptional co-writers on this book, Anika Paris, Coreen Sheehan, Bobby Borg, and Michael Eames.

Michael Eames: I would like to thank my amazing wife, Monica Rizzo, and son, Matthew Eames, for their unconditional love and support and for giving me the inspiration every day to bring my best and be my best. I would also like to thank the entire staff and all clients of PEN Music Group, Inc., who give me the energy and desire on a daily basis to fight the good fight in the ever challenging world of independent music publishing. Many thanks to my mentors Don Willams, Lionel Conway, and Neil Gillis, among many others. Thanks also to Michael Closter, whose referral to Anika Paris resulted in my being involved with this book, and then unending thanks to my fellow authors, Anika Paris, Coreen Sheehan, Bobby Borg, and Eric Corne, with whom it is an honor to be sharing the written word. Many thanks last but certainly not least to John Cerullo, Bernadette Malavarca, Jessica Burr, and the entire Hal Leonard Performing Artists Publishing Group family for bringing me into the fold and showing me how it's done.

Bobby Borg: I would like to thank my family, closest friends, and God. I would like to also send a shout-out to the *Five Star Music Makeover* crew and all those related directly to the creation of Part 5 of this book including my business advisors, business associates and partners, guest speakers at UCLA, proofreaders, professors, clients, students, and associates at major institutions around the world (particularly UCLA Extension, Musicians Institute, and Berklee College of Music where my books and writings are used). A special thanks to those who graciously offered their testimonials, those who provided the rights to use their graphics (Todd Chency, Jessica Rottschafer, Loren Barnese, Sabrina Petrini, and Tania Pryor at PlasticPrinters.com), and everyone at Hal Leonard Performing Arts Publishing Group (especially John Cerullo for believing in the project, Jessica Burr for dealing so well with editorial and other matters, and Wes Seeley for handling publicity). To the readers of this book: Thanks in advance for inviting me to all your parties after achieving your goals. Cheers and best wishes for a successful career.

Part 1

The Voice

With

Coreen Sheehan

Introduction

Most people believe that you must be born with a *gift* to become a professional singer. I believe anyone can develop his or her voice in order to sing. Yes, there are singers born with a gift and natural talent, and others who have to work hard to be just as good. But a gift for singing isn't all that it takes to have a successful music career. For example, you may not be naturally blessed with stamina, great stage presence, original material, or knowledge of how to record and market your songs and get them heard! Most singers need to improve all of these areas to compete in today's industry. Still, whether you are a lead singer or a background singer, you can always start by improving your vocal abilities with training.

Musicians who play an instrument, usually guitar or piano, often believe singing is easily learned, or can be mastered using the same approach they brought to instrumental technique. Many don't realize that the vocal development takes considerable patience and time. For example, while guitarists can practice for hours and hours if they want to, singers should not do this, especially at the beginning of their training. Why not? Because the voice is a physical part of the human body, and has to be trained in short intervals in the beginning, allowing the vocal cords to strengthen properly. Doing this correctly helps avoid vocal burnout and fatigue, or, in the worst-case scenario, physical damage. Over time, singers can begin to lengthen their practice time by applying the proper technique. A regimented practice allows the vocal mechanisms to strengthen and naturally build stamina. In this way, your singing voice can be what it should always be: a natural extension of your speaking voice that comes easily and is never forced.

In Part 1 of this book, we will address getting over fear and other mental obstacles, the vocal mechanisms, breathing, vocal registers, and exercises targeting the falsetto, chest, and mixed voice. In addition, we will learn about vocal stamina, strengthening and control, vowel placement and resonance, how to break down a song, the emotions behind the voice, maintenance tips for a healthy voice, and warning signs of vocal abuse. Get ready to sing!

1 Emerge, Thrive, and Conquer

Moving Forward

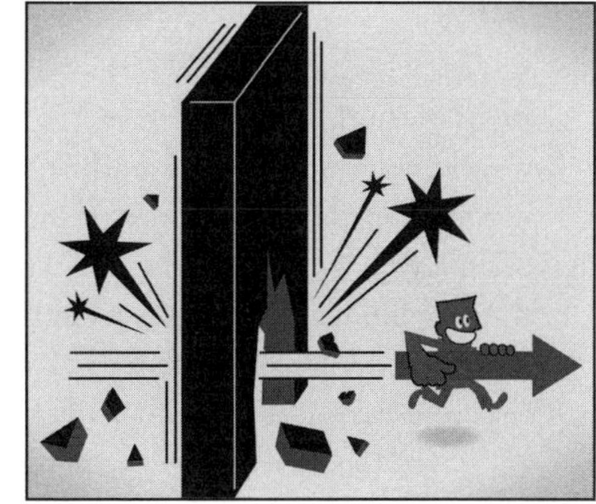

"Emerge," "thrive," and "conquer" are three powerful words that describe your progress through the five chapters and the ten exercises in this section of the book. This chapter will start you moving forward by asking, "What kind of singer do you want to be?," addressing the "fear factor," and creating a mindset that will prepare you to get the most out of chapters 2, 3, 4, and 5.

What Kind of Singer Do You Want to Be?

- Lead vocalist of a band
- Background vocalist
- Singer-songwriter

A singer's job varies depending on his or her role. A *lead vocalist* fronts a band, performing the main melody of songs, no matter who wrote them. A *singer-songwriter* performs original material and provides his or her own accompaniment. A *background vocalist* sings harmony with the lead vocals. A group of *background vocalists* can function as their own section of the band, or that job may fall to guitarists, bassists, keyboardists, drummers, or any other instrumentalists in the band. But, no matter what your role is, you should learn the essentials in order to sing consistently. This means learning about vocal production, vocal strengthening, vocal control, and vocal stamina.

If you are a lead vocalist or a background vocalist, you need to know how to produce the best-sounding voice possible. If you are a songwriter who doesn't sing, you can hire an outside singer and producer to record your material. This way your songs can be shopped to well-known artists or licensed in a movie or television show. You can learn more about how to do this in the next sections of this book: Songwriting, Recording, Publishing, and Marketing. If you do want to sing, this is the place to begin your journey and develop your voice.

The Fear Factor

Singing comes easily to some people but is more challenging to others. Most everyone can sing to some extent. Some vocalists began singing in church, at school, or simply around the house as kids. I bet you sang when you were a child and never worried about how you sounded. You just sang your heart out!

When I was nine years old, I sang for hours and hours in my bedroom. I would practice tons of songs ranging in style from Journey, to Barry Manilow, to Donna Summer, to Ozzy Osbourne. Once I felt confident with the songs, I had the urge to perform them. My parents and neighbors sat out on the front lawn with their lawn chairs and drinks and waited for my show. Upstairs in my bedroom, I connected my Mr. Microphone to my alarm clock radio, propped it up in my window with the speaker facing down to my audience, and from there sang song after song. I felt like a superstar, performing from my second-floor window as the applause and screams came from the front lawn below up to my bedroom stage. An incredible rush of excitement overcame me that lasted long after each show. I couldn't wait to perform again and again. I was 100 percent hooked, and I knew this was what I wanted to do for the rest of my life! I had no fear whatsoever as a child singing and performing—not until I reached the age of fourteen and I joined my first band.

The band's name was Anthem and we began gigging all over Maryland. All the band members were much older than I was, from eighteen to twenty-three years old. After a few months, we were playing in other states along the East Coast. I know what you're thinking—I was only fourteen years old; how did I do this? Well, I simply told my parents I was at a school friend's slumber party when I was gigging in another state. Yep, I know! What a terrible, crazy thing to do! I positively do not advise any youngster to do this! At that time, all I knew was that I *had* to sing and perform. I needed to *gig*!

About the same time I began gigging I became acquainted with the uncomfortable feeling of *fear*. Out of nowhere, I was suddenly worried about what other people thought about my singing and how I looked when performing onstage. I felt afraid before, during, and after our shows, and I had no idea why. I felt this way for a long time, until one day a light bulb went off in my head. I realized that I felt this way because I wanted everyone to like me. I wanted to be taken seriously as a singer, as a performer, and as a musician. I wanted to appear professional in eyes of the audience, promoters, other bands, and the musicians in my band. And I needed to advance my skills as a singer/performer in order to become the musician I wanted to be. At fourteen, I could not attend a music college yet. I bought books and studied singing and styles of music—anything I could get my hands on—wanting to learn as much as possible.

I took private voice lessons and sang in the school choir. I also asked a few lead vocalists I respected from local bands to mentor me. They showed me the ropes and helped me improve my skills. Learning from all of these resources allowed me to grow and become serious about my career path. My mentors helped me set realistic goals for myself as a professional singer, performer, and musician. I realized how I could grow and learn with every experience and could continually test my abilities without fear. Since then, the love of music has always pushed me to work hard and be the best that I can be.

For more than twenty years now, as a vocal coach and music instructor, I have mentored thousands of students—most of whom held on to fear in some way, shape, or form. What about you? What are you afraid of with regard to your voice? Understanding the reason fear is affecting you is the secret to overcoming this roadblock. I've heard several answers to this question, but the top three responses are:

- I don't like the sound of my voice.
- My voice sounds uncontrolled.
- I'm not sure if I can improve my voice.

To overcome fear you must first understand why you feel this way. Having defined our fears more clearly, we can see that each of them has a solution. Once you begin to understand how to use your voice correctly, you will hear improvement with the sound of your voice. Developing your technique will enhance your skills and bring forth the vocal control you seek. And once you have vocal control, your self-confidence will grow!

Creating a Mindset

The first step toward learning about the mechanics of the voice is to become aware of how the vocal mechanism works as a whole—how the parts function *together*. You must understand the theory before you can execute it in practice. At first, this approach may seem a little clinical and technical, but it will lay a solid foundation that is essential before you physically attempt to execute the technique.

> ***YOU MAY BE ABLE TO FAKE YOUR WAY THROUGH CERTAIN THINGS IN LIFE ON THE STRENGTH OF YOUR NATURAL TALENT ALONE, BUT YOU CANNOT TRULY CONQUER SOMETHING UNLESS YOU FIRST GENUINELY UNDERSTAND HOW IT WORKS. VOCAL TECHNIQUE IS NO EXCEPTION TO THIS RULE.***

Let's say that you want to get into better shape, so you decide to start going to the gym. You begin to work out on your own in the hope that you're going to get fit as quickly as possible. Of course, by simply lifting the weights, you will probably see some success from this unsystematic approach. Now let's consider a *systematic* approach, in which you determine what muscles need to be isolated and worked on. With guidance, you can better plan how you are going to get fit by using the correct equipment, the proper weights, and a safe but challenging number of repetitions. Determining what you need to focus on and how you will apply that focus during each workout will help you to reach your fitness goal much more efficiently and with greater results. No time is wasted exercising the wrong muscles with the wrong exercises in the wrong order with the wrong weight for the wrong number of repetitions.

Just as in weight lifting, understanding how our bodies produce sound before physically attempting to employ the requisite vocal techniques will keep you from wasting time on incorrect (and often potentially damaging) efforts. This theory-to-practice approach can help you develop a quality technique, move past common vocal roadblocks, and achieve greater success in your vocals.

Many vocalists are concerned that learning a new technique will change their voice—a voice that they have already become accustomed to. The correct application of vocal technique will enhance the good qualities already present in your voice. You will learn to strengthen and control your vocal output, which will help you to delve deeper into the tonal qualities of your unique voice, the voice that you know and love. And, if you are a beginning vocalist, you will be genuinely surprised at how quickly your voice develops once you start to employ these vocal production techniques.

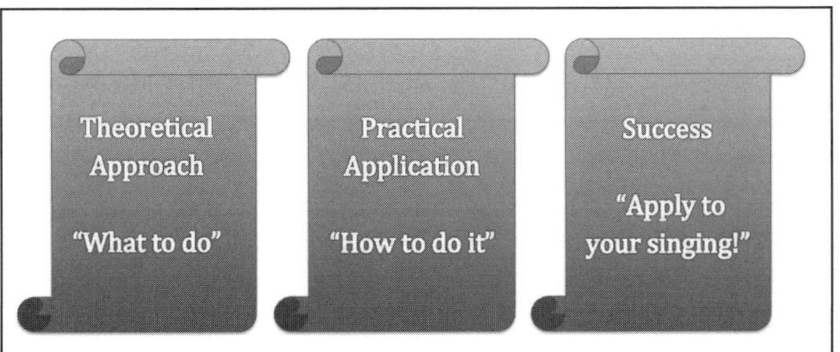

As we have discussed, the first step in good vocal production is to identify and understand what areas need focus. Next come *practice* and *perseverance*. Unfortunately, there's no magic wand for these two elements; your improvement is directly proportional to your focus, determination, execution, and time invested. You may want to be a better vocalist, but the desire alone is not going to make that wish a reality—you have to put the work in, too.

Set aside time to practice at home and reread this section on the voice in your spare time. The more work you put in, the greater results you will see in the long run.

Some of the vocal exercises may seem alien at first, but keep an open mind and allow yourself to "let go." Explore these new methods and you'll soon hear the results as my students have. For example, you might be exercising with some odd sounds—sounds that you are not accustomed to hearing come out of your mouth—in order to get the vocal cords to stretch properly, or to achieve good resonance in an area that needs to be developed. Although a little strange at first, such exercises build muscle memory and allow you to safely achieve sounds you may not have known existed. Such exercises are of huge importance to the development of your voice. Don't let yourself be the biggest roadblock in mastering your vocal production.

Another common question is: "How can I apply this vocal technique to my songs?" The answer is simple: you can't, not at first. Improving the voice doesn't happen overnight. Remember, there is no magic wand. At this point in your journey, you should sing just as you feel comfortable doing, as you have always done. As you start to understand the theory of vocal production, and as you start to attempt the physical execution of that theory, good techniques will slowly begin to take shape in your vocals. You will begin to notice subtle changes in your voice, such as feeling "freer" or able to hit or sustain certain notes more easily than before. Once these baby steps have been taken, you will be able to employ the techniques with more power, focus, and depth; you will be on your way to mastering vocal production!

2 The Foundation of Voice Development

A Consistent Vocalist = A Professional Vocalist

Being a consistent vocalist is important because every performance has the potential to impact your career. If your audience likes you, they'll leave your performance and speak highly to their friends about your show. Hopefully the next time you perform you'll have more bodies in your audience due to word of mouth. But this works the other way as well; if you're having a bad night, people may leave your show and recommend that friends not waste their money going to hear your band. After all, you want the club to have you back again! Word of mouth is powerful advertisement, good or bad, especially at the beginning of your music career. The comments that audiences, musicians, or production staff make can either help or hurt the possibility of you playing out or working with other professionals in the music industry.

If you're lucky enough to be performing in a major city like New York, Nashville, or Los Angeles, the chances are greater that an industry professional will be at your show. Even in smaller cities, you never know who is in your audience or listening to your demo that you've been distributing.

Your performance could be reaching the eyes and ears of

- Record label A&R (short for "artists and repertoire")
- Band managers
- Promoters
- Famous musicians
- Producers
- Actors
- TV personalities

Any one of these professionals could be looking for a new artist to work with or to fill a spot as an opening act for a concert. Sometimes famous musicians will come to a show, then speak to the band's manager and ask to have the band open for them to launch their new CD. I know because it happened to a band that I sing lead vocals for (Whole Lotta Rosies). We all had a blast opening for the Foo Fighters in front of a sold-out audience on the band's Echoes, Silence, Patience & Grace tour. (By the way, the Foo Fighters are extremely cool guys as well!)

Another time, a famous band manager called to tell me that he loved the songs from a demo CD that he had picked up from a friend. He said he had seen a flyer on Sunset Strip for our show at the Cat Club and wanted to drop in and listen to our band. At the club he introduced himself, stayed for the whole show, and told us he loved it and would be in touch about booking us for an upcoming show. Two weeks later, on New Year's Eve, my band (Hottie Knockers) opened for the David Lee Roth Band in front of a sold-out audience at the House of Blues on Sunset Boulevard in West Hollywood. Both the Foo Fighters and David Lee Roth shows sparked interest with promoters, band managers, musicians, and celebrities. As a result, both bands managed to book higher-profile shows and make some money. The consistency in the band's performance and especially the vocals are what got us the gigs. The managers wanted to know that we could deliver a great performance night after night after night.

Being heard and seen in the right place at the right time has led to countless success stories like these. This is why it is extremely important that you should never dip below 90% of your professional level. What this means is, when it's been a rough day for you no one should be able to tell you're having an "off" day.

Being a band's lead vocalist automatically places more responsibility upon you than the rest of the members. When you're a lead vocalist, you are in the spotlight, and everyone's attention is focused on you. Everything you sing, say, and do while interacting with the audience is under scrutiny. To appear professional and compete in the music industry, a lead vocalist must be in control and confident in his or her voice at all times.

When do we begin to feel more confident, secure, and able to function at a consistent, professional level? First you'll need to understand some basics, starting with the internal mechanisms of the voice!

The Mechanisms of the Voice

Understanding the physical mechanisms involved in vocal production and how these mechanisms work together provides a solid theoretical foundation upon which you can later build a strong and functional vocal skill-set. Let's quickly dive into some anatomy.

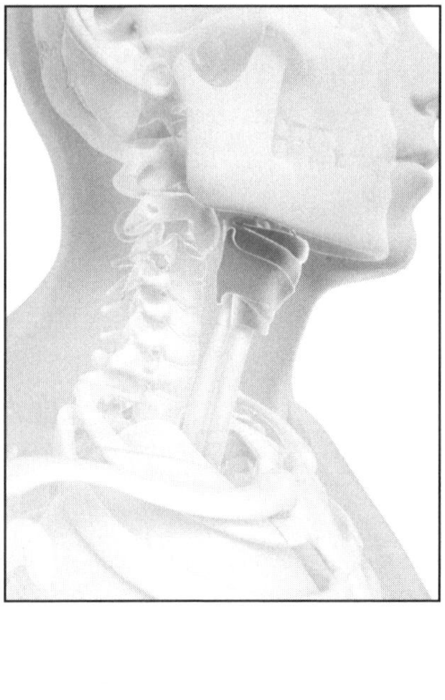

The Larynx

The larynx (commonly referred to as the "voice box") is the most important organ for vocalization. The larynx is a hollow organ in the throat made of cartilage that houses the vocal folds.

The Vocal Cords

The vocal cords (or "true vocal folds," as they are often called in medical terms) consist of two sharp-edged folds of mucous membrane, slightly shorter than one inch in length. They run parallel to each other (side by side) from the front to the back of the larynx. When exhaled air passes through the larynx, the edges of the vocal cords vibrate to produce sound.

Laryngeal Cartilages and Muscles

There are nine cartilaginous structures within the larynx that serve various functions. They range from allowing movement, to preventing foreign bodies from entering the lungs, to giving other parts of the larynx a place to attach themselves to perform their functions effectively. For the purposes of vocal production, we will focus on the most relevant of these cartilages.

Thyroid Cartilage

The largest of the laryngeal cartilages is the thyroid cartilage. The two sides of the thyroid cartilage converge at the front of the throat, creating a distinct ridge. In most males, with the onset of puberty, the uppermost section of this ridge can become noticeably more prominent than in females. This upper section of the thyroid cartilage is commonly known as the "Adam's apple," but is more correctly named the "laryngeal prominence."

To locate your Adam's apple, place your hand on the front of your throat and swallow. You will feel the Adam's apple jump upward and then drop downward. After locating the Adam's apple, if you place two fingers there on each side of your throat and slide your fingers slightly down, you will feel a distinct ridge. The area you are feeling is your thyroid cartilage—the front section of your larynx.

Cricothyroid Muscles

These muscles move the thyroid joints by pulling the thyroid cartilage forward and rotating it downward, stretching the vocal cords.

The Arytenoid Cartilages

The two small arytenoid cartilages sit at the back of the larynx, directly behind the much larger thyroid cartilage.

Cricoarytenoid Muscles

Akin to the cricothyroid muscles, the cricoarytenoid muscles pull at the arytenoid cartilages, causing them to rotate and move upward, stretching the vocal cords backward.

The Upper Register

The cricoarytenoid muscles move in a backward and upward motion, pulling the arytenoid cartilages and stretching the back of the vocal cords backward and upward as they do so. From here on, I will refer to these actions as the arytenoid effort. The thyroid cartilages and muscles hold the front of the vocal cords in a stretched position.

The Lower Register

The cricothyroid muscles move in a forward and downward motion, pulling the thyroid cartilage and stretching the front of the vocal cords forward and downward as they do so. From here on, I will refer to these actions as the thyroid effort. The arytenoid cartilages and muscles hold the back of the vocal cords in a stretched position.

The Middle Register

The arytenoid and thyroid efforts play an important role in producing the middle-register notes. Both of these efforts must become equally strong to handle the transitions in the middle register. The arytenoid effort stretches the vocal cords the majority of the time to produce notes in the middle register.

The Diaphragm and Breathing

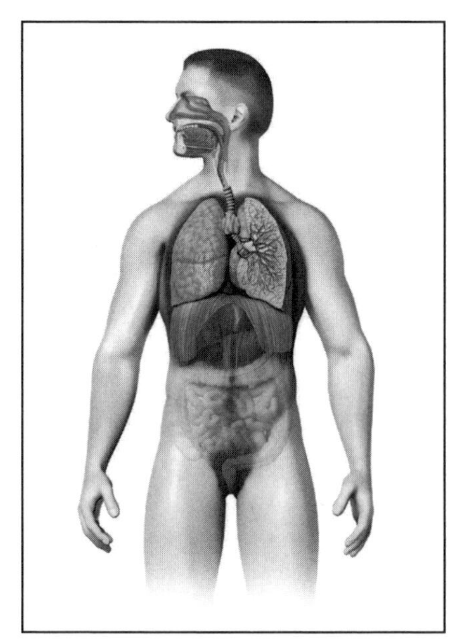

The diaphragm is a large muscle that sits below the lungs, in the lower portion of the rib cage. The diaphragm is not only the engine for the breathing mechanism; it is also the main support system while singing. That is, it is "diaphragm support" that enables the air to flow upward into the larynx, pass over the vocal cords and put them into motion to produce sound. There is a correct and incorrect technique when using diaphragm support to sing. The correct technique allows a natural process of air flow up to the vocal cords. An incorrect technique forces an unnatural air flow up to the vocal cords.

Breathing Correctly

When we inhale, the diaphragm expands out and downward, drawing oxygen into the lungs. This expansion is visible as it pushes the top of the stomach, sides and back outward. When we exhale, the diaphragm contracts and lifts upward, forcing carbon dioxide out of the lungs and pulling the stomach inward. Your breathing process while singing should be as natural as your breathing process while speaking. Both should occur with ease.

Breathing Incorrectly

Breathing with great effort is not necessary and can also be damaging to the vocal cords. Many singers focus too heavily on "diaphragmatic breathing" while practicing or performing. If one pushes too hard (forcing air upwards to the vocal cords) with the diaphragm when singing,

1. The volume and velocity of the air passing over the vocal cords forces them to separate to allow the air to pass through them. This incorrect production, known as *pushing*, will cause fatigue and make the voice crack in the upper register or when singing the first note of a phrase.
2. If the air is pushed up from the diaphragm with great force, the note can go sharp in pitch. This is why consistently sounding sharp is a red flag for singers: it means you are abusing the vocal cords! Eventually, the voice won't sound sharp anymore but instead will sound flat in pitch, as the vocal cords eventually become swollen and will not stretch into the correct position to produce the desired note. Continued pushing will burn out the vocal cords and keep them from producing sound naturally. That is, as the voice begins to sound fatigued, the singer will feel the need to use more muscular effort to sing, abusing the vocal cords even further. (We will talk more about abuse of the vocal cords in the chapter on maintaining a healthy voice.)

Air and the Vocal Cords

Air is crucial for singing. Without air passing over them, the vocal cords will remain static and not vibrate, producing no sound. When we exhale, the diaphragm moves inward and upward, helping to push the air from the lungs. This process puts the vocal cords into motion, causing them to vibrate and produce sound. It is the degree to which the vocal cords stretch or contract that controls the pitch of this sound.

EXERCISE #1: BREATHING

The following exercise will help provide a basic understanding of breathing and voice support. Below are two easy steps to follow:

1. When taking in a breath to sing, always breathe through your mouth and not your nose. When you inhale through your mouth, the back of your throat expands into a relaxed position, ready to sing. When you breathe through your nose, the nasal passages can tighten, and the throat may be slower to open as a result.

    - Place one hand on each side of your throat.
    - Take a breath through your mouth and sing any random (speaking pitch) note. Your throat should slightly expand or feel like it inflates right before you sing and while you are singing that note.
    - Now try the same steps, but take the breath through your nose. Pay attention to any differences you feel between the two approaches.

The majority of vocalists will agree that breathing through the mouth ensures that the throat opens quickly and feels more relaxed than breathing through the nose. Keeping your hands on each side of the throat as a point of reference while breathing in and singing will help if you have a tendency to close your throat while singing. (Closing the throat is a bad habit that some vocalists develop in an effort to control their voice.) If the throat closes, the swallowing muscles that surround the larynx constrict around the mechanisms that stretch the vocal cords. This tension is uncomfortable and can be painful in extreme cases. The throat should always be relaxed and open, whether you are singing quietly or powerfully.

2. Breathe through your mouth and pay attention to the cool sensation of the air that will hit the back wall of the throat. As soon as you feel this cold spot come right in to sing.

    - Place one hand on each side of your throat.
    - Take a breath through your mouth. As soon as you feel the cold spot, come in to sing any random note. There will be enough air to support your voice while singing as long as you have a correct stretch from the vocal cords. (We will cover the correct stretch from the vocal cords in "Strengthening Voice Registers.")

The Jaw

When the jaw moves, the mouth opens! When singing you must open the mouth correctly in order for sound to project outwards. When the voice projects into the microphone, the microphone can easily magnify the sound of your voice, making it sound fuller. If the mouth is closed, there is no possible way for the voice to project correctly into a microphone. Remember, the microphone is outside of the mouth, not inside the mouth! I often witness vocalists singing with their mouths barely open and then complaining that they can't hear themselves in their monitors or P.A. system. Some of these vocalists expect the soundman to work a miracle to make them sound louder, even though their mouths are too closed for the microphone to pick up their sound. Here's an important tip, the soundman can't work a miracle to make your voice sound louder if you aren't opening your mouth to sing! The microphone will only pick up and project what you are projecting! Whether you are singing with soft or powerful dynamics, you must always open your mouth to sing.

There are three ways to open the mouth, but only one of the three is correct in singing:

1. Move the jaw forward to open the mouth.
2. *Drop the jaw to open the mouth.*
3. Move the jaw backward to open the mouth.

Number two is the correct production. Always drop the jaw to open the mouth!

To better understand this concept, let's try an exercise speaking with five words that include five vowel sounds.

EXERCISE #2: THE JAW

1. Place a mirror in front of you so that you can not only feel but also observe the way your mouth opens when your jaw drops to form the vowel sounds.
2. Place a finger on the back of your jaw and below the ear. Keep it there throughout this exercise.
3. *Ee* vowel sound example: Speak the word "he." You should feel your finger slightly move downwards as the jaw drops to open the mouth.
4. *Aye* vowel sound example: Speak the word "hay." You should feel your jaw drop slightly more to open the mouth than it does for the word "he."
5. *Ah* vowel sound example: Speak the word "ha." You should feel your jaw drop significantly more than in the first two examples. A correctly produced ah will involve the largest jaw movement of all the vowels.
6. *Oh* vowel sound example: Speak the word "ho." You should feel your jaw drop as much as in the "Way" example.
7. *Oo* vowel sound example: Speak the word "who." You should feel your jaw drop slightly, as in the "he" example.

Hard Palate vs. Soft Palate and Vowel Placement

The Locations

To locate the hard and soft palates, place the tip of your tongue on the roof of your mouth and behind the two front teeth and glide the tongue backwards. You should feel that the majority of the roof of the mouth is hard (hard palate area) beginning from behind the two front teeth and ending slightly past the middle point of the mouth.

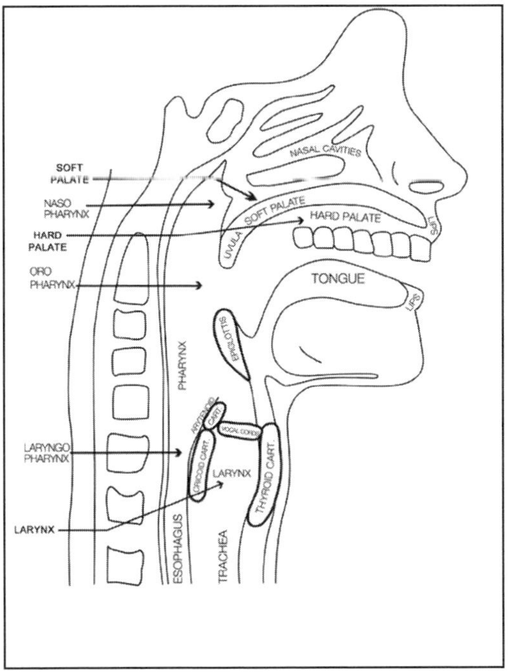

Located behind the hard palate is the soft palate, which will feel softer to the tip of the tongue. The soft palate begins where the hard palate ends and extends all the way to the back of the mouth, in front of the uvula.

The Voice Tone

The difference between the hard and the soft palate vowel placements is in the voice tone. When you sing correctly and there are no obstacles of interference in the path of the air, the sound will travel freely up to the mouth. Beginning at this point, the air of the vowel sounds leans into either the hard or soft palates.

Hard Palate

The hard palate is the foremost section of the roof of the mouth. This area is where we "lean" the air of sung vowels when singing songs in a contemporary style. When we direct the air of the vowels into the hard palate, the air and sound of the voice bounce off the hard palate. From there, the air and sound travel upwards to the head, mask (sinus cavities), and down into the chest. These are the three main areas of the body where the sound can resonate. The head, mask, and chest can resonate in isolation or combined with locations. (We will soon discuss how important resonance is to vocal production.)

Soft Palate

The soft palate is a movable fold suspended from the rear of the hard palate. This area is where we "lean" the air of sung vowels when singing classical and old-school theatrical songs. The air of the vowels and the sound of the voice bounce off the soft palate and then travel to the head, mask and chest areas to achieve resonance.

Because our focus in this book is for vocalists who are singing in contemporary styles of music, such as rock, pop, R&B, country, funk, reggae, and jazz, we will practice directing air against the hard palate in the exercises that follow.

Hard Palate vs. Soft Palate

When singing contemporary styles, we lean the air into the hard palate for a much brighter, fuller, and forward tone. This makes it much easier for the microphone to pick up and project the voice. The soft palate is where we would lean the air of the vowels if we wanted to produce a classical vocal tone. (This tone of the voice is further back in the mouth). But when we are singing contemporary styles, we need the voice to be as forward and projected as possible. Unlike the other instruments in a band, the voice does not have a volume control to turn up to level 10. We need the voice to project outwards for the microphone to pick up and project with clarity over the volume from the amplified instruments.

Hard Palate Vowel Placement

When we sing leaning the air into the hard palate, we naturally direct the air slightly differently for each vowel sound. However, sometimes a vocalist will misplace the air of a vowel sound, moving it too far back or forward and causing the voice to sound uncontrolled or muffled. The *ee* takes the foremost position in the hard palate, followed by the *aye*, *ah*, *oh*, and *oo* vowel sounds.

Let's try the following exercise to better understand this concept.

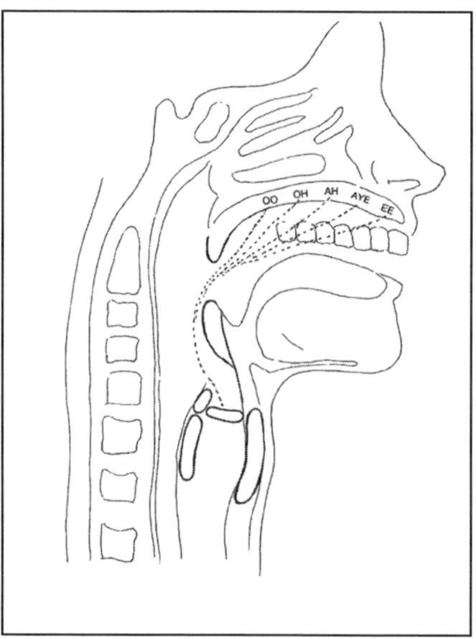

EXERCISE #3: HARD PALATE

Start to sing the word "he" by emphasizing the "H" consonant sound before the *ee* vowel sound. Doing so will allow air to shoot directly forward in your mouth. When forming the vowel sound with your mouth, the air of the vowel sound will lean into the hard palate. Pay special attention to the sensation of the air flowing into the hard palate. Each vowel sound has a slightly different air placement in the hard palate. Refer to the diagram above when doing this exercise.

1. Sit upright on the edge of a chair or stand up with good posture.
2. Inhale quickly through your mouth and begin to sing the exercise.
3. Keep your tongue forward in your mouth. Your tongue should not be sliding backward when pronouncing the words or vowel sounds.
4. Remember that your jaw should drop to open your mouth.

5. Quickly pulse two times the word "he" using the D4 note on the piano (refer to the piano diagram below). Followed by pulsing two times on the word "hay." Then continue to follow the same order by pulsing two times each on the words "ha," "ho," and "who."

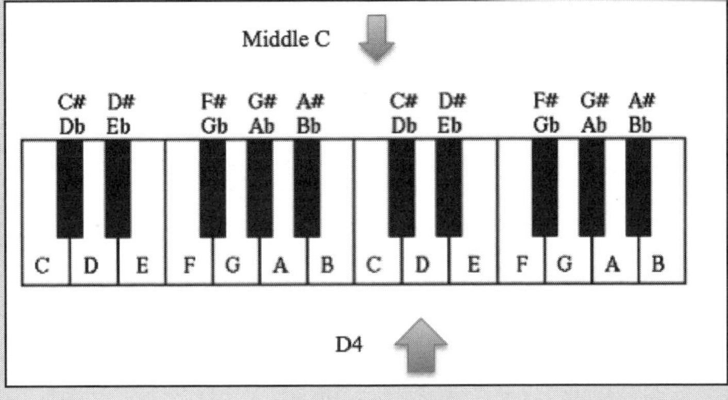

Vowel Sounds

No matter in what language we are singing, we always vocalize using vowel sounds. Why? The only way in which the human voice can flow over a melody is by singing on the vowel sounds. Even when singing in the most extreme vocal styles, you must sing on the vowel sounds.

It is impossible to extend notes on consonants. Consonants are by nature generated by quickly ending or closing vocal production in the mouth. For example, try to sing an extended "K" sound in the word "quick," or a long "T" sound in the word "sight." It is impossible to sing on a consonant! The vocal production ends at the end of the consonant; this is why vowels are so crucial to vocal melody and vocal production.

Breaking this concept into its phonetic elements, in the example below we can see the five distinct vowel sounds.

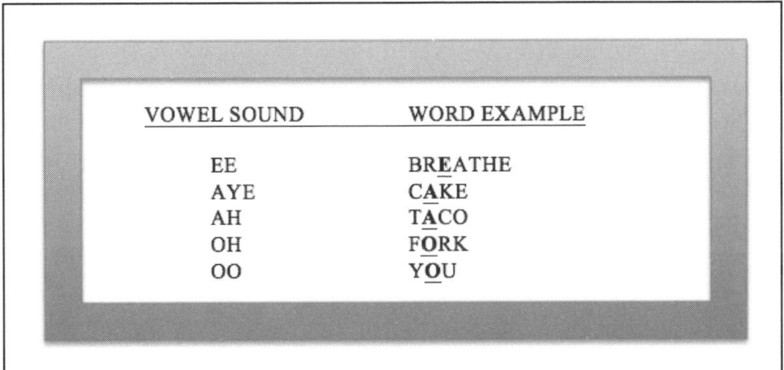

VOWEL SOUND	WORD EXAMPLE
EE	BREATHE
AYE	CAKE
AH	TACO
OH	FORK
OO	YOU

Resonance, Vocal Tone, and Your Voice Identity

A perfect blend of resonance enhances a singer's vocal tone to sound richer and fuller, and also distinguishes the unique original identity of your voice.

Resonance

Did you know that the difference between speaking and singing is resonance? Resonance is extremely important for the voice when you are performing live, recording, rehearsing—in fact, whenever you sing. An easy description of resonance is voiced sounds created by vibrations that bounce around the empty chambers of the mouth, head, sinus cavities (also known as the mask), and chest. For example, have you ever yelled out in a long tunnel, "Hello?" If so, then you would have heard the echo "Hello-hello-hello." Resonance is like an echo in your head, mask (sinus cavities), and chest. Resonance makes the tone of the voice sound much fuller and richer. A perfect balance of vocal tone will be comprised of the following three frequencies:

1. Bottom (bass frequency)
2. Middle (mid frequency)
3. Top (treble frequency)

Let's use a guitar amplifier as an example. A guitar amp has three knobs or dials located on its top front section:

1. Bass frequency
2. Mid frequency
3. Treble frequency

These knobs or dials level and balance the tone of a guitar.

A voice without a perfect resonant tone sounds weaker, smaller in volume, and not as pleasing to the ear as a voice produced using the three above frequencies of resonance.

It is resonance that gives the voice the following three important characteristics:

1. Volume and power
2. Balanced/round tone
3. Sustain

To explain how this works, let's begin by considering an acoustic guitar as an example. Unlike an electric guitar, an acoustic guitar doesn't have to be amplified in order for us to hear its sound. How does the sound of the guitar sustain when you strike the strings? How does it gain volume and power? Why does it have a solid, balanced tone? The way the sound resonates, resounds, and bounces around inside the hollow body of the guitar creates these qualities.

In singing, vocal resonance travels and resounds just as it does in the acoustic guitar example. Here is how it works: First, air travels up from the lungs and strikes the vocal cords into a vibrating motion. While the vocal cords are engaged on a vowel sound from either the thyroid or the arytenoid effort, a pitch, or tone, is produced. The pitch or tone flows upward into the mouth, where, as the breath leans into the hard palate, the jaw, mouth, and lips complete the formation of the vowel. The sound bounces off the hard palate and then travels up into the head, mask, and chest to achieve resonance.

Everyone's voice has an individual, unique tone. Your original vocal tone is not only based on your vocal production from the vocal cords; it's also formed by the way your voice resonates. Everyone's body structure is different. Your face, head, and chest bones are structurally unique, and this is why your vocal resonance differs from all others. Understanding this simple fact will help you develop your original voice.

Everyone who feels resonance describes similar and also different physical sensations in the head, mask (sinus cavities), and chest cavity. Because we all have different body structures, each individual will feel more or less resonance in the head, mask, and chest areas. Everyone can and will be resonating in these three areas. The exercise in the next section will help you tune into what resonance feels like to you.

The Three Locations of Resonance

Each of the three locations of resonance produces distinct physical sensations and effects.

1. Head Resonance

- A tingling or buzzing sensation felt at the top of the head
- Feeling lightheaded
- Sound ringing in the ears and head
- A perception that the sound extends above the head

2. Mask Resonance

- A vibration in the face around the nose area, in the sinus cavities
- Volume that seems much louder in the head than it does with head resonance
- Ears ringing more loudly than they do with head resonance
- A more powerful tone than head resonance
- Sound that feels forward, in front of the face

3. Chest Resonance

- A vibration felt in the chest area, a tingling sensation
- A feeling like the voice is coming from a deeper location in the body than it does with head or mask resonance
- A more powerful tone than head and mask resonance
- The perception of greater volume and a fuller sound than head and mask resonance

Locations of Resonance Exercise

To better identify and experience the three locations of resonance, try the following exercises a few times.

You will need a piano or keyboard. If you do not have one of these instruments, download an app that simulates one of these instruments. Use the keyboard diagram on the next page to locate the notes that you will be playing.

Let's begin with finding head resonance, followed by mask resonance and lastly chest resonance.

EXERCISE #4A: HEAD RESONANCE PLACEMENT

In the following exercise, you will practice *speaking* on a note—a quick action of the vocal cords. You will match your spoken sounds to the pitch you hear, but you will not sustain each word as you would if you were *singing* (which would require your vocal cords to hold their position for a longer time).

Ladies: Play C♯5 three times as you repeat each word in the exercise below.
Gentlemen: Play A4 three times as you repeat each word in the exercise below.

1. Sit upright.
2. Inhale quickly through your mouth.
3. As soon as you feel the cold spot, speak the word "he" three times. Replenish with a new breath, then speak the word "hay" three times. Follow the same pattern for "ha," "ho," and "who." Lean the air of each vowel sound into the hard palate.
4. Focus on your head area during this exercise and feel the head resonance vibration. The sound of the voice should resemble a child's voice. Another name associated with head resonance is a falsetto production.

If any of these notes are difficult to produce using this exercise, descend a whole step to try the exercise again. A half step is also known as a "semitone"—for example, C to C#. A whole step is also known as a "whole tone" and has two semitones—for example, C to D.

EXERCISE #4B: MASK RESONANCE PLACEMENT

Ladies: Play G4 three times as you repeat each word in the exercise below.
Gentlemen: Play C4 three times as you repeat each word in the exercise below.

1. Sit upright.
2. Inhale quickly through your mouth.
3. We'll begin each vowel sound in this exercise with an "N" sound, because the N's vocal production is naturally nasal. This will focus our attention inside the nasal cavities to help achieve mask resonance. You will notice, if you look in the mirror, that your nose will dilate when you make the "N" sound. When you dilate the nose, the soft palate rises, pulling the uvula forward and leaving an open passageway for resonance to travel up to the mask (sinus cavities) area for resonance.

4. Allow the jaw to drop when forming each vowel sound. Doing this will allow the resonance to shift from a nasal, closed sound production to an open, mask resonance production in the nasal cavities. Make sure the nose remains dilated when you drop the jaw to form the vowel sound.

   As soon as you feel the cold spot, speak the sound "nee" three times. Replenish with a new breath, then speak the sound "naye" three times. Follow the same pattern for "nah," "noh," and "new" (with focus on the *oo* vowel sound). Lean the air of each vowel sound into the hard palate.
5. Focus on your mask area during this exercise. The voice will sound bright. Refer to the resonance location descriptions to help refresh the physical sensations associated with mask resonance.

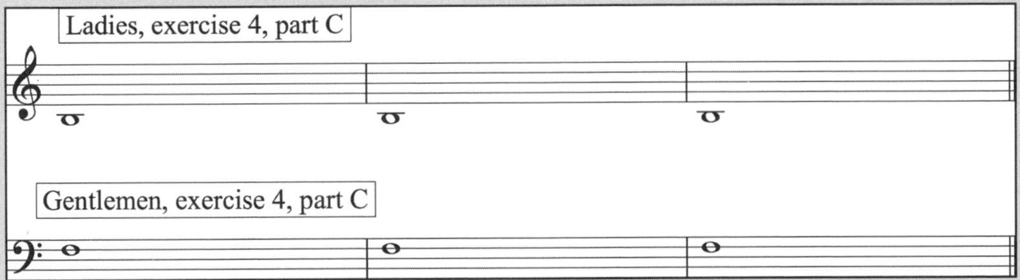

If any of these notes are difficult to produce using this exercise, ascend or descend a whole step to try this exercise again.

EXERCISE #4C: CHEST RESONANCE PLACEMENT

Ladies: Play B3 three times as you repeat each word in the exercise below.
Gentlemen: Play F3 three times as you repeat each word in the exercise below.

1. Sit upright.
2. Inhale quickly through your mouth.
3. As soon as you feel the cold spot, speak the word "he" three times, "hay" three times, "ha" three times, "ho" three times, and "who" three times. Lean the air of each vowel into the hard palate.
4. Focus on your chest area during this exercise. As a point of reference, try placing your hand on your chest while speaking. You will feel the chest resonance vibration against the palm of your hand.

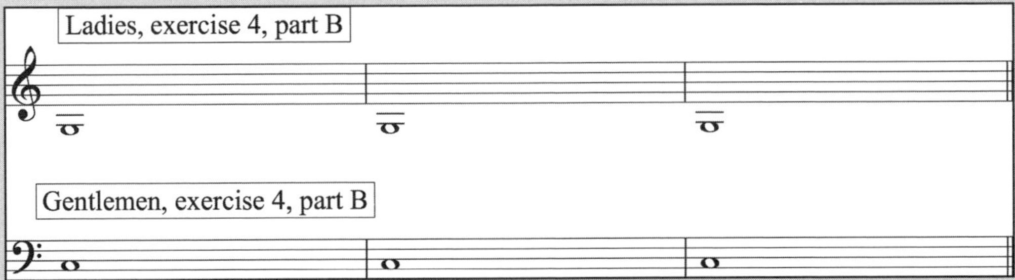

If any of these notes are difficult to produce using this exercise, ascend or descend a whole step to try this exercise again.

Voice Registers: Lower, Middle, and Upper

A voice register refers to three sections of the voice used in singing low, middle, and high notes. Look at the keyboard diagram below to see the three sections of a voice register.

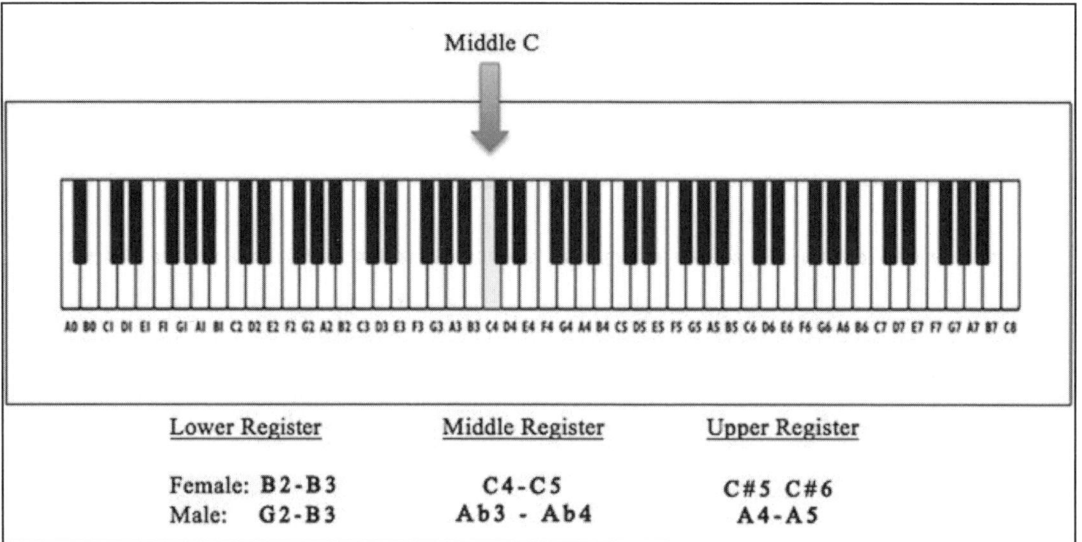

Every vocalist should be able to sing in the lower, middle, and upper registers—so it is important to understand how to produce sound correctly using the arytenoid (upper register) and thyroid efforts (lower register). The lower (thyroid effort) and upper registers (arytenoid effort) must be equally strong to handle the transitions in the middle register of the voice.

In contemporary songs, we sing mostly in the middle register; that is, the average song is sung within the middle register but ascends into the upper register to hit higher notes (the "money notes"). For example, listen to the following songs:

- Aerosmith, "Sweet Emotion"
- Bruno Mars, "Grenade"
- Alicia Keys, "No One"
- Journey, "Separate Ways"

Each song clearly demonstrates the vocalists singing the majority of the time within the middle register and then ascending into the upper register to hit the higher notes.

Less frequently, a song will be sung mostly in the lower register and then ascending into the middle register. For example, listen to the following songs:

- ZZ Top, "La Grange"
- Foo Fighters, " Everlong"

In both of the songs above, the vocalists are singing the majority of the time within the lower register and then ascending to hit higher notes in the middle register.

Some of the artists who study with me are eager to define the range of their voice as soprano, alto, tenor, or bass. Others will inform me at the start that they are within one of these areas and are concerned with training only this range of their voice. All vocalists have a sweet spot in their vocal range, a prime location where they sing the best. However, a contemporary vocalist must sing in all three registers and use chest, mixed, and head voice interchangeably along with dynamics. We will talk more about chest, mixed, and head voice in the next chapter.

Average Voice Ranges

These are *average* female and male vocal range registers. Sometimes a male voice is higher in vocal range and can start or end in a "female" vocal range register. The opposite can be true with the female voice. Sometimes a female voice is lower in vocal range and can start or end in a "male" vocal range register.

Lower Register

Men typically speak and sing lower than most women. The reason this happens is that when a male voice matures, the Adam's apple grows and becomes more pronounced in the front of the larynx. (The Adam's apple is located at top section of the thyroid cartilage.) Thus the thyroid mechanisms stretch the vocal cords slightly more than in females, producing a lower speaking voice. This is why it is often easier for males to sing in the lower register than females. Children often speak at a higher pitch because they are born naturally engaging with the arytenoid effort to stretch the vocal cords. Speaking with the thyroid effort obviously allows the voice to sing better in the lower register. The lower-register notes often resonate in the chest and sometimes in the mask.

Upper Register

Females most often speak higher and also sing higher than most males because of the vocal cords being stretched from the arytenoid mechanisms. Children are born naturally engaging the arytenoid effort, which stretches the vocal cords. When females mature, often the speaking voice will remain higher in range than a male's speaking voice. Speaking with the arytenoid effort allows the voice to sing better in the upper and the majority of the middle register. The upper-register notes often resonate in the head and mask areas.

Middle Register

The middle register is one of the most misunderstood and difficult areas to sing through smoothly. For the majority of singers, the middle register has some notes that are easy to sing and others that are more difficult to control. All singers have struggled in this area at some point in the development of their vocal production. The main reason for this difficulty is that the thyroid and arytenoid efforts must become equally strong in order to handle the transitions in the middle register. The arytenoid effort plays an important role in stretching the vocal cords the majority of the time in the middle register. Thyroid effort handles some notes in the lower section of the middle register. Both male and female voices experience some difficulty in the top section of the middle register when singing up into the upper-register notes.

Singing with the mixed voice production occurs mostly in the middle register. The middle-register notes resonate mostly in the mask, but also simultaneously in either the head or chest areas.

The term "bridging the voice" refers to the smooth transition from the lower register up through the middle register into the upper register. If one of the thyroid or arytenoid mechanisms is weaker than the other, the sound will crack or break during those transitions. A common area where this can occur is when singing from the middle register up into the upper register. It is important that the voice sounds smooth transitioning from one register into another, because most songs require the ability to move between registers. Since the vocal cords stretch into a new position for each single note produced, these transitions require a lot of control from the vocal cords and are difficult to execute in the beginning.

Pitch and Voice Registers

Some vocalists mistakenly focus on practicing in their strongest register. Although this feels comfortable, doing so leaves the other registers underdeveloped, so that either the arytenoid or thyroid mechanisms remain weaker than their counterparts. This weakness creates an imbalance in the vocal cords. When one effort (thyroid or arytenoid) is stretching the vocal cords, the other is holding or "bracing" them. Pitch problems can occur if one effort is stronger than the other.

An analogy I like to use to help make this clear to students involves working out at the gym. Let's say you are right-handed. When you begin to work out, you find that it's easier to perform exercises on the right side, so you work where you're naturally strong. It feels great, but what do you think will happen? As you strengthen the side that is already strong and neglect the side that's weaker, your body will develop a real imbalance!

Vocal training depends upon strengthening your muscles and muscle memory. Let's remember an important rule. The vocal cords adjust and stretch into a different position for each note sung. If you look at the keys on a piano, think of your vocal cords stretching into different positions to sing all those notes. That is an incredible amount of muscle memory that needs to be established to produce a solid pitch with your voice. Where the mechanism is weaker and the pitch is not solid, that weakness needs to be corrected, not ignored, or any imbalance will only become worse.

The Three-Note Student

A few years back, I had a guitar student who wanted to perform his original songs but had never studied voice and didn't know the first thing about singing. In the first five minutes of working with him, I discovered that he could only sing three notes on the keyboard in pitch: G3, A♭3, and A3. If I played B♭3 on the piano, his voice would sing A3—a half step under the note I had played. If I played F3, his voice would wander up to sing G3. If I played any note on the keyboard other than G3, A♭3, or A3, his voice would migrate to one of the three notes that his muscle memory recognized. I tried all the tricks in the book, but he really could not produce any other notes. The student knew he was out of pitch and said, "I know I don't have a wide vocal range but I'm willing to dedicate myself to vocal practice to improve." So I began to teach him about the mechanics of the voice and train him to use his thyroid mechanisms for the notes he could already produce. He was able to identify with the physical sensations associated with thyroid effort when stretching the vocal cords. This made it easy for him to physically feel while also attuning his ears to recognize the correct and incorrect vocal productions. From this point, we were able to establish an expanded lower-register vocal range. Then, in order to build the upper register, I taught him how to identify with the physical sensations associated with the arytenoid effort to stretch the vocal cords.

I worked with this student for forty-five minutes once a week for ten weeks. By the end of the ten weeks he had gained three octaves in range, encompassing the lower, middle, and upper registers. He was able to sing using chest, mixed, and head voice productions and able to apply vocal dynamics in his songs. I was amazed at how dedicated he remained with his vocal practice and determination to strengthen, and control his voice. After a few months, he came back to play me a three-song demo he had just recorded. It was his first demo, and he sounded great. He was now able to able to control his sound and vocal effects, and front his new band with his original songs. He thanked me and called me the Buddha of vocal coaching. I told him that I had only shown him what to do, but his dedicated practice—his blood, sweat, and tears—had gotten him to this point. Pretty amazing for someone who started out being able to sing only three little notes.

3 The Voice Exercises

Building the Muscle Memory

Strengthening Voice Registers

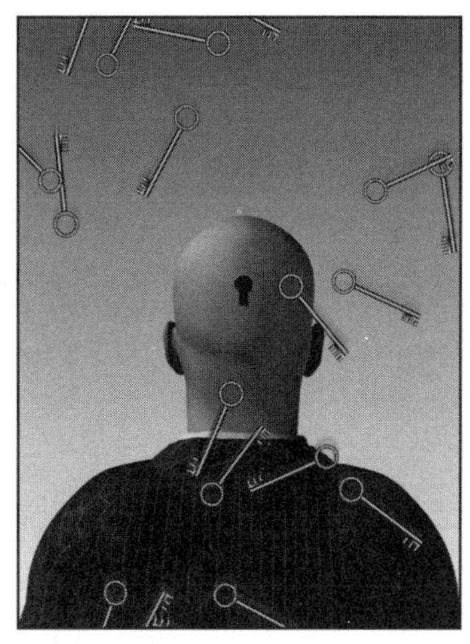

Whether you are a seasoned vocalist who has been singing professionally, an intermediate singer, or a beginner, you can benefit from vocal exercises! I believe that maintaining a weekly practice regimen keeps your instrument well tuned, just as professional marathon runners keep their bodies tuned by practicing and preparing for every race that they run. They don't make the mistake of thinking that once they reach an elite level they don't need to practice anymore, or don't need to warm up before running a race! Just as professional athletes and dancers work constantly to reach and maintain peak performance, you must continue to exercise and care for your voice, which is a physical part of your body! In order to perform well, you must maintain your physical condition!

Practice Journal

Indicate time and duration of practice exercises for each day of the week

FOR THE WEEK OF:	MON	TUES	WED	THU	FRI	SAT	SUN
Time							
Date							
Exercises							
Time							
Date							
Exercises							
Time							
Date							
Exercises							
Time							
Date							
Exercises							
Time							
Date							
Exercises							

It is important to track your practice, progress, and time management in a practice journal. An ideal practice week regimen might look something like this:

Vocal Range

All vocalists should understand their individual vocal range. Knowledge of your range will tell you where to begin vocal exercises (for voice development) and where to warm up the voice prior to singing songs. With diligent warming up and exercising, your vocal range will begin to expand into the lower and upper registers.

Choose Your Easiest Vowel

Practice your exercises using the vowels that are easiest to sing. This will create correct vocal-cord muscle memory. For example, the *ee* vowel sound may be easier for you to produce in the lower register than in the upper register. The next exercise will help you determine which vowels are easier for you.

Determine Your Vocal Range

The lowest and highest notes in a vocal range should be achieved with ease, meaning they are sung without blasting excess volume or air pressure while singing these notes. To better understand your personal vocal range and where to begin your voice exercises, try the following exercise. Refer to the keyboard diagram below to find where to begin singing each note in the lower and upper registers. You will need a keyboard, piano, or virtual keyboard app. The ladies and gentlemen will begin singing from different starting notes in the lower and upper registers.

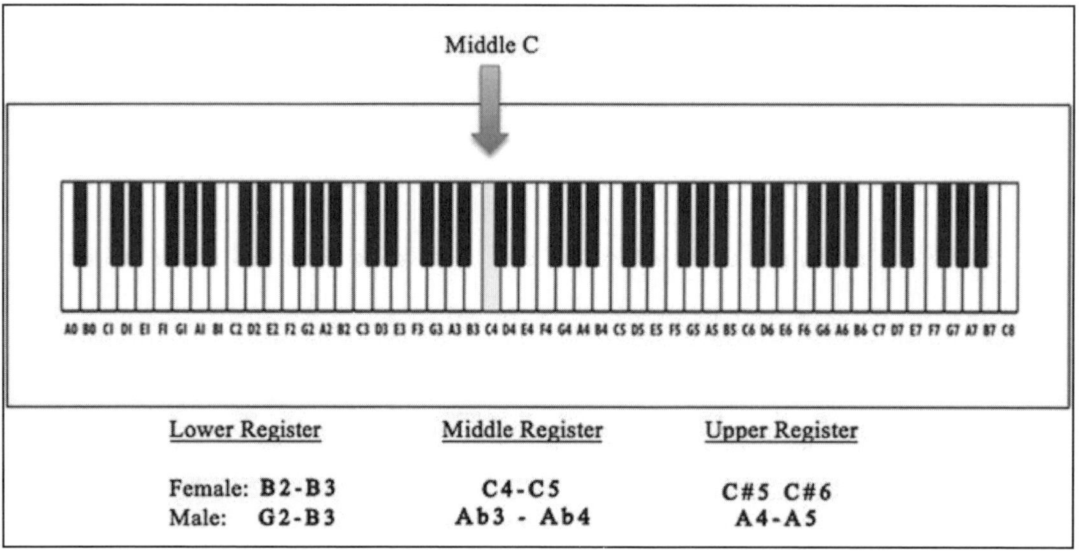

EXERCISE #5: DETERMINING YOUR VOCAL RANGE

LOWER REGISTER

1. Locate your starting note from the lower register on the keyboard diagram.
2. Sing the first note beginning with the *ee* vowel, followed by *aye, ah, oh,* and *oo*. Pay close attention to which vowels remain the easiest to sing throughout this exercise.
3. Proceed down a half step on the keyboard and repeat step #2. Continue descending, a half step at a time, singing through all the vowels on each note. For example, if your starting note was B3, sing all the vowel sounds on B3. Now move down a half step to B♭3 and sing all of the vowel sounds on this note. Then continue down a half step to A3, etc. Continue this process until you sing your lowest *audible* note. An audible sung note means you can hear the vowel sound clearly sung on the note. Distorted "monster" sounds are not "audible!"
4. When you reach your lowest sung note, write in your practice journal the note and vowel sounds that were easiest to sing.

UPPER REGISTER

1. Locate your starting note from the upper register on the keyboard diagram.
2. Sing the first note beginning with the ee vowel, followed by *aye, ah, oh,* and *oo*. Pay close attention to which vowels remain the easiest to sing throughout this exercise.
3. Proceed up the keyboard a half step at a time until reaching your highest *audible* sung note. For example, if your starting note was G4, sing all the vowel sounds on G4. Move up a half step to G♯4 and sing all the vowels on this note. Continue this process up to your highest audible note. An audible sung note means you can hear the vowel sound clearly sung on the note. Distorted "mouse screeching" sounds are not "audible"!
4. When you reach your highest sung note, write in your practice journal the note and vowel sounds that were easiest to sing.

Voice Exercises

The voice exercises that we will be using are divided into two sections. Both sections will cover scale exercises that target the lower, middle, and upper registers, but Section 1 will address the upper and lower registers separately, while Section 2 will focus on the mixed voice that will allow you to sing confidently in the middle register. We will move up the scale in half steps played on a piano or keyboard. You may ask why we are not using longer series of notes, like octave scales, to build the vocal range. In my twenty-plus years of teaching, I have observed that attempting more elaborate scale exercises in the beginning can create bad habits that interfere with building correct muscle memory. When training your voice with new exercises and techniques, working slowly and gradually will allow you to see where your personal difficulties lie, and to improve those areas by practicing forming pitches and vowel sounds correctly. Once all these exercises are easy for you, then you can move on to more challenging scale exercises, such as the ones I compiled and recorded in my Hal Leonard book and CD *Rock Vocals*.

Section 1: Lower and Upper Registers

The exercises in this section will target the thyroid mechanisms (lower register) and the arytenoid mechanisms (upper register). This approach will help build the muscle memory necessary for strong vocal production. You will learn in the first section how to understand the physical sensations associated with the thyroid and arytenoid efforts, and to tune the ear to recognize correct and incorrect vocal production and placement.

Remember, the more you practice, the better your sound will be. Each time you warm up and exercise your voice, you are properly stretching the vocal mechanism and preparing your body for the vocal gymnastics of singing songs. When you sing songs, the voice must move very quickly between one register and another, and the vocal cords stretch into a new position for each single note produced. The degree to which the vocal cords stretch controls the pitch of the sound. Exercising the voice by singing scales correctly develops the correct muscle memory for each single note produced. When the vocal cords develop and strengthen, you will begin to notice the sound of the voice becoming stronger and fuller in tone.

The Lower Register and the Thyroid Effort

The goal of the following exercise is to broaden your lower range by correctly developing the vocal cords to produce lower-registered notes. When singing in the lower register, understanding how to use the thyroid effort is vital. The great thing about using the thyroid effort is the two physical sensations that can be felt:

Vibration: When singing a note in the lower register, you can feel the vibration of the vocal cords at the front of the larynx from the thyroid cartilage.

Movement: As you move from your original note down two whole steps, you will be able to feel the movement of the thyroid cartilage by placing your fingers on the front of your throat. In these exercises, however, we will move just one half step at a time. Practicing these half-step intervals helps us to feel the vocal cords stretch slightly differently for each note produced. But, to get a stronger sense of the downward shift before we get started, you can try descending by two whole steps from one note to another. Both this shift and the subtler half-step movement will help set a reference point when exercising in the lower register.

EXERCISE #6: LOWER REGISTER—USING THE THYROID MECHANISMS

We will descend through the lower register in series of three half steps. Find your starting note on a piano, keyboard, or virtual keyboard and sing the note on an *aye* vowel. On the same breath, descend one half-step and then another. Exhale any unused air, take a new breath, and repeat with the ee vowel. After repeating the series on *ah*, *oh*, and *oo*, descend a half step to the next starting note. Sing the next descending series of three half steps on all five vowels in succession, and continue this pattern until you reach your lowest note. Then repeat the exercise starting with the lowest series and rising half step by half step—keeping the same pattern of three descending notes—until you arrive at the original starting note.

For example, sing the starting note B3, followed by B♭3 and A3. Move a half step down to B♭3 for the next starting note. Sing B♭3, A3, and A♭3, and continue this pattern until you reach your lowest note. Now work your way back up to the starting note, B3. Make sure to follow the same pattern using the three half steps.

When beginning this exercise, try to briefly sustain the notes. When you become accustomed to the exercise, try sustaining the notes longer.

When proceeding through the lower-register voice scales, keep a focus on the following points:

- Look in a mirror while practicing this exercise. Make sure your jaw and mouth remain open and that you are breathing easily. If your shoulders rise when you inhale, your breath is shallow and won't be able to support the voice as well as breathing with diaphragmatic support. Shallow breathing also elevates the larynx into an unnatural position and creates muscle tension around it.
- Place two fingertips gently on each side of your throat below the Adam's apple and keep them there throughout the exercise. Before you sing, imagine the voice's tone sounding rich, deep, and thick. As you sing each note, you will feel a vibration against your fingertips that indicates that the thyroid mechanisms have been engaged.
- As soon as you feel the cold spot, sing the first note. When descending to the second and third note the throat should remain open. The throat can close only when you have finished singing. The vibrations felt on the fingertips should remain constant throughout all three notes.
- Remember to direct the air against the hard palate for each vowel throughout the exercise.
- Note the sensation of chest resonance vibration during the exercise.
- Do *not* sing with vibrato during this exercise. Vibrato is a fluctuating pitch that wavers in and out of pitch very quickly. Many vocalists will use vibrato to help control a note. However, in these exercises we are developing muscle memory for precisely tuned notes. The development of muscle memory is very important when beginning to exercise the voice. All of the vocal exercises in this book should be produced without vibrato. It is important that each sung note be as independently produced as possible.

Ladies: Try step #1 first to get comfortable singing this exercise. When you can sing step #1 with ease, then you're ready for step #2. Follow the same pattern in step #2 as you did in step #1. When you are comfortable singing step #2, move on to step #3.

1. The starting note will be B3. Descend with the pattern described above until you reach the starting note A3 (the lowest note in that series will be G3), and then ascend using the same series, raising the starting note by a half step each time, to the starting note, B3.
2. The starting note will be B3. Descend with the pattern described above until you reach the starting note G♭3 (the lowest note in that series will be E3), and then ascend using the same series, raising the starting note by a half step each time, to the starting note, B3.
3. The starting note will be B3. Descend with the pattern described above until you reach the starting note E♭3 (the lowest note of that series will be C♯3), and then ascend using the same series, raising the starting note by a half step each time, to the starting note, B3.

Gentlemen: Try step #1 first to get comfortable singing this exercise. When you can sing step #1 with ease, then you're ready for step #2. Follow the same pattern in step #2 as you did in step #1. When you are comfortable singing step #2, move on to step #3.

1. The starting note will be G3. Descend with the pattern described above until you reach the starting note E3 (the lowest note of that series will be D3), and then ascend using the same series, raising the starting note by a half step each time, to the starting note, G3.
2. The starting note will be G3. Descend with the pattern described above until you reach the starting note C♯3 (the lowest note of that series will be B2), and then ascend using the same series, raising the starting note by a half step each time, to the starting note, G3.
3. The starting note will be G3. Descend with the pattern described above until you reach the starting note A2 (the lowest note of that series will be G2), and then ascend using the same series, raising the starting note by a half step each time, to the starting note, G3.

EXERCISE #6 SCALE NOTATION DIAGRAM

Ladies, lower register exercise, step 3
Gentlemen, lower register exercise, step 1
Gentlemen, lower register exercise, step 2

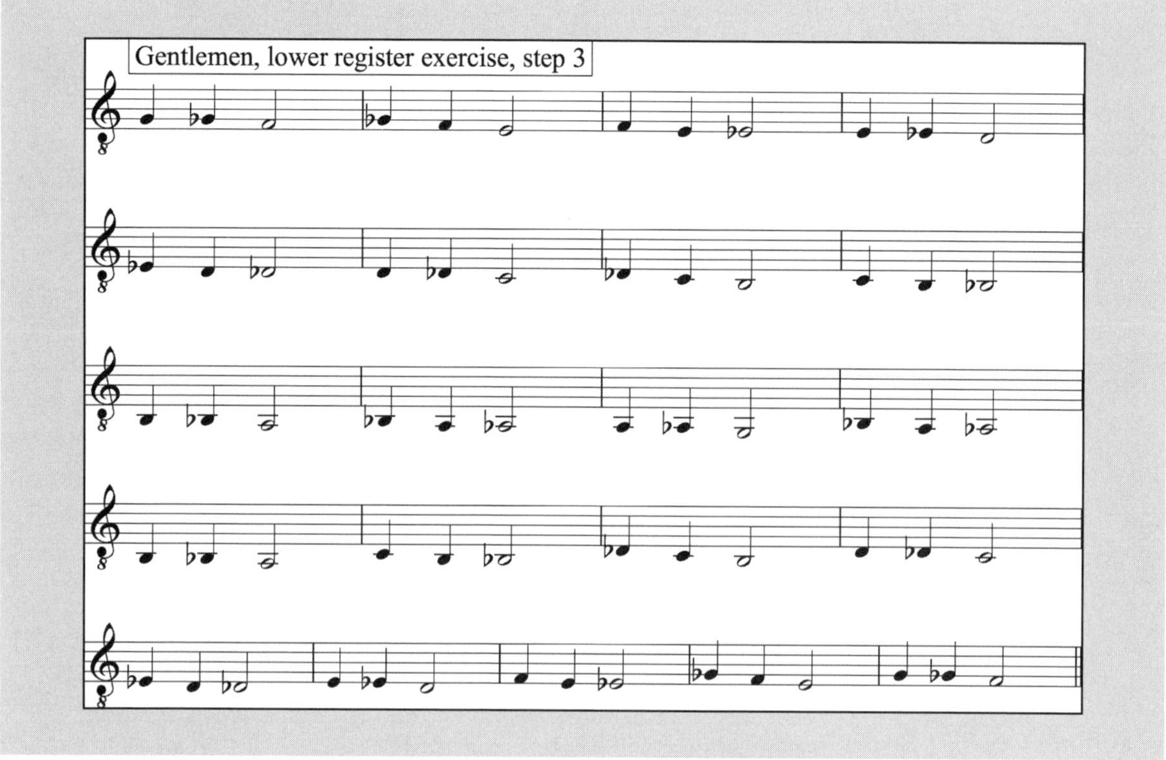

The Upper Register and the Arytenoid Effort

The goal of the following exercise is to develop the vocal cords correctly to produce upper-registered notes. When singing in the upper register it is important to focus on particular sensations and sounds. The physical sensations associated with the arytenoid mechanisms in the upper register are quite different from those associated with the thyroid mechanisms in the lower register. The physical sensations felt from the arytenoid-mechanism movements are more delicate and subtle in comparison to those felt from the thyroid-mechanism movements. Keeping the throat relaxed and open will make it easier to feel the arytenoid and vocal cord movements.

When you engage the starting note of this exercise, you will be able to feel a lifting sensation in the back section of the larynx (where the arytenoid mechanisms reside). In the top section of the upper register, the lifting section can be felt much more. Remember, when we move the voice by half steps, the vocal cords only stretch slightly to proceed from one note to the next, and it may be difficult to register the sensation. If you first try singing the starting note and then descending by two whole steps, you will be able to identify the slight shift from the first note to the second. The physical sensation will help set a reference point for exercising in the upper register.

EXERCISE #7: UPPER REGISTER—USING THE ARYTENOID MECHANISMS

We will ascend through the upper register in series of three half steps. Find your starting note on a piano, keyboard, or virtual keyboard and sing the note on an aye vowel. On the same breath, descend one half-step and then another. Exhale any unused air, take a new breath, and repeat with the *ee* vowel. After repeating the series on *ah, oh,* and *oo,* ascend a half step to the next starting note. Sing the next descending series of three half steps on all five vowels in succession, and continue this pattern until you reach your highest note. Then repeat the exercise starting with the highest series and descending half step by half step—keeping the same pattern of three descending notes—until you arrive at the original starting note.

For example, sing the starting note A4, followed by A♭4 and G4. Move a half step up to B♭4 for the next starting note. Sing B♭4, A4, and A♭4, and continue this pattern until you reach your highest note. Now work your way back down to the starting note, A4. Make sure to follow the same pattern using the three half steps.

When beginning this exercise, try to briefly sustain the notes. When you become accustomed to the exercise, try sustaining the notes longer.

When proceeding through the upper-register voice scales, remember the following points:

- Look in a mirror while practicing this exercise. Make sure your jaw and mouth remain open and that you are breathing easily. If your shoulders rise when you inhale, your breath is shallow and won't be able to support the voice as well as breathing with diaphragmatic support. Shallow breathing also elevates the larynx into an unnatural position and creates muscle tension around it. Focus your attention on the throat area straight back from the thyroid cartilage (where the arytenoid mechanisms reside). While we can't simply place our fingers inside the throat and down into the larynx to feel these movements or vibrations, these subtle movements occurring inside the throat can still be felt. When first attempting this exercise, focus on a lifting sensation when singing the first note and then a slight downward-shifting sensation while descending to the last note.
- Place your hands on each side of your throat to help you focus on keeping the throat open throughout the exercise. The tone of the voice should sound light and thin, with 100 percent head resonance.
- As soon as you feel the cold spot, sing the first note. As you ascend to the second and third note the throat should remain open. The throat can close only when you have finished singing.
- Remember to direct the air against the hard palate for each vowel throughout the exercise.
- Note the sensation of head resonance during the exercise.
- Do not sing with vibrato during this exercise. Vibrato is a fluctuating pitch that wavers in and out of pitch very quickly. Many vocalists will use vibrato to help control a note. However, in these exercises we are developing muscle memory for precisely tuned notes. The development of muscle memory is very important when beginning to exercise the voice. It is important that each sung note be as independently produced as possible.

Ladies: Try step #1 first to get comfortable singing this exercise. When you can sing step #1 with ease, then you're ready for step #2. Follow the same pattern in step #2 as you did in step #1. When you are comfortable singing step #2, move on to step #3 and eventually step #4.

1. The starting note will be A4. Ascend through the upper register singing the descending pattern described above until you reach the starting note C♯5 (the lowest note of that series will be B4. Descend using the same series, lowering the starting note by a half step each time, to the starting note, A4.

2. The starting note will be A4. Ascend with the pattern described above until you reach the starting note F5 (the lowest note of that series will be D♯5). Descend using the same series, lowering the starting note by a half step each time, to the starting note, A4.
3. The starting note will be A4. Ascend with the pattern described above until you reach the starting note A5 (the lowest note of that series will be G5). Descend using the same series, lowering the starting note by a half step each time, to the starting note, A4.
4. The starting note will be A4. Ascend with the pattern described above until you reach the starting note C6 (the lowest note of that series will be A♯5). Descend using the same series, lowering the starting note by a half step each time, to the starting note, A4.

Gentlemen: Try step #1 first to get comfortable singing this exercise. When you can sing step #1 with ease, then you're ready for step #2. Follow the same pattern in step #2 as you did in step #1. When you are comfortable singing step #2, move on to step #3, and eventually step #4.

1. The starting note will be G4. Ascend through the upper register singing the descending pattern described above until you reach the starting note B4 (the lowest note of that series will be A4). Descend using the same series, lowering the starting note by a half step each time, to the starting note, G4.
2. The starting note will be G4. Ascend with the pattern described above until you reach the starting note D♯5 (the lowest note of that series will be C♯5). Descend using the same series, lowering the starting note by a half step each time, to the starting note, G4.
3. The starting note will be G4. Ascend with the pattern described above until you reach the starting note F♯5 (the lowest note of that series will be E5). Descend using the same series, lowering the starting note by a half step each time, to the starting note, G4.
4. The starting note will be G4. Ascend with the pattern described above until you reach the starting note A5 (the lowest note of that series will be G5). Descend using the same series, lowering the starting note by a half step each time, to the starting note, G4.

EXERCISE #7 SCALE NOTATION DIAGRAM

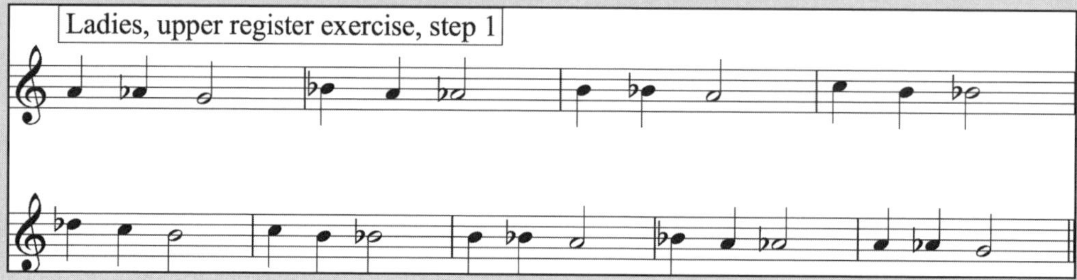

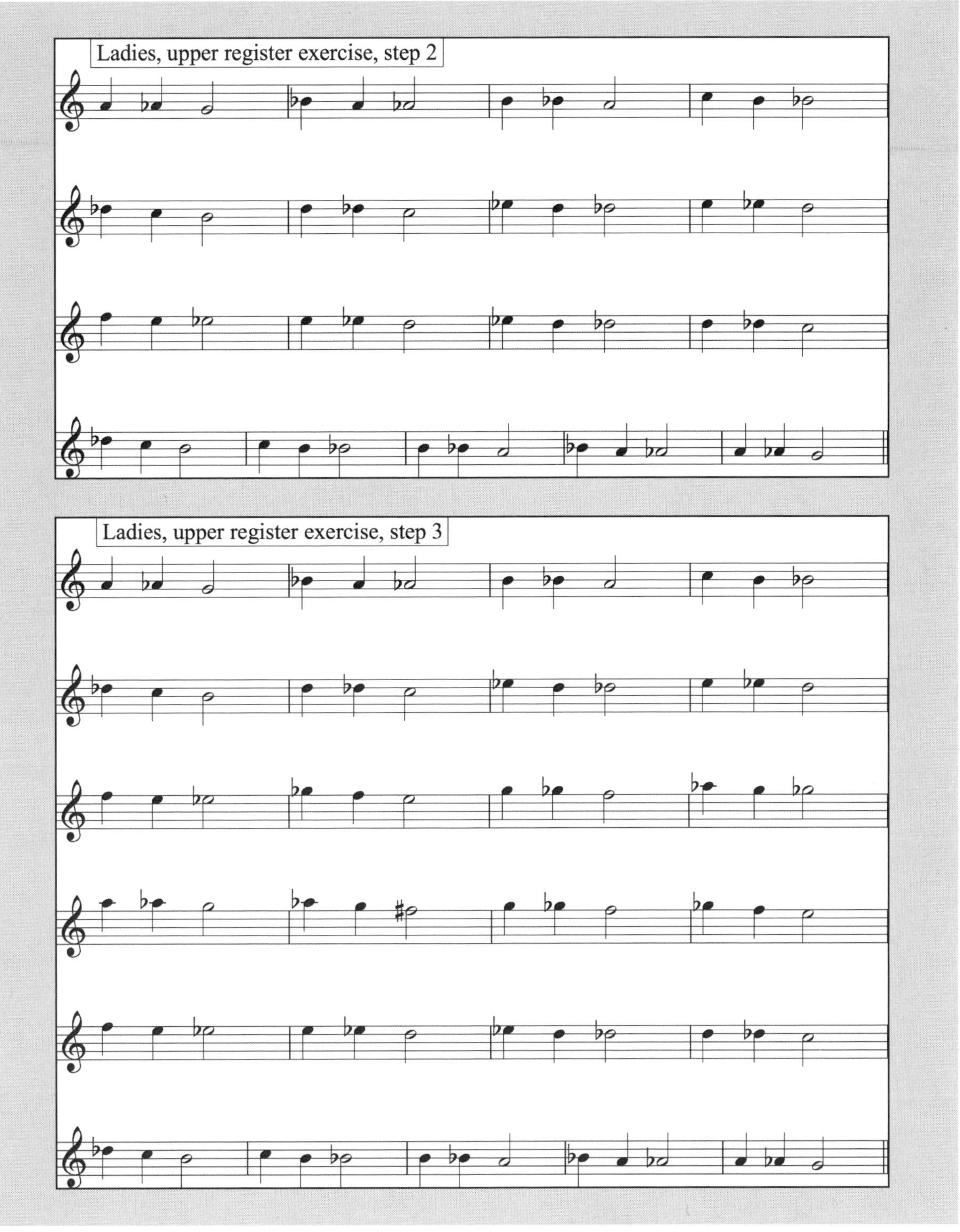
Ladies, upper register exercise, step 2
Ladies, upper register exercise, step 3

Ladies, upper register exercise, step 4
Gentlemen, upper register exercise, step 1

Gentlemen, upper register exercise, step 2
Gentlemen, upper register exercise, step 3

Section 2: Mixed Voice in the Middle Register

The second section of voice exercises focuses on the mixed voice production while simultaneously using head, mask, and chest resonance. You will need a keyboard, piano, or app with a virtual keyboard to do these exercises.

Remember, the more you practice, the better your sound will be. Each time you warm up and exercise your voice, you are properly stretching the vocal mechanism and preparing your body for the vocal gymnastics of singing songs. When you sing songs, the voice must move very quickly between one register and another, and the vocal cords stretch into a new position for each single note produced. The degree to which the vocal cords stretch controls the pitch of the sound. Exercising the voice by singing scales correctly develops the correct muscle memory for each single note produced. When the vocal cords develop and strengthen, you will begin to notice the sound of the voice becoming stronger and fuller in tone.

Light Mixed Voice Production

The light mixed voice is similar to a falsetto sound that uses two resonance chambers simultaneously: 75 percent head and 25 percent mask resonance. Vocalists use this production when they're singing a song that requires the voice to sound light (falsetto/head voice) but still maintain vocal strength. For example, in Radiohead's "Creep" or Muse's "Hysteria," the vocalists sing notes that quickly switch or flip into falsetto (with head resonance) and back into a fuller-sounding production. If you're performing something like this live, you need to be able to use a light mix.

Remember that the sound of the voice you hear on a CD isn't always the true sound of the voice! Singing and performing live is an entirely different situation than singing in a recording session, where the end result can be tweaked to sound much fuller because of the magical mixing process. When we play live or rehearse with a band, the volume projected from the instruments is much louder than the voice. In a live situation, the vocalist must be completely in control of his or her vocal production so that the voice cuts through the volume of the instruments. In a light mixed production, the resonance leaning into the mask area allows the voice to project a bit more fully and clearly than a pure (100 percent) head voice–resonant sound. When the voice projection is fuller, it is easier for the microphone to project through the monitors and PA systems, and vocalists will hear themselves much better!

The combination of 75 percent head and 25 percent mask resonance is the production that should be maintained throughout Exercise #8 below. It will be very easy to fill out the sound of the voice in the lower section of this exercise; however, resist the temptation to sound fuller. The point of focus is to stretch out the vocal cords using the arytenoid effort. To tap into this effort and vocal production, you should sing lightly, without great force or effort. Pay close attention to the notes and vowel sounds that are easiest for you to sing and write them down in your vocal journal. Also, write down the first starting note that becomes more difficult to sing in your journal. Keeping a record of the difficult note in your practice journal will represent a goal to work toward and overcome. Also, keeping a record of your accomplishments reinforces a healthy mindset when practicing your scale exercises. The definition of a difficult sung note is any of the following:

- Muscle tension in the throat area, or a tight or strained feeling or vocal sound
- Hearing an airy or breathy sound, or feeling like you're running out of air
- Feeling like you must push out a lot of air to reach the note

EXERCISE #8: LIGHT MIXED VOICE (75 PERCENT HEAD AND 25 PERCENT MASK RESONANCE)

Find your starting note on a piano, keyboard, or virtual keyboard and speak the sound "nee." Exhale the unused air and take in a new breath, then speak the sound "naye." Continue this pattern with "nah," "noh," and "noo."

Once you become comfortable with speaking the sounds aloud at pitch, try to sing by briefly sustaining the notes. When you become accustomed to practicing this exercise, try sustaining the notes longer.

When proceeding through the light mixed voice scales, keep a focus on the following points:

- Look in a mirror while practicing this exercise. Make sure your jaw and mouth remain open and that you are breathing easily. If your shoulders rise when you inhale, your breath is shallow and won't be able to support the voice as well as breathing with diaphragmatic support. Shallow breathing also elevates the larynx into an unnatural position and creates muscle tension around it.
- To help with the awareness of a closed throat, place your hands on both sides of your throat and take a breath through your mouth. The throat should remain open while speaking or singing throughout this exercise. When you feel the coldness at the back of your throat, speak the first note.
- The larynx and Adam's apple should move only slightly throughout this exercise. To help you focus on this area, place a finger gently on your throat touching the Adam's apple. Ladies, if you are not sure where this is, place your finger on the front of your larynx and swallow. You should feel something move up and then back down; that's your Adam's apple. When the exercises move into the higher range, the Adam's apple might move slightly up, but should never jump up the way it does when you swallow. As you move from speaking to singing, the larynx should be relaxed.
- Keep the nose dilated and the back of the throat open when speaking or singing each vowel sound. If you need to refresh your memory about dilating the nose, please refer to Exercise #4B, Mask Resonance.

Remember, do not use vibrato when singing this exercise.

Ladies: Try step #1 first to get comfortable singing this exercise. When you can sing step #1 with ease, then you're ready for step #2. Follow the same pattern in step #2 as you did in step #1. When you are comfortable singing step #2, move on to step #3.

1. The starting note will be F4. Ascend a half step at a time up to A4, and then descend a half step at a time back to the starting note, F4.
2. The starting note will be F4. Ascend a half step at a time up to C5, and then descend a half step at a time back to the starting note, F4.
3. The starting note will be F4. Ascend a half step at a time up to E5, and then descend a half step at a time back to the starting note, F4.

Gentlemen: Try step #1 first to get comfortable singing this exercise. When you can sing step #1 with ease, then you're ready for step #2. Follow the same pattern in step #2 as you did in step #1. When you are comfortable singing step #2, move on to step #3.

1. The starting note will be D4. Ascend a half step at a time up to F♯4, and then descend a half step at a time back to the starting note, D4.
2. The starting note will be E4. Ascend a half step at a time up to A♯4, and then descend a half step at a time down to the starting note, E4.
3. The starting note will be F4. Ascend a half step at a time up to C5, and then descend a half step at a time down to the starting note F4.

EXERCISE #8 SCALE NOTATION DIAGRAM

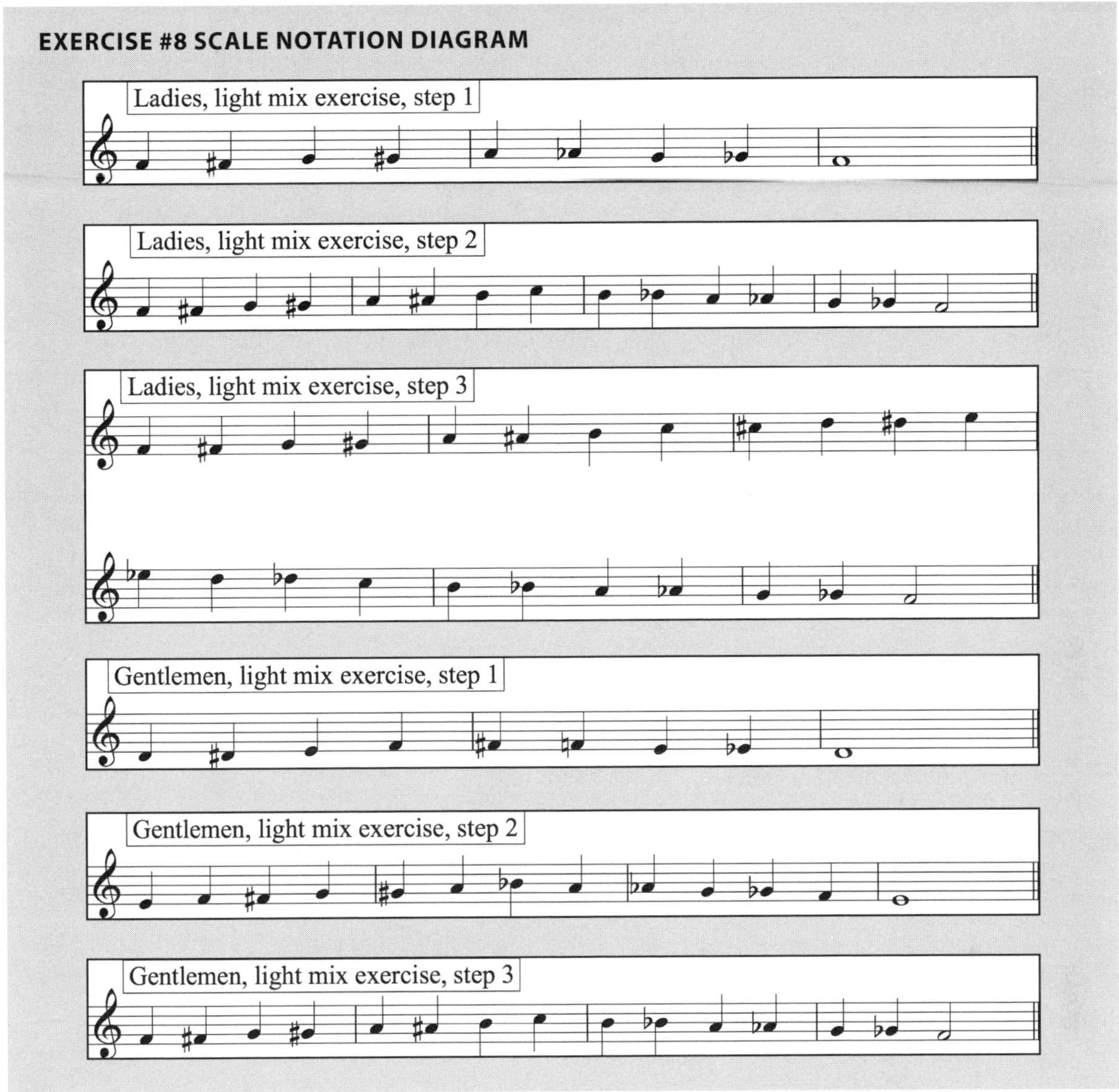

Full Mixed Voice Production

The full mixed voice is similar to a chest voice sound but uses two resonance chambers simultaneously: 75 percent chest and 25 percent mask resonance. Vocalists use this production when singing a song that requires the voice to sound powerful. The full mixed voice production is the most misunderstood technique. Often vocalists push with air pressure, so the resulting sound is louder, but also forced and unnaturally produced. Pushing the voice with air pressure makes the muscles tense around the larynx so that it is impossible to sing with ease. This unhealthy practice will leave you feeling fatigued and burn out the voice over time. It can even lead to injury, as we will discuss in the section on vocal abuse.

An example of a full mixed production is heard in Janis Joplin's "Piece of My Heart." Janis uses her full mix in the opening vocal line ("Come on, come on, come on . . .") and throughout the chorus section. Other examples include AC/DC's "Highway to Hell" and Kings of Leon's "Sex on Fire." These vocalists use a full mixed production in the chorus section and at times in the verse. Many times what sounds like a chest voice is really a well-produced full mixed sound.

Use a full mixed production throughout Exercise #9 below. It will seem easy to fill out the sound in the lower section of this exercise. When proceeding into the midsection of the middle register, allow your voice to lighten up. The point is to keep the full 75 percent chest resonance; however, in the beginning stages of this exercise you may need to revise the percentages of resonance to 50 percent chest and 50 percent mask resonance. It is okay to work with that 50/50 combination while your voice settles in, builds its muscle memory, and becomes strong. Soon, you will be able to create the full mixed production with your voice in a healthy way.

To achieve this vocal production, you should sing as if you are trying to get someone's attention, but not with great force or effort. To refresh your memory regarding chest resonance, reread Exercise #4C, Chest Resonance. Pay close attention to the notes and vowel sounds that are easiest for you to sing and write them down in your vocal journal. Also, write down the first starting note that becomes more difficult to sing in your journal. The definition of a difficult sung note is any of the following:

- Muscle tension in the throat area, or a tight or strained feeling or vocal sound
- Hearing an airy or breathy sound, or feeling like you're running out of air
- Feeling like you must push out a lot of air to reach the note
- Sounding like you are screaming

EXERCISE #9: FULL MIXED VOICE (75 PERCENT CHEST AND 25 PERCENT MASK RESONANCE)

Find your starting note on a piano, keyboard, or virtual keyboard and speak the sound "nee." Exhale the unused air and take in a new breath, then speak the sound "naye." Continue this pattern with "nah," "noh," and "noo," and "newe," a modification of the vowel oo.

Once you become comfortable with speaking the sounds aloud at pitch, try to sing by briefly sustaining the notes. When you become accustomed to practicing this exercise, try sustaining the notes longer.

When proceeding through the full mixed voice scales, keep a focus on the following points:

- Look in a mirror while practicing this exercise. Make sure your jaw and mouth remain open and that you are breathing easily. If your shoulders rise when you inhale, your breath is shallow and won't be able to support the voice as well as breathing with diaphragmatic support. Shallow breathing also elevates the larynx into an unnatural position and creates muscle tension around it.
- To help with the awareness of a closed throat, place your hands on both sides of your throat. Take a breath through your mouth. The throat should remain open while speaking or singing throughout this exercise. When you feel the coldness at the back of your throat, speak the first note.

- The larynx and Adam's apple should move only slightly throughout this exercise. To help you focus on this area, place a finger gently on your throat touching the Adam's apple. Ladies, if you are not sure where this is, place your finger on the front of your larynx and swallow. You should feel something move up and then back down; that's your Adam's apple. When the exercises move into the higher range, the Adam's apple might move slightly up, but should never jump up the way it does when you swallow. As you move from speaking to singing, the larynx should be relaxed.
- Keep the nose dilated and the back of the throat open when speaking or singing each vowel sound. If you need to refresh your memory about dilating the nose, please refer to Exercise #4B, Mask Resonance.
- The *oo* vowel sound can be troublesome to use during this exercise. When the time comes to use the *oo* vowel sound, enunciate the "N" sound in front of the vowel. As we sing higher using the medium mixed production, we must modify the vowel to allow the sound to open more of its projection. "Noo" eventually becomes "newe" (the *ewe* sound is the one you may make when you're grossed out).

Remember, do *not* use vibrato when singing this exercise.

Ladies: Try step #1 first to get comfortable singing this exercise. When you can sing step #1 with ease, then you're ready for step #2. Follow the same pattern in step #2 as you did in step #1. When you are comfortable singing step #2, move on to step #3.

1. The starting note will be A3. Ascend a half step at a time up to D♯4, and then descend a half step at a time down to the starting note, A3.
2. The starting note will be A3. Ascend a half step at a time up to F4, and then descend a half step at a time down to B♭3.
3. The starting note will be B3. Ascend a half step at a time up to A♭4, and then descend a half step at a time down to B3.

Gentlemen: Try step #1 first to get comfortable singing this exercise. When you can sing step #1 with ease, then you're ready for step #2. Follow the same pattern in step #1 for step #2. When you are comfortable singing step #2, move on to step #3.

1. The starting note will be F3. Ascend a half step at a time up to B♭3, and then descend a half step at a time to G3.
2. The starting note will be G3. Ascend a half step at a time up to D4, and then descend a half step at a time to A♭3.
3. The starting note will be A♭3. Ascend a half step at a time up to F4, and then descend a half step at a time to the starting note, A♭3.

Once you can sing with a full mixed production reaching the top note with ease (A♭4 for ladies and F4 for gentlemen), the next step will be to use the medium mixed production continuing up throughout the entire middle register. Soon we will cover the medium mix exercises.

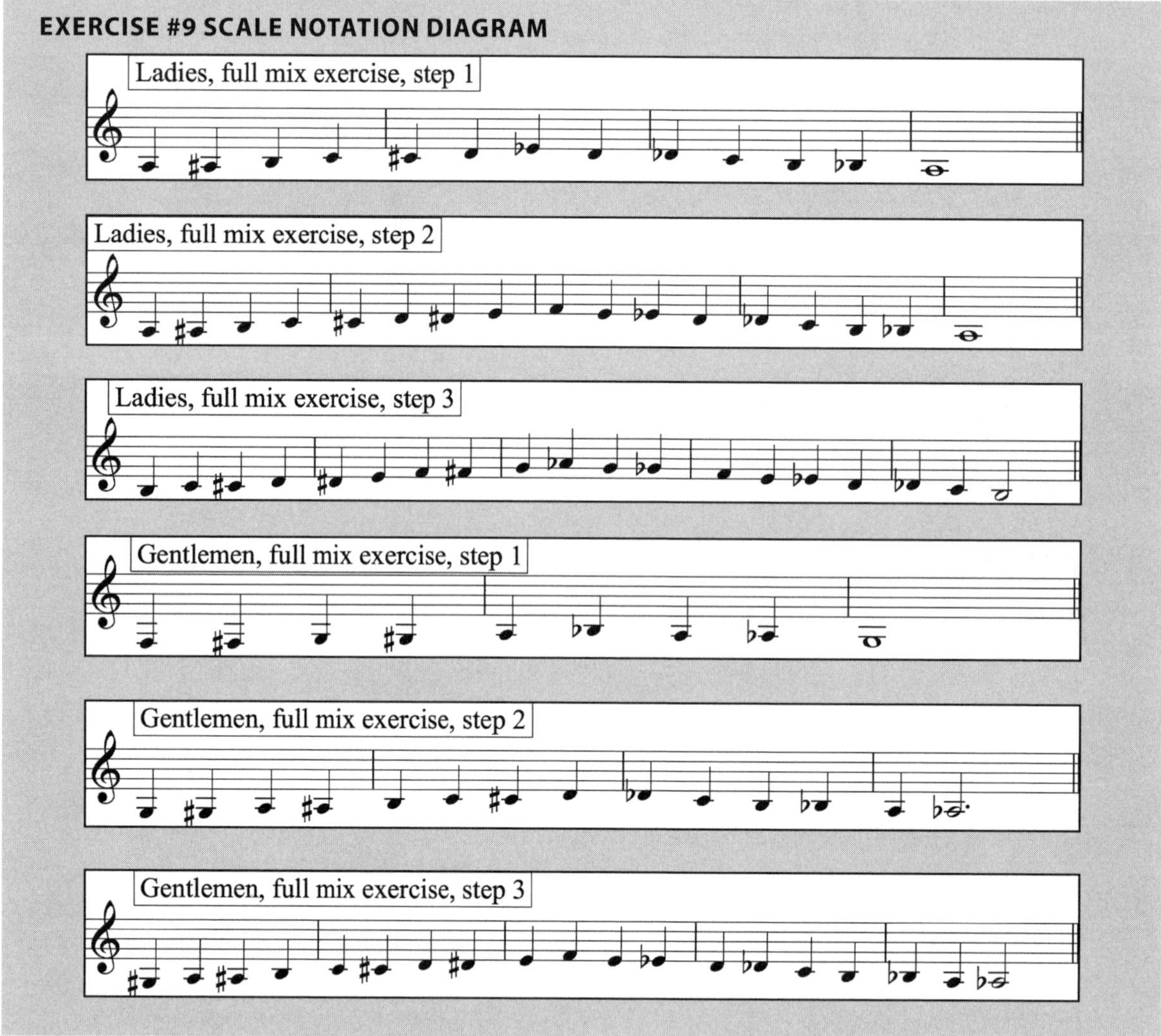

Medium Mixed Voice Production

Like the light mixed voice and the full mixed voice, the medium mixed production uses two resonance chambers simultaneously. In this production, mask resonance is the constant, and you will add either chest or head resonance depending on which notes you're singing in the middle register. The mask area is always at 75 percent with its resonance, with 25 percent resonance in either the chest or head. When using a medium mixed production in the bottom section of the middle register, we will combine 75 percent mask and 25 percent chest resonance. In the top section of the middle register, we will combine 75 percent mask and 25 percent head resonance. Vocalists use this production when singing a song that requires the voice to sound bright (not heavy, like a full mixed production) but powerful. Examples of this voice production include Paramore's "Ignorance," where the medium mixed production is heard on the higher notes in the chorus section, and Led Zeppelin's "Black Dog," where we hear the medium mixed production and other mixed productions throughout.

The medium mix is the most difficult out of the three mixed voice productions. Vocalists who have trained using this production will agree that this technique takes the longest to solidify because it targets the break areas of the voice in the middle register. As a reminder, the break areas are on different notes for ladies and gentlemen. The average areas where the voice breaks or cracks are A♭4 to C5 for ladies and E4 to G4 for gentlemen.

Patience, discipline, and dedication are a must while you allow your vocal cords to build the necessary muscle memory and strengthening for this production. The goal here is to be able to sing smoothly without interruption (no voice breaking or cracking) and with complete control throughout the top section of the middle register bridging the voice into the upper register. Often vocalists will push with air pressure to achieve more volume, but this makes the voice sound forced and unnaturally produced. As mentioned above in the full mix section, when the voice pushes with air pressure, the swallowing muscles will tense around the larynx, making it impossible to sing with ease. Untrained vocalists do this because they don't know how to maintain this production correctly. This unhealthy practice will leave you feeling fatigued and burn out the voice over time. It can even lead to injury, as we will discuss in the section on vocal abuse. (By the way, vocal cord damage is most often found in the voice break areas that we just talked about.)

I'm often asked, "How will I know where to switch my voice from 25 percent chest to 25 percent head resonance?" The answer is not universal, because every vocalist has a unique voice range and development. If you are dedicated and disciplined with your vocal practice, the voice will strengthen over time. After practicing all the mixed production exercises you will notice that singing these exercises gets easier and you are able to sing higher. When this happens, you are ready to try to expand your range of 25 percent chest resonance by moving a half step up each week if you practice consistently. There will be a limit to how far you can take the 25 percent chest resonance into the top section of the middle register before you need to switch to 25 percent head resonance; however, the 75 percent mask and 25 percent head resonance will begin to sound much stronger. The voice will sound fuller and more powerful as it maneuvers through the transition of chest to head resonance notes. When you are first beginning to do this exercise, however, if you need to switch to 25 percent head resonance while you are still in the lower section of the middle register, you may.

To tap into this vocal production, you should speak/sing with a focus mainly on the mask area and dilate the nose throughout the exercise. (To refresh your memory regarding mask resonance, reread the Exercise #4B, Mask Resonance.) The notes sung in this exercise will move a half step at a time. Pay close attention to the notes and vowel sounds that are easiest for you to sing and write them down in your practice journal. Also, write down the first starting note that becomes more difficult to sing in your journal. The definition of a difficult sung note is any of the following:

- Muscle tension in the throat area, or a tight or strained feeling or vocal sound
- Hearing an airy or breathy sound, or feeling like you're running out of air
- Feeling like you must push out a lot of air to reach the note
- Sound like you are screaming

EXERCISE #10: MEDIUM MIXED VOICE (75 PERCENT MASK AND 25 PERCENT CHEST SWITCHING TO 25 PERCENT HEAD RESONANCE)

Find your starting note on a piano, keyboard, or virtual keyboard and speak the sound "nee." Exhale the unused air and then take in a new breath to speak the sound "naye." Continue to follow this pattern for "nah," "noh," and "newe," a modification of the vowel *oo.*

Begin by speaking with the medium mixed production on the given notes. Once you become comfortable with speaking, try to sing by briefly sustaining the notes. When becoming accustomed to practicing this exercise, try sustaining the notes longer.

When proceeding through the medium mixed voice scales, keep a focus on the following points:

- Look in a mirror while practicing this exercise. Make sure your jaw and mouth remain open and that you are breathing easily.
- Check your diaphragm support throughout this exercise by placing a hand on your diaphragm. You will feel a slight kick inward when speaking or singing each note. Sometimes vocalists will hold their breath when attempting this production.
- To help with awareness of a closed throat, place your hands on both sides of your throat. Take a breath through your mouth. The throat should remain open while speaking or singing throughout this exercise. When you feel the coldness at the back of your throat, come right in to speak the first note.
- The larynx and Adam's apple should move only slightly throughout this exercise. To help you focus on this area, simply place a finger gently on your throat touching the Adam's apple. Ladies, if you are not sure where this is, place your finger on the front of your larynx and swallow. You should feel something move up and then back down; that's your Adam's apple. When the exercises move into up into the higher notes, the Adam's apple might move slightly up, but should never jump up the way it does when you swallow. As you as you come in to speak or sing the larynx should relaxed.
- The *oo* vowel sound can be troublesome to use during this exercise. When the time comes to use the *oo* vowel sound, enunciate the "N" sound in front of the vowel. As we sing higher using the medium mixed production, we must modify the vowel to allow the sound to open more of its projection. "Noo" eventually becomes "newe" (the *ewe* sound is the one you may make when you're grossed out).
- Keep the nose dilated and the back of the throat open when speaking or singing each vowel sound. If you need to refresh your memory about dilating the nose, please refer to Exercise #4B, Mask Resonance.
- Do not use vibrato during this exercise.

Ladies: Try step #1 and step #2 first to get comfortable singing this exercise. When you can sing steps #1 and #2 with ease, then you're ready for step #3. When you are comfortable singing step #3, move on to step #4, and so on.

1. The starting note will be B3. Speaking or singing using 75 percent mask and 25 percent chest resonance, ascend one half step at a time to D4, and then descend one half step at a time to the starting note, B3.

2. The starting note will be F4. Speaking or singing using 75 percent mask and 25 percent head resonance, ascend one half step at a time to C5, and then descend one half step at a time to the starting note, F4.
3. The starting note will be B3. Ascend one half step at a time to F4 using 75 percent mask and 25 percent chest resonance. Beginning at F♯4, ascend one half step at a time and switch the combination of resonance to 75 percent mask and 25 percent head as you continue up to C5. Then descend one half step at a time from C5 to F♯4 using mask and head resonance. Beginning at F4, switch the combination of resonance to 25 percent chest with 75 percent mask as you descend to the starting note, B3.
4. The starting note will be B3. Ascend one half step at a time to G4 using 75 percent mask and 25 percent chest resonance. Beginning at A♭4, ascend one half step at a time and switch the combination of resonance to 75 percent mask and 25 percent head as you continue up to C♯5. Then descend one half step at a time from C♯5 to A♭4 note using mask and head resonance. Beginning at G4, switch the combination of resonance to 25 percent chest and 75 percent mask as you descend to the starting note, B3.

When you can sing through step #4, continue to expand your range by moving up one half step at a time using 25 percent chest resonance from the G4 to A♭4 to A4 and so on. Do the same with the top notes; expand your range by moving up one half step at a time using 25 percent head resonance from C♯5 to D5 to D♯5 and so on. Testing your range in a safe manner is always a good plan of action when this exercise becomes easier to sing. If you focus throughout your exercises, your voice will always continue to strengthen and grow.

Gentlemen: Try step #1 and step #2 first to get comfortable singing this exercise. When you can sing steps #1 and #2 with ease, then you're ready for step #3. When you are comfortable singing step #3, move on to step #4, and so on.

1. The starting note will be G♯3. Speaking or singing using 75 percent mask and 25 percent chest resonance, ascend one half step at a time to C4, and then descend one half step at a time to the starting note, G♯3.
2. The starting note will be E4. Speaking or singing using 75 percent mask and 25 percent head resonance, ascend one half step at a time to G4, and then descend one half step at a time down to the starting note, E4.
3. The starting note will be G♯3. Ascend one half step at a time up to C4 using 75 percent mask and 25 percent chest resonance. Beginning at C♯4, ascend one half step at a time and switch the combination of resonance to 75 percent mask and 25 percent head as you continue up to G4. Then descend one half step at a time from G4 to C♯4 using mask and head resonance. Beginning at C4, switch the combination of resonance to 25 percent chest with 75 percent mask as you descend to the starting note, G♯3.
4. The starting note will be G♯3. Ascend one half step at a time to C♯4 using 75 percent mask and 25 percent chest resonance. Beginning at D4, ascend one half step at a time and switch the combination of resonance to 75 percent mask and 25 percent head resonance as you continue up to A♭4. Then descend one half step at a time from A♭4 to D4 using mask and head resonance. Beginning at C♯4, switch the combination of resonance to 25 percent chest with 75 percent mask as you descend to the starting note, G♯3.

When you can sing through step #4, continue to expand your range by moving up one half step at a time using 25 percent chest resonance from the C♯4 to D4 to D♯4 and so on. Do the same with the top notes; expand your range by moving up one half step at a time using 25 percent head resonance from A♭4 to A4 to B♭4 and so on. Testing your range in a safe manner is always a good plan of action when this exercise becomes easier to sing. If you focus throughout your exercises, your voice will always continue to strengthen and grow.

EXERCISE #10 SCALE NOTATION DIAGRAM

Gentlemen, medium mix exercise, step 3

4 Breaking Down a Song

Polish and Go!

Vowel Breakdown

A common practice method is singing all the way through a song over and over again. Sometimes this method works with songs that are easy to sing. But, when a song is more challenging to sing, repeating the song over and over again most likely will not resolve the difficult areas. Instead, repetition will likely reinforce bad habits without resolving the problematic sections.

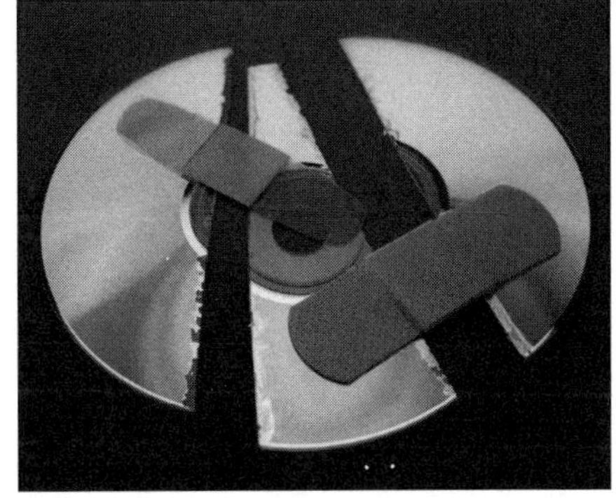

One of the most important skills to learn is opening up the vowels in a challenging song. Vowels are the key to singing freely through any series of notes in a song. Every word has consonants and vowel sounds. For example, the word "run" has two consonants, the letters R and N. When we sing the word "run" over several notes, the *uh* vowel sound sometimes becomes closed off because we anticipate the N at the end of the word. In order to avoid this, we should briefly enunciate the R, then quickly open to the *uh* vowel sound over the series of notes, ending by briefly enunciating the N consonant after the last note is sung. The only way humanly possible for the voice to flow over a melody is to sing with open vowel sounds.

In the following "Vowel Breakdown and Word Analysis" section, use a piano, keyboard, or keyboard app, and try to sing each word with an emphasis on the vowel sound over any series of notes of your choice. Exploring the vowels in these word examples will help you to understand and correctly sing each vowel sound in a song. Be sure to sustain as you sing, so that you can clearly hear the vowel sounds.

Vowel Breakdown and Word Analysis

1. *Ee* as in the words "feet," "breathe," "weak"
2. *Aye* as in the words "way," "fake," "may"
3. *Ah* as in the words "palm," "ha," "stall"
4. *Oh* as in the words "go," "broke," "woke"
5. *Oo* as in the words "you," "Sue," "brew"
6. *Eh* as in the words "bet," "tent," "went"
7. *Ih* as in the words "think," "if," "wink"
8. *Uh* as in the words "love," "stuff," "trust"
9. *Ow* as in the words "cow," "how," "mouse"
10. *Aw* as in the words "walk," "brawl," "saw"

Diphthongs

Vowels may follow one another in distinct syllables, or may merge in one syllable. When they merge, they form what is known as a diphthong: a complex speech sound or glide that begins with one vowel sound and gradually changes to another vowel sound within the same syllable. An example of a diphthong can be heard in the word "house," in which the "ou" part of the word obviously consists of two distinct vowels, but there is no syllabic break between the two. When singing the word "house," the *ou* sound will modify to an *ow* sound. When singing a diphthong, always stress the first part of the vowel sound.

Vowel Breakdown with Word and Syllable Analysis

When singing a word with more than one syllable, try breaking down each word and practicing the vowels in each syllable. Once again, sustain singing on each syllable for each word.

- SITUATION— si (*ih*) / tu (*oo*) / a (*aye*) / tio (*uh*) n
- AWFUL— aw (*aw*) / fu (*uh*) l
- SOMETIMES— some (*uh*) / ti (*ah*) mes
- AFRAID— a (*uh*) / frai (*aye*) d
- ENOUGH— e (*ee*) / nou (*uh*) gh
- TIMING— ti (*ah*) / mi (*ih*) ng
- COUNSELING— cou (*own*) / se (*eh*) / li (*ih*) ng
- UNBELIEVABLE— un (*uh*) / be (*ee*) / lie (*ee*) / va (*uh*) / ble (*uh*)
- BASIS— ba (*aye*) / si (*ih*) s
- SUPERUNKNOWN—su (*oo*) / pe (*uh*r) / un (*uh*) / know (*oh*) n

In the next exercise, the notes of a melody are written out above a lyric. Slowly sing each word on the given melody, matching words to notes as indicated and using a keyboard as a reference.

EXERCISE #11: VOWELS AND MELODY

The Melody: A A3 A3 D3 / E3 D3 / C4 A3 A3 A3 / D3 / E3 D3 C3 / A3
The Lyrics: This pain has ta- ken a- hold of me, con- su- ming my world

Let's try breaking down these lyrics using the vowel sounds we've identified above. First sing slowly through the vocal melody to discover which vowel sounds to use. Some words will have two or more syllables; sing on each vowel sound throughout each syllable. You will notice that you must remain open with the vowels to ensure that the voice flows (has a smooth transition) through each word in the melody.

Your vowel breakdown might look like the layout below. Try singing the vowel provided for each note to sing through the lyrics again, using a piano or keyboard.

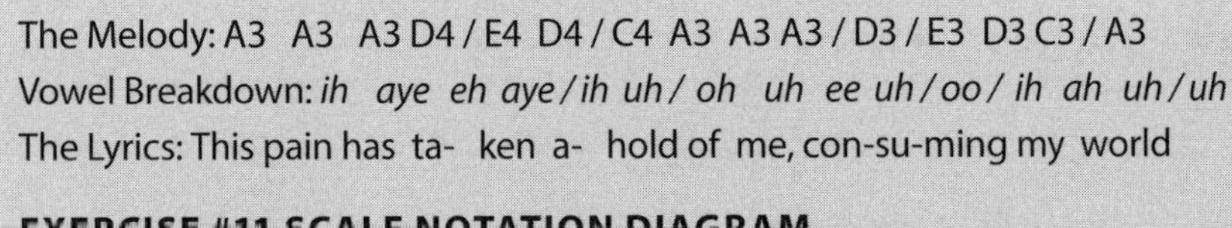

The Melody: A3 A3 A3 D4 / E4 D4 / C4 A3 A3 A3 / D3 / E3 D3 C3 / A3
Vowel Breakdown: *ih aye eh aye / ih uh / oh uh ee uh / oo / ih ah uh / uh*
The Lyrics: This pain has ta- ken a- hold of me, con-su-ming my world

EXERCISE #11 SCALE NOTATION DIAGRAM

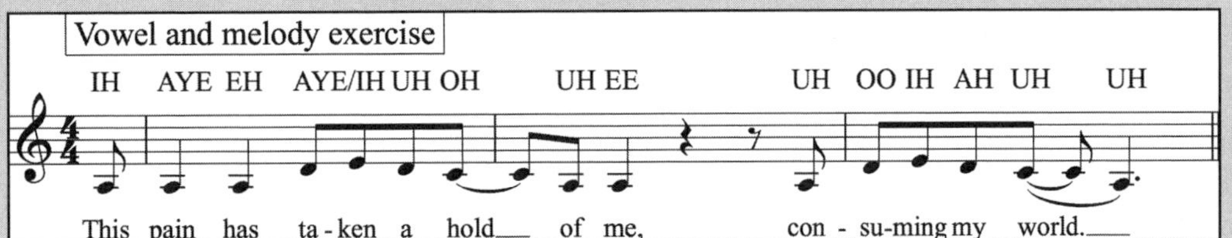

Diagnosing the Obstacles

Now it is time to test this approach with other songs. Choose a song and break down the section that is giving you difficulty, following the same guidelines as above. First, write out each note of the melody. Second, write the lyrics for the melody that you are singing. Third, sing each word slowly to figure out which vowel sounds to use for each note. Now write out the vowel sounds above the lyrics. Practice singing the melody at a slow tempo to help build the muscle memory for these precise pitches so that you can sing comfortably. Once you are singing with ease, pick up the pace until you are back into the actual tempo of the song. Giving time and attention to this detail work will help you fine-tune your vocal production when singing songs.

It is important to address the most common obstacles that vocalists encounter when practicing songs so that you can spot areas that may be troublesome with your own practice.

The most common pitfalls for singers include

1. Vowels and pitch
2. Consonants
3. High notes
4. Tempo
5. Memorizing lyrics
6. Emotion

Vowels and Pitch

We achieve correct pitch by employing the correct stretch of the vocal cords and the muscle memory that has developed from practicing scale exercises. But failing to open our vowels can affect the pitch of the voice. A natural reaction from the body when we sing with "closed" vowels will be to push the note out to help control it. The excess air pressure we create can force the vocal cords to go sharp on the note. Closing on the vowels can also trigger the swallowing muscles to become tight. Muscle tension makes it difficult for the thyroid and the arytenoids to stretch the vocal cords properly. The pitch can be affected and go flat. If you are experiencing these issues, do the following:

- Determine which area of the song is challenging to sing.
- Place your lyrics in front of you to help you identify which vowel sounds and words need your attention.
- Place your hands on each side of your throat to remind you to keep the throat open while singing.
- Sing through the vocal melody after you feel the cold spot.
- Begin by singing the excerpt a cappella (without accompaniment) and at a slower tempo. This will help you identify which vowel sounds are giving you trouble.

Consonants

It is impossible to extend sung notes using consonants. Consonants are by nature generated by quickly ending or closing vocal production in the mouth. Just try singing an extended "T" sound in the word "treat," or a long "K" sound in the word "took." It is impossible! Vocal production ends at the end of the consonant. A common problem can occur when, for example, vocalists sing a one-syllable word on two notes and use the second note to enunciate the consonant instead of the vowel sound (think ruN, triP, or bridGe). Singing on the consonant is a closed production inside the mouth and the sound of the voice will not be able to project as well as it should. When we try to sing notes on consonants, the swallowing muscles tighten around the larynx, creating an uncomfortable pressure or pinching sensation within the throat. This closed voice production will also make vocalists overcompensate with air pressure to increase the voice volume if they cannot hear themselves properly when being accompanied by instrumentation. Over time, this can easily fatigue the voice and affect the length of time spent practicing, performing, or recording. This can also lead to vocal abuse, which we will cover in the next chapter.

Being prepared with the following guidelines for singing consonants when you are at the beginning stage of practicing songs will help you in preparation for future band rehearsals, gigs (live performances), and recordings.

- When a word begins with a B, P, or T, pronounce the consonant more softly when singing into a microphone. The B, P, and sometimes the T create a harsh popping sound that the microphone will pick up and amplify through the P.A. system. No FOH (front of house) soundman or ME (monitor engineer) stage monitor man at any venue will appreciate your popping consonants into the microphone. If they hear you doing it, they will decide you are unprofessional and lack experience—and they will turn down your mic to the minimum volume in fear that you could damage their equipment. I'd also like to mention how annoying those popping consonants sound through the PA system that your audience is listening to. So pay attention to harsh-sounding consonants, as in words like

B—BUT, BRAKE, and BLAME
P—POP, POWER, and PROBABLY
T—TRICK, TAUNT, and TREAT

Lightly pronounce the "T" and "G" sounds in words that contain contractions, like

CAN'T, DIDN'T, and WON'T
TAKING, BRING, and MAKING

When singing words that have a double consonant, drop one of the consonants. Most often you should drop the first consonant in a double-consonant word. As you can see, in the examples below the first consonant is crossed out.

BE~~T~~TER
WO~~R~~RIED
CU~~R~~RENT

When a word ends with a consonant and the next word begins with the same consonant, drop the first consonant. As you can see, in the examples below the first consonant is crossed out.

- WIL~~D~~ DOGS
- FAS~~T~~ TRACK
- WIL~~L~~ LEAD

High Notes

Many singers never realize how important the vowels are in mastering a challenging song. For example, it's not necessarily the case that a high note is difficult to sing or out of your vocal range. It's usually the vowels you sing prior to the high note that cause problems. If the vowels of the prior notes are closed, the high note will be even more closed—and that means your swallowing muscles have tensed around the larynx. Many vocalists never realize that this common vocal problem is standing in their way.

An easy way to work through this problem is do the following:

- Place your lyrics in front of you and focus on the words prior to and including the high note.
- Sing that line a cappella, at a very slow tempo.
- Listen to each vowel sound on each note and check that you are singing on the most open vowel sounds.
- Pay special attention to whether your throat is open and your breath is propelling your voice forward.
- You should be able to determine which vowel sound was closed prior to the high note. You may find that you were singing on the wrong vowel sound. Change the vowel sound and follow the above process again.

Tempos

Whether singing with slow, moderate, fast, or odd-meter tempos, you must be able to memorize the tempo by feeling the rhythm! If you are experiencing difficulties with tempo, try the following:

- Practice listening to (not singing) the song first. Listen and let the rhythm sink in, then, using your body as a whole, begin to move and sway in tempo. (That is, do not tap your foot, smack your hand on your lap, or clap your hands! Sometimes the feet and hands become tired and you will fall behind the beat and lose the tempo of the song.)
- Then sing only the first verse of the song while moving your body with the song's tempo. After successfully singing and keeping time with the first verse, sing the chorus.
- After successfully singing and keeping time with the chorus, put the first verse and chorus together and sing and move to the tempo. Keep practicing with this method and address each section of the song.
- After using the above steps, repeat them in time with a metronome set to the tempo of the song. Continue to practice with the metronome, and eventually you will begin to hear a song's tempo in your head and be able to keep time correctly throughout a song.

Memorizing Lyrics

When memorizing lyrics, the first thing you should do after listening to the song a few times is to read the lyrics without the music. Whether the lyrics are yours or someone else's, you must understand the story. That will help you memorize the lyrics and deliver a better performance, too! Once you understand what your story is about, try the following steps:

- Play the music and read the lyrics out loud a few times. This will help you to memorize the vocal melody and the phrasing of each word of the song.
- Now practice singing along with the song. Start with the first verse and sing it a few times through with the lyrics in front of you.
- Then practice the chorus a few times through.
- Add the first verse and chorus together and sing them a few times through.
- Continue practicing by adding in the rest of the verses, choruses, and bridge.
- After singing the entire song, practice singing the song alone, without the recording. If you can sing the song on your own and remember all your lyrics, you've memorized it!

Emotion

The emotion of a song is the final ingredient to add to your learning process. In a way, it's the most important step of all, since the pure emotion conveyed through the message of a song is what singing is honestly about! The emotion put into the song by the songwriter and the performer is what draws in a listening audience, whether at a live performance or on a recording.

Most artists will agree that performing their original material is much easier than covering someone else's lyrics. However, all vocalists should be able to sing and add their emotion into any song given to them to sing.

Original songs: An original song is normally inspired by someone or something in the artist's life. There is emotional truth in writing out those lyrics and then creating a melody to carry them. The melody flows from an emotion that energizes the song, and this is what an audience feeds off of when listening.

Cover songs: Artists may choose to cover someone else's song because of a feeling that moved them. It could have been the lyrics or message, the texture of the voice in a performance they heard, or the feeling of the music or instrumentation that energized their desire to sing or play the song.

To emote fully in performance, you must allow yourself to let go. Letting go means not worrying or doubting yourself. Focusing on what might go wrong prior to performing will vibe-slay the performance. Most commonly, singers will ask themselves,

- What if the audience doesn't like my song?
- What if I look stupid on stage while performing?
- What do I say to the audience in between my songs?
- What if my voice cracks on the high note?
- What if I forget my lyrics while performing?
- What if my band messes up the difficult section of the song? How will I cope with that?

If you fill your head with doubt and worry before getting on that stage, you've already psyched yourself out of a great performance! Instead think of how much time and work you've put into your songs and what inspired you to write or cover these songs. The object here is to tap that original emotion, that place where you were when you were first inspired to write or to cover the song. If you can tap that emotion, that energy, you will certainly deliver a spectacular performance.

Tips, Tricks, and Tidbits

There will be times when a difficult vocal situation will present itself to you. If you understand how to get through these challenges, you will be able to move forward and continue to do what you want to do, which is sing! The tips, tricks, and additional tidbits in this section will help you prepare for the unexpected and difficult problems that vocalists face when singing, performing, or recording.

1. **Tongue position:** Always keep the position of the tongue forward in the mouth when you sing. If the tongue slides back (even slightly) the epiglottis will move backward and downward, covering the top of the larynx, which will muffle the sound of the voice. Doing this will also trigger the swallowing muscles to become tight around the larynx, making it difficult for either the thyroid or arytenoid mechanisms to stretch the vocal cords correctly. The tongue sliding backward can also make the air of the vowels misplace in the hard palate. The epiglottis moves to a closed position (covering the larynx) when it is ready for the function of swallowing. The epiglottis moves to an open position when speaking or vocalizing.

The tongue moving backwards in the mouth is a common bad habit that may creep in when a singer is trying to sing difficult notes or vowel sounds that are troublesome. The best way to address the issue is to place a mirror in front of you and check to see whether the tongue is remaining forward as you sing. There are two correct tongue positions:

- Average tongue size: The tip of the tongue is touching the front bottom row of teeth.
- Large tongue size: The tip of the tongue is resting above the front bottom row of teeth.

Pay close attention as you sing to make sure that your tongue doesn't slide back, especially when singing higher or when sustaining notes.

2. **Harmonies:** When singing background harmonies or a duet with another vocalist, you must sing the same vowel sounds simultaneously to secure a perfect blend of harmony with one another. For example, if the lead vocalist is singing the word "way" and sustains the *aye* vowel sound, then the background vocalists should sing it the same way. If the background vocals sing the word as "wayeee" and emphasize the *ee* vowel sound, the blend of harmonies won't lock in tightly. Timing, too, is key. If one vocalist is slightly late opening the mouth to sing a vowel sound, the harmony won't sound smooth. A great tip for vocalists is to *always* rehearse with *all* the vocalists who are preparing to sing together. When practicing harmonies, face one another and look at each other's mouths as you sing. You will quickly not only hear but see whether everyone is on the same vowel sound and opening up on the vowel at the same time. If you're having trouble finding your pitch when harmonizing, play the note or notes you must sing on a keyboard or other instrument. Look at the notes as you play; then, after hearing your notes once or twice, sing along while you play. The more vocal practice you do with picking out harmonies, the better you will become.
3. **Remaining hydrated when performing:** When singing live, you should always have room-temperature water onstage. Singing will quickly dry the throat because of how much air we use while breathing to support the voice. If you do not have water, or can't see your water because the insane, out-of-control smoke machine has made it impossible to see onstage, gently bite the sides of the tongue to release saliva into the throat area. Swallow and repeat this to get your throat moist. (See "Healthy Voice Maintenance" in the next chapter for more on keeping your throat and body hydrated.)
4. **Earplugs:** When performing or rehearsing (lead or background vocals), you should always have earplugs in case you cannot hear yourself in your monitors. It is wise to practice using earplugs *before* singing live or in a rehearsal to test this approach and get used to it! The best way to do this is to first practice the song you must learn without using the earplugs. Once in the song is in good shape, try wearing one earplug as you record yourself singing the song. (You can use a smartphone for this exercise; no elaborate recording equipment is necessary.) You will notice that the sound appears louder inside your head with the earplug in. Resist the urge to push your voice to become louder in the room. Listen back to your recording and evaluate yourself. You should sound just as relaxed singing with one earplug as singing without the earplug. Once you feel you're becoming accustomed to singing with one earplug, try singing using both earplugs. Record yourself again and listen to your recording. Once again you must resist the urge to push your voice to sound louder.

5. **Cupping your hand:** If you don't have earplugs in performance or rehearsal and you cannot hear yourself in the monitors, cup the palm of your hand at a close distance from your ear to hear yourself better. Try this now. Sing any comfortable note out loud and use the palms of your hands to create a cup shape about seven inches away from the front of your face. Slowly move your hands from in front of your face towards your ears, and stop when you hear your voice at the loudest volume inside your head. Take note of where your palms are. This hand position will come in handy (no pun intended) when you forget your earplugs and need to hear yourself sing.
6. **Preparing for a performance when ill:** If you have fallen very ill, canceling a live performance is never a wise option. You must prepare yourself hours before the show by doing the following.

- Rearrange the order of the set list for the show. You may have to take out the songs that feature higher notes and replace them with songs that are easier to sing.
- You may want to ask your guitarist to extend some solos for the show. Your guitarist will probably be happy about this.
- Sleep as much as possible! Sleep or rest up until four hours before the show, then eat something light and drink a lot of water.
- Begin to warm up your voice first in the upper register. Use Exercise #7 from Chapter 3 of this book. Begin with step #1, then try to move to step #2. Expect that it will take some time to warm up, so allow an hour and a half to proceed at a slow pace through this process. Do not freak out if you don't reach your normal highest notes when exercising your voice in the upper register. Remember, you're very sick. Be patient with yourself and stay positive in your head.
- After warming up with scale exercises, listen to some of the songs you will be singing that night. Try singing just a few sections of some of the songs, but don't try to belt out the songs out right now. Stay relaxed and save your energy for the show. It's amazing what adrenaline does to energize your performance and help you pull through the gig.
- When you get to the gig, go straight to the dressing room and chill out. Don't talk a lot; save your energy and voice. If you don't have a dressing room, stay in the car or some location in the venue that's private. Talking too much before the show can burn your voice out before you even get onstage to sing.
- Make sure your monitors are hot (loud in volume) so you won't overcompensate for any congestion that's blocking your hearing by pushing your voice to get more volume. Sometimes when we are very sick and the body is very fatigued, our muscle memory may respond more slowly than usual to stretch the vocal cords to sing.
- Have a lot of water onstage with you while performing.

7. **Song selection for auditions and performing live:** When performing live or auditioning, sing songs that you have rehearsed to perfection—songs that sound vocally spectacular! Do not choose songs that you don't sing perfectly! If you can sing the song at 98 percent, that's still not good enough. Find a way to correct that 2 percent or choose something you can sing perfectly. For example, if the 2 percent is a higher note that is difficult to sing, then sing a lower alternate note that showcases you at 100 percent. However, if it's something else you can't fix in time for the gig,

audition, etc., choose another song. Think about a time when you went to a show and the vocalist sang great up to a point and then suddenly hit some bad notes. What did you remember from that show? The bad notes are more than likely what you remembered. Most people won't say, "Well, let's ignore all the flaws in that performance and only think about the good parts." In the real world, it doesn't work out that way! Obviously there are mistakes live, but if there's a problem that you know about in advance, avoid showcasing it until you've solved it by working out the vocal issues that are giving you trouble. If you love that song, you can always sing it at a later time.

8. **Choosing the right song for auditions:** It is important to select the right songs for your audition! If you are instructed to choose two songs for the audition, choose an up-tempo song and a slower-tempo ballad. Sing the up-tempo song first in the audition, and then sing the ballad. If you are instructed to choose one song, choose an up-tempo song to audition. Many vocalists think that singing a ballad is better for some reason. But they may not realize that the judges have been auditioning vocalists all day, or for days! And guess what the judges have been listening to all day long? Ballads. If you sing an up-tempo song, and you sound awesome, you will energize the atmosphere. Grabbing the judges' attention immediately will help your performance stand out from the rest. So, once again, choose a song that you are going to kill when you perform it.
9. **Recording preparation:** When recording, especially in a recording studio, always prepare in advance the songs you are going to track for the scheduled session day and time. Two copies of your lyrics should be printed out: one copy for the producer or engineer (sometimes the engineer is the producer) and one for yourself that you can refer to when recording.

   Be vocally warmed up and ready to sing when you arrive at the studio. Be well rested so that you can be your best attentive self during the long hours of intense focus you will need to put in when working with a producer. It may seem obvious that you should show up for the session prepared to sing! But I've seen some crazy scenarios with lead and background vocalists unprepared for their recording sessions. I've witnessed vocalists burning their voices out, either because they'd been rehearsing like crazy or because they hadn't maintained their voices in a healthy condition prior to the recording.

   When you record in a studio, time is money. You waste precious time when you are not healthy or not prepared. Your producer and engineer are making money during the entire session, whether or not you're ready to work with them. However, they will likely be annoyed if the vocalist isn't ready to track and appears to be unprofessional and not serious about recording. Let's look at this from another perspective: if you're not ready to sing, do you think you are going to be 100 percent happy with your recording? Vocalists frequently need to re-record their songs because they weren't prepared enough the first time. If you know you are going to record your songs, be prepared and well rested so that you are in excellent condition to sing spectacularly.
10. **Sound check preparation:** Know what you are going to sound check prior to getting on stage. Nothing looks more unprofessional than a band whose members are looking at one another and wondering, "So what do you want to sound check?" "I don't know, what do you want to sound check?" "Well, we could sound check this song . . ." "No, I think we should sound check this other song . . ." While you're taking your sweet time—that is, time out of your sound check—the production staff waits patiently to do their job for you. They also acknowledge that they are dealing with unprofessional musicians on the stage. If they see that you are inexperienced, they are

less likely to provide any extra special attention to help your band sound incredible through their P.A. and monitor systems. No one will take a band seriously if this is how you present yourself with a simple sound check. Always know what section of a song or songs you are going to sound check prior to arriving at the venue. Always be respectful and remember the production staff names and their job titles. These are the people who are in control of your sound!

5 One Voice That Lasts a Lifetime

Good Habits vs. Bad Habits

Any professional vocalist will agree that it can be difficult to keep the voice in excellent condition when touring, recording long hours in the studio, and keeping a busy schedule. Maintaining a healthy physical condition is imperative for a vocalist! If you are a young artist, remember that you won't be young forever! The best way to sum up what I'm about to cover in this chapter is this: you have only *one voice* that needs to last you a lifetime! If you burn your voice out, damage it, or lose it, you can't go down to the local music store and buy yourself a new set of vocal cords. What you have inside your larynx is what needs to remain in tip-top shape. Remember, it is consistency that gets you labeled professional! You can never allow yourself to be anything else less than absolutely spectacular with your voice condition. If you are tired, your voice is tired. If you are sick, your voice is most likely fatigued. If you are hungover, your voice is hungover. If you haven't slept, your voice is not rested enough. Your voice is like a radar, constantly informing you of your body's condition. In this chapter, we will cover healthy voice maintenance, unhealthy habits for the voice, and vocal abuse.

Healthy Voice Maintenance

Good Nutrition

How many times have we heard "you are what you eat"? Drinking or eating junk food or dairy products is not a smart idea prior to singing. Dairy products and fatty foods produce phlegm. Fatty foods can also generally weigh you down, causing you to feel full and tired. Whether you're singing in a vocal lesson, a session, a band rehearsal, a show, or a recording session, be aware of what you eat and drink prior to singing. I tell my artists to pack their food and drinks for the day, since they have very busy schedules that make it difficult to follow a healthy diet. Try to eat your three meals a day, or else pack some snacks (nuts, protein bars, fruit) and water. If you spend one hour once a week on shopping for the entire week, you can be ready and armed to eat healthy for whatever busy schedule you maintain. When I tour in the U.S. or abroad, I always pack healthy trail mix, Power Bars, tea, and honey sticks. This way if I'm starving I won't resort to eating junk food at a convenience store or elsewhere.

Physical Shape

Staying in great physical shape can be a touchy subject for some artists. I am always brutally honest and will not candy-coat this topic! If you are a performing artist, lead or background vocalist who wants to perform or currently performs onstage, you need to maintain a healthy physical condition for two reasons. One reason is that we all like to believe that the music industry and public, judges us solely on our musical talent. I'm here to tell you that 98 percent of the time this thought is not true! I'm not saying you need to look like a model or anything like that. What I'm saying is that you need to look in a good physical shape when you are a performing artist. Photos, video, and film are a standard element of performing. When A&R people call me and ask if I know any lead vocalists or background vocalists to audition for a national act that is getting ready to tour, I'll ask, "What are the requirements for this audition?" Below is just one example, but the requirements usually go in this order:

- Female, blonde hair (sometimes height request)
- Must be between the ages of twenty and twenty-three and look in good shape
- Must sing pop-rock styles and sound something like Kelly Clarkson, Pink, and Paramore

Shocking, huh? Not really—they are looking for vocalists that fit a certain image as well as demonstrate the necessary talent for the gig. So staying in good physical shape will give you a shot at getting more gigs!

The other reason to remain in great physical condition is to give you the stamina you'll need for those gigs. You might be performing three fifty-five minutes sets per night, or two hours in a row when on tour—up to six nights a week. Also, you are not normally standing still for the entire show. You most likely will move or run around onstage when you are singing. If you are out of shape, this will be physically draining—and the voice is the first part of the body to become exhausted. Overcompensating for fatigue with muscle tension and excess air pressure will only damage the voice. To ensure that you have the stamina to perform consistently, you need to be in great physical shape before you go on tour!

Sleep/Relaxation

The voice is a delicate and sensitive instrument. Relaxing during down times in your busy schedule is imperative! Even if you only have enough time to take power naps, they can help to recharge the body and voice. It can be very difficult to do when you are touring and have gigs every night in a new city or country. When I'm out on tour, and traveling by plane, train, and car, I close my eyes and rest or sleep. Mel, my bass player for Whole Lotta Rosies, has this down! I've seen her asleep on top of her bass amp at a motorcycle festival. Do you know how loud it is at an indoor motorcycle festival? I had to wake her to get ready to go onstage. She always replies when waking, "Sleep is overrated. I'll try and rest wherever and whenever." Mel is the queen of resting up, becoming recharged with energy and ready to rock out. Getting plenty of rest and a good night's sleep is important for maintaining a healthy voice and energy for any situation.

Water

Vocalists always need to drink lots of water (room temperature) because it helps to keep the throat and body hydrated. When we sing we inhale through the mouth, which makes the throat dry. Water is the best remedy for dryness. Some vocalists say that they don't like water, so they drink flavored water or sports drinks instead. Many times this results in phlegm being present. Phlegm is a sticky fluid that can drip down from the throat into the larynx and hang on the vocal cords. Phlegm can add extra weight to the vocal cords, making it difficult to achieve a natural vibration. Water helps to wash away phlegm that has been kicked up from the vocal cords or is present in the throat passageway. Why is room-temperature water important? Imagine playing guitar; you've been warming up and practicing for twenty minutes, and you then place your fingers on a block of ice for a couple of seconds before going back to practicing. Your fingers are going to be a little stiff, and the same is true of vocalists who chill their throats.

Steam

Breathing in warm steam is great for a vocalist suffering from a sore throat or nasal/head congestion. Steaming helps to soothe the swollen membranes and loosen congestion in the head and sinuses. A steam machine is effective because you can place your nose and mouth into the mask, creating a direct flow of steam to the membranes. Steam machines are inexpensive and should be available at your local pharmacy or online. Steaming with this remedy will take fifteen minutes of your time. It's best to do this in the morning and at night before going to bed, when congestion is usually at its worst.

If you don't have a steam machine, try the old-school approach by pouring boiling water into a bowl. Pull a towel over your head and put your face over the hot water. Inhale through the nose and exhale through the mouth. The water will become cool quickly, so this steaming method will most likely take ten minutes of your time. Once again, it's best to do this in the morning and at night before going to bed.

The Neti Pot

The nasal cleansing pot known as the Neti pot is becoming more popular among singers. Vocalists who are suffering from head congestion due to allergies or illness use this technique to wash and remove dirt, pollen, excess mucus, and other irritants from the nasal cavities. The nasal passages become soothed and moistened after using the Neti pot. However, daily use is not recommended because not only the bad but also the good bacteria in the nose rinses away. Nasal mucus contains good bacteria that have beneficial qualities in fighting respiratory infections. When all the good bacteria rinses away it leaves the body in an unstable condition, susceptible to other illnesses. Good bacteria help you fight off illness, so you need to keep them present. I use the Neti pot when I'm just beginning to get sick and am feeling the first symptoms of head congestion. I'll use it once in the morning and once at night, but never more than three days in a row. I make sure to eat healthy, stay hydrated, and get plenty of rest to kick whatever is going on. I should be fine in three days, and if not, I'm off to see the doctor.

Teas

Some vocalists find temporary relief from throat irritation by drinking certain teas. However, drinking tea does not make your vocal cords feel better, only the throat. When we swallow, the fluids we drink go from the mouth to the throat and down the esophagus, and not into the larynx. Remember, the epiglottis closes over the top of the larynx when we eat and drink. Tea will also dry the throat, especially teas that contain caffeine. Some singers will stay away from drinking tea altogether for this reason. But others will drink tea with caffeine to help dry out the phlegm that is present in the throat. A favorite tea among vocalists is

"Throat Coat" tea. If you need to sweeten it up a bit, add honey to it instead of sugar. Peppermint tea is soothing for the throat as well. You can find both of these teas in the grocery, health food, or vitamin stores.

Unhealthy Habits and Irritants for the Voice

As mentioned above, maintaining a healthy physical condition is extremely important for a vocalist. However, sometimes vocalists derail off the healthy path onto a not-so-healthy regimen that can damage the vocal cords. The areas of the vocal cords that most frequently become affected are the back inner edges that help produce voice in the upper register. When the back inner edges of the vocal cords became irritated and swollen, the higher notes become more difficult and challenging to sing. If you're dealing with any of the following sources of irritation, learning what can happen and what you must do to counteract their effects is crucial. Understanding what exercises to do will help the voice get through these challenging times.

Smoking

Everyone asks this question: "Does smoking affect my voice?" The answer is yes! Hot tobacco smoke burns the vocal cords. The heat and chemicals from cigarettes and marijuana irritate the vocal cords. When this happens, the cords begin to swell and become thick. Once again, the area primarily affected is the back inner edges of the vocal cords. The majority of vocalists who smoke agree that singing in the upper register can be difficult.

I used to smoke half a pack of cigarettes a day. I always had a strong upper register, but when I smoked it took a lot longer to warm up my voice, especially if I had smoked a lot the night before. Depending on how much you smoke and how your individual body handles these irritants, the effects can vary from person to person—meaning that some vocalists will develop more damaging effects more quickly than others.

When you quit smoking, the lungs go through a clean-out period. The lungs are lined with small hairs called cilia. When you stop smoking these hairs become active again and begin to clean out the mucus that has built up in your lungs. Although this is healthy, you are now coughing up a lot of phlegm. The lungs can clean out like this for several months.

When I quit smoking, it took six months to get all the crap from my lungs to clean out. I'd quit before, but the phlegm I coughed up while my lungs were releasing toxins was such a nuisance when I sang that I always went back to smoking. I'm glad that I finally quit, because after six months of not smoking and dealing with the phlegm issues, I felt better than ever. My voice was so much easier to warm up, I could sing for longer durations, and I had more energy while performing onstage. Let's remember, you only have one voice that lasts you a lifetime!

Coughing and Clearing the Throat

When you cough or clear your throat, the vocal cords rub together. If you do this constantly, the vocal cords can become irritated and swollen. The back inner edges of the vocal cords are primarily affected; this will make singing in the upper register difficult. Take care not to cough too loudly when trying to clear any phlegm inside your throat. Sometimes you will feel phlegm on your vocal cords. The urge to clear the throat ("hm-hm-hm") just before singing can be a difficult habit to break. Some vocalists have developed this bad habit due to phlegm but also because of nervousness. When you feel that phlegm is present on your vocal cords, try the following tips:

- When you notice phlegm during your warm-up exercises or songs, sustain the note you are presently singing. Your voice might sound interrupted or distorted because of the phlegm, but keep sustaining that note. When the vocal cords vibrate, the phlegm that is present will shake off the cords. Once the phlegm flies off, it usually kicks back up into the throat. Quickly swallow water to wash it down the esophagus.
- You can very gently clear your throat if you are dealing with an excessive amount of phlegm. You should also be flushing your body with water to clear out the phlegm from the throat.

Stress

Stress is difficult to avoid. Let's face it, we all get stressed out, sometimes not even realizing what that stress is doing to our bodies. Stress or nervousness can produce muscle tension in the body, which can hinder the vocal cords from their natural processes. Why? Muscles surround the vocal cords and mechanisms inside the larynx, and when one muscle becomes tense a chain reaction of muscle tension is set into motion. When this happens the vocal cords can't stretch naturally. All artists need to figure out what they need to do to reduce their own stress or nervousness. Whether you do yoga, relax in a Jacuzzi, take a long walk, etc., create a list of ways to help you relax!

Illness

When you're sick with a sore throat, the lymph nodes can become swollen, which makes the throat feel closed or tight. Head colds and congestion can clog the ears, making it difficult to hear accurate pitches, or to gauge whether you're singing with too much volume. These issues can make a vocalist overcompensate and engage the vocal cords incorrectly. This is one reason that understanding how to warm up the voice is so important. The muscle memory that you have established from practicing scale exercises will provide an easy and safe warm-up process so that you won't risk damaging your voice when you're sick.

Fatigue

Your voice is usually the last part of your body to wake up in the morning, and the first indication that you are getting tired at night. When you first wake up, the voice sits lower, deeper in register than normal. When you get tired, the voice once again drops deeper, lower in pitch—the body's first signal that you are becoming fatigued.

It will be very difficult to maintain a normal vocal production when fatigued. Because a musician's schedule is hectic and demanding, offering little time to relax, it's important to know how to warm up the voice when you're tired. Be sure to check out the list of recommendations in the later section "Warning Signs of Vocal Abuse" to learn how to treat a tired voice with care.

Acid Reflux

If you are prone to acid reflux, it is not recommended to eat for at least two hours before your performance. Singing after eating can kick up stomach acid, which in turn can produce phlegm. It also is not recommended to eat for at least two hours before sleeping. When you lie down, the acid attempting to digest the food in your stomach continues to travel up the esophagus, and can even reach the level of the vocal cords. In severe cases, the stomach acid can burn the cords and cause them to swell. If your symptoms are mild, simply identify what you are ingesting that is acidic (pineapple, tomato sauce, coffee) and cut it out of your daily life for a week or so to test whether your symptoms subside. If this is a major case of acid reflux, then you may need to see an ear, nose, and throat (E.N.T.) doctor.

I had the worst acid reflux years ago and did not understand at the time what was wrong with my body and my voice. My symptoms began with heartburn after eating sometimes, then progressed to burning sensations in my throat when I woke up in the morning. My voice sounded much lower in pitch than normal and was taking much longer to warm up. Then I started waking up from fluid in my mouth (stomach acid). I was pale and completely fatigued, with no energy whatsoever. My voice never seemed to warm up properly and I could no longer sing with ease. I finally went to the doctor after six or more months in this condition—way too long. The doctor suspected what was happening from hearing my symptoms. He put a camera (scope) down through my nose to my esophagus, and there we saw on the monitor screen the damage from acid reflux. I had several burns and bleeding throughout my esophagus, and the stomach acid was burning my vocal cords as well. I went on a strict diet and medication for more than six months in hopes that my esophagus and vocal cords would naturally heal. I was lucky and was fine in nine months. My advice is never to ignore acid reflux. Even if it's minor, see an E.N.T. doctor before the problem gets worse.

Warning Signs of Voice Abuse

Most vocalists don't like to talk or even hear about this topic out of fear that learning about it brings on some bad karma. Often the disorders of vocal abuse and misuse are reversible. The best treatment is to identify and eliminate the vocal behavior that created the voice disorder. In many cases, voice therapy or instruction can help by teaching good vocal techniques such as proper breath support for speech or eliminating forceful vocalizing. Sometimes eliminating the abuse or misuse and voice therapy or instruction isn't enough. In some cases, medication to block the production of stomach acid may be helpful. In other, more extreme cases, a surgical procedure may be necessary to remove growths from the vocal cords. Unfortunately, most disorders of vocal abuse easily recur following surgery. If the vocal misuse continues, therapy with a speech-language pathologist after surgery may help prevent recurrence of the problem. A speech-language pathologist is a health professional trained to evaluate and treat people who have a voice, speech, language, or swallowing disorder that affects their ability to communicate.

In my experience, artists who have not been good to their voices usually go through a typical series of warning signs that something is wrong. I call it the three-warning-sign order. The three-warning-sign order is a series of red flags indicating that real trouble with the voice is on its way! So if you show signs of the problems I am about to describe, take note and take charge of these issues.

1. After singing, or the next day, the voice sounds a little bit hoarse, scratchy, and lower in pitch than the pitch of your normal speaking voice. The best thing to do for your voice is to rest, sleep, and abstain from alcohol and smoking. The next day, warm up the voice by singing falsetto, stretching out the vocal cords using the arytenoid effort. (To refresh your familiarity with the falsetto production, refer to Exercise #7.) Do not practice your lower-register exercise or any mixed voice productions. It's important to work only in falsetto to help reduce the swelling on the back inner edges of the vocal cords. Usually, it is this area of the vocal cords that receives the most abuse from vocalists. The falsetto is the healing part of the voice.

2. The voice sounds lower and hoarser than before, breaking and cracking when you try to speak. You are burning your voice out with bad vocal technique! When this warning sign appears, rest completely for an entire day without speaking. Over the next few days, continue to get plenty of rest, avoid alcohol and smoking, and warm up the voice by singing falsetto, stretching out the vocal cords using the arytenoids effort. (To refresh your familiarity with the falsetto production, refer to Exercise #7.) Do not practice your lower-register exercise or any mixed voice productions. It's important to work only in falsetto to help reduce the swelling on the back inner edges of the vocal cords.
3. The voice sounds completely hoarse. When you try to speak or sing, only air comes through at first, followed by the voice abruptly sounding. The voice feels completely tired and sounds much lower in pitch than the normal speaking voice. Pay special attention; this is a major red flag! Complete rest is a must for the next few days, and if you cannot get the voice to warm up with singing falsetto, it's time to go to see the E.N.T. specialist! Don't mess around with this condition. Get to the doctor.

The four most common disorders resulting from vocal abuse and misuse are:

1. **Laryngitis**
   Laryngitis is an inflammation of the larynx and swelling of the vocal cords. The vocal cords can still vibrate and produce sounds, but not at their normal capacity. If a voice is suffering from laryngitis for more than two weeks, an examination by an otolaryngologist (a physician/surgeon who specializes in diseases of the ears, nose, throat, head, and neck) is recommended. Laryngitis may be caused by excessive use of the voice, bacterial or viral infections, acid reflux, and other irritants like inhaled chemicals.
2. **Vocal Nodules**
   Vocal nodules are small benign growths on both sides of the vocal cords. They form at the area that receives the most pressure when the cords come together to vibrate and phonate. Vocal nodules first appear as swollen spots that can develop into harder, callus-like growths. Nodules will grow and become stiffer with continued vocal abuse. A voice that is suffering from vocal nodules usually sounds hoarse, scratchy, breathy, and lower in pitch than normal.

   Vocal nodules are the most common disorder among singers and are the result of incorrect vocalizing. The majority of vocalists who have suffered from vocal nodules either didn't know the warning signs or chose to ignore them. Being scared that the doctor will find something wrong with you is not a bad thing, because addressing what is wrong will help you get back on the road to recovery and singing up a storm again! Ignoring the signs and making excuses for not seeing a doctor prolongs the inevitable and delays the recovery process.
3. **Vocal Polyps**
   Vocal polyps are benign growths that are similar to a vocal nodule but softer and more like a blister than a callous. They most often form on one side of the vocal cords. A vocal polyp develops from vocal misuse, gastroesophageal (acid) reflux, or long-term cigarette smoking. Vocal polyp symptoms often produce a hoarse, breathy voice that is lower pitched than normal. The majority of vocalists who have suffered from vocal polyps either didn't know the warning signs or chose to ignore them. It is best to see a doctor to begin recovering from this condition.

4. **Contact Ulcers**
   Contact ulcers are often experienced by people who use too much force when bringing the vocal cords together to speak. The excessive force causes ulcerated sores, or a wearing away of tissue on or near the cartilages of the larynx that move to bring the cords together. These ulcers are also found in people who have gastroesophageal (acid) reflux. Symptoms of this condition are an easily tired voice and pain in the throat, especially while speaking.

Scientists who study vocal abuse and misuse are conducting in-depth studies of the tissues of the vocal folds to determine how various types of stress affect these delicate tissues. They are especially interested in determining why particular behaviors in some individuals lead to vocal nodules while similar behaviors in other individuals may lead to mild laryngitis, vocal polyps, or little or no voice change. The best ways we know to protect your voice from all of these ailments, however, is to practice good health habits and good vocal technique! Take care of your one voice so that it really will last a lifetime!

Conclusion

Singers have the freedom to express their story and emotion through singing. Whether your goals are to become a professional musician or to sing just for fun, embrace your passion, move forward, and enjoy every step of the way. You never know what lies ahead and where your path will lead.

Set goals for yourself that you can achieve by taking baby steps toward them every day. Take chances and sing when the opportunity comes your way, but also learn to seek those opportunities out. No one will come knocking on your door offering a chance of a lifetime. You'll need to knock on many doors yourself to make it happen!

Every year, music evolves, grows, and changes, embracing new styles, new genres, new artists, new songs, new equipment, new recording techniques, new music business rules and procedures, and new licensing and publishing laws. Music doesn't remain in a static state! Read on through the next four sections and absorb all the vital information. You have nothing to lose, only incredible knowledge and skills to gain.

The power of music is life-changing and rewarding. Go out there, create, sing, perform, and, most of all, take the steps to make your dream a reality!

Part 2
The Art of Songwriting

With
Anika Paris

Introduction

It all begins with a song. Whether it's performed at the piano, grabbing your guitar, or singing over beats, a great song should be able to stand on its own. The question is, what kind of song, what style, and what signature sound is right for you? Why did you choose to be a writer? There are no "pure methods" of songwriting, but there are ways to spark your inspiration, and to help you understand what you want to say and how to say it. The rest is pure and unexplainable "magic"—a voice paired with a lyric and melody that resonates with audiences, transcending the individual songwriter and taking on a life of its own. With a worldwide audience, and a multitude of musical styles that appeal to the seven billion people on this planet, there's a place for you.

I've been writing since I can remember, on napkins, on Post-its, on steamed bathroom mirrors, on sidewalks, in wet cement, and sometimes even on paper. Whenever the muse comes to visit I tattoo the world with lyrics and songs. Yes, songwriting is exciting, freeing, and inspiring, but it is also a discipline that needs practice, much like singing or learning an instrument. It is an endless dedication, I believe, to an art one never truly masters.

A common mistake is to get discouraged and throw in the towel after writing only two or three songs. Another is rushing to immediately record every song, thinking *this* will be your big break. Unless you give yourself time to write, your best work has yet to surface. My motto is you have to write a lot of mediocre songs to get to the good ones. Some writers are born with an innate quality, a gift that only gets better with time. Others have to work harder to write as well. But you won't know your true potential until you put in the work.

We writers are of a different ilk than most, hearing melodies and lyrical whispers that wake us from a deep sleep, drawing us into the arms of our muse, each time thinking *this* song will be the best of all. I'm sure your friends who are not artists won't understand when you're in the "writer's zone." That's when you fall off the face of the earth, disappear from time's agenda, without realizing hours, sometimes even days, have come and gone. But I wouldn't trade it for the world. I'm guessing you feel the same! So, if you're interested in exploring the process of songwriting through a variety of disciplines and creative insights that I've learned over the years, let's get started.

6 You and the World of Music

Without music, life would be a mistake. —Friedrich Nietzche

Call it hyperbole, but music is a primal element of human nature. Perhaps it predates even language. The role it plays in our everyday lives and throughout history is as natural as life's breath. It is the invisible friend accompanying us throughout time, an expression of the emotions we hold deep within our souls. How profound that we, as a species, are communicators in voice and tone, therefore first and foremost musical beings. As early as tribal chants and intonations, to ancient hymns, to symphonies and beyond, music is an integral part of who we are. To know its roots and have an understanding of music evolution is invaluable for songwriters. I believe most artists desire to leave their mark one day. Perhaps we even fantasize about a future civilization discovering our music and playing it aloud for all to hear long after we are gone. When looking back on history, it is the arts—books, theater, architecture, film, poetry, and music—that remain, defining an era and reminding us of our human evolution. To be a part of that tapestry is a gift. And as sure as technology grows exponentially, we will continue to grow with it. We will use computers and terabytes to store libraries of music, upload data to clouds, and transmit mp3s and sound waves through cyberspace. We may eventually lose all physical hard copies of music. If so, can we ensure that our work survives? It is something to consider. Why? Because your work and your songs have a life of their own, beyond you.

Earliest Written Song

Here's an example. The oldest piece of music known to us was written 3,400 years ago. That's a long time ago. The music was carved on clay tablets that were discovered during an archeological dig in the ancient Syrian city of Ugarit. These tablets had symbols resembling "guitar tablature" for lyre strings in cuneiform script, the earliest writing system. Dr. Richard Dumbrill discovered thirty of these musical texts, but only one clay tablet was preserved well enough to be transcribed into modern musical notation. Many scholars still argue about its true melody. But you can look it up online and hear interpretations of it played by various artists on piano, on lyre-guitar, and even in symphonies. What an eye opener—the thought that we could all have our musical legacy shared for thousands of years to come.

Looking back, we must acknowledge the many influential artists who paved the way for us to continue in their place. Music has always intertwined with art, fashion, dance, and the societal pulse defining each decade. It's the soundtrack of our lives. From ragtime at the turn of the century, through the vast musical pilgrimage leading up to the birth of rock 'n' roll, and today's electronic dance movement, we have seen many musical genres influence entire generations of listeners. Even the way songs were delivered, from the hand-cranked Victrola to digital streaming online, keeps pushing us into new playing fields. How have time and technology changed music? Where are we going, and where do you fit in?

Our musical history is so vast; it is difficult to cover everything in one book, or even to research its lifetime by rummaging through libraries filled to the brim with texts, artifacts, instruments, songs, and scores. Still, I think you will find it empowering to learn how new styles, trends, and technology merged and evolved into today's popular music. I also believe a knee-deep understanding of genres will greatly enhance your songwriting. If this is something of interest, you can go to Chapter 13 for a more in-depth look. There, I touch upon trends and the evolution of western music, giving you a broader perspective.

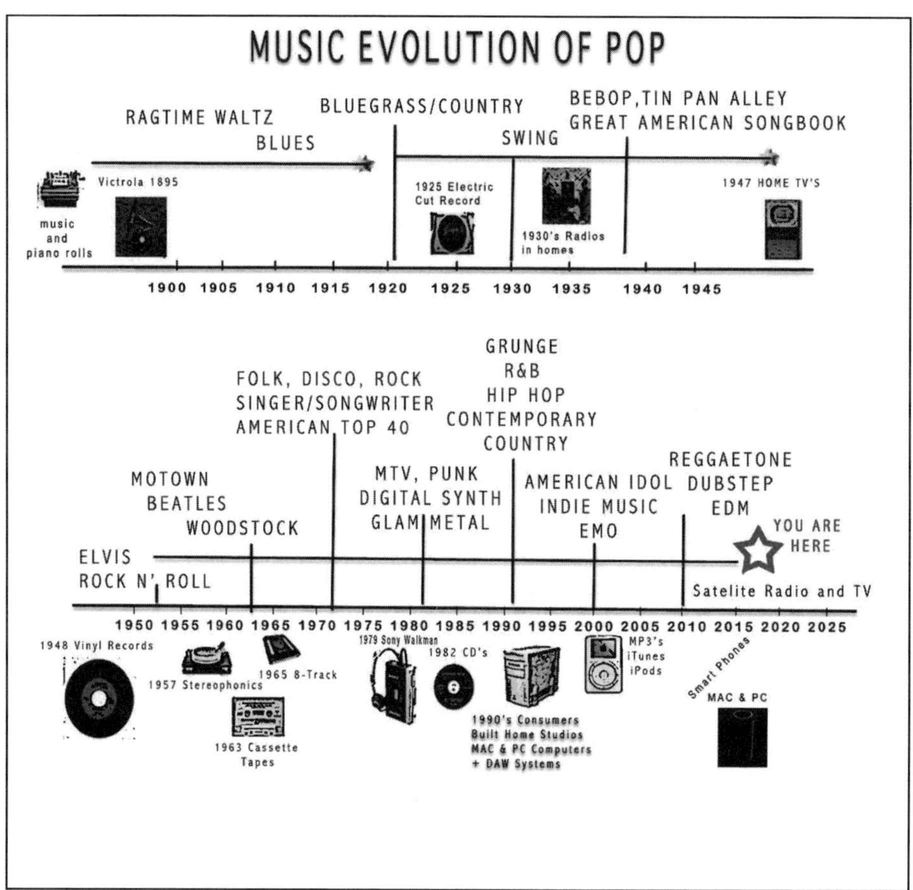

Popular Music Trends

As songwriters we must participate in what's going on in the world around us. The hunger for something fresh and new is built into the human psyche. It is the latest craze of sound we all are chasing. Like a fast-moving train, music bolts through our lives and we want to catch it. People cringe when I say the word "pop," but it is simply an abbreviation of the word "popular." The term "pop song" was introduced into our vocabulary as early as 1926. It started when ragtime was considered "pop!" Since then, a new rhythmic rage of "pop" seems to appear every twenty to twenty-five years. Today's artists, whether they know it or not, are borrowing from past trends and sounds that evolved over time, and adding the new flavor of the minute. Quincy Jones said it best: "The melody stays the same, but each generation has its own rhythm."

I think it's important to understand that each generation develops and pushes forth a new musical style for the future, like a snowball effect collecting sounds that we all keep building upon. Did you know that English and European traditions in music became heavily influenced in America by African-American sounds and culture? Much of the music we know and love today is because of a black influence on music, starting with ragtime. Without these predecessors there would be no rock 'n' roll, blues, jazz, country, soul, pop, and everything in between. Robert Palmer, a musicologist and journalist for *Rolling Stone* magazine, said this about its roots: "Rock 'n' roll was an inevitable outgrowth of the social and musical interactions between blacks and whites in the South and Southwest. Its roots are a complex tangle. Bedrock black church music influenced blues, rural blues influenced white folk song . . . blues and black pop influenced jazz, and so on. But the single most important process was the influence of black music on white."

Old Sounds, New School

Today's American music is a melting pot of sound and continues to grow with multicultural influences and ethnic genres. And retro sounds keep coming back in new mediums and new budding stars. Beyoncé borrowed Tina Turner's grit and moves; Bruno Mars borrowed the song styles of Elton John, Billy Joel, seventies funk, and even fifties doo-wop. Amy Winehouse mixed up the Motown flavor of Diana Ross with a touch of Billie Holiday's jazz style. And Sam Smith brought back the smooth sounds of R&B soul reminiscent of Sam Cooke. Even pop diva Lady Gaga brought together different generations by singing and touring with legendary jazz singer Tony Bennett. Talk about full circle.

So the one thing that remains is "music" and audiences that crave it. That musical train keeps on running. What's coming next? And what will you create before your last stop?

7 Raising Your Antenna

Inspiration flows through you, and although it is with you, it belongs to no one. —August Tygier

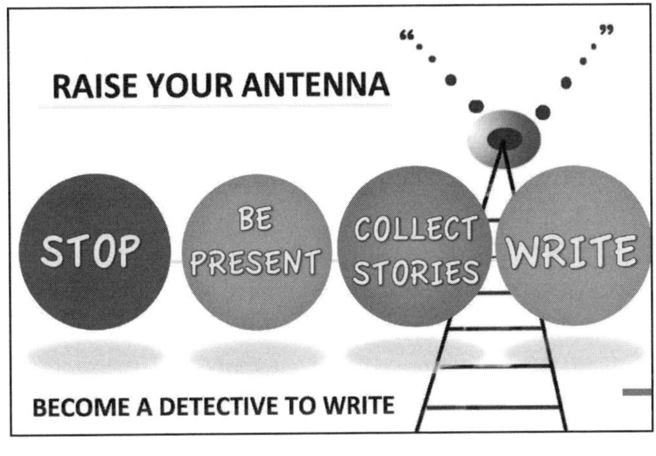

Broadcasting the way we see the world is an artist's blueprint and design. We didn't choose it. We are simply the conduits. Pablo Picasso says, "The artist is a receptacle for emotions that come from all over the place: from the sky, from the earth, from a scrap of paper, from a passing shape, from a spider's web." In other words, as writers we need to raise our antennas and listen to the signals going off all around us. We must live as detectives, collecting information, stories, and truths, and reveal how we feel about them. As musicians, we must create a musical palette to color our lyrical interpretations. Merging the two is often the challenge. We all experience life in a different way, whether culturally, religiously, ethnically, or geographically. Music unites us by bridging the gap and the yearning that exists deep within us all; it lets us know that we are not alone. In this chapter, we will discover creative ways to live with a songwriter's mindset.

Think about your relationship to the world. There's your internal world and your external world—what goes on around you and what goes on inside you. We experience life through all our physical senses—sight, sound, taste, touch, and smell. And we experience life by how we feel about it, and how it affects us. As writers, we live by expressing this.

And yet, there will always be barriers to stop us from writing. Whether it is writer's block, or time constraints, or fear of what people might think that holds you back, I suggest you start to train your mindset by writing something down every day, even the simplest of things you've noticed. What stood out to you, what do you remember from your day? You can also write about the dreams and visions you see in a deep sleep. Buy yourself a special journal to collect little bits and pieces of inspiration daily. Make sure to write them down when the details and the emotions are crystal clear. Record your thoughts, observations, and lyrics when they come to mind. I promise you will not remember your brilliant idea later that day or the next morning. So even if it's in the middle of the night, or in the middle of a conversation, wherever this surge of creativity appears, get up, excuse yourself, and catch it while you can.

Writer's tools are a must. These might be a favorite pen, a journal, a smartphone or recorder, a thesaurus for synonyms, a rhyming dictionary, or a fabulous app I use called Master Writer. Whether you write on paper or electronically, make sure not to erase your original ideas or lyrics. You might find when you go back through the work that the original draft is the one you like the best. So it's important to have options to choose from once all your ideas are fleshed out. And don't forget to back up everything.

I have used many methods to spark inspiration. Sometimes I read other people's lyrics or get out into nature, read a book or watch a movie, lose myself in someone else's story. Most of the time, I write about my experiences, but that too can be daunting. If we don't have a specific idea in mind, the project of writing a song can be overwhelming because we are all experiencing a multitude of things simultaneously and may not know where to begin. I try to dial into a story, or an emotion prevalent in my life, so as to be more decisive about the topic before beginning. I still have pages and pages of half-written lyrics and ideas, hundreds of audio clips of melodies I've yet to work on or complete. But I believe the ones that are meant to be finished will never leave the room inside your mind, and you'll keep returning to them. The rest you'll abandon. Not every song you sit down to write needs completion. Perhaps these brainstorms and song segments are a way to clear the cobwebs in order to make way for the keepers. Even so, there are little jewels buried deep inside you that need to be excavated.

Tuning In

I recently read about a family that goes on "technology fasts." They unplug for an entire day, once a week from morning until evening: no phones, no television, no computers, nothing that can pull them out of the present moment, or away from hearing their inner thoughts. I challenge you to try it. I'm not sure I could do it for an entire day, but I consciously put my phone away when writing—turn off chat, Twitter, and anything that can interrupt my flow. I let people know I'm going into the writer's dungeon.

I find that people don't observe each other anymore. It's almost as if it's socially unacceptable just to sit and "be." We don't have to be occupied every millisecond. Being online, or constantly tethered to our phones, disconnects us from experiencing the real world, because we are more concerned about a virtual world. If it's not posted, did it really happen? Yes, it did. Tweeting #hadthebesttimetoday#, or posting a snapshot or a five-second commentary, is not being musically creative and opening up our imaginations. Instead, paint the picture with lyrics and music, and take us on a journey that rekindles the emotions you are trying to express. A songwriter's purpose is to allow the listener to feel. That's what makes you an artist. It's okay to have space and mystery in our lives. To organically experience being a part of this world cannot be a pastime; it is a huge part of what life is about, and especially important if you want to write.

Awakening Your Senses

We've talked about raising our antennas, getting into the mindset of a writer, unplugging, and tuning in. We need to make room to dip the pen deep enough, and open those doors wide enough, to see the broader picture. And we need to awaken our senses to find the space between reality and our imagination. I give the same advice to performers about performing. Before stepping on stage, they need to flip the switch from "everyday person" to "performer." And writers must practice accessing that energy and discipline, too, from being an everyday person to adopting the mindset of a writer, because inspiration comes and goes like the wind. Here's how.

Do You See?

DO YOU LOOK, OR DO YOU SEE?

SEE THE CRACKS IN THE SIDEWALK BENEATH YOUR FEET, THE ABANDONED PAPER CUP ROLLING BY, THE LEAVES AND WATER FLOWING DOWN THE GUTTERS, ALL THE DIFFERENT SHOES.

SEE THE PEOPLE WALKING BY YOU THEIR FACES, BODY LANGUAGE, CLOTHING AND ATTITUDES.

SEE THE LEAVES ON THE TREE TOPS, THE CLOUD FORMATION IN THE SKY ABOVE, THE RAIN GUTTER AT THE TOP OF A BUILDING, HIGH WINDOWS, SHOES HANGING OVER TELEPHONE WIRES. SEE A FAR AWAY HORIZON, SIT AND WATCH A TEENY TINY ANT.

Let's take an ordinary day and have some fun. Whether you walk or drive to work or take public transportation, you can start to experience your daily routine differently. In our homes, we see the same décor and objects daily and probably have a photographic memory of what they look like because they are stationary. We've probably all had to call home and ask someone there to locate something particular for us, while we describe in great detail where they should look to find it. When we are in the outside world, however, everything moves and interacts, creating changes daily. As you pass through your day, try observing everything in detail. Pretend your eyes are a camera filming along the way. Look at the shape of clouds, the tops of trees, the brim of a building, its windows, doorways, sidewalks, and gutters. Look for small, insignificant things, like shoes hanging from a telephone wire, a discarded cup, and a poster on a telephone pole. Think to yourself, "What's the story here?" Observe people, their faces and their body language. Describe what you see by writing about it. You can also do this in any new environment, even if you are sitting in a coffee shop, a lobby, a bus or train stop, a park, your car, anywhere you go. Write down all that you see and create a story. The more you have in your mind's creative room, the more easily you will be able to recreate imagery in songs.

Do You Listen?

This is one of the hardest for musicians and writers, because I think we probably all have a supersensitive reaction to sound. The world is polluted with noise, and music is pumped through every clothing store, mall, and restaurant. In quieter moments, try to sit and listen and identify all the sounds you hear. See if you can differentiate between nature's sounds and man-made sounds. Listen to the sound of rain, the wind, and birds singing . . . versus cellphones ringing, cars driving by, and sirens blaring. You can even listen in on people's conversations; this makes for great song ideas. Listening for detail is a great way to train your ears as well. When it comes to music, I have spent years in the recording studio sitting in front of studio monitors ranging in price from \$300 to \$20,000. I've learned to listen from a mixer's point of view. I've learned about the "sweet spot," finding exactly where to place my chair between two studio monitors when listening to a song. I've learned to

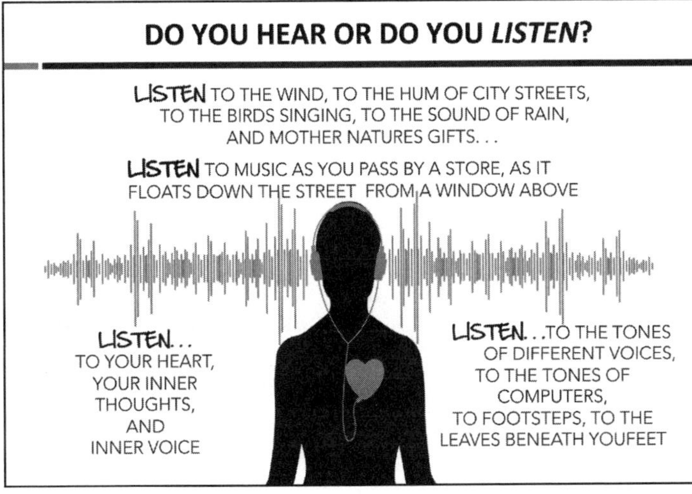
DO YOU HEAR OR DO YOU LISTEN?
LISTEN TO THE WIND, TO THE HUM OF CITY STREETS, TO THE BIRDS SINGING, TO THE SOUND OF RAIN, AND MOTHER NATURES GIFTS. . .
LISTEN TO MUSIC AS YOU PASS BY A STORE, AS IT FLOATS DOWN THE STREET FROM A WINDOW ABOVE
LISTEN. . . TO YOUR HEART, YOUR INNER THOUGHTS, AND INNER VOICE
LISTEN. . .TO THE TONES OF DIFFERENT VOICES, TO THE TONES OF COMPUTERS, TO FOOTSTEPS, TO THE LEAVES BENEATH YOUFEET

identify different frequencies (highs, mids, and lows). Try closing your eyes to hear a song in its entirety, not just focusing on the vocals. Tune into specific sounds. For example, listen to each instrument, and see if you can identify them all. If you rehearse or perform with a band, turn out the lights, face one another, and try to isolate every part and every instrument that is playing. Don't simply focus on your performance. Listen for transitions, solos, and the overall dynamics of the song and its various textures. Recognize how all parts paint this sound. We need to train our ears and become highly aware of soundscapes to fill up our mind's creative room with melodies and textures. Take notes.

Do You Taste and Smell?

DO YOU TASTE AND SMELL?

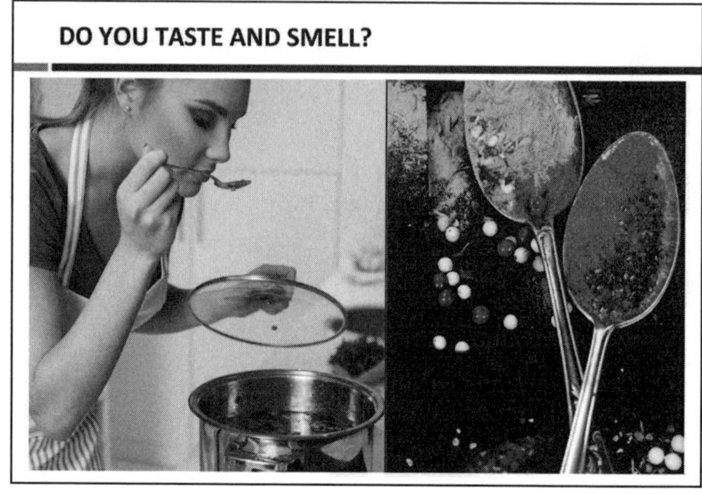

Ever since college, when I had to eat quickly between classes, I've found myself cramming in a fast meal before rushing off to the next thing. Yes, I love chocolate, a nice glass of wine, and fine cuisine. But most of the time I'm in a hurry, talking about something intense—or trying to unwind by watching television. European cultures have long lunchtimes and afternoon breaks, and hours to enjoy food while socializing. How often do we take the time to truly enjoy a meal, savor it and really appreciate it? I just watched a fabulous movie called *The Hundred-Foot Journey*, about a poor Indian boy who ends up becoming the top chef in Paris. It is based on a true story. And to watch him prepare a meal was like watching Renoir paint a masterpiece. He would take trips to the local market and pick fresh-dewed vegetables with vibrant colors and textures, then cut them into perfect bouquet shapes and place them one by one into a hot sizzling pan of oil and garlic. He took Indian spices from tiny glass jars, gently dipping his fingers into the earth-toned grains, tasting them first, then sprinkling them like rain over a creamy white truffle sauce. Watching the steam rise from the pan in slow motion made my mouth water. Although I could not smell the food, it was so beautifully filmed, it heightened my sense of awareness.

If I were to describe the fresh smell of coffee brewing, or the aroma of cinnamon rolls seeping from the oven, your olfactory sense would remember. In fact, smell is highly associated with memory. Simply visiting my grandma's house takes me into the past, just like the smell of honeysuckle bushes from my childhood catapults me back through space and time. I'm sure it's the same for you. Notice smells as you go through your daily rituals. Notice the scent of your shampoo, the aroma of a pizza joint, cigarette smoke, a scented candle, perhaps smoke from a chimney that instantly reminds us of winter and Christmas. There are so many aromas to experience. And for your next meal, take the time to enjoy it, taste it and smell it, and relish the experience. Describe it in writing.

Do You Experience Touch?

The one we don't fully pay attention to is touch. Well, okay, we do when it comes to either pleasure or pain. But what about all the sensations "in between," and our physical relationship to everything around us? You are most likely sitting right now while reading this book. Are you aware of the chair underneath you, your feet on the ground, the weight of the book in your hands, how it feels? Do you have to hold it open to read it? Are your fingers hot or cold? Is the paper rough or smooth? If you are reading it on your computer, how does the mouse or the touch screen feel when you click or scroll to move the page? Is it hot or cold, smooth or sticky? Are you truly aware of your physical being? Next time you brush your teeth, focus on the feeling of the brush, the temperature of the water, and the texture of the toothpaste as if it were your first time. When you shower, take a moment to feel the warm water on your back. Feel the movement of your fingers on your scalp when shampooing your hair. Feel what it's like to hold a warm cup of coffee or cold iced drink. What does it feel like to walk on hard cement versus soft grass or choppy gravel, or barefoot on a fuzzy carpet? Take a deep breath and hold it. Feel the edges of your body. Be aware of its relationship to everything around you. Be in the moment. Try describing it in words.

How Do These Exercises Help You in Writing?

We interact with the external world on a physical level via sight, sound, taste, touch, and smell, and on a concrete level via time, locations, seasons, events, etc. Then we interpret these in our internal world via emotions, thoughts, beliefs, feelings, opinions, etc. When we compose a song, we need to express our relationship to all three with lyrics, melody, and a musical mood.

The role of a *songwriter* is to create an experience for the listener.
The role of a *musician* is to create a mood imparting the emotion of the song.
The role of a *lyricist* is to describe that emotion.

Put all three together to create an experience.

1. Internal world (thoughts, feelings, and emotions): *This sadness is overwhelming.*
2. External physical effect of emotions: *My hands are shaking, my heart is aching.*
3. External world (place, location): *You left me here inside this empty house.*

In my song "Another Sleepless Night," the music is soft and haunting and dreamy. You feel the emotion of the singer longing for another. And the visual of a person in bed, thinking out loud, and traveling between reality and fantasy keeps it interesting. There are references to internal thoughts, external physical effects, and many of the five senses interwoven through the story.

OH ANOTHER SLEEPLESS NIGHT

Oh another sleepless night another moment counting sheep	Internal Thought/Physical sleeplessness—*Sight*
If only you were by my side maybe I could fall asleep	Internal Thought Physical sleeplessness—*Sight*
Can you see me smiling as I thinking of you	Internal Thought—*Sight*
If I walked into you dream where would we run to	Internal Thought—*Sight*
Maybe Paris in the middle of the fall	External Place—*Sight*
Oh another sleepless night beneath the vast and endless sky	Internal Thought/Concrete World Sky—*Sight*
I left the window open, and the breeze is softly blowing like a lullaby	External/Concrete World Room—*Sight, Touch, Sound*
Can you hear me as I'm calling out your name	Internal/External Sound—*Sound*
If I walked into your dream what would you say	Internal Thought—*Sight*
Come and dance with me in this masquerade	Internal Thought—*Sight*

Raising your antenna allows you to be more present. The more present we are in life, the more we have to draw from when we write. It also keeps us in touch with our physical and emotional connection to the world inside us and around us.

The Obstacles of Writer's Block

Songwriting is very often an all or nothing experience. You can be writing, and writing, and writing, and then it is as if you've run out of melodies and come to a dead end. Other times you may be staring at a blank page for hours, trying to find the right word to complete a line. There is nothing wrong with you. I often think of the movie *Forrest Gump*, when the title character is running and running across the country, and then he says, "One day I just stopped running." Sometimes getting stuck can also be indicative of the subject matter and your relationship to it. So how do we get around these roadblocks?

One of my students was having a hard time finishing his songs. We listened to three of his hip-hop tunes, which were pretty good. My job was to listen to him speak, and help him find a way back into his writer's flow.

STUDENT: I call these my party songs. I'm pretty happy with them. But now I've got all these new tracks I've written, and I can't write.

ANIKA: I like your songs—great beats, good solid feel, and they are engaging. I've noticed a lot of your lyrics are the same in many songs. Are you aware of that?

Student: Yeah, I guess so, I feel like I've already said a lot and now I'm drawing a blank.

Anika: So, what are you wanting to write about?

Student: I want to write about my future. I want to be rich and famous, and a celebrity.

Anika: Okay, is that all you want to say?

Student: I don't know. What do you mean?

Anika: What do you want your audience to walk away with after hearing your music?

Student: I never thought about it. I guess I want people I grew up with to see me rich and famous.

Anika: Why?

Student: Because I was bullied growing up biracial.

Anika: I wouldn't know that from your songs.

Student: Well, I was under a lot of pressure and discrimination. There were other kids too who were not rich enough and didn't fit in either. It bothered me the way we were treated. So I want to show the ones who bullied us that they didn't stop me from living my dreams.

We spoke more in depth about his feelings towards these judgmental kids, their discriminatory behavior, and how music was a great way of attaining some closure.

Anika: Write about *that* emotion and *that* truth. Tell them how you *feel* about what they did. Don't hide it. Give yourself and the other kids a voice. I think your writer's block may be in part because there's more to your story than you're allowing yourself to let out."

Student: Man, I didn't realize that until now.

The beauty of writing is getting that second chance to say what you wished you had said the first time. What would you tell a younger version of yourself when looking back on a situation? Or what would you say to someone else going through the same thing? We all need songs to dream to and dance to, but being a songwriter can't only be about partying and being rich and famous—especially in hip-hop music. It is a cultural genre that started in the streets. It gives a voice to the social injustices that often go unseen. And there's so much lyrical room.

My student talked about his feelings and observations regarding corporate greed, apathy in adolescence, searching for love, growing up in a technological world, and even traveling to impoverished countries to build schools for kids. We listened to his favorite rappers and analyzed why he liked their music and their subject matter. I told him how rich his life was and how wonderful his philosophies were, and that these things were not reflected in his songs. I explained that he would inevitably hit writer's block because he was avoiding his real emotions and using partying songs as a Band-Aid on a bigger wound, a deeper story. We all love fun music, but we also need music to heal ourselves. I suggested he write down everything he was thinking about, without editing himself, while it was fresh in his mind. And I gave him the assignment to come in the following week with a different story to his song.

Ever since our first lesson, waterfalls of ideas have come pouring down. He's written and recorded five new songs, all on different topics, in less than a month. I've watched his transformation first-hand. If you are in tune with your convictions and use music as your tool, the floodgates will surely open.

Music Soundscape

Changing the music soundscape you write to may also help you. Try juxtaposing a dark musical palette with powerful, uplifting lyrics, or taking poignant lyrics and creating an up-tempo, feel-good musical vibe. Experiment with this approach—you may not believe it will work, but in fact it may drive the message home even more. Sia's pop song "Chandelier" sounds epic and festive, but she's singing about facing the demons of alcoholism. And one of my favorite songs, written by Charlie Chaplin, is called "Smile." Michael Jackson sang it. Lyrically it is about smiling through a broken heart, but musically it is so sweet and beautiful that if you don't listen carefully you might think it is meant to be a happy song.

Everyone wants the writing process to happen with ease and to end up with great songs. Finding that perfect expression of ourselves musically and lyrically is the journey. Once you open up your senses, and tune into what you want to say, the creative process begins to unfold. What kind of artist do you want to be? What's your artistic voice? Artists like Bruno Mars, Earth Wind and Fire, and Pharrell Williams are known for feel-good music, love songs that make you want to dance. Katy Perry, Lady Gaga, and Madonna sing pop anthems about relationships and self-empowerment. The infamous Sex Pistols, Bob Marley and the Wailers, and Rage Against the Machine perform mostly politically driven songs. And music by Robin Thicke, Barry White, and Prince is often seductively sexy. Many of your favorite artists are expressing what's important to them. Perhaps it's how they cope with problems and their observations about the world. They use their music as a way to inspire, enlighten, entice, and provoke their audiences into thinking, feeling and, in the best-case scenario, making a change. Music is one of the most powerful mediums. So how will you use yours? Consider the following:

- How can you continue to raise your antenna, your senses, and stay in tune?
- What is important for you to express artistically?
- How do you want the listener to feel after hearing your music?

If you keep these things at the very core of your artistry, you're off to a good start.

8 An Overflow of Lyrical Madness

Hooks, Lines, and Sinkers

Poetry is when an emotion has found its thought and the thought has found its words. —Robert Frost

We've touched upon you and the world of music, talked about raising your antenna to uncover what kind of writer and artist you want to be. Now we are entering the woodshed. Everywhere you look you'll see words, words, and more words. Our constant electronic communications are a rekindling of the written word. I remember beautiful letters I would get from my father, handwritten in ink on rice paper, telling me of his European excursions and concert tours. Today those letters have evolved into e-mails. That is one of the advantages of modern technology; we are back to communicating through writing via texts, tweets, e-mail, blogs, and posts. So today, as in poetry, the visual aspect of the word is as important as its meaning. And lyric videos, where a song's lyrics are displayed as a visual, have become very popular. With that thought in mind, take a good look at the slogans, advertisements, storefronts, menus, books, movie titles, street signs, and banners you pass by every day—and you can collect an ocean full of lyrical inspiration. But how do we put it all into a sensible flow? How do we make something from nothing? How can we move our listener, paint the emotions of the story, relive conversations, and leave an imprint?

I suggest you learn from studying other songwriters. I turn to my favorites—John Mayer, Ed Sheeran, Ray LaMontagne, Sting, Paul Simon, Tom Waits, Joni Mitchell, Annie Lennox, Peter Gabriel, Bob Dylan, Leonard Cohen, Lennon/McCartney, Bernie Taupin, Carole King—and hit songs throughout the years for inspiration. And turn to poetry when you are "speechless from grief or joy," as Stanley Kunitz said. As a poet myself, I find that poetry provides a larger canvas, and a freedom with words without the added pressure of needing to sing well or fit into rhythmic meter. Poetry allows the imagination to be blown wide open. So reading contemporary poetry —like Billy Collins' "I Ask You," Charles Bukowksi's "A Smile to Remember," Maya Angelou's "Still I Rise," Langston Hughes' "I, Too," Pablo Neruda's "Don't Go Far Off," Robert Frost's "The Road Not Taken," and many more—can help spark new ideas about using language. Research contemporary poets (http://www.poemhunter.com), and study lyrics from songwriters in your genre (www.azlyrics.com), analyzing how they write. Note the clever verbal twists and turns in an up-tempo pop song by Taylor Swift, and the more reflective tone of a pop-folk ballad by Mumford and Sons. In rap, songs can be raw and uncensored with unique cultural phrases and rhythmic patterns and a much larger body of lyrics. And poetic songs create a unique imagery and feel, like many of Ray LaMontagne's songs. It is a definite art to compose a lyric of substance that not only imparts your song's message, but sings well and fits your musical genre.

For a writer it helps to have a natural sense of metaphor, and the desire to express an idea in a unique way. You can practice what I've discussed thus far: journaling, unplugging, collecting information, and listening to your inner voice to open up your muse. There are various ways to begin writing a song. Sometimes I start by simply sitting at the piano, singing gibberish to a chord progression until a song evolves organically. Or I'll begin writing with a specific quote and/or title I've set aside. And once I choose my approach, the process begins.

From wordplay, to hip-hop's free style, to internal rhymes, to double entendres, there are many tricks a writer can use to spice up a lyric. It's all in the approach and how you think. Sometimes a lyric is intended to be simple and conversational, other times clever and fun, and many times illustrating a scenario we all have been in at one time or another in our lives. But a great writer is also one who can say it like it has never been said before. In this chapter, we will explore different ways to make your lyrics sing.

You Can't Copyright a Title

BOOKS CAN BE INSPIRATIONAL

- A THOUSAND SPLENDID SUNS
- WHERE THE WILD THINGS ARE
- THE PERKS OF BEING A WALLFLOWER
- I GAVE YOU MY HEART BUT YOU SOLD IT ONLINE
- THE SOUND AND THE FURY

You Can't Copyright A Title

A creative way to inspire a song is using titles of movies or books as starting points. Titles are not copyrightable. You can Google best films of the year, surf through cable program lineups, or look up *New York Times* best-selling books to find titles that open your mind. As an exercise, take them and integrate them into a lyric. Of course, think about the style of music you'd like to pair them with.

Take a look at these creative templates of movie and book titles. I write for television and film and love to use metaphors and imagery, so the lyrical style I'm drawn to is evident from the titles I've chosen. Here's an example of a workable lyric from combining book and movie titles to begin creating a story.

I hear the sound and fury
in this house of sand and fog
As I set my heart to sail across the sea
Searching for an answer beneath a thousand suns
Lost within a requiem of dreams

MOVIE TITLES CAN INSPIRE SONGS

- REQUIEM FOR A DREAM
- THE HOUSE OF SAND AND FOG
- LOST IN TRANSLATION
- THE COLOR OF MONEY
- WHERE EAGLES DARE
- THE HEARTBREAK KID

You Can't Copyright A Title

I would then go back and take out the obviously recognizable titles and rewrite until the lyric felt right. You can choose titles and tailor them to your original writing style. To exemplify, let's take bands we know and pair them with a title that might be closest to their style of songwriting.

- *A Thousand Splendid Suns* would fit perfectly with Coldplay's ethereal style of music and poetic imagery.
- *Where the Wild Things Are* would be a good title for one of Imagine Dragons' edgy pop songs.

- Lorde might turn her spacious vocal style and nonconformist energy to a lyric using *The Perks of Being a Wallflower*.
- Linkin Park's rock and rage could incorporate *The Sound and the Fury* into a song.
- Blake Shelton could have fun writing a country song using the title *I Gave You My Heart, but You Sold It Online.*

There are many other titles that could be incorporated or used as springboards to create a theme and musical palette for your song, but this should give you a good example of how to do it.

Writing on Assignment

Someday you may be called to write for a scene in a movie, or for a commercial, or an artist looking for material. When hired to write on commission, you have to deliver quickly. Writing assignments can help you sharpen your craft, put you to the test, and prepare you for any given moment. And the song created can end up being great.

American Sniper is an Oscar-nominated film. I thought that would be a hard title to use in a song, but why not engage in the challenge? What could one do with this title? Perhaps it could be incorporated in a rap lyric or a rock song; metaphorically everything has its place. You can use it as a point of reference. To be less obvious, bring the story home to the listener by comparing it to a war many have in their everyday lives. Talk about all the shooting and killing that takes place in America. Who is hunted and who's the hunter? The right to bear arms, the right to kill—when is it ever right? What laws of war and peace can there be?

I had a student I was working with in artist development, meeting weekly to work on songs. He is an emerging hip-hop artist and goes by the name G5avage. I mentioned using book titles and movie titles for lyrical inspiration. I gave him "American sniper" in a verse as an assignment to see what he'd come up with as opposed to me. I did the assignment first and wrote a verse in my style:

An American sniper in the infrared light
I am the prey bearing no civil rights
Zip codes and borders blurring the lines
Release, aim and shoot, but you're not colorblind
Big Brother police with Baltimore force
Money and power in the bloodiest war
One nation under God but the battlefields here
With liberty and justice for all that you fear

Here's G5avage's. He likens his lyrical style to that of Kanye West, Common, and Bun B.

Dark night . . . no sounds . . . empty street
stands a fifteen-year-old with a pistol in his jeans
Handshakes to seal the deal and give the piece you ate in exchange for currency
over and over daily, looking over his shoulder
never knowing when his day will be
Up the mountain we watch 'em climb

with self-independence to push his grind
to a heavenly reach 'til the day he went insane
Lost his mind at a corner store for the Nutri-Grain
Such as an American sniper in the battlefield, we see this every day
asking for the right direction but nobody truly knows the way
Hustle to survive thinking it's the only means of pay
until you get sent upstate, and you wonder why things will never change.

Anika: What were you thinking about when you wrote this?
Student: I was thinking about my home, 36th Street in Tucson, Arizona.
Anika: Why, how does that relate?
Student: Because, in South Tucson, this is a specific area known for drug dealing and gang violence.
Anika: In reading your lyrics, are there hidden messages or the kind of speech only some will understand?
Student: Yes, if I were to break it down for you, it's about struggling to get out the hood, by doing what you got to do with what resources you have.
Anika: Okay. And when you wrote "Handshakes to seal the deal and give the piece you ate in exchange for currency," what does this mean?
Student: It's a Southern under-the-tongue trick, where you hide drugs. And "seal the deal" is the handshake, and the "munna" (money) you get for the drugs. Well, that's how Chicago kids talk.
Anika: What other choices do you feel you have?
Student: On any bad side of town I'm sure it's the same thing. You either go pro sports or you gang bang. Depending on your parents and if they even care, school is also an option. I chose music.
Anika: Is this a true story?
Student: It's real. I know people who have been through situations like it, but it's about hood life in general.
Anika: Did you know the person in the story?
Student: Yes, I knew him.
Anika: What happened to him?
Student: He got shot.
Anika: How did that affect you?
Student: It hurts. He was a friend of my dad's, but like family. I called him Uncle.
Anika: Would you record this for him to honor him?
Student: Yes. It will be called Diddyville.
Anika: I suggested "American sniper" to you. Did that spark a fire?
Student: The concept did more so than the name.

Hit in a Hat

I also conduct a Songwriters in the Round workshop for more advanced writers. Every week we meet at Amp Studios in North Hollywood, a funky rehearsal studio with carpeted walls, tight parking spaces, and noise leaking from the adjoining rehearsal rooms. We sit on the floor or the couch, coffee and tea in hand. It is a fabulous writers' circle, great artists playing new songs for feedback and critique. Every week there is a new assignment to push everyone to his or her limits.

One was called the "hit in a hat." Everybody writes down three titles or a pairing of words and places them in the hat. We then blindly choose three and vote on one. The words can be the main theme, or incorporated into a verse, or simply used as inspiration to write a new song. I ask each to explain their process. Danny Byrne and Josh Misko, writing partners (a.k.a. the band Everett Coast), ended up writing a fabulous song called "So So Bad" from this exercise. Here's how it happened, in their own words.

> Well, first off, talk about a fun way to write a song! Our "hit in a hat" words were "cigarettes and coffee." It's funny, sometimes words just click with you. We flew through the song that night! Neither of us smoke, but traditionally it seems caffeine and nicotine go together hand in hand, so it only felt right to associate "coffee" with one of our favorite places to get a caffeine fix—Coffee Bean! Then, staying true to Everett Coast fashion, we found a way to transition it into a love song. The lyrics flowed one after another as we painted a turbulent love affair where the significant other is just so, so bad, but so everything you need. Just like cigarettes and coffee are to many people around the world. Thus "So So Bad" was born.
>
> **SO SO BAD**
> Mama said when I was young that I'd meet girls like you
> She never told me 'bout the wild and crazy things you'd do
> Now I'm strung out on your love just like a drug
> Like an addict to your lovin', and you can keep it comin'
> I'm sorry, Mom, I'm in too deep and there's no going back
> She had me hooked with just one look and now I'm seeing black
> You got me strung out on your love just like a drug
> Like an addict to your lovin', and you can keep it comin'
> Oh, you take me, and play me like a symphony
> *Chorus*
> You're like my cigarettes and coffee bean
> Baby you're my nicotine
> That's so so bad and so everything I need
> You're like Veuve Cliquot and limousines
> The cocaine to my Charlie Sheen
> So so bad, oh you're so so bad . . .
>
> I love this song. It was just released on their latest EP, and all from an assignment.

Capturing the Listener with Opening Lines

The first few lines of a song are extremely important if you consider pulling in the listener from the get-go. Yes, the music, track, and singer have to be great as well, but challenge yourself to write an opening line that hooks the listener.

"Eleanor Rigby" is a classic song by the Beatles and sets a scene with a woman picking up the rice in a church where there's just been a wedding. The music is dark and mysterious, stirring up our curiosity and making us wonder what comes next. We soon find out that the song is about all these lonely people's stories, including this woman who watches and cleans up after weddings but never has her own.

"Bohemian Rhapsody" by Queen is another great classic. In the opening line, a young boy confesses to his mama that he's just killed a man by taking a shotgun, pointing it at his head, and pulling the trigger. The music is simple, mostly an acoustic piano and Freddie Mercury crying through the lyric at first, then leading us into an epic operatic ride that will not disappoint. Still, that first line is enough to make any heart ache.

In a more contemporary vein, John Mayer's song "Slow Dancing in a Burning Room" is a keeper. The title in itself lets the listener know something's ending badly, and the visual is brilliant. Mayer opens the song talking about the breath of a deep and dying love that isn't working. The ending of a relationship is a more common scenario than the Beatles or Queen songs. Most listeners have lost in love, but the way John Mayer renders this universal theme is painstakingly eloquent.

Adele's song "Someone Like You" is a great example, too. The narrator shows up uninvited to wish an old lover the best in his new marriage—though as she wishes him well, her words are full of pain. The opening verse paints a picture of this woman doing what most people would not have the strength to say or do. It touches a deep wound in all who have lost in love—and captures our hearts so that we listen to the song from beginning to end.

To pull the listener in immediately, your opening lines need to impress. Don't forget memorable music to support them, and a gifted singer to sing them—but if you have those few great opening lines, the song will sail, and the listener will follow.

Four Categories of Lyrical Styles

Now that we've looked at several different approaches to lyric writing—how to find titles as inspiration, strong opening lines, and writing exercises to get there—let's talk about how to give your songs character. Here are four categories of lyrical styles I've identified that may help you refine your lyrics.

1. Nonsensical
2. Narrative
3. Conversational
4. Poetic

Nonsensical

Lyrics don't always have to be perfect, poetically beautiful, painting pictures and provoking emotions. They can also be fun and playful and have a bit of ridiculousness. I call these lyrics nonsensical. Think of songs from your childhood, like "Supercalifragilisticexpialidocious"—a made-up word from *Mary Poppins* that makes no sense but sings well. Or think of pop songs like "Ob-La-Di, Ob-La-Da," by the Beatles; "De Do Do Do, De Da Da Da" by Sting, "Love Shack," by the B-52's; "Hey Ya," by Outkast, and Gwen Stefani's "Hollaback Girl" and her famous "banana breakdown" in the song. I don't even want to talk about Nikki Minaj's lyrics—her song "Four Door Aventador" would have us placing a sticker on this book for explicit language. Still, half of the time I have no idea what she's singing. Frequently we won't know the definitive meaning of a song's lyrics, but the flow and production can still make people sing along and dance.

Narrative

Narrative songs, or storytelling songs, usually lend themselves best to folk, pop, and country music. The lyrics take you from the beginning to the end of a situation in a linear fashion. Many of the most famous narrative songs are longer than the typical three-minute pop formula, some even as long as eight minutes. Bobbie Gentry's "Ode to Billy Joe" is a story about a farming family that learns of a local boy's suicide when he jumps off the Tallahatchie Bridge. The song "American Pie," by Don McLean, is rumored to be dedicated to the death of Buddy Holly. It was a number one hit song for four consecutive weeks. The legendary "Stairway to Heaven," by Led Zeppelin, and more contemporary songs like Carrie Underwood's "Jesus Take the Wheel," Eminem's "Stan," and Miranda Lambert's "The House That Built Me" are also great narrative songs. The list goes on and on.

Conversational

Many of the songs I love are favorites because of the way they sing. Singing is simply elongated speech, and great lyrical phrasing makes for memorable songs. Reading your lyrics out loud is a strong indicator of whether the emotion and cadence of the spoken words matches the melody you've written. If so, you've got a song based on a conversational type of lyric. For example, speak this line from the chorus of the Gnarls Barkley hit song "Crazy": "Does that make me craaaaaaazy?" The phrasing is exactly how you might speak it in conversation. Paul McCartney's "Yesterday" is another example. The inflection of each word invoking "yesterday," when his "troubles seemed so far away," could be sung or spoken, and the only true difference would be placing it in a key and setting it to music. Some other great examples are "Isn't She Lovely," by Stevie Wonder; "I Can't Make You Love Me," by Bonnie Raitt; and "My Heart Will Go On," by Celine Dion. If you take these lyrics and read them aloud with the emotional intent behind them, they sound the way they sing.

Poetic

Artists such as Leonard Cohen, Bob Dylan, Joni Mitchell, Sting, and Coldplay fall into the category of poetically driven lyrics. In contrast to the literal lyrics of narrative songs and the trendy lyrics of pop, Sting's fields of gold, Coldplay's starry skies, Joni's desire to drink a case of you, and Leonard's confession of stepping on an avalanche are ethereal concepts with a lot of room for interpretation.

Spices in the Spice Rack

What's in your spice cabinet? There are fun ways to bring words to life. Sometimes it's creating a new phrase, or pairing words as no one else has done, and then there are writer's tricks and traditional methods.

Oxymoron

Oxymorons are great for imagery and emotional conflict. Today music is more in-your-face than ever before, so using an oxymoron in your song is trendy. An oxymoron is a figure of speech in which contradictory terms are used together, for example:

quiet revolution	tame beast	dry pond	beautiful nightmare
terribly pleased	real fantasy	a new classic	enormously small

A great song that uses an oxymoron in the title is Sheryl Crow's "My Favorite Mistake," or "Bullet with Butterfly Wings" by the Smashing Pumpkins. If you wanted to include an oxymoron in a punk song, a title like "Life's Suicide" could work. You might use "Hello Again to Another Goodbye" for a ballad; for a political song, "Bombing for Peace." All of these oxymorons paint vivid pictures and can be provocative in allowing the writer to make a statement with words.

Alliteration

Alliteration is using the first letter of a word consistently throughout a sentence to create a sound, as well as a visual. We've all tried to say the tongue twister "Peter Piper picked a peck of pickled peppers"—well, that is an alliteration. It can be clever and fun not only for the tongue, but also for the ear. Write one that easily rolls off the tongue, and consider the sound of the alliteration for rapping or singing. I would avoid P's and T's or other hard consonants because they pop when using a microphone. S's would be a little softer, for example:

> So say you'll stay for summer suns and Saturdays
> Say you'll stay, and I'll be satisfied

You can try incorporating some alliterative lines into your verse to keep the lyric fresh and catchy.

Simile

A simile is a figure of speech in which two things are compared; one thing is "like" another, or takes action "as" another. A lot of clichés we've all used or heard are similes (cute as a kitten, busy as a bee), but you can also find similes in classic literature. Celia in Shakespeare's *As You Like It* tells her friend Rosalind, "I found him under a tree like a dropped acorn." There are many songs that incorporate similes into their lyrics. Elton John sings about living "like a candle in the wind," and Simon and Garfunkel immortalized friendship that stands "like a bridge over troubled water." Madonna's "Like a Prayer" and Far East Movement's "Like a G6" were also huge hits. It's all in how you choose to use those similes.

Metaphors

Metaphors are more direct than similes. A metaphor is a word or phrase applied to an object or action to which it is not applicable. William Shakespeare's "All the world's a stage" is the most famous of all. While similes maintain boundaries with those little words "like" and "as," metaphors cut straight to the bone. For example:

> Simile: You are *like* a sunlight beam as soon as the rain stops.
> Metaphor: You are my sunlight after the rain.

"Titanium," a beautiful song written by David Guetta, is a brilliant metaphor. He sings about being bulletproof: that no matter how much you fire away at him, he will not fall because he is *titanium*. A classic song by the Eagles also incorporates metaphor in referring to "Hotel California's" *lovely face.* Metaphors are everywhere in music.

You can take an intangible object and mix it with a literal metaphor. A prodigy student of mine, Natania Lalwani, and I each took on the metaphorical theme of "boxing up" feelings. My song is a ballad called "What Do I Do," and hers is a fun, up-tempo song called "Box You Up."

WHAT DO I DO
What do I do
with the rest of my love
tell me where does it go
should I put it in a box
and bury it outside under the snow
I can't go on until this love is gone
and I don't feel it anymore
How can I take
all this pain in my heart and
send it overseas
to a place I'll forget that we ever met
somebody tell me please
I can't go on until this love is gone
and I don't feel it anymore
Chorus
What do I do with the rest of my life
where does it go from here
how will I know when to let go
What do I do
Should I pretend that
you just need some time
Until all my hope fades away
How will I know when to let go
What do I do

BOX YOU UP
I've been going crazy lately with
all these feelings I've got filled up
inside me need to get them out
need to get them out need to get
rid of them without a doubt
Got my keys got my car I'm
heading down the UPS store need
some cardboard to fill
my heart's up to the brim
it's about to spill
Chorus
I'm gonna box you up
I'm gonna box you up
Make sure they remember if
undelivered don't return to sender
I'm gonna box you up
I'm gonna box you up
Maybe it'll ship across the sea
Maybe you'll find someone
you'll meet oh oh oh

Wordplay

Try to make your lyrics clever. It's not that easy, but a cool twist or image will help your lyric last longer for the listener. For some reason food is a great reference in pop music. "Milkshake," "Who Pumped the Wind in My Doughnut," "Big Black Horse and the Cherry Tree" . . . I have no idea what it all means, but it works. Another catchy play on words is the song "All About That Bass," sung by Meghan Trainor. She says she's "all about that bass"—referring to her hips—then sings "no treble," which also sounds like "no trouble." So the musical play between the bass and treble gains a double meaning and a hint of fun. Gwen Stefani wrote "Hollaback Girl," I'm not sure what a hollaback girl is, but she coined a new word saying she "ain't one." Start thinking of cool ideas and ways to play with your words.

Rhyme Scheme

Creating rhymes in song lyrics can be done in a variety of ways. However, once you've established a particular rhyme scheme, you should follow it throughout the song. So if your verses rhyme every line, or every other line, at the beginning or end of the phrase, keep that pattern going. The first example demonstrates simple pairs of rhymes:

Baa, baa, black sheep, have you any *wool?*
Yes, sir, yes, sir, three bags *full*
One for the master, and one for the *dame*
And one for the little boy who lives down the *lane.*

But there are other, more complex ways to add rhymes to your lyrics:

- **Internal rhyme:** I love internal rhymes, which fall in the middle of the phrase.

So *typical*, another sunset fades *away*
I'm *cynical* 'cause you are still not here *today*

- **End syllabic rhyme:** Beauti*ful*, wonder*ful*, memora*ble*, laugha*ble*, careful*ly*, loving*ly*.
- **Loose rhyme:** These are rhymes that are not exact, but when sung they can work because the vowels are close enough to feel as if they are a rhyme. For example, the extended *eh* vowel sound at the end of each line below will match closely enough to suggest a rhyme:

Was it all in my *head*
That our love came to an *end*

Verbal Tense

Why is verbal tense so important? If the tense is inconsistent, it can confuse the picture you're painting with your lyrics:

MIXED	PRESENT
We *had* love in a perfect place	We *have* love in this perfect place
And I'm *holding onto you* tonight	And I'm *holding onto you* tonight
I *didn't* want to let you go	I *don't* want to let you go
Until the morning light	Until the morning light

Pay attention to tenses, and you'll find that simply changing the tense of your song can make a huge difference in the emotional arc of your story. Writing in the present tense has the greatest impact. The person listening to your song is the one receiving the story and living it vicariously through you. Past tense doesn't engage the listener as readily, but if the story is happening as we listen, it can be a great way to bring your song new life. For example:

GIVE ME THE STRENGTH

(past tense)
I *drove* to your house
My thoughts *were* turned up way too loud
There's so much I *had* to say, and I *wasn't* feeling very proud
Wished that night *was* far behind me
I *was* so scared to be alone
I *got* too tired to keep forgiving
Still it *was* hard to let you go

(present tense)
I'm *driving* to your house
My thoughts *are* turned up way too loud
There's so much I *want* to say, but *I'm* not feeling very proud
I wish this night *were* far behind me
I'm so scared to be alone
But *I'm* too tired to keep forgiving
Still *it's* hard to let you go
Chorus
Oh God give me the strength to leave you
Give me the strength to say goodbye
God give me the strength to leave you
Give me the chance to say goodbye
Cause sometimes love is not enough

Because the chorus describes a mental and emotional struggle, it's more vibrant and interesting in the present tense, where listeners can feel as if they are going through the scenes with you.

Of course, it can be useful to evoke or reflect on events from the past in a song. But you'll find that many of the songs that do this still connect the past with the present. A perfect example is Carrie Underwood's "Jesus, Take the Wheel," which relates a physical and spiritual journey that took place "last Friday" but pulls the listener into that experience with the present-tense chorus: "Take it from my hands / 'Cause I can't do this on my own. . ." Here's another example.

LOOKING BACK

Back in '84
We were young and so naïve
I was just a dreamer
Couldn't wait to leave
You had other plans in mind
A solid job, a simple life
I was running out of time
with songs and hopes and city lights

We went our separate ways, on that brokenhearted day
Chorus
Here I am again thinking 'bout you
Wonder where you are tonight
Has life been good to you?
I know we must be different now
But still inside my heart's
A tiny place I've saved for you
A place where you still are

The point is to be conscious about what tense you are using, to be consistent within scenes or sections, and to go for the strongest emotional impact.

P.O.V. What's Your Point of View?

Besides present and past tense, consider *who* you are singing to, and what your *point of view* is in a song. We can use the first, second, or third person to create a perspective in a song.

- When writing in the first person, the song is about the singer. The lyrics use pronouns such as *I, we, me, us* and the possessive forms *my*, *mine*, *our*, and *ours*.
- When writing in the second person, the song directly addresses the listener. Lyrics use pronouns such as *you*, and the possessives *your* and *yours*.
- When writing in the third person, it is usually a story about somebody else. The lyrics use pronouns such as *he, she, it, they, them*, and the possessive forms *his, hers, its, their*, and *theirs*.

I think the first person (*I, me, my*) and second person (*you*), like present tense in a song, have the most impact. The famous song "I Will Always Love You," written by Dolly Parton and sung by Whitney Houston, is a perfect example of this. You can mix the third person (when you're singing about someone else—*he or she or they*) with direct address (a.k.a. first person), if you're clear and consistent. For example, the verse could be in the third person, and the chorus in the first person.

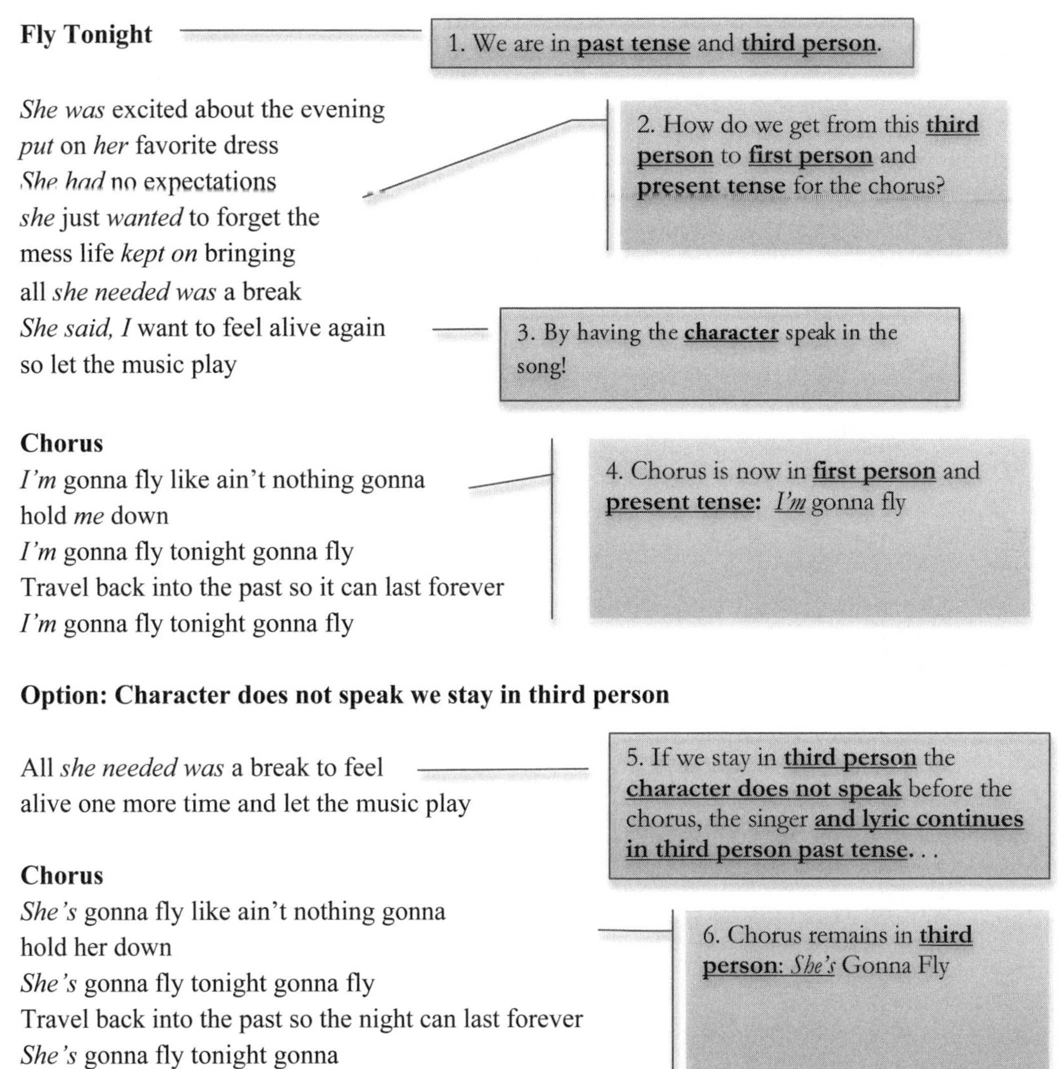

Fly Tonight
1. We are in **past tense** and **third person**.
She was excited about the evening
put on *her* favorite dress
She had no expectations
she just *wanted* to forget the
mess life *kept on* bringing
all *she needed was* a break
She said, I want to feel alive again
so let the music play
2. How do we get from this **third person** to **first person** and **present tense** for the chorus?
3. By having the **character** speak in the song!
Chorus
I'm gonna fly like ain't nothing gonna
hold *me* down
I'm gonna fly tonight gonna fly
Travel back into the past so it can last forever
I'm gonna fly tonight gonna fly
4. Chorus is now in **first person** and **present tense:** *I'm* gonna fly
Option: Character does not speak we stay in third person
All *she needed was* a break to feel
alive one more time and let the music play
5. If we stay in **third person** the **character does not speak** before the chorus, the singer **and lyric continues in third person past tense**. . .
Chorus
She's gonna fly like ain't nothing gonna
hold her down
She's gonna fly tonight gonna fly
Travel back into the past so the night can last forever
She's gonna fly tonight gonna
6. Chorus remains in **third person:** *She's* Gonna Fly

In general, when a song is written in the third person the listener is not part of the experience. Remember, people either like to sing along with you, so they can express emotions that they feel as their own, or to feel as if you are singing directly to them. Most contemporary music is in the first person.

When writing a narrative song we mostly use third person (*she, he*, or *they*). But it is important to address the listener and to allow the character to have a voice; otherwise, there's no relationship being developed. Using names of people, places, and cities in your song can help to create that relationship, too. In one of my songs, a true story called "Sweet Alice," we learn about a woman who helped everyone in the crumbling Los Angeles neighborhood of Watts. One day a huge storm tore her house down, and the entire community she had been so good to, came to her rescue, rebuilding her home to give back to her—a "pay it forward" type of song. As you read the lyrics, notice the narrative lyric style, the direct address to the listener, the metaphors, similes, imagery, and rhyme scheme.

SWEET ALICE

Verse
Just southeast of Holly*wood*
The <u>ghetto streets are dressed in</u> *concrete and wood*
And <u>all the children play against the odds</u>
There's an angel in Watts giving out *wings*
on Lou Dillon Avenue where all of their *dreams*
can finally come *true* for *you*

Verse Rhymes and Metaphors

1. Exact Rhyme: "Hollywood" & "wood"
2. Metaphors: "ghetto streets are dressed in concrete and wood" and "children play against the odds"
3. Slant Rhyme: "Wings and Dreams" Sung on the vowel "EEE"
4. Internal Rhyme last line: "true" and "you"

Pre-chorus
She's planting *gold*
and <u>dusting off their worn out *hope*</u>
Somehow she *knows* just how to make a young heart *glow*

Pre-chorus

1. Loose and Internal Rhyme: "gold, know, glow" sung on the vowel "OH"
2. Metaphor: Dusting off their worn out hope

Chorus
Oh Sweet Alice Oh Sweet Alice
she will take you into her *arms*
Oh Sweet Alice Oh Sweet Alice
with the magic in the back*yard*
And she's singing "Hallelujah
bless the sun shin*ing* down on your *face"*
And she's singing "Hallelujah
for all the beauty pour*ing* out this *place"*
Singing "Hallelujah, Glory, Glory, Glory Hallelujah"

Chorus

1. Loose Rhyme: "arms," "backyard" sung like "ARR"
2. Internal Rhyme (ending): "shin*ing* and pour*ing*"
3. Perfect Rhyme: "face & place"

Verse 2
Caught somewhere between heaven and *hell*
November skies pummeled rain and *hail*
and washed her castle far *away*
She cried "Oh sweet Lord how can this *be*"
And all of the people came because they *believed*
Their angel now was the one in *need*

Verse 2: Developing Rhyme

1. Rhyme on words:	"Hell" "Hail" "Away"
Sung on the vowel:	"Ell" "Ale" "Ay"
2. Rhyme on words:	"Be" "Believed" "Need"
Sung on the vowel:	"EE" "EE" "EE"

Pre-chorus
Rebuilt her *home*
Refilled her boxes full of *hope*
They touched her *soul*
and thanked her for her heart of *gold*

Pre-Chorus

1. Rhyme on words:	"Home" "Hope" "Soul" "Gold"
Sung on the vowel:	"OH" "OH" "OH" "OH"

Syllabic Rhyme and Repeat

2. Rhyme on words:	"Rebuilt" "Refilled"
Sung on the vowel:	"Re-ill" "Re-ill"

Words That Don't Sing Well

Try and avoid words that are too cerebral. We speak from the heart, not the head, and beginners often confuse being analytical with being lyrical. When you look at the lines below, you can tell right away that they won't work as song lyrics. Why not?

Love is a human emotion.
A relationship is useful.
Dealing with rejection can be challenging.
Loneliness is inconvenient, especially on the weekends.
Are you optimistic about the future?

While the ideas expressed may be legitimate, the phrases above are completely lacking in emotion, action, point of view, and imagery. How can we take the same concepts and create a verse lyric?

Love is a human emotion. I find this funny, because we are not reading a science book. The sentence doesn't begin to get across how important love is to us as human beings. To do that, we might say: "Oh, I just can't live without you."
A relationship is useful. I don't think "useful" quite explains it; a manual is "useful" when you buy something at Ikea. A relationship is a much more significant part of our lives, part of our identity; so we might say: "You're the very air I breathe."
Dealing with rejection can be challenging. We use words like "challenging" to talk about our physical fitness goals; rejection is heart-wrenching if it's from someone you love. We might say, "If you leave me now, you'll take my heart from me."
Loneliness is inconvenient, especially on the weekends. True, but how do we connect this rather clinical observation with our personal experience? We need emotion, action, location, risk: "It's Friday after midnight / I'm still listening for the door."
Are you optimistic about the future? When speaking to someone about love, we wouldn't use the same words we'd apply to our job prospects or the stock market. We'd speak from the heart, with a question like "Don't you think our love is worth fighting for?"

Oh I just can't live without you
You're the very air I breathe
If you leave me now, you'll take my heart from me
It's Friday after midnight
I'm still listening for the door
Don't you think our love is worth fighting for?
Chorus
How many times, and how many ways,
how many words do I have to say tonight
To get back to where we used to be, you and I
How many nights and how many days,

how many vows do I have to make it right
To get back to where we used to be
To feel your love again at least for a little while

In order to create a lyric that is engaging and connects with the listener, keep the following tips in mind.

- Use conversational language to say or describe things, and keep it vivid via metaphor, oxymoron, and coining new phrases.
- In the verse describe the events and situation.
- In the chorus express your reactions and emotions.

Vowel and Syllabic Placement

Another important factor is where the stresses and syllables fall, rhythmically and melodically, as you sing the lyric. Let's take the song "Happy Birthday," since everybody knows it, and replace the original lyric with words that do not sing well.

Ly-rics need real good vo-wels
Syll-a-bles in pro-per pla-ces
Should-n't be so mech-a-ni-cal
that the fee-lings fall short.

The example shows that there is already a problem in the first line. Words with strange diphthongs (gliding vowels of two adjacent sounds) need to be taken into account. So "owls" in "vowels" sounds funny when sung on a single note.

In the second line, we end up stressing the last syllable of the word "syll-a-BLES," so that it sounds like "bulls" when sung with this melody. But when the word is spoken, the strong accent is on the first part of the word: "SYLL-ables." It doesn't work.

In the last line, we are ending a melody on a closed consonant in the word "short." We end up singing "orrrt," which is not a very nice sound either. So these lyrics are what you would not want to do!

Still, taking the melody of a famous song and replacing the original lyrics with your own (an exercise I teach called "ghostwriting") can be a good way to practice matching words to music. If you try this yourself, you'll notice where the open vowel sounds fall within the melodic phrases, how the lyric fits rhythmically within the song, how the lyrics enhance the story and emotion of the song, and how your lyrics compare. It is an excellent exercise to get into the mindset of the original composer.

Summary

To review, here's a quick list of important questions to guide your writing process:

1. What type of song are you writing? (narrative, poetic, conversational)
2. How can you capture us? (opening lines)

3. Who are you singing to? (point of view: yourself, one person, the world)
4. Where are you? (visual imagery, relationship to the external world)
5. When did it happen? (past, present, or future)
6. Are you spicing it up? (using metaphor, simile, alliteration, oxymoron, coining words)

Make sure to keep us coming back for more. Use the spices in your spice rack, the stories in your creative mind and in the world . . . and your own words to share the feelings that you've never shared before.

9 Shaping Your Melody

An Octave Above the Rest

Music is the melody whose text is the world. —Arthur Schopenhauer

Let's talk about structuring melodies. How can we make our songs sound as if they are "an octave" above the rest? How can we write that melody that gets stuck inside your head?

I believe the melody is the first element that drives a song home. Think about it: how many times have you been singing along to a song and get to the point where you're mumbling the lyrics even though you know the melody? Or find out that you've been singing the wrong lyrics for years! We've all been there. We absorb and recall melodies first, but can also use melodies to help with memory. In college, I would write songs using my science definitions as the lyrics so I could remember them when taking finals. I'd have to sing under my breath during exam time, which could annoy the person next to me, but for some reason it was much easier to memorize when the facts were set to sound. Scientists use music to trigger memory for people with severe dementia, Alzheimer's, and debilitating brain disorders. Music can awaken a portion of their patients' brains to total musical recall.

What does that tell us? Think about how we learn our ABC's, or nursery rhymes we've sung as children. They are simple, easy, catchy, and fun. Melodies help us absorb information to develop our memory and help us tap into memories that never go away. And the combination of a great melody paired with a lyric is what forms emotional snapshots creating lifelong memories for all of us.

Greek mathematicians established a theory of the "golden mean," the most pleasing and harmonious proportion, for example, between the height and width of a temple. It has been applied to art, architecture, and composition, and I believe it can be applied to songwriting. As one element of the song becomes more complex, other elements of the song become less complex. There must be a balance. The human ear can only absorb so much information, and inevitably, instinctually, songwriters must privilege one element over the other. For example, if a song chord structure changes often, and is rhythmically complicated, then the melody in contrast should remain simple and flow easily on top. If the musical score is less complicated, then there is room to play with a more rhythmic and moving melody.

An important factor in writing a great song is to affect the listener emotionally. There must be some *payoff.* Otherwise, you get a reaction like, "Eh . . . it's okay." I'd rather hear, "I hate that song," or, "I love it." The melody should always be the highlight of your production. And when you're not singing, of course, there are instrumental melodic hooks as well. Great productions, grooves, bass, the layering of instruments, and the vibe of the song are there to support the voice and message of the song, not drown it out. The track cannot be competing or more important than the singer, and balancing the two is what makes the song work, whether it is a ballad, mid-tempo, or up-tempo.

When composing a melody, we must consider the following:

Does the artist's voice sound great in the song's key, style, and production?
Does the melody fit the mood of the lyric and story of the song?
Do the melodic and rhythmic patterns fall into singable or memorable phrases?
Does the melody provoke an emotional reaction?

In this chapter, we will explore these topics and many useful tips for writing great melodies.

Key, Tempo, and Rhythm

Defining the key, tempo, and rhythm of a song may sound obvious, but it isn't always that simple. When writers struggle over why a song isn't working, it's frequently one of these basic elements, or even all three, that needs adjusting.

Shooting for the Stars

Let's start with vocal range. Don't aim too high. If you write a melody that requires a singer to *wail* in his or her highest register, be sure you don't write something that's impossible for the particular singer who will present your song (which may be yourself) to sing. It can't be so wide in range that only a few great singers can pull it off. "So what," you're thinking to yourself, "I'll hire the best demo singer in five states to cut the vocal." But if you're shopping the song, make sure it's in the vocal range for the artist you are shopping it to. Just a heads up: artists like Mariah Carey, Celine Dion, and Ariana Grande have the entire world pitching them material. Of course, there are other magically gifted singers, but make sure you know them. And if you are writing a song in this vein for yourself, you'd better be able to pull it off.

Too Low to Feel

The opposite of aiming too high is a song that is set too low for the singer and thus lacks energy. If you feel something just isn't gelling, try modulating up a step or two and see if it makes a difference. In the end, the key has to be in the correct register for the singer. We all have a certain area of our voice that has a rich flavor and translates the best. The way you buy clothes to fit your body type is the same way you need to choose a key, tempo, and style for a particular singer. The song must be tailored to match.

Major or Minor

Shy of going into heavy music theory, I am going to offer some simple ideas for you to use when writing songs. I call myself a songwriter who plays piano. I don't break out into heavy solos and riffs. So you don't have to be a phenomenal pianist or guitarist to write songs. The most important thing is to understand chord progressions and basic relative pitches you can go to when your song needs a change. I often say, "When in doubt, leave your hands out"—that is, if you hear a melody, sing it without playing and then find the chords, or find someone who can write it out for you. Your ear may be more advanced than your hands. There are numerous online theory classes and YouTube videos you can watch to help teach you.

Reading about harmony without the ability to hear or demonstrate can be challenging, but I will give you some options below that can help.

Chords often affect us physically. In the mockumentary *This Is Spinal Tap*, there's a funny scene where the lead character sits at the piano and plays a ballad. He plucks D, then F-natural, then A on the piano, popping and chewing gum, and proclaims, "D minor is the saddest of all keys." When asked the name of his song, he says, "Lick My Love Pump." We laugh out loud because the melancholy sound of the piano, and the chord, doesn't match the ridiculous title of the song. Develop a harmonic vocabulary; learn to identify and use major, minor, suspended, slashed, and seventh chords and a variety of voicings. Consider your chord choices and how they match the mood and rhythm of your song. And you're off to a strong start!

Harmonic Structure: Four Chords

You can easily write a song over a simple and commonly used four-chord progression, C–G–A minor–F. You can play these four chords on guitar or piano and sing many famous melodies over the same progression. Maroon 5's "She Will Be Loved," Journey's "Don't Stop Believing," Lady Gaga's "Poker Face," and Jason Mraz's "I'm Yours" are a few. There's even a musical comedy group called Axis of Awesome whose song "4 Chords" runs through dozens of examples from hit songs. I also demonstrate this phenomenon every time I give a songwriting workshop. I'm continually shocked at how many *new* hit songs I add each year to fit over those four chords. (You can also start later in the progression on A minor, the sixth chord, and play A minor–F–C–G instead. You'll be in good company.)

Pop Chord Progression	**Alternate Progression**
I V VI IV	**VI IV I V**
C G Am F	Am F C G
Other Simple Progression	
I VI IV V	**VI V IV V**
C Am F G	Am G F G
Ballad progression descending bass line	
I VII VI V IV V	

Another great way to study songwriting and chord voicings is to look at sheet music. You can follow along with the chord progressions located above the staff, play the progressions from hit songs, and practice writing a new melody over them. You'll learn by example where changes should occur, how to develop a melody, what chords and keys and tempos you like, and what song form feels best.

Melodic Choices over Chords

I also urge you to try writing melodies that don't always start on the first, third, or fifth note of the scale or key as many songs do. We hear these melodic intervals and harmonies every day! Consider the songs and nursery rhymes we grew up singing; "Mary Had a Little Lamb" in the key of C starts on the third (E); "Twinkle, Twinkle, Little Star" begins on the first or tonic note.

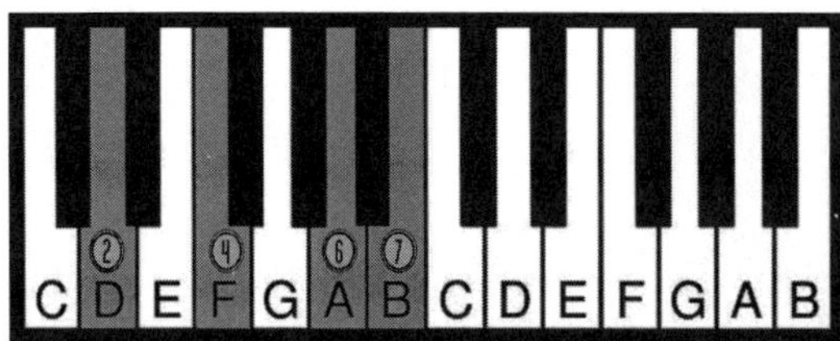

For a different approach, try singing a melody starting on another note of the scale (second, fourth, sixth, or seventh) and see if that adds something fresh. In the key of C this would be D, F, A, and B as shown. You can apply this to any key.

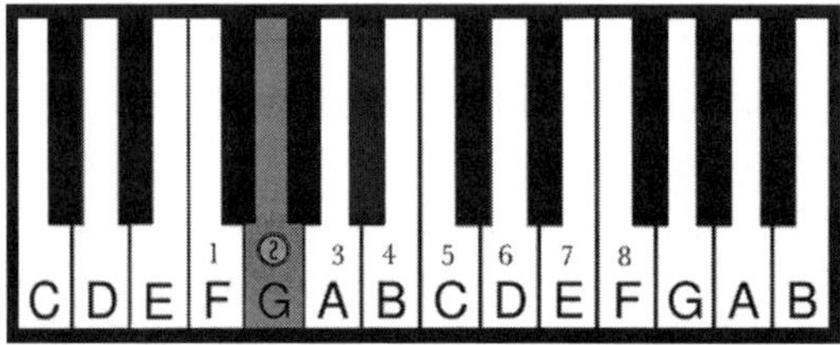

Paul McCartney's song "Yesterday" starts on the second scale step—G over an F chord—before moving into A major to resolve on D minor. Note how the movement from G to F on the word "yesterday" is echoed by E to D on the words "far away."

In "Wrecking Ball," by Miley Cyrus, the chorus melody starts on the fourth scale step, B-flat of the F chord ("I came in like a wrecking") and resolves a half step down to A on the word "ball." This "suspension" creates such sadness and tension in the chorus.

The melody of America's classic seventies song "Ventura Freeway" begins on the seventh scale step, C-sharp of the D major chord. A more modern reference might be One Direction or any kind of vocal harmony group.

"Landslide," written by Stevie Nicks, was recut by the Dixie Chicks. The first note of the chorus, which is so stunning, is on the sixth scale step, E of the G chord.

Tempo and Rhythm

The speed of your song (which we measure in beats per minute, or BPMs) is so important. You want to make sure it is not too fast or too slow. When you're writing a song, click on the metronome and see if the tempo feels right. Make sure we can understand the words, and that there's enough room to deliver the melody. Try speeding it up or slowing it down. I remember working with one particular medium-tempo ballad, and deciding to speed it up. We kept playing it back, first at 86 BPMs, then taking it up to 89 BPMs . . . and then finding at 92 BPMs that it had a new life and new meaning. Six BPMs doesn't sound like a lot, but it changed the entire feel.

You never know if a song would work better with a different approach until you try it out. I recently had an artist bring in a song along the lines of John Mayer's "Waiting on the World to Change" or Colby Caillet's "Bubbly." He didn't like that his song had a vibe that felt too poppy, so he told me he planned on recording it faster. I said, "Actually, it's way too fast if you want a blues vibe." When I played him the Mayer and Caillet songs, he realized their tempos were slower, and his tempo did not allow enough space to bend notes for a more bluesy vocal approach. I had him sing his song to a slower tempo, and he loved it.

Correct tempo is when the phrasing and emotion of the song feels right. Of course, a song can have more than one life. Think about why remixes and remakes of songs are so popular. Maybe you'll find your original idea of tempo is better as a great follow-up or remix version of your song. So again be open to experimenting with your tempo and time signature and try a few out until it feels right. Then you can remix it, or play it differently live with a new arrangement, and maybe even hear other artists covering your song with a new interpretation.

Keep in mind that your vocal style and texture should fit your song. Some singers are balladeers, while others are very good at quick, tight rhythms, so consider where your vocal phrasing falls best, and allow your song to feature your strengths. In my classes students who don't have an "original" song ready for showcasing can perform a cover song, but they have to find a new style or twist for it. For example, one of my students from Bermuda did a version of Adele's song "Someone Like You" with a reggae feel. Another student decided to sing Christina Aguilera's "Genie in a Bottle" as a sexy, slow, blues rock song. Both performances were amazing. The singers, the styles they chose, and the tempos all seemed to flow naturally. A great example of one of the first remixes was "Tom's Diner," which Suzanne Vega originally sang a cappella on her 1987 CD *Solitude Standing*. In 2003 DNA, a British production team, took her vocal and made a very cool dance version of the song. It was vastly different approach, and the song became a big hit.

The Verse Curse

A common songwriting mistake is thinking the chorus can carry the entire song. The first part of a song, the verse, is just as important; if you lose your listeners there, they never get to the chorus. Think of paving an eye-catching or mysterious way to the castle. It's not easy to write something that has that *magic* factor. And, even when we do write a chorus with a killer hook, we need to make sure the verses leading up to it are memorable and interesting—that they are building your song.

Variety and Phrasing Are Key

Variations help build your melodies, but they have to make sense. Decide carefully where and when you'll move the melody, and how it should propel the emotion of the song. I always say by your second verse, excite us by doing something melodically unexpected. In fact, these days the traditional verse/chorus and verse/pre-chorus/chorus song structures have almost been tossed out the window, and there are hooks throughout the entire song, not just in the chorus. Perhaps song structures became too predictable, so writers now play with variations of structure to avoid monotony.

Some of the best advice I ever got was to reevaluate the strength of my melody by trying different ways of singing the line. This includes paying attention to word emphasis. We don't want the strength of the melody to fall on insignificant words and prepositions; *is*, *of*, *in*, and *to*. I wouldn't say, "I'm madly IN love." I would say, "I'm MADLY in LOVE!" Where should the emphasis of the words fall? Where should the volume and intensity increase and decrease so that they carry the story or emotion forward?

In the lyric below, the words in bold can easily tell the story on their own. However, to construct a sentence that makes sense, we need more than just the descriptive bits. So when writing a melody you want to make sure those are the words that sing with the most conviction.

There's a **bridge** that we have **built** that **lies between us**
And **through** the **years grows old**
But **we keep finding ways** to **cross on over**
With all the **rusty nails exposed**

Let's take the first line and play with it to demonstrate how many choices we have when writing a melody. Say these out loud, emphasizing the bold words and letting the others play as passing words in the phrase. When speaking through the lines out loud, there's a rhythmic pattern that will naturally develop. Now think about adding a simple melody to it. Let the bold lyrics stand out melodically from the rest. Even within those phrases you can move emphasized words melodically up or down the scale to create impact. Play around with it.

There's a bridge that we have built **that lies between us**
There's **a bridge** that **we have built** that **lies between us**
There's a **bridge that we have** built that lies **between us**
There's a **bridge** that we have **built** that lies **between us**

There are so many choices. You can change the melody until you the find the perfect one. Consider the tone of the song. If you are asking a question, does the phrase remain unresolved and ascend at the end? If you are making a statement, does the phrase hit hard? If you are emphatic, scared, confused, angry, are the chords or suspensions you choose in major or minor?

Let's take the famous song "All by Myself," written by Eric Carmen and covered by Celine Dion. The melody and the lyric of that song are perfectly paired. The melody line makes the words *by* and *my* emotional and vulnerable, like the lyric. In the key of A major (F# G# C#):

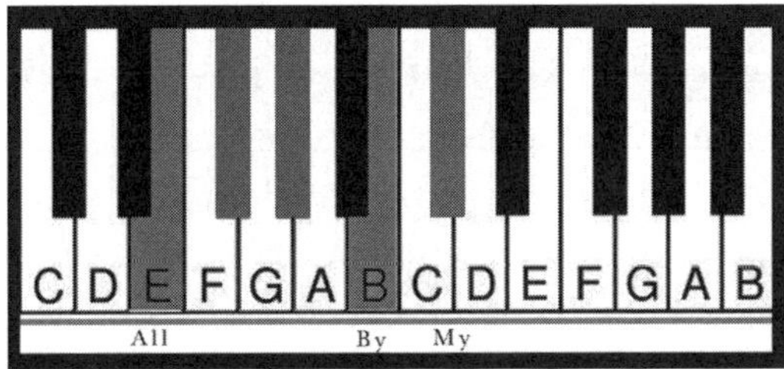

The chord progression of this song is complex. But the melody is achingly beautiful. After the instrumental bridge, the final chorus builds by moving up the scale. The singer doesn't want to live *by myself . . . a-ny . . . more*; but instead of the expected F major we hear C# major! The classical guys call this a "deceptive modulation." We call it the "money note"—the most climactic point of a song, the highest note that is both dramatic and emotionally stirring.

Consider two- and three-syllable words, and how you can use the accent within that word to designate the focal point. We don't say forev**ER**, we say for**EV**er. Make sure the accent and stress of the word falls properly.

Where Celine's vocal in the song "All by Myself" is crying and sad, Bruno Mars' "Locked out of Heaven" is sad and emotional but exciting as well. Listen to the shape of the melody on "you make me *feel like . . .*" He uses the same melodic emphasis when he talks about being "locked out of *hea-ven . . .*" and again when he continues, "for so long." Stretching out the vowel (*lawwww-awwww-awwwwng*), and moving it up and down in whole steps, Mars creates a literal example of the melody and lyric paired at the right moment in a phrase, and demonstrates how the open vowels (*ahh, eh, eee, ooh, ooo*) can be elongated for impact. Whether old or new, slow or fast, the melody and lyric paired at the right moment in a phrase makes all the difference.

Musical Motifs: The Art and Style of Repetition

In a great song the lyric, the measures, the phrasing, are important, but above all there must be an ear-catching motif, a feeling of wanting to return to a musical hook or chorus. That same feeling of wanting to return to the top should happen in songs after the chorus and after each verse section. We are ready for a repeat; the ear is teased and following along and anticipating the next round. Try to pull the listener in and create something people can sing along to!

Warning: More advanced musicians should be careful not to get too fancy by writing something so complex, with crazy chord structures, melodic runs, and rhythmic changes that no one can follow along. Only musicians will think it is cool, and the general public will think, "What the heck was that?" I love fusion, I've seen some amazing players, but after a while I think they must have spent a lot of time practicing in a room alone. The wow factor is there, but can I remember a single riff? Can I join in? No way. I'm more of a spectator; it's like watching the Olympics. I'm in awe and enjoy it immensely. Popular music is intended for listeners who want to be participants. They want to sing along to the song. They want to sing with the radio in their car at stoplights, and in the shower and around the mall or at home. I suggest composing contemporary music with simple, flowing melodies and give the song room to build to an emotional payoff. When approaching a melody or motif, there are a few choices you can make.

Three Musical Motifs: Linear, Circular, and Square

A linear motif by definition is repeated notes and not a lot of movement melodically. So, if you were to look at the actual page of music, we could connect the notes and draw a nearly straight line across the measures. One example of a linear melody is the verse in Jefferson Airplane's song "White Rabbit." There are two chords in the verse, and the melody is very linear, staying pretty straight. The song does increase in intensity with a payoff at the end.

A circular motif is one that has minimal leaps, but creates a smooth melodic line and a serene feeling. If you were to draw a line across the notation it would look like small waves, as if you were going on a smooth, gentle ride. "All of Me," by John Legend, and Richard Marx's "Right Here Waiting for You," are both very beautiful songs that use circular motifs.

A square motif uses larger intervals and melodic leaps to produce an emotional rise. The music creates an atmosphere of adventure, happiness, or despair with extreme feelings and emotions. Listen to Sia's song "Chandelier." She sings about wanting to swing on a chandelier, and her melody covers more than an octave. "Somewhere Over the Rainbow," written by Harold Arlen and sung by Judy Garland, starts with an octave leap on the word "some . . . where," literally taking us "over the rainbow." Sam Smith's "Lay Me Down" is another example of a motif with large emotional and melodic leaps. Octaves can create contrast in songs in other ways, too. In Nirvana's "Smells Like Teen Spirit," the Goo Goo Dolls' song "Iris," and Ellie Goulding's "Love Me Like You Do," the verses are sung an octave lower, and the chorus an octave above; this definitely creates an emotional impact or payoff for the listener.

Create Contrast

If your verse melody travels up the scale, try traveling downward melodically in the chorus to create contrast. Make sure the first note and chord of your chorus distinguish it from the verse or pre-chorus, so we get a feeling of change when we get to the chorus. If A minor is the final chord of your verse, the chorus cannot begin on A minor.

Warning: Don't give up the money note of your melody in your verse or pre-chorus. Wait until the chorus to feature that highlight; you don't bring out the cake until the climax of the birthday party! Study popular songs that you like and analyze how they create memorable melodies within each section of the song. There are often (not always) patterns of eight bars for a verse, two to four bars for a pre-chorus, and a chorus of anywhere from eight bars to a double chorus of sixteen bars.

Let's review and make sure you consider the following:

- Create a motif, a musical idea that reoccurs, and a melody that shows a distinctive shape.
- Determine whether your song should be slow, mid-tempo, or up-tempo.
- Use the correct range or key for the singer so the vocal texture expresses the song's mood and vibe. Decide whether you want to use a major or minor progression.
- Establish the rhythmic cadence of the words and a tempo that allows the lyrics to be emotionally impactful or to roll off the tongue.
- Write a lyric and hook line so that the payoff comes in the chorus, not the verse.
- Use contrast to heighten the emotions in the verse, the chorus, or both.

10 Song Structure

Piecing the Puzzle

If it weren't for the rocks in its bed,
the stream would have no song. —Carl Perkins

To the average listener, it might sound like a song is just thrown together for us to sing along to, but there are definite patterns, forms, and ways to write a song following structure. Let's study the most popular forms of contemporary writing:

AAA Song Form

A song in this form progresses straight from one verse to the next; AAA = verse, verse, verse. It is a great song structure for telling stories where the first or last line is a repeated lyric and melody, or a "refrain" revealing the title of the song. Writing in this style, the verses complete on their own, rather than setting up a scenario that needs to build up into a chorus release. Famous songs like Bob Dylan's "Blowin' in the Wind" and Simon and Garfunkel's "Bridge Over Troubled Water" are written in an AAA structure.

AABA Song Form

This song form is the same concept as the AAA form, except it has a bridge. AABA = verse, verse, bridge, verse. The B section or bridge is written to break away from the verse pattern. Bridges are also called "middle eights" because they usually occur in the middle of the song and often take up eight bars. A lot of jazz standards use this AABA song form. Paul McCartney was a huge Cole Porter fan, so many of the Beatles' songs used the AABA form. Sting has recorded songs in AABA, including "Every Breath You Take." So it is evident in multiple genres, including contemporary music.

Pop Song Form

The most common structure that emerged out of rock 'n' roll in the fifties is verse/chorus or verse/pre-chorus/chorus. Ideally, this creates an emotional melodic ride you take the listener on, so contrast is key. Imagine the following:

The verse gives information about where you're going, as if you're in your car on your way to a party.
The pre-chorus is the build of the story, creating anticipation, like the steps leading up to the front door of the party.
The chorus is the payoff: that door opens and you're in the party.

Verse/Chorus

This song form is rather straight ahead: a verse followed directly by the chorus. Listen to Avicii's "Wake Me Up," Foster the People's "Pumped Up Kicks," and Beyoncé's "Drunk in Love" as examples.

Verse/Pre-Chorus/Chorus

This is the same as a verse/chorus song, only it has a pre-chorus—a transition connecting the verse to the chorus. If your verse and chorus are too close in melody or the same key, a pre-chorus will give a change to the harmony and create a buildup to the chorus. For example, Mark Ronson's "Uptown Funk" breaks down the song to build it back up. Bruno Mars, the featured vocalist, actually says "break it down" in the song. The music drops to just a kick drum and an eight-bar vocal build, adding some keys in the last two bars when Mars tells us, "Don't believe me, just watch," and the big chorus release. "Bad Blood," by Taylor Swift, features Kendrick Lamar rapping the verses and Swift singing a vocal pre-chorus about "how sad it is to think about the good times" and then holding "I" (*ahhhh*) over the dance build that brings us into the chorus, where now they've got "bad blood."

Art Song

An art song does not follow a prescribed form. Lyrically and musically it's recorded to provoke a reaction. Art songs can be set to poetry and quite beautiful. For example, the political song "Strange Fruit," sung by Billie Holiday, is a poem set to music. For more examples of art songs, listen to more experimental artists like Laurie Anderson and Bjork.

Epic Song Form

An epic song contains multiple hooks and distinct sections with their own rhythmic and harmonic identity. This form takes you on an extensive ride that goes on longer than a normal three-minute song, sometimes even as long as ten minutes. This form was very popular in the sixties and seventies, giving rise to songs like the Beatles' "A Day in the Life," Queen's "Bohemian Rhapsody," Led Zeppelin's "Stairway to Heaven," and Michael Jackson's "Thriller." Take a listen and hear how those artists crafted these brilliant songs.

Today, as long as there are hooks for the audience, almost anything goes with popular music. The traditional song form can get tired if it's not done well. Listeners want more. A perfect example of something that sounds simple, but once analyzed and broken down is very well crafted, is Coldplay's "Paradise."

- The song is 4:20 in length, which is considered long for today's pop standards, but if the music is interesting enough it doesn't feel long.
- Coldplay opens with 37 seconds of music, with the chorus sung in *ahhs*, then delivers the first verse and the chorus an octave down.

- A musical interlude follows where Chris Martin is singing the verse melody in *ahhs* an octave up.
- The second verse is followed by the first pre-chorus, and then a new melody is introduced with a second pre-chorus before the double chorus.
- This time the double chorus is in stacked octaves singing the hook "paradise."
- Then there's an instrumental bridge without any vocals until the fifth bar, and the first pre-chorus melody returns, leading us back to a double chorus with new ad libs that play out until the end of the song.
- In the outro, Martin sings the intro melody over new variations and inversions of the original chords to keep the listener interested.

There's no pure structure, but the repetitions take us on a carnival ride. EDM, dubstep, and hip-hop also play with song forms these days. Take a listen to your favorite songs and see what form they follow. In your own work, be sure to keep the listener interested and unable to predict the next line you will sing, or the next change you will make. Then use hooks and payoffs to entice them to sing along. How we get them there is where creativity plays a big part.

Writing the Same Song Over and Over

I believe we can write the same song over and over again. If you listen back, you'll find you're repeating yourself more than you realize. Here are some suggestions to challenge you to keep getting better as a writer. Write using different instruments than you normally would. If you are a piano player, write on guitar, or vice versa. Even a ukulele or a nylon-stringed classical guitar will bring a different feel than a simple acoustic. Alternate tuning also helps in creating new ways to compose.

There are so many choices on a synthesizer as well. Use a Fender Rhodes or cool synth sound, or an orchestral plug-in, as opposed to an acoustic piano sound. Another way to approach your writing differently is by creating a soundscape. Take some sound you find interesting, record it on a smartphone app or digital recorder, and write to it. I once recorded the heart monitor in a hospital, took it home, tuned it, and wrote a song using its rhythm and key as a backdrop. The ticking of a clock, microwave beeps, the hum of a fan, anything you hear that's interesting can create a mood to inspire a new song. I also suggest pulling up any drum groove in a DAW (digital audio workstation) system to help with a habit of writing only slow songs. Even write to different time signatures; try 6/8 or 3/4, or change between 4/4 and 6/8 within the same song. And, as we saw in the previous chapter, sometimes speeding up the tempo can give your song a complete facelift.

Top-Liner

A "top-liner" composes melodies over an existing track. Many songwriters and singers pair up with producers who compose beats, and then collaborate to create songs. There are also lots of websites where you can purchase or license beats to write on. The drawback in those situations is that you can't change the harmonics. If you feel you want the melody to move where the chords are not leading, you're stuck, because the track is completed. But if you are in the studio with the producer and you write together, he or she can always change the track so the song doesn't suffer. This is most popular means of collaboration for writers and artists in the pop/R&B, rap, and EDM genres.

Deconstructing a Song

Deconstructing songs is a great study. The one thing about popular music is it is ever changing, and what is current may quickly become overused. Keep in mind some songs become hits because of outside factors such as when they were written, who sang them, and which people in the industry heard them. There's a famous saying, "Preparation meets opportunity"—not to mention "timing is everything." Still, there are essentials we always want from a song. And a great song, if given the right opportunity, can take on a life of its own. So I suggest you listen to lots of music, and evaluate why you like it and why it's popular. We still have standards and classic hits that will remain in our musical playlists for a long time to come. The key is to keep listening to new songs, and to write ones that are competitive today, or at the very least ones that will transcend pop trends and bring you joy and satisfaction.

Jason Derulo's song "Want You to Want Me" has charted. When listening to the song, you will hear the chord progression E-flat major to C minor in the verse and E-flat major–C minor–A-flat major–C minor in the chorus. We anticipate that the last chord in the chorus will resolve to the E-flat major chord, but it lands instead on C minor again (the vi chord or the relative minor), whereas the obvious route would be to land on a dominant chord (B-flat major) and then return to the tonic, E-flat major, for the first chord of the verse. The chord progression is simple but still leads you through the song with intention. In addition, the melody played against the rhythmic track is in Derulo's falsetto range, standing out above the track.

In contrast, Sam Smith's "Lay Me Down" is a ballad and sparse in production. It also uses just two chords in the verse, E and A, but its simplicity allows room for the melody to move lushly on top. The pre-chorus pushes and pulls us toward the chorus until Smith opens up, singing the payoff note (G-sharp, the root of the E major chord) for the chorus in full voice. The melody highlights the lyric as it opens up into emotional crooning: *Ahhh laaaaay byyyyyy yoooour saaaahhhhide.* Then, on "next to you," Smith toys with a vocal hook on the *ooo* vowels, ascending over B, C-sharp, E, F-sharp, G-sharp, B (derived from the pentatonic scale) over the chords F-sharp minor to A major and ending back on E major. The second verse's first chord is again E major, but Smith sings on D-sharp, the major seventh of the chord, and continues to build upon the existing melody and rhythm to create a new feel. The bridge rhythmically pulses in eighth notes and creates anticipation as the production builds slowly with Smith's voice over an eight-bar bridge leading us again back to the final chorus. This last time, instead of the anticipated crescendo, Smith sings the chorus soft and pianissimo, creating a feeling of coming full circle.

There are so many ways to write a great melody, the key to keeping songs playing in our heads. Marrying that melody to a lyric is a crucial part of being a great writer. Sometimes it's one person who writes the melody and lyric, like Ed Sheeran. Sometimes a songwriting team is established when a lyricist and a melody writer collaborate, for example Elton John and Bernie Taupin. In pop music it is mostly producers and top-liners working together; for example, Taylor Swift's "Bad Blood" has four writers: Taylor Swift, Kendrick Lamar, Max Martin, and Shellback. However you go about it, the idea is always to make sure the song represents what the writer or singer wants to convey. Does it move you? Do the little hairs on your arms stand up? Do you want to get out of your chair and let go? Is it lifting your mood, soothing your soul, healing your heart? That's what great songs do when you hear them. That's what you as a writer are aiming to achieve.

11 Writer's Playground

My father would take me to the playground and put me on mood swings. —Jay London

There are times when we all need inspiration. When the well has run dry, and you find yourself staring at a blank page, turn to the next few pages to find a playground where you can explore. Here are some of my favorite exercises to get the creative juices flowing!

Exercises for Songwriters

Inanimate Object Point of View Exercise: Write from the point of view of an inanimate object. Your object can be anything non-living (sidewalk, lollipop, mirror, toothbrush, window, shoe—anything). Take on the voice and persona of that object. Think about what your object experiences every day. What is a day in a life of that object? How would it see itself in the world? How does it feel about people and how they interact with it? What is its personality? Is it happy, funny, sarcastic, arrogant, shy, depressed, jealous, or needy? Write a story about this object, and be creative. Use descriptive words and adjectives to keep us interested, but do not reveal what you are. In the end, the reader or listener will have to guess from the clues you provide.

Drawing Exercise: Focus on an object in the room, or something you place in front of you, and recreate it with one single line drawing. Take a pen and draw a line without lifting the pen or looking at the paper. Once you complete the drawing, start writing whatever comes to mind. Do not edit yourself; let your mind roam freely.

Color My World of Emotions: Grab some colored pens, pencils, crayons, whatever you have in your house. Take a sheet of paper and draw what you are feeling. Pick a color, shape, or abstract image that expresses your emotions. In this exercise, you'll focus entirely on painting what you're feeling. When you finish, write.

Peel Me a Lemon Exercise: Close your eyes and hold an imaginary lemon in your hand. See the bright yellow color. Feel its weight and shape and the texture of its skin on your fingertips. Smell the lemon. Now take your fingernail and make an incision into the skin. Now smell it again. Squeeze a little lemon juice on your tongue. Can you taste the sourness? Start writing.

A Person, Place, Event: Draw two lines down the middle of a page to form three columns. In the left column, list every type of person you know: friend, retail clerk, teacher, doctor, family member, policeman, even a fictional character like a "Batman." In the middle column, write down different geographical locations and places you go to, from Starbucks to the Egyptian pyramids. In the last column, list a specific time period or famous historical event, for example, "man landing on the moon" or "the eighties." Combine a person, place, and event and experiment with writing about that particular situation. You can try as many as you like!

Dream Exercise: Many people have recurring dreams—of flying, of being chased, of being in a particular location or situation. Write a lyric about such a dream that uses repetition to capture its obsessive nature. Try to repeat fragments rather than simply initial words or complete sentences; let the repetition interrupt the flow of the dream-story.

Fairy Tale Exercise: Write a lyric in which you adopt the persona of a character from a fairy tale. For example, you could describe the way Snow White feels while she sleeps inside her coffin, or how the Prince feels as he holds Cinderella's glass slipper in his hand.

Google It: Select a random topic like hummingbirds, or new technology, or trash art, or whatever you think of, and look it up on as many reference sites as you can find. Learn as much as you can about this new topic. Take notes and see sparks of new ideas.

Body Exercise: Make a list of fifteen physical experiences that you've had, such as falling out of a tree, riding a roller coaster, or jumping on a trampoline. Choose one from your list and use images to create a lyric about the experience.

Unplug Exercise: Take a full hour without electronics, and go outside and observe your world. Let the inner chatter fade while you take it all in and write about it:

- *Word collector:* Study billboards and advertising slogans, go to bookstores either in person or online, review your favorite movie titles and search for new ones, remember store names, street signs—anything with words.
- *Use other people's lives as inspiration:* Eavesdrop on people's conversations in coffee shops, in restaurants, at airports, etc.
- *Be a novelist*: Observe travelers on buses and trains, and people walking the streets, sitting in waiting rooms or at stoplights. What's their story? Where are they going, where are they coming from? What's going on in their lives? Create a story based on their expression, their interactions with others, how they are dressed, etc.

The Five Senses: Be truly present in the moment.

- *See:* Study the world around you, all the way from the street gutters to the sidewalk cracks, to building facades, to trees, to birds, to skylines. From top to bottom, look at everything you drive or walk past in a day. See if you notice something new in your daily routine, and write it down.
- *Smell:* Breathe the air, the rain, flowers, trees, fresh-cut grass, coffee, garlic, cinnamon rolls, and your favorite food. Pretend you are a dog and smell your way to your destination.
- *Taste:* Eat chocolate and try to describe it in words. Indulge in your favorite cheese, fruit, meal, wine, bubbly drink, anything you love. Close your eyes when you taste it and describe it in every detail.
- *Touch*: Feel the sunlight against your skin when you are outside. Take a moment to really feel the water running down your back when you are in the shower, the cold texture of ice, the softest skin, a fluffy blanket, a textured surface, etc. Describe the sensation.
- *Hear:* Listen to the city traffic and hum. Listen the quiet of a room, the sound of a soft breeze, the birds singing—wherever you are, see how many different sounds you can isolate, identify and describe.

Field Trip Exercise: Go somewhere serene or hectic, whatever you choose—to a park or a city café, for example. Describe everything you experience. Pretend you are a camera picking up all the images for us to see when you return and play them back. Also describe feelings you have while there.

Scissors Exercise: Print out a lyric you have that you cannot finish. Cut the lines into phrases that make sense, and try rearranging them in different orders. Add whatever you need, but keep playing with it until it works.

Confession Exercise: Confess to a crime you didn't commit. You can create any circumstance. Who are you confessing to? A lover, a parent, a priest, a therapist, a police officer? Turn your confession into a narrative lyric in which you describe the events leading up to your crime.

Alliteration Exercise: Create alliterative sentences, meaning that the first letter of each key word is the same). For example: "She saw Steven stalling on the sidewalk." Write two or three random ones and use at least one of these images in a lyric.

Death Exercise: Write about your first experience with death—perhaps a person you know, or your pet. Then write about your most recent experience with death. Combine the two into a narrative lyric.

Erotic Exercise: Make a list of everyday chores and activities—doing laundry, making breakfast, washing dishes, shopping, etc. Choose one and describe it in detail, every action that is required, all the little sensory moments involved. Take the details and images and use them to write a lyric in which you make this mundane experience sound erotic.

First Line Exercise: Take one line from a lyric of your own that is unfinished or a lyric by another writer as a first line. Once you've written your lyric, erase the first line.

First Time: Write a lyric about your first kiss, the first time you rode a bike, your first day at school. Then write a lyric about that last kiss, the last time you rode a bike, your last day at school.

Good and Evil Exercise: Good and evil are often described as "light" and "dark," sometimes "white" and "black." Write a lyric that reverses expectations. In other words, write about what is uplifting, intriguing, and beautiful about the dark, and a lyric about what is scary, terrifying, and uninviting about the daylight.

Gesture Exercise: Go to a public place and observe people's gestures, no matter how subtle: the way a youngster adjusts his hat or an elderly woman carefully balances herself, the way a woman plays with her hair, how people coddle their phones. Choose one gesture and what you think it tells you about the person.

Home Exercise: Revisit your childhood home in your mind. Try to remember it inside and the outside (the front yard, back yard, patio and swing, etc.). Focus on your favorite place. What did you do there, what do you remember? How did you feel at that age? What did you dream of?

Isolation Exercise: Write a description of one particular element in a larger setting; for example, one face in a crowd, one duck in the pond. Describe how it compares and fits into the group, and what distinguishes it from the others. Turn your description into a lyric.

Newspaper Exercise: Pick one story from the paper and take on the persona of someone involved in the story. Write from that person's point of view.

Photograph Exercise: Find a picture and write a lyric that describes the person or scene.

Syllabic Exercise: Write a lyric that is composed of only one-syllable words, or a lyric that alternates between one- and two-syllable words. Try three-syllable words. Play with rhythm.

Window Exercise: Write a lyric describing a scene outside your window. Do this even if your window faces a brick wall or a boring landscape; use your imagination to make it interesting.

Free Style Circles: Grab a pen, colored pencils, crayons, whatever you choose. Set your timer for three minutes and fill each of these circles up with words, sketches, doodles, whatever comes to mind. When you're finished, see what stands out to you. Use it as a springboard for a song or lyric or thought-provoking concept.

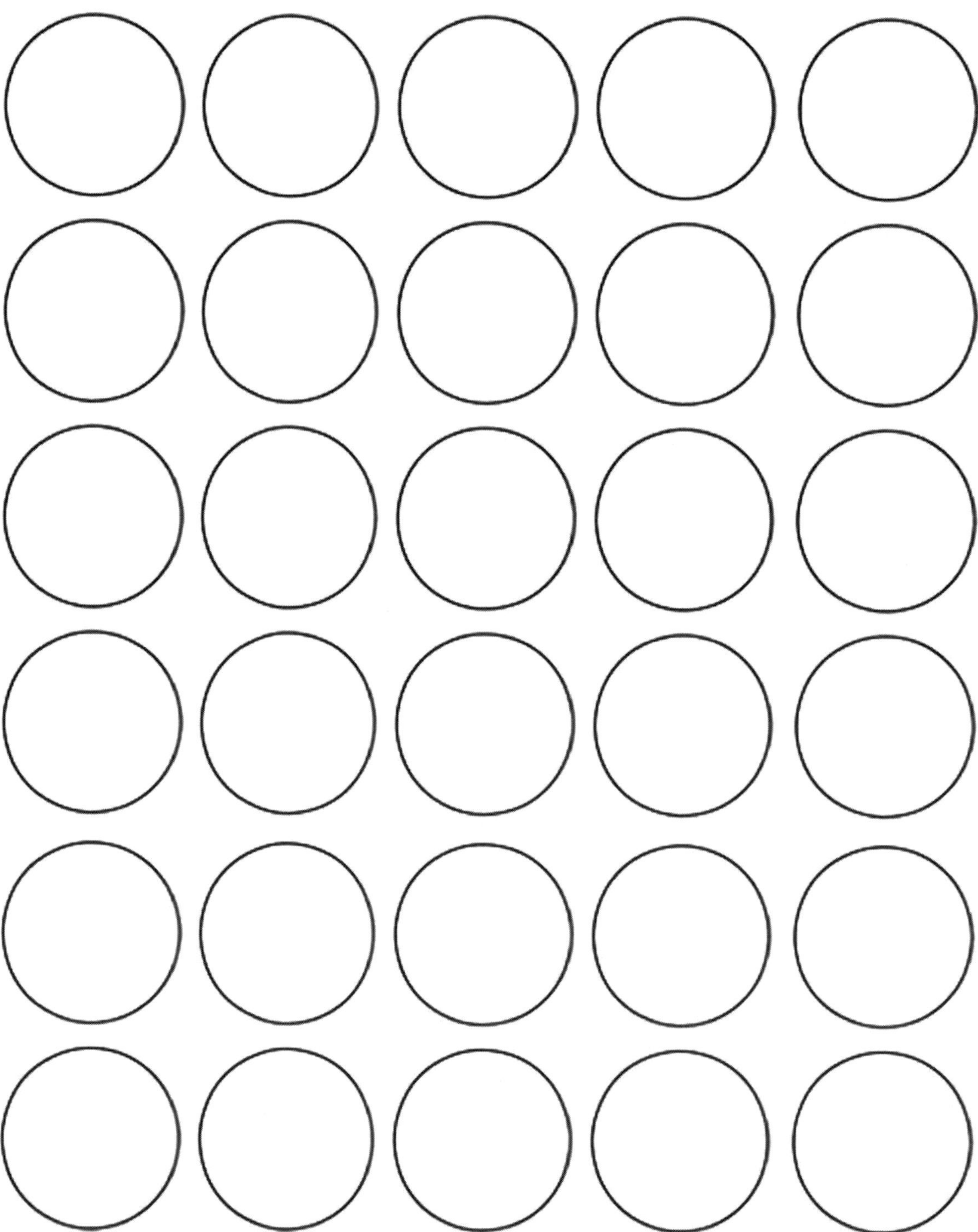

Song Analysis: Writing the Right Song for You

We now know we can do many different things to collect information, open up our senses, and fill that creative mind of yours, but when putting it all into song form we don't want to end up disappointed. This can happen if you really don't know what style you want to write in, what you are attracted to, and what is best for you vocally. So perhaps this next exercise can provide new insights for you.

Pick some of your favorite songs and let's analyze them. Take your time to think about them. Remember the ones that moved you. There was something about the words, the melody, the instrumentation, and the feel that took you to another place. When did music first touch your life? Where were you? What song was playing? Think about a song that inspired you to start writing because the song said it better than you could. Think about a song that allowed you to completely let go, or songs that accompanied you through stages of your life. Write down a few that come to mind and answer the following:

1. Where does the song fit on the spectrum or musical timeline?

   ____

   Classic, Current, Progressive

2. Is there a common factor when listening to a song?

   ____

   Tempo, Style, Era

3. What's the rhythmic pattern?

   ____

   Up-tempo, Mid-tempo, Ballad

4. What's the instrumentation?

   ____

   Organic and Raw, Full and Lush, Electronic, A Combination

5. What's the identifying sound of the vocal?

   ____

   Personality or Quality (Clean, Gritty, etc.)

6. How does it make you feel?

   ____

   Happy, Sad, Inspired

7. What is the song about?

   ____

   Party Fun, A Story, Political, Abstract and Interpretive

8. Are any of your songs the kind of music you want to write?

____

9. Does your voice, style, or instrument fit that genre?

____

Analyzing what draws you in can help you in your journey as a writer. What kind of song do you want to write, and what do you want to say? How do you want your listener to feel? You may have even discovered that we don't always write the music that we love. But what's important for you to discover is what you want to express. That's key. And don't make any apologies for your need to express yourself.

Art Chooses You

It may take a lifetime to write those few songs that stand an octave above the rest. In the meantime, keep listening, keep learning, and keep on keeping on. Ride the tide, get pulled by the undertow, navigate the rapids, but surf that wave. Being an artist is a life of ebb and flow. There are no shortcuts; many work their entire lives, and only a few get lucky. Art chooses you. If you have to ask yourself whether you should be an artist or not, I say quit right now. That question should not even take thought. Don't confuse that with the realistic concern of whether or not you will be able to make a living. You'll figure it out—because that "pull" should be so strong you can't find a way around it. You can't help but surrender and breathe in the oblivious madness and all its glory. And so I share with you this edifying quote from Rainer Maria Rilke, who says it best when addressing a young poet:

> Find out the reason that commands you to write; see whether it has spread its roots into the very depths of your heart; confess to yourself whether you would have to die if you were forbidden to write. This most of all: ask yourself in the most silent hour of your night: must I write? Dig into yourself for a deep answer. And if this answer rings out in assent, if you meet this solemn question with a strong, simple "I must," then build your life in accordance with this necessity; your whole life, even into its humblest and most indifferent hour, must become a sign and witness to this impulse.

12 Celebrity Songwriters Speak

Interviews with Allan Rich and Lindy Robbins

All is fair in love and songwriting. —Norah Jones

I always learn from the experiences of other songwriters and artists. Some of the artists and songs mentioned in the book so far can be directly linked to Allan Rich and Lindy Robbins. Both are platinum-selling songwriters who have experienced different career paths in this ever-changing music industry.

ALLAN RICH is a Brooklyn-born songwriter who has written for Barbra Streisand, Tina Turner, Dolly Parton, Oleta Adams, Rod Stewart, Luther Vandross, Patti LaBelle, Gladys Knight, Chaka Khan, Ray Charles, and Barry Manilow, to name a few. He had a hit single, sung by Whitney Houston, on the biggest-selling soundtrack album of all time, *The Bodyguard.* He has been nominated for an Academy Award, a Golden Globe, and a Grammy Award, and has had a Broadway musical debut in London. When I asked him what it's like to keep on after thirty years in the business, he spoke of the importance of networking—"You never know who's next to you"—and his passion and devotion to writing songs with an emotional impact. "No matter how technologically driven music production can become," he said, "it's still all about a great song."

Q: You wrote "Run to You," which Whitney Houston sings on the soundtrack for *The Bodyguard.* It is honestly one of my all-time favorite songs. I get chills every time I hear it. The sweeping melody and emotional impact that song has on listeners is truly magical.

You cowrote that with Jud Friedman. Can you tell us the story behind writing that song and getting it to Whitney? Was that song actually written for the movie *The Bodyguard*?

A: Yes. The song was actually written specifically for *The Bodyguard.* Here's how it happened. All the publishers in town were given a written breakdown of the songs that they needed for the movie. I still have it hanging on my wall! One of the songs was a "breakup" song. I was going through a breakup at the time so I channeled my feelings into a verse and chorus that I wrote at my steering wheel as I watched that person walk away and go up the steps of the building. The original chorus was:

I wanna run to you, I wanna run to you,
Like I always did before, come knocking at your door
I wanna run to you, how I wanna come to you,
But you're not there to run to anymore

I gave it to Jud Friedman, my writing partner of over twenty-five years now, and he put the most beautiful music to it, and then we finished the rest of it together. We tried to be strategic about it because we knew the odds of landing it were like winning the lottery. My product manager at MCA music publishing, Carole Ware, sent it to Gerry Griffith, an executive at Arista Records. He loved the song and passed it on to Clive Davis. Shortly afterwards, I came home and there was a message on my answering machine from Clive Davis himself. It said, "Hi! This is Clive Davis and I think you're going to like this message. Whitney and I really like your song. Please call me." I started shaking. Jud and I called Clive immediately and he said how much he and Whitney loved the song. But we had only done a piano vocal and Clive wanted us to add drums before he sent it to the film company. Since we did the piano vocal out of time, it was incredibly difficult to do the drums. In fact, it was a bitch and took hours! If you heard the demo, you would definitely hear all the stops and starts. But it still had magic. One day the director, Mic Jackson, called us and said, "We love your song. But we've changed the scene from a breakup scene to a 'take a chance on me' scene." It wouldn't be too difficult to rewrite the lyric to adapt to the new scene, right? Jud and I thought we were going to have a heart attack, but we said, "No problem." When we got off the phone Clive called us and said "Rewrite the lyric, and before you send it to Mic, send it to me." An angel must have been watching over us, because we rewrote the lyric and sent it to Clive and he called back to congratulate us on a terrific rewrite. He sent it to the film company and the rest, so to speak, is history.

Q: You've also written others songs for some of music's biggest icons: Smokey Robinson, Tina Turner, Chaka Khan, Barbra Streisand, Barry Manilow, Patti LaBelle, Luther Vandross, Ray Charles, and more. These are the kind of artists that will go down in history. During their heyday, a time when only the crème de la crème were recognized, the wall you had to climb over to get your song heard by the A&R record executive was Mt. Everest high. The DIY market today, a saturated industry that appears to be easily accessible, holds a very different playing field for young writers and artists. If you were starting out today as a writer, what would you do differently and what do you believe remains the same?

A: Well, when I started out, those were the days when if you wrote a great song, there were places you could pitch it and eventually get it cut. For instance, our James Ingram song "I Don't Have the Heart" was the first song Jud and I ever wrote. And it was a number one pop song. I didn't know James, I just thought he could kill it and somehow found his address and sent it to him. He was on tour with Quincy, I think, but a year or two later, he listened to a box of songs that had accumulated in his house and called me and said, "Are you Allan Rich?" I said, "Yes." He said "I listened to your song and it was the only one in the box of hundreds that made me want to cry." Then he said he was going to cut the song. Now the practice of writing a song for the sake of writing a song and trying to pitch it is almost non-existent. When I started out, the songwriter wrote the song and the producer produced the song. There wasn't too much overlap. But once the artist and the producer caught on that there was money to be made in songwriting and publishing they "suddenly" became songwriters as well. Today's market is much more track- and groove-oriented. And track guys and producers are king. If you're not in a producer's writing camp, or an artist's camp, it's pretty difficult to get your songs cut. Not to say it can't be done. But you're swimming upstream and there's a serious current getting in your way. If I were starting out today, I'd try looking for producer/track guys to work with—ones who have their finger on the pulse. One who you believe has got something special. Or I'd try to go to a publisher that I might know and have them hook me up with some of their producer/track guys. If you're just starting out, you will have to probably pay your dues a bit and eventually, hopefully, one of your songs will be so good that some producer you send it to, or someone at ASCAP or BMI or ASCAP Expo will hear it and recommend you to some producer/track guys who are happening. Or I'd try and find a young, unknown artist who I believed in and write with them in the hopes that they were going to break and I would along with them. Believe me, I'm trying to do that today, as we speak.

Q: Since you've had some of the all time greatest singers sing your songs, is there someone in particular you want to write a song for, or who you wish would sing one of your songs?

A: I wish Aretha or Celine had sung one of our songs. I think Jennifer Hudson could kill one of our songs, and so could Ariana Grande. But, even with my credentials, it's hard to get it through to them.

Q: What do you believe constitutes a "hit" song? Do you know when you are writing one?

A: I think I know when I've written a special one, but that doesn't necessarily mean it will be a hit song. I think a great title, like Katy Perry's "I Kissed a Girl," is important, or telling a great story in an unusual way, like Magic's "Rude." Or a song just creates a special atmosphere, like Gotye's "Someone That I Used to Know." The minute I heard them, I knew they'd be hits. One of my favorite songs that has been out recently is Nick Jonas's "Jealous." Great story, great vocal, and a sexy hook. One of my all-time favorite songs is Ryan and Macklemore's "Same Love." The lines in that song were unforgettable, unique, and anthem-like. Or maybe it's a really catchy melody or groove like Pharrell's "Happy." I knew Ellie Goulding's "Love Me Like You Do" would be a smash, because I hated that I couldn't stop singing that chorus. Not one of my favorite songs, but I knew it was a hit. And Ellie has a unique sound that is totally her own.

Q: Are you a better songwriter today than when you started?

A: I'm probably better than when I started. But there was something magical about the struggle and being young and bright-eyed and so full of ideas. I've been writing for over thirty years, and the disappointments and the ups and downs of the business and the way you get treated wear you down after a while. It's like a boxer. The older you get, the harder and slower it is to get up. At least, that's true for me.

Q: I have notebooks filed with titles and lyrical ideas, and MP3s of melodies and verses that constantly visit me. Do you still write songs when your muse is scratching at your door? Or do you only write for work?

A: I write a lot less than I used to. In the early days, Jud and I would write five days a week from morning 'til late afternoon. We'd just try and write great songs for the sake of writing a great song. Not anymore. We write when there's a project, or an artist we're working with or a producer. But it doesn't seem worth it to just write anymore and have all these songs that you don't know what to do with.

Q: You must know that everyone dreams of having a hit song and getting nominated for an award. There's truly only a handful of people who can say they are a two-time Academy Award, Grammy, and Golden Globe nominee. Does it change you? Did you ever say to yourself, "I've made it?" Or is that a myth? Do you still strive to continue to get better?

A: I feel very lucky and privileged to have had those nominations. No one can ever take them away. But I still want to have hits and feel relevant. I still feel I have a lot to say. But, honestly, you're only as good as your last hit. And you're on the A-list one year, and the next, you're not getting your calls returned. Or your phone isn't ringing with artists requesting you on a project. You really have to do some inside work on yourself or else you can go crazy.

Q: What do you dream of now? What's next?

A: The magic thing about this business is, out of the blue, something could happen and change everything. I still believe in that. I would love to be surprised with a big hit single, or a sample of one of our songs being used. Something I wasn't expecting to happen. I would love for *The Bodyguard*, which was turned into a musical and was a huge hit in London, to come to Broadway. And I'd love to be nominated for an Academy Award again but this time WIN! And Jud and I have cowritten several songs with an artist that Quincy is producing, and I'd love for us to have a hit together.

LINDY ROBBINS grew up in Los Angeles singing from a very young age with her father, also a gifted musician. She was actor, cabaret performer, and comic before hopping coasts to New York City to join and perform with a vocal quartet. She soon realized songwriting was more of her passion then performing and gave up the spotlight to hone her craft from behind the scenes. She moved back to LA in 1997 to write songs full time, never knowing it would lead her to becoming the multiplatinum songwriter that she is today.

Q: Today the digital format of music has completely changed the industry as well as songwriters' rights. Your career began right during this shift and survived the transition. We are now back to a single-driven world and a very "instant success mentality." Since the advent of home studios, Facebook, social media platforms, YouTube, Vevo and shows like *American Idol* and *The Voice*, songs are readily available for people to download virtually overnight. And today listeners are used to getting them for free. The value of music and its craft is quickly declining. Musicians now are giving their songs away for free. How do you feel about this? What would you say to songwriters and artists?

A: This is not only a complicated but a constantly changing issue, so it's hard to comment too much on the technical side. I will say, though, that streaming is not going away, and I pray for a fair marriage to be arranged as laws that are outdated and unfair get revamped. Songwriters get the short end of the stick by far. Regarding musicians giving songs away for free: I understand promotion is different, and if people want their music heard for free on clouds. . . then that is understandable. But, if someone wants to have a song in their library, then downloading it illegally for free is no different than going into a restaurant and eating the food without paying; the creators make their living; pay their mortgage, healthcare, rent; feed their families from the music they write and should be fairly compensated.

Remember, artists make a lot of their money from touring, merchandise, appearances . . . whereas pure songwriters have only their music to support them. Streaming needs to be properly monetized, and the public needs to be informed and educated so they realize they're literally stealing when they illegally download a song. Pay for streaming, buy songs you love, and support the writers of the music you love so that they can keep writing.

Q: Currently, you have a top pop single with Jason Derulo, "Want You to Want Me" with over 12,000,000 views on YouTube. Congratulations! And it is number five on the charts! Is this your biggest hit? And, with record sales virtually gone, can a songwriter make it rich on a "hit" song today?

A: This looks to be a very big hit for me. As we speak, it's number four on both mainstream radio and iTunes and moving up. I'm incredibly grateful. I have had other big hits: "Dangerous," by David Guetta, featuring Sam Martin, was number one in France, Germany, and many other European countries; "Tonight Tonight" and "Classic" were both top ten hits for me, as were my first hits, "Incomplete" and "What's Left of Me." But, fingers crossed, it looks like "Want You to Want Me" will be the biggest one yet.

In regard to whether or not a songwriter can make it rich on a hit song today, there are a lot of factors. Is it a domestic or worldwide hit? The length of time it spends on the charts, and if it's used for a lot of synchs, has to be considered, too. (Synchronizations are paid when a song is licensed for TV, film, etc., and hit songs can be used frequently depending on the content of lyrics.) It also depends on the writer's situation—if he or she has a co-publishing deal as opposed to an administration deal, a manager, etc.—but, in short, if you have a top ten radio hit there is still very good income to be made. I'm also very happy to be administered by Kobalt, who is on the forefront of technology, fighting for fairness for songwriters, and looking to the future in a positive way. Also, my managers at AAM are always looking out for their songwriters, so it's good to have the right people on your side through these difficult and changing times.

Q: I'm sure once people know who you are they want to write with you. Even writers without any kind of success probably ask you to collaborate with them, hoping it will catapult their careers. What would you say to an up-and-coming writer about advancing in the music industry?

A: You need to be aggressive and determined, but you also need to make sure you are good enough. It took me many years developing before I was ready to be in the room with A-list writers. I would say get trustworthy and honest feedback on your songs before you pursue people for co-writing. Go to as many open mics and showcases as you can, like the ASCAP Expo, to find collaborators. Also, I highly recommend getting a reputable publisher or manager to represent you. I don't respond to people I don't know who send me links on Twitter or Facebook or somehow find my e-mail address; I ask that they go through my management, who I hired to help me choose the best cowriters and opportunities. There is also an opportunity for up-and-coming writers to get signed to an established producer or songwriter. I don't look for writers to develop and sign, but many do, and this can be a good way to go, as it can open a lot of doors for a beginning writer or producer.

For me as a top-liner (that means melody and lyrics), I either look for a producer who is established or up-and-coming with great beats. If I add another top-liner, it will be either an artist who writes, or someone who sings well, which is a huge plus as they can sing the demo. I was very aggressive when I started; I used ASCAP (Brendan Okrent helped me early on) to get me meetings with publishers, who started to put me in with their producers and writers, but it was a process. I also won an international songwriting contest called Unisong in 1997 (founded by Alan Roy Scott) that led to my first deal in 1999 with Polygram. I had my first hit in 2003. So, six years of learning, taking every session I could get, and working very hard to get my first big single.

Q: There are two other women who have achieved your Olympian level of songwriting success: Diane Warren and Kara Dio Guardi. Your discography is amazing and you've been writing for years. What do you honestly believe makes you successful?

A: Thank you for the kind words! I know of many successful and fiercely talented women in music, and I look forward to the ones coming up as well. I believe what makes me and keeps me successful is a combination of many things: luck, perseverance, and the ability to always keep learning; I never feel like I know it all. I love working with young songwriters who help keep me current. I listen to the radio every day and study the charts. I love bouncing between genres, and pride myself on being able to write a lot of different styles. In sessions, I don't like to be "right." I like to listen to my collaborators and make sure we are all excited. I think I've learned more about songwriting in these past couple of years than ever before. Simplicity is deceptively difficult. I also think I've been fortunate to surround myself with great talent, and to have a good ear for up-and-coming writers who keep me fresh. I feel incredibly blessed and fortunate with my success. I'm probably more inspired now than ever. I travel often to writer's camps and to sessions in other countries as well to keep it interesting. I've increasingly tried to work less but have it mean more, to experience life, spend time with friends and family, and take more time off in order to keep from getting burnt out. The balance has been very helpful to my longevity.

Q: Do you have a favorite song you've written? Can you tell us a story about it?

A: I would say "Skyscraper" is one of my favorite songs I've cowritten. It was originally written with Kerli (and Toby Gad) for her record. Then, when she changed labels and didn't use the song, it was recorded by Jordin Sparks but didn't make the record. I never stopped believing in it with all my heart—I believed in it from the moment the song was written. When Demi Lovato recorded it a couple years later, I knew the universe had been waiting for her, and for her journey to coincide perfectly with the message of the song that seems to have touched a lot of people. That is what I strive for—that a song I have been a part of can touch someone emotionally, make them happy, dance, and feel alive.

Q: Is there someone in particular you've always dreamed of writing a song for?

A: I had always wanted to have a song recorded by Kelly Clarkson, Britney Spears, and Maroon 5. They actually all did record one, but they were never released, so maybe someday. I would also love to have a song recorded by Barbra Streisand, who is my childhood idol.

Q: Most artists sacrifice their lives trying to make a living. Many never give up their desire to share stories through music and songs. Success or no success, could you ever walk away from songwriting? What does music mean to you?

A: I love songwriting more now than ever. I often feel as if I am channeling ideas as they flow through me. I still feel it in my heart and soul. Honestly, it's the only thing I want or know how to do. I think in years to come the form may change; perhaps I will write a musical or more songs for TV and film. I also see myself working less in later years, but for the foreseeable future I can't ever imagine walking away from it. That said, if people take songwriters for granted, try to take away our copyrights and imagine we should not be paid for our creations, it does take a lot of the fun out of it; I pray with all my heart for all creators in music that we can have a happy and fair resolution so that everyone wins, and songwriters are still inspired to create.

Q: What do you dream of now? What's next?

A: I want to keep doing what I'm doing, but always with an open heart, mind, and soul; to let in ideas and create what is in my heart or what feels fun or new; to share the creative process with people I enjoy writing and spending time with (both my regulars and new people, who can always teach me something); to focus on a balance of work and life so that I can enjoy the world and travel, enjoy my relationships, and hopefully be creating as long as I walk this earth.

13 The Evolution of Pop Music

Music is a moral law. It gives soul to the universe,
wings to the mind, flight to the imagination,
and charm and gaiety to life and to everything. —Plato

We've learned about the mechanics of songwriting and different ways to help you see the world with a creative mind. Yet there still exists a vast body of music and history that, when explored, can help expand your artistic development even further. The evolution of music is fascinating and, I believe, empowering for both artists and songwriters. If you've come to this page, you've got an inquiring mind. Knowledge is power, and as you develop your writing, you may draw upon a musical style you were not aware of had you not done your homework.

Music has always reflected art, fashion, dance, and the societal pulse of each decade. Folk, pop, blues, rock 'n' roll, and country music all stem from the blending of West African, Mexican, Cuban, Irish and Scottish sounds, instruments, and traditions. As I mentioned, many of today's artists are recycling sounds of pop music from eras before they were even born. Try researching some of the names and styles you don't recognize and infuse what you've learned into a unique sound and style of writing. We'll begin at the turn of the century.

RAGTIME— BLUES —BLUEGRASS/COUNTRY — SWING — BEEBOP —
ROCK —MOTOWN —DISCO — DIGITAL SYNTHPOP —GLAM METAL —
GRUNGE —CONTEMPORARY COUNTRY — R&B HIP HOP —INDIE MUSIC
EMO—

1900–1920s: Ballroom Dancing, Victrola, Ragtime

Before the advent of radio, music brought people together for public gatherings and dances. Ballroom dancing, which originated in Europe, became very popular in America at the turn of the twentieth century. Where religion had frowned on couples dancing in an embrace, now with the Viennese Waltz and popular dances, people found greater opportunity to express themselves—a development that became a dominant theme during this era in music as well as in dance.

At the same time, barbershop music was also popular. It originated with African American men singing spirituals in four-part harmony while waiting their turn for a shave and a haircut. This style of performing and singing was adopted by white society, and soon enough barbershop quartets were performing for crowds who gathered at the town square in front of the five and dime on Saturday nights. Song pluggers, too, would travel to the town square, carrying their upright pianos on horse-drawn buggies to play shows and sell their sheet music for a quarter. Music was the main attraction for social events of that era.

Today I would compare the song pluggers to street performers on city sidewalks or in subway stations who sing, dance, and sell their CDs. When I listen to barbershop quartets, I can hear their influence in later contemporary music, such as Frankie Valli and the Four Seasons and early Beatles songs, the Temptations and Motown groups, the Bee Gees, folk harmonies in Crosby Stills Nash and Young, and even many boy bands from the Backstreet Boys up through today's One Direction. Female groups like the Andrews Sisters, Diana Ross and the Supremes, Wilson Phillips, the Spice Girls, and Destiny's Child are part of this tradition as well. And although ballroom dancing is still popular on television shows like *Dancing with the Stars* and *So You Think You Can Dance,* today most young people prefer to express themselves at EDM festivals and raves, wearing GloFX glasses and the latest styles. DJs can earn $250,000 per night by triggering electronic devices and mixing music to elaborate light shows for thousands of fans.

Waltzes weren't the only tunes inviting Americans to dance in those early days. Ragtime music was considered pop music from the late 1800s through the turn of the century. Black pianist and composer Scott Joplin was its most noted artist. Its style is a modification of marching band music. The only way it works is by syncopating or "ragging" the rhythm, creating a "jerky" effect that gets people moving their hips. Originally performed for strippers in the red-light district, and behind closed doors, it was thought to be degrading and a lowering of your moral standards were you to dance to it. But ragtime eventually made it to mainstream society and the legitimate stage. Following World War I, New York's high society hired African-American ragtime bands so they could dance these "nasty" dances called the One-Step and the Turkey Trot. And ragtime music began evolving into newer musical styles that came to be known as jazz and blues.

The actual "birth of blues" is not exact. Many scholars believe blues music began in Mississippi sometime around 1900, where groups of black workers in fields and chain gangs and churches would sing in prayer for better days, sounding a call and answer, a cry and holler of bent notes and melancholy lyrics. Eventually, blues singers began performing solo rather than in groups. Mamie Smith's "Crazy Blues" was the first female solo blues record that sold over a million copies, and was inducted into the Grammy Hall of Fame.

One of the first devices to play records back then was the hand-cranked Victrola. It's not an easy thing to play. I bought one at a yard sale, and you have to physically crank the handle to spin the turntable. To get the correct speed is hard, and when the turntable spins too fast or two slow, you get some funky-sounding results. You've probably seen the famous picture of the dog looking into the flaring horn of a Victrola.

That was the logo of RCA Victor Records, also known as RCA Records. Artists such as Elvis Presley, Ray Charles, Count Basie, and Benny Goodman eventually signed to RCA. By then, the hand-cranked Victrola days were long over, and instead phonographic records spun electronically at seventy-eight rotations per minute.

We must recognize how easy it is to collect and play music these days. With a click of a button, and a thirty-second download, you can have any song you dream about. And computer programs with premade loops and plug-ins allow the recording process to be easily accessible to the average person. Early on the record industry was concentrated in New York City, where musicians would travel to record their music. Ralph Peer of RCA Victor Records, who supervised Mamie Smith's "Crazy Blues," was a producer and publisher who discovered many star musicians. He traveled all the way down to Tennessee with a portable studio to capture what people were calling "hillbilly music," heard in the Appalachian mountain regions. Irish, Scottish, and English immigrants played traditional music on instruments like the fiddle, guitar, mandolin, dobro, and upright bass. African Americans who were free from slavery and working in timber and coal mining influenced this new music by adding banjo and a blues feel. Peer thought it could be the next "new" sound. He recorded local musicians in hotel rooms, ballrooms, or empty warehouses. In time, this "new hillbilly" sound became popular and is known today as country and bluegrass. Peer even went on to record the Carter Family, June Carter's parents. Their song "Wildwood Flower" sold over 100,000 copies. That same June Carter would grow up to record hit songs of her own, and would marry the one and only Johnny Cash.

1920s–1930s: Swing, Jazz, Bebop

Following the hardships of World War One, people indulged in new styles of dancing and dressing and rejected all moral standards. Life in America brought happier times: easier work weeks, a new generation of women coming of age with the right to vote, and people enjoying life. And it was all about listening and dancing to jazz that put the "sin in syncopation." From New Orleans to Kansas City, Chicago, and New York, this slurring and bending of musical notes known as jazz played on. An element of improvisation known to African-American culture influenced jazz as well as the development of swing and bebop. We start to witness music moving farther and farther away from notes on paper. The first great jazz musician, Louis Armstrong, was known by all other musicians as the cat who never allowed himself to repeat the same solo. Bebop soon followed with Dizzy Gillespie, who played a bent trumpet with a unique sound. Vocalists would scat, stringing together vowels and syllables instead of words, to fit complex musical figures. And swing, the so-called "devil's music," made people dance wildly to the Charleston, the Shimmy, and the Black Bottom. These popular dance moves, derived for the most part from dances brought by slaves from Africa, were adopted by mainstream white celebrities and featured in movies. Music and rhythm had found their way into the secret places of our souls, hit the big screen, and were soon to be broadcast in every home.

Radio Was the Internet

By 1940, more than 80 percent of households had a radio, and the average person spent more than four hours a day listening. Just like today's Internet, television cable, and subscription programming, people tuned in to live music, performances, singers, comedians, news, educational shows and more. *Billboard* magazine began publishing music charts for pop, rhythm and blues, and country and western songs that got the most radio play. Broadway shows ached for "hit" songs. And many composers refined their skills on Tin Pan Alley. Writers would lock themselves away in piano rooms in the buildings that lined West 28th Street between Fifth and Sixth Avenue in New York City. Just imagine an entire city block dedicated to music. Rumor has it the name came from the clatter of all the pianos playing different songs simultaneously—as if a thousand tin pans were being clanged together. Writers like George Gershwin, Sammy Cahn, Cole Porter, Irving Berlin, Harold Arlen, Jerome Kern, Richard Rodgers, and Oscar Hammerstein wrote songs so popular that many are still recorded today. Songs such as "It Don't Mean a Thing If It Ain't Got That Swing," "Fly Me to the Moon," "Somewhere Over the Rainbow," and "Stormy Weather" formed a canon we now call the Great American Songbook. It was a time when music was booming.

1940s: Movie Stars, Crooners, and American Idols

By 1940, Frank Sinatra, a crooner who sang over lush orchestrations, had become our first "American idol" and star of the silver screen.

A new fan base of teenagers in bobby socks lined up outside theaters and movie houses, and would faint and swoon at his shows. At the same time, western swing–singing cowboys like Roy Rogers and Gene Autry hit the big screen. Hollywood had a new glimmer and shine. RCA Victor sprayed Glenn Miller's recording of "Chattanooga Choo Choo" in "gold" for having sold more than one million copies. And great music innovators like Bing Crosby, Perry Como, Doris Day, the Andrews Sisters, and Nat King Cole graced the new "long play" records that quickly became the standard. As opposed to a noisier and faster seventy-eight revolutions per minute with less than five minutes of music per record side, the LP (invented at Columbia Records in 1948) revolved thirty-three and a half times per minute, resulting in a better sound and a longer play of twenty minutes of music per record side—meaning more music for fans.

When the gift of sound was most glorious, discrimination was center stage. Black band members were only allowed to enter through the backs of clubs, while white players and singers got first-class treatment. On the brink of an emerging Civil Rights movement, a voice in protest filled the airwaves when Billie Holiday's song "Strange Fruit" graphically depicted the lynching of young blacks, hanging from poplar trees. Afraid of retaliation, Holiday was scared to perform it, but in honor of the victims she braved the storm. She added it to her set as her final song and requested that even the wait staff stop working as, over a moment of silence, she sang to honor those who had lost their lives.

1950s: Elvis and the Electric Guitar

The roof was about to be blown off with Elvis Presley, the king of rock 'n' roll. This new musical storm, created from a crosscurrent of electric blues, boogie, gospel, and country, blew in on a new guitar, the solid body electric. Producing over thirty-two number one hit songs and eighteen number one albums, Elvis was more popular than Frank Sinatra and the biggest artist of his time. The censors of the time found it a good thing to forget how Sinatra had made the girls swoon, but were "shocked" at how Elvis made them scream. It was a teenage rebellion in the fifties. Rock sounds, rhythmic changes, and Presley's gyrating hips while he sang

"Don't Be Cruel" on the *Ed Sullivan Show* created a huge controversy. He became known as "Elvis the Pelvis" and stirred up critics, priests, teachers and parents. Ed Sullivan's producers insisted he could only be photographed from the waist up!

Elvis rose to fame by bringing black music to white audiences. Meanwhile, Little Richard, Chuck Berry, the Coasters, Chubby Checker, Fats Domino and the black originators of his sound were pushed aside. Particularly notable among these greats is Carl Perkins, who wrote "Blue Suede Shoes" and other rockabilly hits—a cross-pollination of "hillbilly music" and rock. Paul McCartney has said that without Carl Perkins, there would be no Beatles. And, of course, without blues and gospel, there would be no rock 'n' roll.

The 45 single replaced the full LP. Bill Haley and the Comets' "Rock Around the Clock," Patti Page's "Tennessee Waltz," and Bobby Darin's "Mack the Knife" were major hits. A softer sound in comparison still existed in country music with Pat Boone, Hank Williams, Patsy Cline, and Connie Francis. On a more soulful side, Motown was on the rise with rhythm and blues, blending jazz, doo-wop, blues, and gospel, for singers like Sam Cooke, the Drifters, and Ray Charles.

1960s: Sex, Drugs, Rock 'n' Roll, and the Beatles

The sixties was a "Coming of Age Era" for young hopefuls, when popular rock music dominated the charts. With the invasion of the British sound of the Beatles, there was no turning back. Music was more in-your-face, and performers were much freer on stage. There was a huge hippie movement, championing sex, drugs, and rock 'n' roll and representing the anti-establishment and anti-war movement during Vietnam. Motown's rhythm-and-blues sound garnered attention with Marvin Gaye questioning our involvement in Vietnam with his song "What's Going On." Other artists like Stevie Wonder, the Temptations, Gladys Knight and the Pips, the Four Tops, Diana Ross and the Supremes, and the Jackson Five followed right behind.

In the late sixties, outdoor music festivals took off. The most famous festival of all was Woodstock, a three-day event where 500,000 people gathered to hear provocative rock bands like the Who, the Grateful Dead, and Jefferson Airplane and introspective folk artists like Arlo Guthrie, Joan Baez, Simon and Garfunkel, and many more. Much like the days of Tin Pan Alley, during the sixties songwriters like Carole King, Gerry Goffin, Burt Bacharach, Paul Anka, Neil Diamond, and Phil Spector crammed into cubicles in the Brill Building on Broadway and 49th writing hit songs.

1970s: Album-Oriented Radio, Disco, and America's Top 40

The seventies were all about the journey of a song. It was an album-oriented time when rock stations would play entire records without a single commercial break. Progressive rock bands like Yes, Led Zeppelin, Pink Floyd, Genesis, Queen, and Emerson, Lake and Palmer filled the airwaves. Many songs were longer and more epic in production. For example, Led Zeppelin's "Stairway to Heaven" lasted eight minutes. It felt as if there were no musical boundaries. And a new psychedelic vibe of electric guitars and synthesizers helped create a fantasy or journey for the listener. Many of the bands toured for years on the road honing their style and sound before hitting it big. Car stereos became common for drivers; then eight-track and cassette tapes were introduced. *American Top 40* broadcast its first show, with Casey Kasem, on the weekend of Independence Day, 1970. The nation would tune in to hear the biggest-selling artists on the countdown to number one every Saturday morning. The first song Kasem ever played was Marvin Gaye's "End of the Road"; thirty-four years later, in 2004, he ended his run with Outkast's "Hey Ya." The biggest news of the decade was the Beatles' breakup. But Paul McCartney and John Lennon went on to successful solo careers, while new sounds and styles began to emerge on America's dance floors.

The newest breakout was disco: the beat of four on the floor, sixteenth notes on the hi-hat, funky bass lines, and falsetto male vocals that got everyone grooving. That sound has reemerged today in Daft Punk songs, Pharrell's productions, and some EDM music. The Bee Gees' soundtrack for *Saturday Night Fever*, a film starring John Travolta, sold fifteen million copies. KC and the Sunshine Band, Earth, Wind and Fire, and the Jackson Five also helped fill disco clubs with people dancing the night away. Donna Summers' disco hit "I Feel Love" incorporated synthesizers and the Mini-Moog, sounding a lot like today's dance music. The Mini-Moog was also evident in the Beatles' 1969 *Abbey Road* on songs such as "Here Comes the Sun" and others. The manual manipulating of sounds through oscillators is recycled today in EDM, dubstep, and electronica music. Progressive rock also incorporated synthesizers and a new wave sound that lent itself to punk music. However, punk and new wave music had shorter songs, stripped-down instrumentation, and the anti-establishment messages of Blondie, Talking Heads, the Velvet Underground, David Bowie, and more. On the softer side, rock bands such as Bread, America, and the Carpenters were popular. And singer/songwriters James Taylor, Joni Mitchell, Cat Stevens, Linda Ronstadt, Elton John, Billy Joel, and Barry Manilow had big careers.

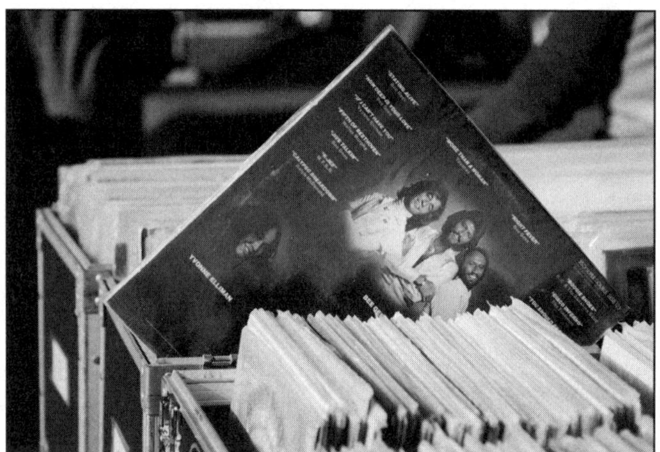

1980s: MTV

Video "killed the radio star" with the cable "music television" channel MTV. It used to be you rarely knew what artists looked like unless you bought their records or went to see them in concert. There was a mystique that allowed the music to be the most important factor. We could listen for hours and let the music speak for itself. Now it wasn't just what you sounded like; it was the "look": the fashion, the video, the bells and whistles. I remember Madonna's first cassette tape, which came without a picture and had a solid black

cover. Her music was a huge hit in gay clubs in NYC. But no one saw her face. She had a high-pitched voice and poppy rhythmic synth songs produced by Jellybean Benitez that were catchy and new. But it was MTV that was truly a game changer for her. Music became even more electrified. Super-slick productions with gated drums, big reverb on vocals and electronic keyboard of all kinds. It was a big sound to match the videos, the big hair, big shoulder pads, and bright colors. The eighties were about abundance, money, and clout—the more, the merrier. VH1 also launched during the eighties, playing videos 24/7 and introducing a new platform for artists daily. Michael Jackson's *Off the Wall* and *Thriller* albums dominated the world.

I waited in line for hours to purchase *Thriller* at the record store. Jackson's ability to merge rock, R&B, and pop remains unmatched in my opinion, and his stage performance was one of a kind. Whitney Houston also rose to megastardom alongside glam rock band Bon Jovi. These icons dominated the world charts and sold in the mega-millions.

We had pop/punk/new wave artists Devo, the Pet Shop Boys, the Police, Duran Duran, Cyndi Lauper, Pat Benatar, the Cars, Devo, Boy George and the Eurythmics, as well as R&B urban artists such as; Prince, Janet Jackson, and Lionel Richie. In addition, we had hard rock, heavy metal, and glam metal artists; Van Halen, Poison, Def Leppard, Guns and Roses, AC/DC. Male artists like Bruce Springsteen, Phil Collins, George Michael, and Bryan Adams were dominating the charts. And rap/hip-hop artists like Grandmaster Flash, Run DMC, Queen Latifah, LL Cool J, and the Beastie Boys began to cross over.

As technology connected us all more globally, musicians began using their art to bring awareness to causes. Benefit concerts hosting many rock artists were formed to stop world hunger and to help fund a cure for AIDS. Songs like "We Are the World," produced by Quincy Jones, featured a who's who of celebrity singers and soared to huge success.

1990s: Grunge

The pendulum always swings in the opposite direction, and after the big sounds of the eighties, music in the nineties brought the onset of grunge. Distorted electric guitars, broken-down verses with huge dynamics accompanied by gritty vocal textures and lyrical angst landed center stage. The back-to-basics sound of garage bands like Nirvana took the world by storm.

An empowered group of singer-songwriters also came center stage with Lilith Fair. This concert tour hosted an all-female line-up reflecting the seventies era of the singer-songwriter. With artists such as Sarah McLachlan, Alanis Morissette, Sheryl Crow, Shawn Colvin, and Fiona Apple, a simple performance showcasing the music and the message itself was the focus, as opposed to big theatrics, costumes, and over-the-top visuals.

Latin-infused music won new fans thanks to artists such as Ricky Martin, Selena, Marc Anthony, and Carlos Santana. And vocal divas Mariah Carey and Celine Dion sang to the highest heights. We also had R&B sensations Luther Vandross, Mary J. Blige, Brian McKnight, Brandy, Destiny's Child, Usher, and many more.

Disney's television show *The Mickey Mouse Club* introduced new music pop sensations Britney Spears, Christina Aguilera, and Justin Timberlake. Writers and producers would craft these teen television performers into superstars.

The addition of Auto-Tune to the vocal track of Cher's dance tune "Do You Believe in Love" paved the way for a newly accepted tool to manipulate a singer's voice. We were no longer hiding its effect, but rather featuring it. It was the golden age of hip-hop music and sampling. There was no need for formal training, and DJs would put together sound collages mixing in funk, R&B, soul and hints of rock 'n' roll for rappers to rap over. Artists such as Ice Cube, Snoop Dog, Sean Combs, Dr. Dre, DMX, and Jay-Z were at the top of their game. The popularity of Auto-Tune and sampling shifted the focus in writing and production from finding new grooves and instruments to computerizing vocals and using prerecorded samples of works instead.

With the creation of the file-sharing service Napster, developer Shawn Fanning shook the music world. EMI, Warner Brothers, BMG, Universal, and Sony, sued to shut down the service, citing alleged copyright infringement. But digital music sharing had already changed the industry for good. Digital music creation software became available for home computer users, and compression of songs into MP3s for digital distribution seemed to eliminate the need for record companies. Artists now had complete control and were able to write, record, produce, and distribute their own music. The middleman was gone, and the music industry was now more in the hands of the artist and the buyer.

2000: Fast Forward

On January 9, 2001, Apple iTunes and iPods were released to the public and became the new record stores. The early years of the millennium saw a complete change in the way music was delivered to the buyer. Record label mergers began, and others shut down completely. Record stores went out of business, but artists kept making music. A new music platform was in place, and artist development days were over. Televised singing competitions came to act as the newest record labels, collecting endorsements for newcomers from a panel of celebrity judges and turning viewers around the world into A&R executives. Voting virtual unknowns to winner's status on *American Idol* and *The Voice* catapulted them to instant stardom. Singles were uploaded virtually overnight to iTunes and solo records released within a few months once the show ended. Kelly Clarkson was the biggest pop-rock star, next to country artist Carrie Underwood, selling tens of millions of records.

New metal, EMO, garage bands, post punk, and electronic instruments again became the focus when it came to Eurodance. Attention spans shortened with an overload of information; compression and over-the-top pop production peaked. Latin artists such as Jennifer Lopez, Shakira, Selena Gomez, and Enrique Iglesias became multiplatinum sellers. Many pop groups broke up with solo artists Beyoncé of Destiny's

Child, N' Sync's Justin Timberlake, and Rob Thomas of Matchbox Twenty stepping out alone. On the rock side, artists like Avril Lavigne, Pink, and Gwen Stefani brought the rebellious side of women into focus. And R&B pop singers Usher, Justin Bieber, Alicia Keys, and Leona Lewis lit up the stage.

Country crossed over to pop radio and the pop market by commercializing the sound with artists such as Shania Twain, Faith Hill, the Dixie Chicks, Taylor Swift, and Lady Antebellum. Contemporary country pop became its own genre, paying homage to its roots with just a slight vocal twang, a slide guitar here and there, and nontraditional story lines.

With his "no holds barred" way of rapping about controversial and social issues, Eminem became the most successful white rapper in the music industry, selling 172 million albums and charting #83 on Rolling Stone's *100 Greatest Artists of All Time.* In rap, artists explored and crystallized distinct stylistic differences between the East Coast, the West Coast, and the "Dirty South."

Pop punk bands such as Blink 182, All-American Rejects, and Green Day also gained popularity. In grunge and rock, the Foo Fighters, Red Hot Chili Peppers, Creed, Nickelback, the White Stripes, Hoobastank, and Daughtry gained a following with less angst and more anthemic songs. Subgenres fusing Latin music such as merengue and reggaeton with hip-hop became popular, with artists like Rihanna bringing this flavor to the mainstream. A British sound returned once again, with Radiohead, Oasis, Coldplay, and Mumford and Sons all rising to the top. One Direction and Imagine Dragons also had Top 40 success by the end of the era, as did solo newcomers Jason Mraz, John Mayer, Adele, Lady Gaga, Miley Cyrus, Lorde, Katy Perry, Ariana Grande, Sia, Bruno Mars, and Ed Sheeran, to name a few. And social media offered the DIY artist new opportunities to achieve mass success. One Republic went viral on MySpace and got signed to Columbia Records. And Psy's "Gangnam Style" debuted in South Korea, but then went viral with over 2.3 billion views on YouTube and a hit single in thirty different countries.

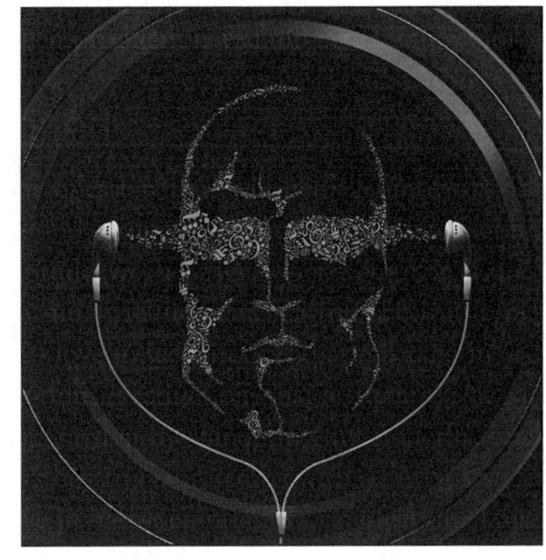

As a projection of social norms, computers became integrated into most live shows. Stadiums full of fans gathered to watch DJs create spectacular, sonic-driven beats synched up to theatrical light shows and displays. EDM's Dead Maus, Zedd, Calvin Harris, and Avicii remixed popular hit songs, vaulting them past the multi-million-selling mark. A new form of musical art and expression took on a life of its own and dominated the scene.

Looking to 2020

Today, millennials spend a majority of their time on their smartphones or computers surfing the Internet, where every genre, producer, and song is available at our fingertips through services such as Spotify, iTunes, Apple Music, Google Play Music, Sound Cloud, Pandora, and YouTube's Music Key. Most millenials have never paid for music—never owned an album, a cassette, perhaps not even a CD. And by 2020 all young listeners will only know music as purely "intangible." They will create their own radio stations, playlists, and video channels in an endless virtual world. They can travel back through time through a library of songs, all the way back the first blues recording of Mamie Smith "Crazy Blues." It's a new world for both the listener and the creator.

And until 2020 and beyond, music continues to be the soundtracks of our lives.

Part 3

Recording and Production

With

Eric Corne

Introduction

The previous sections of this book highlighted the importance of great songs and performance chops. The next step is to create a standout recording of your songs to be sold at shows, streamed online, played on the radio, and synched in film, TV, and ads.

Music production, the craft of making sound recordings, can take many different forms. It could be recording your band in the garage, producing music in your bedroom on your computer, working with a great producer at a killer studio, or a combination of these. Whatever your process, to succeed in today's music business, independent artists require a combination of creative and technical skills.

Music production involves tasks like selecting the right songs, keys, and tempos; honing the structure; rehearsing the songs and parts; building arrangements; choosing and recording the instrumentation; and enhancing and balancing the sounds into a cohesive, visceral final production.

The following five chapters explore the music production process: Preparing to Record (Preproduction), Creating and Executing a Production Plan, DIY Recording, Mixing, and Mastering. The goal is to help you create productions that truly represent who you (or the artists you're producing) are, and to give you the know-how to do it at a professional level.

In decades past, the cost of producing a record was so prohibitive that few could imagine making their own records. Record labels truly were the gatekeepers of the music industry, and without a record deal you were unlikely to make a record in a recording studio.

With the rise of digital recording and more affordable equipment, the price of entry was greatly reduced, forcing big studios to lower their rates. As a result, starting in the late 1980s to early 1990s, we saw a rise in independent producers working outside the label system and the beginning of the proliferation of home recording, which really exploded in the new millennium.

But becoming a successful independent recording artist does not happen overnight. You may have great ideas, but it takes skill to execute them. You may get lucky with a cool sound, but it takes knowledge to repeat that sound. It's not enough to just be in love with the *idea* of having a career in music. You also have to be in love with the *work*. It's the people who love the work, the process, who build successful careers, block by block, week by week, month by month, year by year. If that sounds like you, then I think you're going to find this section of the book very informative and inspiring.

14 Preparing to Record (Preproduction)

A lot of the work in music production takes place before you even hit the "record" button. Preproduction is the stage where you take a song, fine-tune its chord structure, lyrics, and melody, and begin experimenting with the arrangement and instrumentation.

Here are some preproduction tasks to help you prepare for the recording stage:

1. Listening to music analytically
2. Song analysis
3. Honing the song
4. Finding the groove
5. Demoing the song

Listening Analytically with Your "Producer's Ears"

Every great artist or producer has studied the masters in his or her genre. When most people listen to music they don't analyze the structure, arrangement, and instrumentation of a song, but serious artists and producers do. This is the difference between listening to music casually or with your "producer's ears."

It's one thing to respond to the groove, lyrics, or melody with your heart and soul, but it's a whole other thing to dissect a song's structure, arrangement, and instrumentation. This is a key skill in a producer's tool belt; and while it is certainly a skill that takes time and work to develop and excel at, you should benefit from this process immediately.

This type of deep listening can reveal many mysteries behind a great production, and the more you listen in this analytical way, the better you'll become at identifying specific instruments when they enter and exit the arrangement, the octave range/register they're playing in, doubled parts, panning, effects, and other subtle textures. As a result, your productions will become more sophisticated and/or visceral, and you'll become better at determining the right approach for each song and artist.

As a teen, Neil Young was dissecting the sound of 1950s instrumental rock 'n' roll bands like the Shadows and researching the instruments they played. When Bob Dylan first started he was practically a Woody Guthrie clone and later drew greatly on Nashville and Chicago blues productions. Dangermouse studied everyone from Ennio Morricone, to DJ Shadow, to '60s psychedelia. Trent Reznor points to David Bowie, Rush, the Cure, and others. Noel Gallagher's (of Oasis) deconstruction of The Beatles is well documented. And this isn't true just for music. Talk to any great painter, filmmaker, or athlete and I bet they can tell you who they've studied and what they learned.

I'm not suggesting you copy your favorite artists. I'm not talking about ripping off chord progressions or melodies. I'm talking about observing the details of the sound, performance technique, and arrangement from a wide variety of productions and discovering yourself as a producer in the process.

Let's take a look at the drums as an example: Are you paying attention to the points in a song where the drummer is on the hi-hat, as opposed to the ride cymbal, or whether or not the hi-hats are opened or closed? This is key to evolving the dynamics of the song. When does the switch from side stick (on the rim) to full snare occur? Is the drummer hitting the middle of the snare without striking the rim or including the rim for that extra *crack*? Are the drums muted with tape, blankets, and pillows, or wide open with a long decay? Is it a vintage kit or more modern? How are the drums tuned, low or high-pitched? How does the sound differ when a drummer hits hard or soft? Is the kit close-miked or does it sound more *roomy*? What about the feel? Is it straight, or swinging/accented? Is it laid back or driving? Is it in 4/4 time or an odd time signature?

These factors make a huge difference in a production where a lot of little details contribute to the final result. Observe the points in a song at which sound or texture changes occur, and this will further inform *your* productions. Take this approach in analyzing all the instrumentation and vocals in a production and you will begin to hear, think and react like a producer.

Sometimes when I suggest this listening approach to young artists or new producers they tell me that they aren't sure how to identify or recreate a sound they've heard in a song. My response is twofold. Number one, do some research! A simple Google search can reveal everything from what gear was used to what techniques were applied. Secondly, there are many paths to the mountaintop! Sometimes I think it's actually cooler to hear something that grabs you and have it inspire you to experiment and find your own way of doing it. The result can be a little more unique.

Eventually, this kind of analytical work becomes natural, ingrained, almost unconscious, and you'll find yourself in sessions beginning to react more in the moment with your instincts, your gut.

Let's take a look at an example of a song analysis. If possible, I suggest listening to the song while reading the analysis and re-reading the song analysis after you've finished the mixing chapter.

Song Analysis

"Time to Pretend" by MGMT

Sound

This entire record has a very distinct sound. It's a hybrid of styles and approaches. This, along with its brilliant keyboard and vocal hooks, and Dave Fridmann's production, are what make the album unique. The addition of new layers in each successive section gives the arrangement a nice evolution.

Refined

The fact that the track is so densely layered with instrumentation and effects lends it a lot of its production value, giving it a more refined sound.

Punchy and Ambient

The drums sound gated, or perhaps the hi-hat and toms were overdubbed separately. The drums also sound layered with samples, adding an electro texture. These techniques give each drum a punchy sound with more separation. There is ambience on the drums, vocals, and some keyboards, which lends the track some nice contrast between textures.

Vintage and Modern

The analog synths and seventies drum sound give the song a vintage element; however, other parts of the production and modern processing give the track a modern edge, as well.

Structure and Instrumentation

Intro

- Mono synths (possibly Moog) with plate or spring reverb producing layers of bubbles, crickets, and bird-sounds. The low synth has some cool random pitch bends.

Refrain 1

- Stereo synth enters: right side plays quarter notes / left side plays offbeat accents. This creates a cool ping-pong effect.
- Lead mono synth enters midway through the fourth measure playing a repeating phrase, as the "wild" intro sounds fade out. It has a little reverb, possibly with a pre-delay.
- There's the odd accent with a bell every couple of bars and a slightly random high-pitched chirp with ambience.
- Syncopated snare fill with reverb leads into the first verse.

Verse 1

- Simple mid-tempo groove with added kick drums on the sixteenth note before beat three
- Closed hi-hats on the offbeats
- Drum sequencer with triggered delays loops under the drums
- Distorted, polyphonic synth plays chords (this is the main synth in the song). It has some repeated variations in its sound that create some great movement.
- There is no bass. The synth covers the low end.
- Lead vocal is doubled and has some delay and reverb on it.
- Two quiet eighth-note claps with ambience every four bars
- After eight bars a high legato synth enters with vibrato and reverb.

Pre-Chorus 1

This is the long B section with the instrumental section in the middle.

- Legato synth from the verse pedals (pedaling is when an instrument doesn't play the chord changes but rather holds the root chord).
- Toms play a sixteenth-note pattern.
- Drum sequencer pans left and right.
- Intro stereo synth returns left/right (possibly with pitch modulation on right side).
- Multiple layers of vocal (lead melody) and harmonies enter with delay and extra reverb. The vocals are wider than in the verse, with some layers panned.

- Instrumental break brings back verse groove
- Bubbly synth with a dotted feel leads back to a repeat of the chorus chord changes with tom beat and exits with a nice chordal climb into the chorus refrain.

Chorus Refrain 2

The refrain serves the role of the chorus but is slightly different from a traditional chorus in that it just repeats a couple of words from the song title.

- Chorus refrain repeated over the refrain instrumentation, with lead synth.
- Vocal is layered, but there is no harmony.
- An electric bass, panned right, plays some octave runs in a higher register.

Verse 2

- Drums lay out.
- Chirpy intro synths return.
- A synth panned to the right plays the chord changes.
- Another horn-like synth pedals through the chord changes.
- Main synth re-enters after three bars with crashes on the drums.
- Drum fill leads back into second half of the verse. It starts with quarters on the kick, builds to eighth notes, and then sputters on the snare and toms.
- Full verse instrumentation, including the high legato synth, comes back in.
- The panning drum sequencer sounds more prominent.
- The refrain's stereo synth creeps back in midway through.

Pre-Chorus 2

- The elements from pre-chorus 1 return, and the horn-like synth from verse 2 is added, giving the section a nice lift.
- A new high synth sweeps over the top.

Chorus Refrain 3

- All the regular chorus-refrain elements return.
- The electric bass, panned right, plays some octave runs and fills in a higher register.
- A little synth phrase plays on the 1 of every fourth measure.
- The chorus refrain gives way to another hooky chorus of "yeah, yeah, yeahs" with harmony. This is set up with a drum fill.
- Tambourine hits enter on the right side towards the end.
- Tom part re-enters and leads into a "cut" ending with a hi-hat accent on the and of 4, allowing us to hear the nice reverb tail from the synth lead.

Honing the Song

Before starting the actual production of your songs it can be helpful to do some preproduction to hone a song's structure, work out the groove, and flesh out its instrumentation with some demo (demonstration) tracks. Since songwriting was already covered earlier in the book, we will keep our discussion here somewhat limited.

First, it's important to choose the right songs. I like to choose songs that best represent what's cool and unique about an artist's style, and play to the artist's strengths as a performer. A group of songs should fit together well stylistically but vary somewhat with respect to mood and tempo. Careful consideration should be given to the key and tempo of each song, and the words, melody, and structure should be honed and refined as much as possible *before* production begins.

Like any artistic pursuit, songwriting takes not just talent, inspiration, and life experience, but also, skill, style, and craft, developed over hours and hours of listening analytically to song structures, learning songs on your chosen instrument, and, of course, writing and performing your own songs. As you do, you pick up tricks, styles, and techniques and blend them together into your own thing.

I think it can help to set up goals of, say, learning one song per week and writing one song per week. Then songwriting becomes very disciplined and develops much like a muscle that will fire when called upon.

There are of course many different ways to write a song, but for the scope of this chapter let's assume you've written it on either guitar or keyboard. Next, record it into a handheld recorder. Your phone works great for this. Listen, refine it, and repeat this process. Possibly bounce it off some other writers you admire for feedback, but that's up to you. Once you are completely satisfied with the chord structure, melody and lyrics, double check that you have chosen the best key and tempo.

While the instruments should be considered when choosing the key (perhaps you want the open E string ringing, for example), the most important consideration is the vocals. So pick a key that allows you to best express the mood of the song, be it breathy and sexy, sweet or sad in falsetto, or confident in your power zone.

With respect to the tempo, the groove and the vocal phrasing are the two most important considerations. Be sure they neither rush nor drag.

Next, it's time to start to work out the drum beat.

Finding the Groove (Drum Machines)

Now we are coming to what I would consider a fundamental skill for any artist who wants to produce music, and that is being able to count in time. Being able to count in eighth- or sixteenth-note subdivisions will allow you to unlock the kick/snare patterns implied by your strumming hand on guitar and generally your left hand playing keyboards. In addition, it will give you the ability to communicate with drummers in their language. You will hear the beat you want, and, by being able to give clear, simple direction to any musician, you will maintain a much more positive, communicative vibe in the session.

It can be frustrating for a drummer, or any musician, to receive vague, uninformative feedback like "Can you try something different?" However, if you say something specific like "Can I hear what it sounds like with the bass drum on the '1' and the 'and of 3'?," then that's what you're going to hear! I find it also helps fuel everyone's creativity as the process gets more positive momentum and collaboration is encouraged. That's when chemistry can help lead to results that are greater than the sum of their parts—and that's where the real magic happens.

Here's a chart to help illustrate different subdivisions: quarter, eighth, and sixteenth notes.

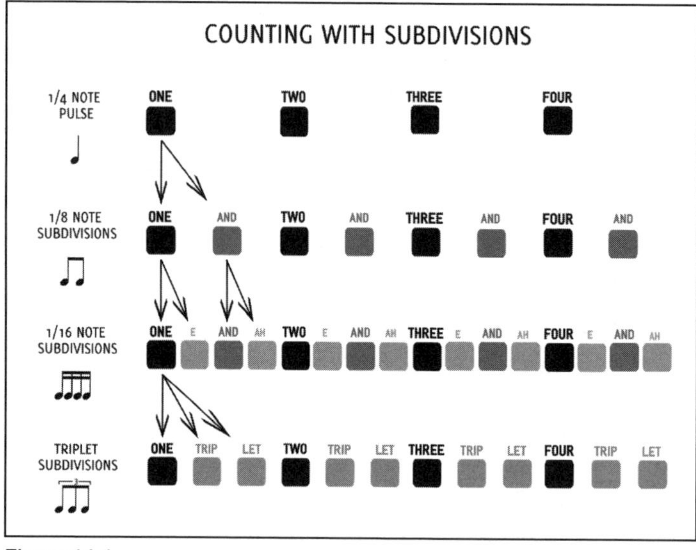

Figure 14-1

The ability to hear the right drum beat did not come to me immediately. I started out singing in bands and was focused on other things like lyrics, melody, and performing. Then, as I grew as a musician and began to discover a passion for music production, I realized that I needed to develop this skill of finding or unlocking the groove. What this means, nine times out of ten, is knowing where to put the bass drum. The bass drum defines the groove. Let's look at how to develop this skill.

First off, you'll need a step drum machine. A step drum machine is a sequencer that allows you to program and store drum patterns. You can use a hardware drum machine, a virtual one in your digital audio workstation (DAW) of choice, or even a smartphone app. Some DAW-based examples would be Ultrabeat in Logic, Boom in Pro Tools, or ReDrum in Reason.

The first step is to program a basic beat with the bass drum on the 1 and 3 beats, the snare on the 2 and 4 beats, and eighth notes on the hi-hat. You will probably notice right away that this basic beat is the beat in many famous songs, including "Billie Jean" by Michael Jackson. Because the kick and snare are playing downbeats and the bass is playing the upbeats (the eighth notes in between the kick and snare), the two instruments create a very cool counter-rhythm together.

Here's how it would look programmed on a step drum machine displaying eighth-note subdivisions.

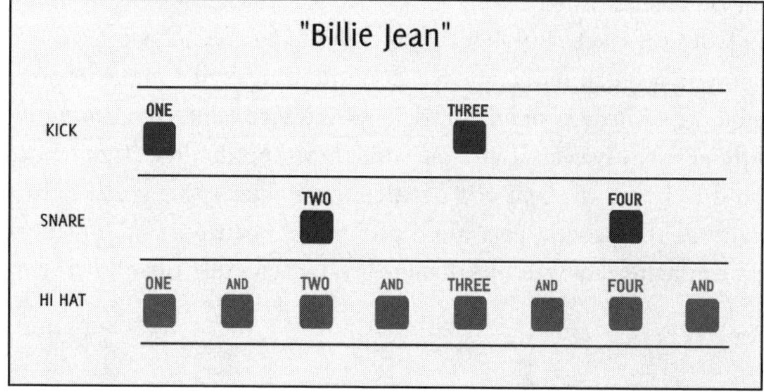

Figure 14-2

Next, adjust the beats per minute (BPM) of the session to match the song you're currently working on. Make sure it feels good to sing and play at that tempo. Once it feels good, try it slightly faster or slower to be sure the tempo is right. You may even want to record a short piece and listen back to really ensure the tempo feels right.

Now, while playing along with the drum machine, try to move the bass drum until it matches your strumming pattern. As I said, for me, it's the bass drum that really defines the groove of the song. Most rhythm guitar and keyboard parts are implying a kick/snare pattern in their strumming/playing patterns. You need to tap into that and unlock the groove. The other option is to create more of a counter-rhythm like in "Billie Jean"—and of course, there are many other more complicated things the drums can do. It just depends on what you're going for and what else is in the arrangement.

This process will teach you how to count better and communicate in the language of time and meter. In addition, it will improve your ability to pick out drum beats in songs you like and to create drum beats for your songs, or at least to find a good starting point for working with a drummer or band.

If you plan to use the drum machine as a part of your production, rather than just as a writing tool, you will want to explore its other parameters, such as velocity and swing, to help "humanize" it and achieve different feels.

Demoing the Song

Once you have a solid drum pattern worked out you can begin to sketch out the arrangement, laying down guide tracks and other instruments or virtual instruments. A **guide track** or **scratch track** is one that is recorded to demonstrate the form of the song and give the other musicians something to play along with. It won't necessarily be used in the final production.

With that said, however, I would strongly urge you to perform a guide track like it could be "the one." You may not be able to use it much of the time, but there are a number of obvious advantages, if you can. For one, it's one less overdub to have to do on the record, so it saves time. Second, there can be a fresh, unique magic the first time you sing or play something that can often be difficult to repeat. Third, the better the scratch track, the more inspired the musicians playing along to it will likely be. And, finally, it's just another opportunity to hone your performance skills.

A guide vocal with guitar or keyboard is enough to get started recording drums, if you plan to use live drums. However, it can be worthwhile to flesh out more of the parts and instrumentation with real or virtual instruments first. This way you'll have more of a template to draw from when producing the final recording.

Even though I like to be prepared and have strong ideas when I begin a production, when I bring in great musicians to play on it, I would feel remiss if I didn't allow them to get a "first impression" of the song before I make any suggestions or show them any ideas. Remember, you've always got your ideas to fall back on, but if you snuff out the potential for creativity, you may never know what you're missing.

I would recommend using a click track when recording the guide/demo tracks. A **click track** is a metronome in your DAW that sets the tempo/BPM (beats per minute) of the track. Most of the time we record with a click—not just for demos, but for all tracks. The only times I'll consider *not* using a click track are when the band is very well rehearsed or comprised of top session musicians, they are recording at the same time, *and* the song and style of music work better with a "looser" feel.

Now, let's move forward to the next chapter and take a look at production.

15 Creating and Executing a Production Plan

A song's production is key to how it's received and interpreted by the listener. It determines the mood, structure, instrumentation, and arrangement of the song. It requires vision, skill, and organization.

While production can be a pretty sprawling topic, we are going to distill it down to three topics:

1. Formulating a production vision
2. Building a strong arrangement
3. Executing a production plan

Formulating a Production Vision

Can you imagine a movie director starting to shoot a film without a vision and a plan? Well, the same can be said for a music producer. Before beginning a project I try to identify an artist's strengths and influences to help develop a production vision for the recording. By formulating a vision for the sound and style of the recording, you are much more likely to end up with the kind of recording that represents who you are as an artist. You have to know what you're going for before you can figure out how to get there.

I've met a lot of artists and bands who tell me their influences and what genre they fit into, only to listen to the music and hear something completely different. This is usually because they didn't do their homework, the preliminary work of studying great productions and analyzing the sound, structure, and instrumentation. For example, does it sound "punchy" or "ambient," "raw" or "sculpted," "modern" or "vintage"? It's important to understand these terms when working with other studio professionals, be it producers, engineers, or musicians. Using the proper terms will help you get the result you're after more consistently and more quickly.

Let's look at some different goals and how to achieve them.

Punchy or Ambient

If your goal is to make a punchy-sounding production, you will want to bear that in mind right from the beginning by picking the right instruments. In addition, you'll want to "treat" those instruments to sound punchy. For example, with the drums you could achieve this through a combination of tuning, muffling, and drumhead choice. This is a topic we cover in more detail on p. 178–179, in the DIY Recording chapter.

Dynamic and condenser mics will sound punchier than ribbon mics; however, if you have the option, a ribbon can still add a little extra depth. (More on microphones on p. 171.) Positioning the mics, amps, and players for minimal bleed will also allow you to process each instrument for maximum articulation. This can be achieved using baffles, isolation booths, even by building a kick drum tunnel with mic stands and packing blankets.

In addition, try having the bass player use a pick and driving the bass amp harder by turning up the gain for some extra sizzle. In addition, try using the bridge pickup and boosting the treble on the bass.

For a punchy sound I'd also consider minimizing or not using any reverb on the guitars, as reverb diminishes the punch or impact by washing out the attack and making things sound further away. (For more tips on reverb, see p. 203.)

If, on the other hand, you're after a more ambient sound, be sure to record more room mics (unless you have a bad-sounding room with ugly reflections, in which case you may be better off using artificial reverbs at the mix stage). We tend to associate ambient-sounding recordings with a more "live" feel. Consider having the musicians play together in one room, as they would in a live setting. The resulting bleed may be an asset if an ambient sound is an important piece of the production vision.

This might be a good opportunity to "open up" the drums more by tuning the drumheads for more resonant tones and removing materials used to "dampen" or "mute" the drum kit's decay. (Please see "Drum Tuning" on p. 177 for more info). Reverb, delay, and other time-based effects pedals on guitars à la the Edge (U2) or Johnny Greenwood (Radiohead) will lend themselves nicely to an ambient recording, as will pads like electro piano (Wurlitzer, Rhodes), organs, strings, horns, and other synth or vocal pads.

Then, at the mixing stage, more ambient effects can be applied to the vocals and instruments. These types of considerations during the recording stage will pay dividends at the mix stage, as you won't be struggling to compensate for poor decisions made earlier in the production. There should always be a through line between production and mixing. Mixing should bring the production vision to fruition.

Raw or Refined

Another important question that will help define your production vision is whether you're going for a raw and visceral sound or one that's more refined and sophisticated. It's the difference, say, between being influenced by the Stones or the Eagles, Jack White or Jason Mraz, Amy Winehouse or Sarah Brightman.

Sometimes too much refinement can rob the music of its humanity, feeling, and sincerity. Humans are imperfect, and I love to see and hear that reflected in art. Performances that are honest and real appeal directly to our emotions. Productions that are quantized, edited, pitch-corrected, and layered can mask the true character of expression by smoothing out imperfections where this very humanity lies. Certain artists and subject matters beg to be presented with a rawer, sparser approach to the production, with individual performances that emphasize emotion over perfection. This is true for artists like Neil Young, Jack White, or Tori Amos, to name a few. Artists like this embrace these imperfections as part of the performance.

Of course, there is a big difference between the imperfections in a vocal or guitar solo by *those* musicians and the rest of the general population, but the main thing is that, if you see yourself as this type of artist, you have to be willing to put in the time necessary to develop your performance chops, because this is likely where you will make it or break it.

When a band or artist and I decide to take a rawer approach, we tend to do fewer overdubs and just let each instrument have its own space in the arrangement. We also tend to process the sounds less with effects, instead going for a more natural/organic approach to the sound. Finally, we tend to choose performances based on emotion rather than perfection.

A more refined approach will generally mean more repetition of grooves and phrases with less room for variation. It will also be more precise in every aspect of the music, from the timing to the pitch to every arrangement detail. In today's commercial pop music, it's very common to edit all the instruments to a tempo map or grid, making the groove a little more mechanical, robotic, and, well . . . perfect.

Similarly, the pitch of all the instruments and voices would be pitch-corrected, sometimes slightly, other times perfectly. In addition, parts would usually be more layered, giving the music more of an overall gloss or sheen. Finally, these types of productions can be highly arranged, from the register of the instruments to when precisely they enter and exit the arrangement.

I think certain styles of music—like mainstream pop, pop/rock, pop country, hip-hop, and electronic music, for example—all lend themselves to this more quantized, synthesized, layered, and sculpted approach to production. Other styles—like folk, blues, alt country, roots rock, indie rock, jazz, reggae, etc.—are more performance-based and often involve ensemble playing. Both approaches are valid and sometimes a hybrid of the two can be just the ticket.

Vintage or Modern

The trend in modern production has been towards a more compressed, processed, in-your-face type of sound that is loud, present, and exciting. The trade-off is that the sound is often less dynamic and doesn't breathe as much as classic sounds of the past. This might be the difference, say, between country artists like Jason Aldean (modern) and Sturgill Simpson (classic), or One Republic (modern) and the Alabama Shakes (classic).

If you're gravitating towards a more vintage sound, one of the important factors will be the instruments you use. And it's not always the expensive ones you want. Again, it's just a question of doing your homework. On more occasions than I care to count, I can remember a drummer coming into a session and telling me he wanted to get that "John Bonham" (Led Zeppelin) drum sound, only to pull out a modern drum set with the heads tuned for punchy modern rock. Had these guys done their homework, the way serious musicians do, they would have come in with a vintage Ludwig or similar kit, with thin heads, large shell sizes, no blankets or pillows in the bass drum, and no hole in the bass drum, giving it a warmer, less "clicky" sound.

Similarly, if you are into artists like Beck, the White Stripes, or the Black Keys, you'll want know that they often use cheap old Japanese or Sears and Roebuck guitars like Harmony, Supro, Teisco, Airline, and Silvertone. Doing your homework on the artists and productions you admire is part of your training, like in any profession. The sum of your influences and how you personally combine and interpret them through the filter of your life experiences will be what makes your art unique.

When it comes to mixing for a vintage sound, I lean more towards my room mics over my close mics (still blending them, though), especially on drums, guitars, and pianos. I would tend to also use fewer tracks and do less layering, as that wasn't done as much in earlier eras.

Of course, it can be a lot of fun to mix and match these approaches, too. I love using vintage instruments with modern processing techniques. Independent and alternative-leaning projects in most genres can benefit from this approach. Even electronic music, which is intrinsically forward thinking, has retro niches, from 8-bit video game sounds to old-school vintage hardware units like the 808 drum machine and Akai MPC samplers, to vintage synthesizers like Moog, the CS-80V, Jupiter, and ARP.

When working on a more modern-style project, I'll usually look to give the overall production more of a polished sound by adding layers, doubling and tripling parts, making sure they are really locked in time, often quantizing them to the tempo grid. I also pitch correct vocals and look for creative ways to push the boundaries with musicians, manipulating parameters on various effects, editing, and sound design.

Because modern sounds are typically more aggressive, distorted, compressed and "in your face," drum sounds tend to be drier, with an emphasis on the close mics over the room mics. This allows for a punchier sound with more transient attack to cut through the multiple, dense layers of guitars, keyboards, and vocals.

Guitar and keyboard effects are going to be key in determining your sound, so remember that there's a big difference between hip and retro and old and dated. Make sure you know the difference. Ultimately, it comes down to taste, and it's that taste that defines you.

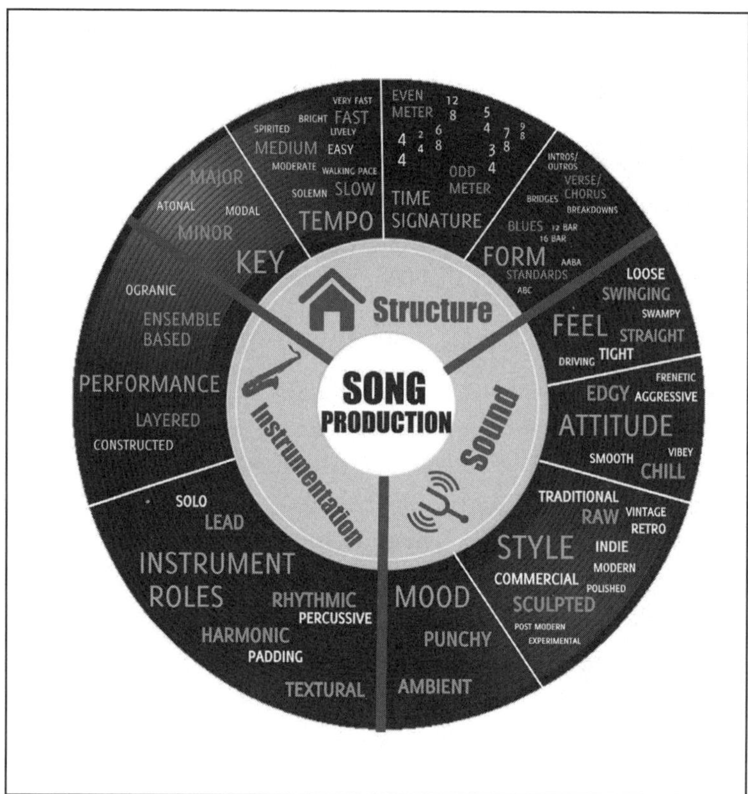

Figure 15-1

Building a Strong Arrangement

A song's musical arrangement refers to the instruments and voices added to the basic melody and what, where, and how they are played. Many new producers suffer from one of two problems: they either struggle to generate ideas past the song's original chords and melody, or they have too many ideas. The result is a production that sounds unfinished and boring or cluttered and lacking focus.

By ensuring your productions have some key ingredients, you should be able to produce music that has a strong groove and melody, with the right balance of texture and contrast to enhance and reinforce, rather than interfere and clutter.

The Key Ingredients (Groove, Melody, Texture, and Contrast)

The groove is the heartbeat of the production and something that people connect with physically. The bass and drums usually determine it, sometimes with a complementary guitar or keyboard rhythm.

The melody is more like the soul of the song. It's the thing that people connect with emotionally, along with the lyric, if there is one. It's essential that the melody be performed in a manner that truly expresses the intended emotion. Once you've characterized this emotion, be it joy, sorrow, nostalgia, or anger, it can serve as a light to help guide the rest of the production.

I make a point of considering the groove and melody when adding new elements, and if anything is distracting from or interfering with either one I reconsider it. Now, I'm not talking about reinforcing elements like doubled parts or keyboard pads. These add texture. Rather, I'm referring to contrasting elements like instrument fills, countermelody lines, or rhythms. There usually isn't room for too many competing ideas at the same time, so watch out for that.

Here's an example of what I mean. Let's say you're adding a second guitar part to a production and you play a guitar fill over top of the vocal. When I hear that, I pause and listen for the spot where the vocal stops and try moving the fill there. Not only does this leave more space for the vocal, but it also helps build the story of the song by responding to the vocal and adding to the conversation.

Another important production consideration is texture. We'll go into more detail in the recording and mixing chapters, but suffice it to say now that your choice of tool profoundly influences the texture and vibe of the sound. We're talking about drumsticks vs. brushes or blast sticks, bass or guitar played with fingers or a pick, as well as the thickness of pick, a trumpet with a plunger, tremolo on a keyboard, modulation on a synth, vocals sung in chest voice or head voice, and so on.

Pads are a great way to add some extra texture underneath to support the melody. **Pads** are long-sustaining notes or chords played by strings, horns, woodwinds, organ, accordion, electric piano, synthesizer, guitar with time-based effects, or even vocals. Sometimes they can be almost subliminal, other times more out front in the mix.

Arrangement Drivers (Emotion, Rhythm, Vibe, and Genre)

When building the arrangement of the song I look for certain elements to play off to help generate ideas. We've already talked about one of these, the **emotion** of the vocal and lyric. Now, sometimes that might mean something more predictable, like adding cello in a sad song, and other times it might be juxtaposing happy instrumentation with sad lyrics. Here are some good examples: "Hey, Ya" (Outkast), "Maxwell's Silver Hammer" (the Beatles), "Pumped Up Kicks" (Foster the People), "Up the Junction" (Squeeze), "Brown Sugar" (the Rolling Stones), "Jump" (Van Halen), and "Mamma Mia" (Abba).

Another good arrangement driver is the **rhythm**. If the song is very upbeat, I would likely look to add parts with drier, less ambient sounds, possibly played with choppier or more staccato rhythms that might work nicely with a driving, up-tempo beat.

A song with a slower, moodier rhythm, on the other hand, might work well with the vibey sustain of a ride cymbal or the drone of a tom-tom groove, along with pads or guitars with washes of reverb.

Furthermore, how about the **vibe** of the chord progression? How does the combination of chords make you feel, and how can you play off major or minor chords to embellish their intention? Also, try combining an upbeat groove with a sad, minor-key chord progression or vice versa. These types of juxtapositions can yield interesting, unexpected results.

Genre can also play a role in influencing production. Let's say I want to add a pad. If it's a pop/rock production, I might add a string pad; if it's a blues or roots rock song, I might use a B3 organ; and if it's an indie pop song, I may elect to go with an analog synth.

Finally, sometimes the way to be innovative is to combine elements or genres in atypical ways, like adding banjo to jazz (à la Bela Fleck), or hybriding genres like blues and hip hop (à la Beck).

All of these examples are just aimed at stimulating ideas. They aren't intended to represent any particular rules of thumb, or anything. Those choices are up to you. But, I think, as you build your arrangements, considering elements like emotion, rhythm/tempo, vibe, and genre will help generate production ideas that match your vision.

Arrangement Checklist

Now let's finish off our discussion about arrangement with a few things to watch for. First off, does your production have **balance**, both in terms of frequency (lows/mids/highs), as well as stereo image (left/right)?

The key to a great mix is a great arrangement. Spread instruments out across the octave ranges for frequency balance. In addition, consider where to pan each new part and counterbalance it with something on the other side of the stereo field (please see p. 189 for more on "Panning").

As you add new elements to the production, consider the register or octave range of each part. I think this is really important and a common downfall of inexperienced producers. It's okay to have two instruments in the same register and pan them left and right, because they will not be right on top of each other. As you continue to add more parts, however, you will usually hear those and the existing parts better if they are playing in a higher or lower register.

There's a reason why a string quartet, for example, has cello, viola, and violins, or a choir is broken up into bass, tenor, alto, and soprano sections. They all play or sing in different registers and hence produce sound in *different* frequency ranges.

Let's look at it another way. Every musical note produces a central, or fundamental frequency. For example, the A above middle C on a keyboard has a frequency of 440 Hz (this is the standard pitch used for tuning musical instruments). Now think about it: if you keep adding new musical parts right around middle C, you are going to have a lot of parts producing sound in the same frequency range. And, if you think of a frequency range like a piece of land, there is only so much territory to go around. As a result, if you record multiple parts in the same register and pan them in a similar position in the stereo field, you are going to find that they just cover each other up. The result can be a production that lacks definition, distinction, and depth.

If instead you move that new part up or down the keyboard or fretboard a couple of octaves, you will find that you can hear both parts more clearly, assuming that's your intention. If your intention is to create more of a sound wash or a thick stew, then it might work to stack parts up in the same register. It just depends what your goals are.

A second quality to aim for with your productions is **evolution**, both of the arrangement and the mix, in terms of size, space, width, and/or depth. Having arrangements build up and break down during the song can help paint a much more interesting picture than a static arrangement. The latter might be more real/live-sounding for a four-piece blues or jazz band, but if we're talking about production with pop elements, an ebb and flow to the arrangement makes things more exciting and interesting.

Sometimes it can be important to hold back certain parts in order to allow the arrangement somewhere to go. Assuming the song lends itself to this approach, I try to find a couple of points that I can make more minimal, like an intro or a verse after a big bridge. I also like to reach a couple of dynamic peaks, say in a bridge, last chorus, or outro, for example.

In addition, I find that in the latter stages of the production, it can help maintain and build interest to add extra reinforcing layers with pads, harmonies, percussion, or contrasting elements, like countermelodies and rhythms.

Furthermore, I can follow through on these types of efforts at the mix stage by evolving the sonics of the production, automating my sends and effects to have them increase or decrease at various points throughout the production (please see "Automating" for more on this topic on p. 206).

Finally, no discussion of production would be complete without mentioning **dynamics**. There are so many little things you can do during a production to vary its dynamics: palm muting a guitar, foam under the strings of a bass or finger muting, opening and tightening the hi-hats, playing side stick on the rim of the snare, vocal dynamics, volume swells, turning distortion pedals on and off. Reminding performers about controlling the dynamic arc is really important and really rewarding when you hear the results. Then, at the mix stage, dynamics can be further enhanced with volume, effect, and send automation.

To sum up, try to arrange the song with an eye (and an ear) toward the mix, and it will make mixing much easier and more enjoyable, and yield better results.

Executing a Production Plan

An important part of achieving your production goals is executing a well-thought-out production plan. It's okay for it to be a fluid plan that adapts to things that happen "in the moment," but being organized will help keep you on target.

The Budget

Whether you are working with a professional engineer/producer in a commercial studio or embarking on an independent production in a project studio, it's smart to prepare a budget and prioritize how funds are allocated. Consider the cost of the studio for all tracking and overdubbing, the engineer/producer, musicians, mixing, mastering, hard drives/tape reels, guitar strings, drumheads, instrument rentals, meals, artwork, and manufacturing. Add up the expenses, determine what you can afford, and work on those two sides of the equation until they balance.

In my experience as a producer, a typical recording budget for an indie record would be between $1,000 and $3,000 per song. This largely depends on who is involved and where it's done. There are always ways to record more cheaply—home recording, minimal overdubs, getting your friends to work on it. Just be sure not to compromise the quality, or this could undermine your overall career goals.

The Schedule

Another responsibility of a producer is scheduling. It's important to prepare a schedule designating when each part of the production will be recorded, mixed, and mastered, and to book the studios, musicians, and engineer for these days. Your schedule is an important part of staying organized and prepared throughout the production process. It helps keep you on time and on budget.

Charts

Basic chord charts and lyric sheets will make the sessions go much more smoothly and efficiently.

I also find it helps to keep a "to do" chart with song titles and instruments listed for each song. I cross them off as they are completed. This serves as a visual aid to help you manage all of the recording tasks throughout the production.

Agreements

While no one likes to anticipate having a dispute, it's always better to have the terms of an agreement laid out prior to beginning a project. This includes agreements with labels and producers/engineers, and work-for-hire agreements with musicians. Be sure to do your homework and have a music attorney you trust advise you on the deal points of any agreement before signing.

Casting

Casting is perhaps an underrated part of producing a record. Carefully consider what instruments and style you envision and cast the musicians and engineer who match this vision. Just because someone is great on their instrument doesn't necessarily mean they're great at every style. In addition, the chemistry of your team is very important, both musically and personally. The same can also be said for the studio you choose. Consider whether you need a big room, isolation booths, what instruments they have, the recording equipment, the location, price, and overall vibe.

Collaborating

There are many different ways to make a recording today. One of the best things to come out of the recent technological changes in the industry is how they've facilitated hybrid productions, moving easily between the bedroom and professional studios. It's also helped give independent artists the ability to collaborate with other musicians, engineers, and producers, even high-profile ones on different continents. This can add tremendous value to your productions, particularly in the areas of recording drums and mixing, two areas that require more advanced skill sets.

If you do plan to collaborate with different people and work on different systems, sending files over the Internet, there are a few things to know to ensure everything goes smoothly.

- Cross-fade all your edit points.
- Consolidate all files starting at bar 1 in your DAW to ensure they line up.
- Only bounce tracks with effects and automation on if they are intended to be part of the final mix
- Use consistent file types, for example, 24-bit/48kHz WAV files.
- Indicate the BPM and include a separate click track.
- Sometimes tracks can be sub-mixed into stems.
- Provide reference tracks as a guide for what you are looking for.
- Give clear direction.

One final point to make about production is that it also benefits from good "people skills." A producer needs to be a little bit like a psychologist or a bartender. He or she needs to understand what makes people tick and how to get the best out of them. In addition, producers and engineers spend long hours, days, weeks, and months working with artists, so it's important to have a good demeanor and be a "good hang," so to speak.

16 DIY Recording

Now that we've talked about the production process, let's focus in more on the nuts and bolts of do-it-yourself (DIY) recording, with a look at:

1. Optimizing your recording space
2. Getting the right gear
3. Getting the sounds you're after

Optimizing Your Recording Space

As an independent artist you will of course want to optimize your own workspace. If you are building a studio, you'll definitely want to read a book more devoted to this specific topic and/or consult a professional studio designer who has the necessary expertise. However, there are some good tips I'd like to share on:

- Room Shape and Setup
- Sound Isolation
- Sound Absorption and Diffusion

Room Shape and Setup

Where and how you set up your work area, the shape of the room, and materials in the room will all contribute to how lively or how flat it sounds, frequency-wise.

Parallel walls are problematic for sound, and if you're constructing walls you should bear this in mind. Square rooms are the worst, of course, because they have four parallel walls. The main problem with parallel walls is that the reflections of sound bounce back and forth like a tennis rally, eventually creating what are called "standing waves." Standing waves hinder your ability to clearly hear the lower frequencies. (We will talk more about this in more detail when we look at "Phase Cancellation" on p. 175.)

Since space is limited in most project studios, it generally works best to set up the room lengthwise, so that you're facing one of the shorter walls. Also, try not to put the speakers too close to the walls (1ft. away or more is best) or near the corners, as it can result in bass buildup and phase cancellation. Finally, set up your work area with your speakers at ear height, making an equilateral triangle between the two speaker cones and your ears, as illustrated in the diagram on page 166.

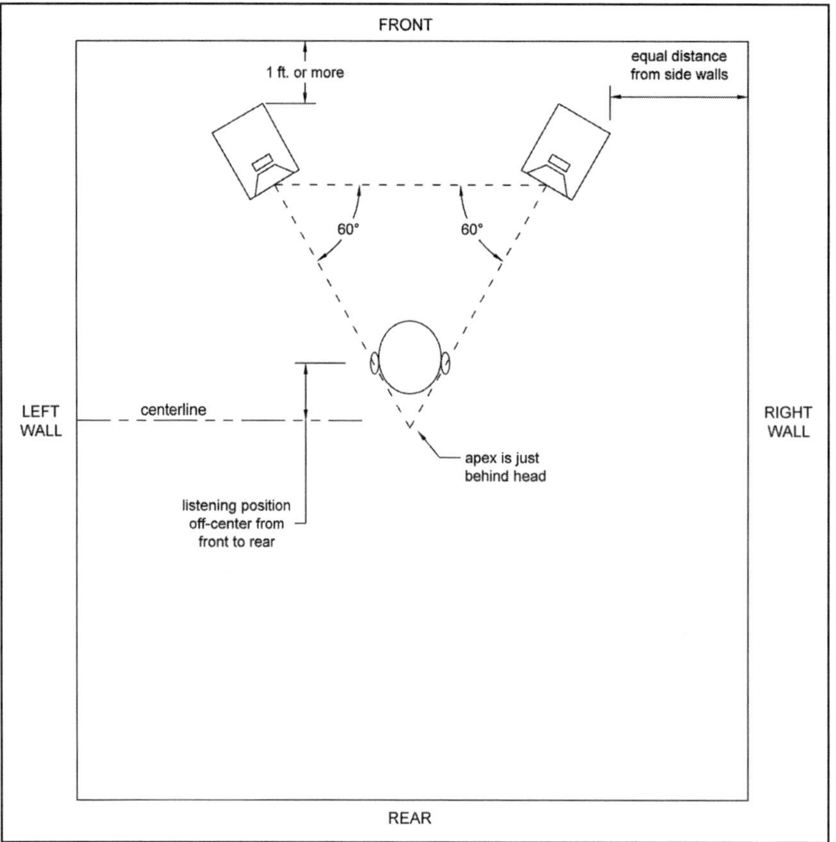

Figure 16-1

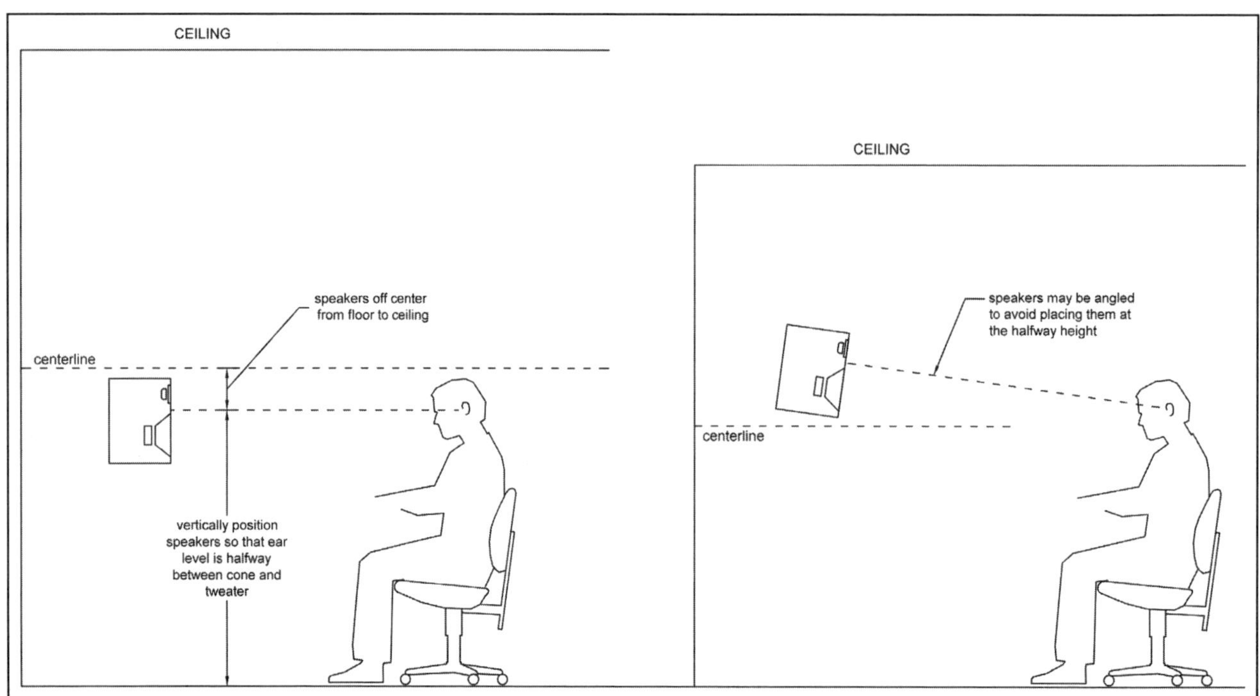

Figure 16-2

Sound Isolation

Sound isolation utilizes construction methods aimed at preventing sound from traveling between different spaces. One of the ways you do this is by preventing any hard surfaces from touching one another. Much like how most metals conduct electricity, most solid building materials like concrete, wood, drywall, nails, and screws conduct sound. That is, they act as sound conduits, carrying the sound through the walls, floors, and ceilings to other areas of the house or building.

By placing softer absorptive materials between any hard surfaces, you can prevent them from touching one another, greatly reducing their ability to act as sound conduits. One way you can do this is by using spring-loaded metal channel clips, attaching those to your 2 x 4 studs and then attaching 5/8" drywall to the channel clips. Then you can spread a thick layer of sound-dampening glue onto the drywall and attach a second sheet. The idea is to prevent the two pieces of drywall from touching, so don't be stingy!

If you have the space, you can soundproof further by building a double wall with an air pocket in between the two walls. Essentially, this is like building a new room inside the existing room. This creates an extra little sound barrier that helps cut down on sound getting in and out of the studio.

Finally, you can use a soft acoustic sealant in place of a harder silicone one to prevent the drywall from touching the floor, as well as between any joints. Just rest the drywall on spacers while you screw it in to your 2x4 studs, remove the spacers, and fill the gaps with acoustic sealant.

Sound Absorption and Diffusion

Once the construction is complete, or if you are in a pre-existing space, there are some other things you can do to treat the space and optimize its sound. First, you should distinguish between the priorities of recording and mixing, with the recording space typically being a little more "live" than the mixing area. If you only have one room (no isolation booth), one suggestion would be to make the mix area a little more "dead" or absorptive, and the other side of the room, slightly more live.

One way you could do this would be to use sound absorption panels/materials in the mix area and sound diffusers in the recording area. The difference is that **sound absorbers** are designed to absorb and eliminate as many of the reflections as possible, whereas a **sound diffuser**'s job is not to absorb the sound reflections, but rather to scatter them into little pieces. By doing this, they help preserve the "liveness" and sustain of the room, but with fewer problematic reflections.

It's much easier to deal with high frequency reflections than low ones. Really, anything made of soft material will cut down on high frequency reflections—a bed, sofa, curtains, rugs, clothes, etc. Low frequency reflections are a bit trickier to deal with. For this you may need more specific materials like bass traps or thicker 4" panels, as opposed to the more typical 2" ones. Try placing these in the corners of the room, as low frequency buildup is the worst there.

Most of these room treatment solutions can be hand-built on your own, if you are handy and have the time. You just have to research and buy the right materials. You can also buy them assembled from many different stores, and they aren't too expensive. A 24" x 48" x 2" panel may run you $60. The bigger the room, obviously, the more coverage you will likely need.

Getting the Right Gear

With the number of options today, a discussion on recording equipment can be endless, but we are going to keep our focus pretty streamlined by limiting it to:

- Interfaces
- Speakers
- Midi Keyboards
- Computer/DAW

First, I would suggest trying to come up with an overall budget. Then, I would try to prioritize the allocation of that budget based on who you are and what your greatest needs are. So, if you're a singer, devote a bigger chunk of your budget toward a good microphone. (We will discuss microphones in the next section, "Getting the Sounds You Are After.") For a producer/mixer, speakers are more of a priority.

The Interface

When it comes to interfaces, there are a few different things to consider, like:

- The quality of the sound card
- The number of inputs/outputs
- The quality of the preamps

The **sound card** is a component of the interface that uses an analog-to-digital converter to change the format of an analog signal from a microphone or instrument into a digital signal that a computer can receive. Similarly, it would use a digital-to-analog converter to convert the digital signal coming from your computer into an analog signal for your headphones and speakers. Since all of your recorded signal will be affected by the quality of the sound card, this is one of the most important criteria for choosing an audio interface.

An inferior sound card can sound harsh or strident, less open and clear, especially as the track count builds up. As your work gets better it will demand higher-quality equipment to help you continue to raise the bar.

Another important consideration when purchasing a sound card is the number of **inputs** it has, especially if you plan to record your own drums.

Most interfaces have two inputs. For drums, I think you need a minimum of three or four inputs, but if you plan on recording your own drums regularly, I would recommend an interface with at least eight inputs/preamps.

A third consideration when choosing an interface would be the quality of the **preamps**. The microphone preamp is an amplifier used to boost the level of the signal for recording. The quality of recording technology has progressed to the point where even many "prosumer"/"budget" interfaces come stocked with fairly adequate preamps. However, you want to do your homework and get good advice, because not all are created equally, even within the same price range.

Of course, if you already have a good quality external preamp or channel strip, then the quality of the sound card should probably take precedence. A **channel strip** is a hardware unit that usually includes a preamp, a compressor, and an EQ.

Speakers

When it comes to choosing audio monitors/speakers I would start by asking yourself what you plan to use them for. If you only need them for recording and playback and don't intend or aspire to do any serious mixing, then you should be able to get by with some smaller, less expensive speakers. I still, however, think it's important to have pro audio monitors and not consumer stereo speakers to ensure making good accurate decisions about what you're hearing.

If you are intending to mix and even master on your speakers, I would keep a couple of key factors in mind:

- Frequency Response
- Speaker Size

First of all, I would recommend choosing speakers with a relatively flat frequency response. Some speakers have an EQ curve that colors what you're hearing. For example, the speakers may boost both the low and high frequencies, creating what is often referred to as a "smiley face" EQ curve.

The problem with this type of speaker is that while it may sound great, when you listen somewhere else on different speakers, your mixes may very likely sound thin and dull because they lack low and high frequencies. This is because you were hearing more than you actually had. If, instead, you mix on "flat" speakers, your mixes will translate much better. All speakers come with illustrations and specs of their frequency response curves.

The second factor I think worth mentioning is the speaker size. Most speakers less than eight inches in diameter won't be able to produce the lower octave range very well. It really just comes down to physics, and smaller speakers are generally unable to stay "flat" at lower frequencies. Larger speakers are going to be more expensive, and this is why I think it's important to consider your goals and priorities when making this decision.

I would recommend taking some music (CD quality WAVs, *not* MP3s) you know really well to a pro audio store and listening to some different speakers. Ask who among the sales staff is the most knowledgeable about speakers and get some input from them that you can cross-reference with the research you've already done online.

Midi Keyboard

In addition to acoustic instruments, you will likely want to have the ability to use virtual instruments like synthesizers or keyboards, string or horn patches, percussion, etc., triggered by a midi keyboard. Three things to consider when purchasing a midi keyboard are:

- The inclusion of knobs and sliders
- The number of octaves
- Whether or not it has weighted keys

If you primarily make electronic music, it would be useful to have a midi keyboard with knobs and sliders that can be assigned to various parameters of the virtual instruments. If your keyboard doesn't include knobs and sliders, these parameters can probably be programmed, drawing automation in your DAW, but there can be a real benefit to doing it manually—and it can also be more fun.

If you are a serious keyboard player, rather than someone who is just using the keyboard to trigger sounds, you will probably want to consider how many octaves the keyboard has and if it has weighted keys that provide the "action" closer in feel to a real piano.

Portability and on-board sounds may also be a consideration for live gigs.

Computer/DAW

System requirements will include:

- A modern Mac or PC
- A minimum of 4 to 8 GB of RAM
- A 7200 RPM hard drive (It's recommended to record on a separate hard drive, other than the one the software is installed on.)

Every DAW has its strengths and weaknesses:

- Pro Tools excels at recording and editing audio.
- Logic excels at composition and midi functionality.
- Ableton Live is a favorite of electronic producers and live DJing.

A couple of general setup rules apply:

- Set your buffer size low for recording and high for mixing (check your DAW's instruction manual on where to find this option).
- Turn "low latency" option on when recording and off when mixing.
- Turn "delay compensation" off when recording and on when mixing.

Lower buffer sizes will reduce latency when recording. Higher buffer sizes will allow you to run more tracks and plug-ins, ideal when mixing.

Finally, unless you plan to create strictly instrumental electronic music, any project studio is going to need at least one microphone. Since is this is a much bigger topic, let's begin our discussion of recording techniques with a look at microphones.

Getting the Sounds You Are After

In this section we will take a look at how your choices for microphone selection and placement will influence the sound. In addition, we will introduce techniques for stereo miking and preventing phase cancellation, as well as share tips for recording specific instruments.

Microphones

In recording, like in any profession, it's important to choose the best tool for the job at hand. The biggest factor influencing your choice of microphone may have less to do with the actual instrument you're recording and more to do with the particular *sound* you have in mind for that instrument. This is something that is sure to change from time to time, so formulate a goal before choosing your microphone, or any processing tool, for that matter.

There are three main categories of mics:

- Dynamic
- Condenser
- Ribbon

Within these categories, microphones can vary greatly. As a result, we'll talk about these categories first in broader, more general terms to establish the basics. As you get these under your belt you can begin to investigate the characteristics of specific models to hone in further on finding "that sound."

Dynamics

Dynamic microphones are probably the most common. They're also the least expensive and most physically durable mics, two factors that make dynamics the most popular choice for live sound. Frequency-wise, they tend to capture less information in the lows and highs and instead accentuate the mid-range frequencies, which, depending on the particular microphone, could be between 1 and 10kHz.

For this reason dynamics tend to sound great on instruments that live in this frequency range, like guitars and drums, particularly the snare. Another reason I think they work great on these instruments is the somewhat "grittier" quality of their sound. This is due in part to a thicker diaphragm.

The **diaphragm** is a thin metal plate that vibrates when struck by sound waves, triggering a conversion of acoustic signal into an electrical signal. Because the diaphragm of a dynamic mic is thicker, it vibrates more slowly. Think of it like capturing fewer frames per second with a camera. It captures less transient detail, which results in a grittier sound. Much of the time, this is preferable.

A **transient** is the initial attack of a sound. For example, on a drum it would be the moment the stick or beater hit the drumhead, that initial strike. Other examples would be the initial strike of the pick across the strings of an acoustic guitar or the consonants of a vocal.

Another important characteristic of any microphone is its polar pattern. The polar pattern determines the directions from which the microphone records sound in a three-dimensional space, the front, back, top, bottom, and/or sides. There are four main polar patterns and general rules linking them to the three different microphone categories. (See image on page 173.)

Dynamic mics are almost always **cardioid**, so they reject sound from the back while capturing it from the front and sides. In addition, they can handle very high sound pressure levels (**SPLs**), another factor that makes them an excellent choice for loud, close sounds.

Some popular examples include the Shure SM57 and SM58, Electro Voice RE20 and Sennheiser MD 421.

Condensers

Condenser mics differ from dynamics in many ways. First off, they have a lusher, more full-bodied sound that tends to accentuate the low and high frequencies. As a result, they are very popular for recording vocals, cymbals, and acoustic guitar, to name a few examples. They are very sensitive, helping make them more adept at capturing hushed, nuanced tones, like ghost notes on a snare drum or breathy intimate vocals. Also contributing to this is the fact that condensers have thinner diaphragms, resulting in a faster transient response, capturing more sonic detail.

Condenser mics are fragile, and the larger ones incorporate a shock mount rather than a traditional mic clip to prevent the microphone from vibrating. They can't be hand held while singing.

They also require an extra power source (in addition to the preamp) in the form of either their own power supply or 48 volts of **phantom power**. If the mic doesn't come with a power supply you can find the phantom power on the preamp or interface. A condenser microphone won't produce signal without phantom power or the power supply unit.

Always make sure that phantom power is turned off when making a connection with the microphone, because it can produce a loud "popping" sound, which isn't good for the mic or the speakers.

Some condenser microphones come with switchable polar patterns, and some are only cardioid. If the mic is switchable, it's up to the manufacturer whether it's two patterns or four or more. For example, the legendary Neumann U47 microphone can switch between cardioid and omni polar patterns, whereas the lesser-known U48 is cardioid and figure 8. Other than that, they are identical. In fact, the Beatles used the U48 as often as the U47.

There are different types of condenser mics. Large-diaphragm condensers (**LDCs**) have a hotter output and are more sensitive than small-diaphragm condensers (**SDCs**). This makes them preferable on quiet or distant sources. In addition, LDCs have a "deeper low frequency response" and capture a wider area, making them a better choice for vocalists, who are not as stationary as most instrumentalists.

Another distinction is whether the mic is made with tubes or transistors (solid state). Tubes tend to sound warmer, with softer highs, and solid-state condensers sound more transparent.

Some other popular classic examples of large-diaphragm condensers include the AKG 414, and Neumann U87. Other preferred small-diaphragm condensers include the AKG 451 and Neumann KM84, to name just a few.

Ribbons

Ribbon mics preceded both dynamic and condenser mics and were the microphone of the day from the 1920s through the 1950s. They continue to be among the most popular microphones in recording today. Overall, ribbon mics sound the most natural, closest to what the human ear hears. They have a smooth bottom end that's warm and sometimes even a little dark in a romantic or mysterious way.

One of the things that make ribbon mics sound different is their figure 8 polar pattern. Figure 8 or bi-directional mics record sound from the front and back, rejecting from the sides. This helps result in a bigger, deeper, more full-bodied sound.

I love to use ribbons on any instrument that can be shrill or strident, like trumpet or violin. They have a terrific, velvety sound on drums, guitars, piano, and vocals; however, in most modern music applications (even music with a vintage vibe), condensers and dynamics get chosen for that extra presence and air, especially on vocals.

Ribbon mics are very fragile, particularly vintage ones. These mics cannot handle loud sound pressure levels (SPLs) from close-miked drums or electric guitar. Some newer ribbons like the Royer R121 are stronger and can handle fairly high SPLs, but as a precaution it's recommended you tilt the microphone forward about 20 degrees off-axis from the sound source. Also, beware of phantom power/48V because it can destroy the ribbon. Always make sure it's off whenever a ribbon microphone is connected.

Most ribbon mics have a fairly low output and require a fair amount of gain from the preamp. For this reason, sometimes I won't use them on very delicate, quiet sounds because I'll end up with too much room noise. Other times, I love that extra room/wild sound. The key is knowing the difference.

Some popular examples include the RCA 44/77, Royer R121, AEA R84, and Coles 4038.

To recap, any microphone can be suitable on any instrument. The key is to have a goal in mind for the sound you want (gritty, lush, natural), and then choose the mic whose characteristics best match your goal. Keep in mind that our discussion was in general terms as we took an overview of the three categories. I suggest you research specific models once you know the type you're looking for.

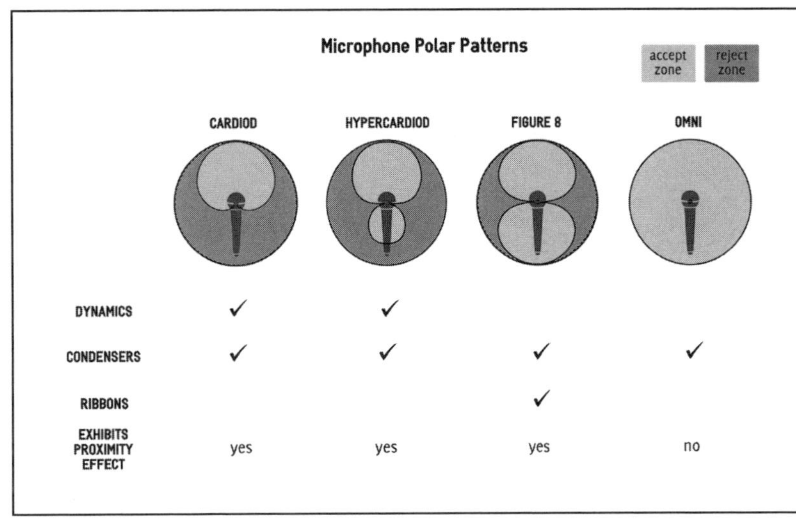

Figure 16-3

Mic Placement

Once you've chosen the best mic for the job you need to decide where to put it. Listen to the room and how the instrument's sound changes as you move around it. Make sure you are happy with how the instrument sounds in the room *before* you listen through the speakers. This is key to being a good engineer. If you have the time, experiment with different mics and different placements, and keep a notebook of what you discover so you can refer back to it to re-create past successes.

Here are a few things I take into consideration when placing a microphone:

- Position and Axis
- Height
- Proximity

First, how bright do I want the sound? The brightest spot will usually be the center of the sound source. This is true whether it's the bell of a saxophone, the cone of a guitar amp speaker, or the mouth of the singer. The **position** and **axis** of a microphone's placement can influence its tone. If you want the sound brighter you place the microphone directly on center and on-axis to the source (see the illustration on p. 174). If you want to darken the sound slightly, move the mic off center and/or off axis (see the illustration on p. 174).

So, with something like a violin, if the arrangement calls for more body I'll sometimes mic the violin from underneath or across the top, not pointing directly at it. If, however, it needs to cut through a fifty-piece orchestra, pounding drums, or distorted electric guitars, it may need a brighter tone with more transient attack, in which case I would point more directly at the sound source using a brighter mic, like a condenser.

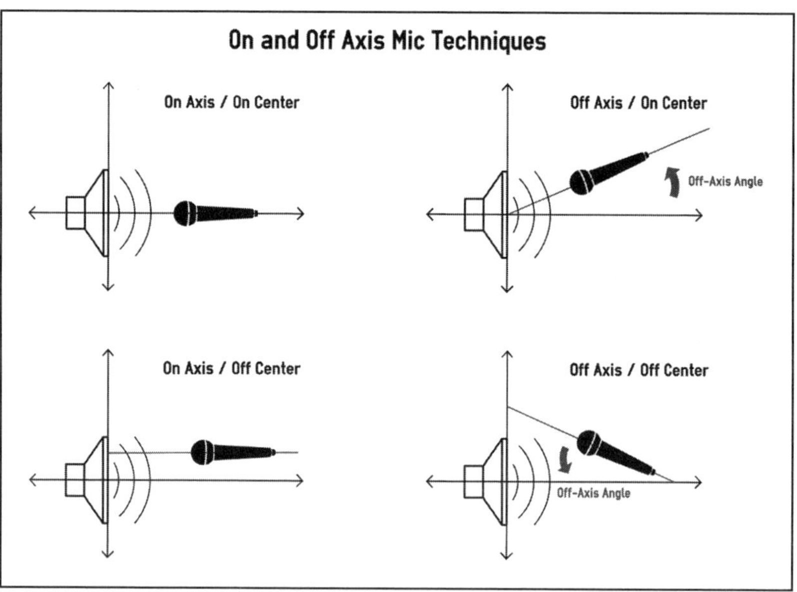

Figure 16-4

Another consideration is the **height** of the mic placement and whether I want it more focused on the low or high frequencies of the sound. For example, with a room mic on a guitar amp or drums, I'll emphasize the lows or highs more by raising or lowering the microphone. If I want more bass drum, I'll place the mic lower. If I want more cymbals with fewer lows, I'll place it higher.

Finally, a third consideration for mic placement is **proximity**. Do you want a more present, intimate, in-your-face type of sound with a lot of transient attack, or do you want a more airy or roomy sound that emphasizes depth and size over presence and intimacy? Of course, you can always record both, if you have another preamp and mic. Then you can blend the two sounds together. If you do so, however, you need to be aware of the potential for phase cancellation (discussed in the section below) that may arise when using more than one mic at a time.

Another thing to be conscious of when close-miking is **proximity effect**. This is an artificial bass boost that can result when the mic is placed extremely close to the sound source. This is true for every polar pattern except omni, which does not exhibit proximity effect. (More on polar patterns below.) It can also be used to good effect, when a bassier tone is what you're after.

While I often prefer just one mic on an instrument, other times I combine two or more mics on a single source to blend their different tones. For example, I may use a ribbon and a dynamic mic on an electric guitar amp. Other times, I blend different mics to capture a close sound *and* a room sound. This has many advantages, including extra depth, body, and potentially stereo imaging. It's very specific to what else is in the arrangement, but, especially with sparser arrangements, I like to spread the panning of a close mic and a room mic. Other times, I prefer to pan them the same to keep the sound more focused.

Phase Cancellation

Whenever you record two or more mics at the same time on the same sound source, phase cancellation is a concern. Phase cancellation is the result of two waveforms that are polar opposites, but they don't need to be 180 degrees apart to cause a problem.

The further you place a microphone from the sound source, the more latent the waveform. As a result, when using both a close mic and a room mic on, say, a guitar amp, or several mics at varying distances on a drum kit, you will end up with the sound of the room microphones lagging behind that of the closer microphones.

How can you determine whether or not two mics are out of phase? They will sound thin (lacking low end), quiet, and sometimes a little bit swirly. In addition, you can zoom in on the waveforms and visually analyze them. Ideally the two waveforms should be moving in the same direction above or below the zero line at any given location, or at least at the beginning of the waveform (please see the illustration below).

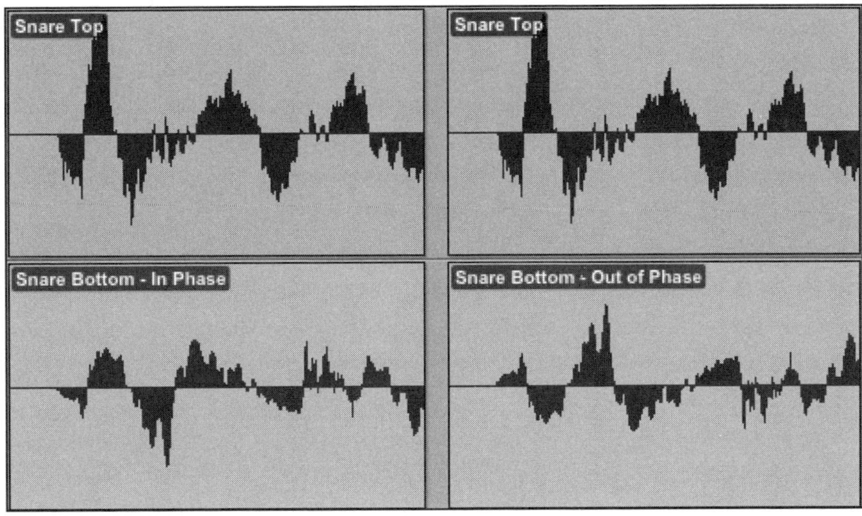

Figure 16-5

Let's go over two principles of microphone placement that will help prevent phase cancellation.

- The equidistant rule
- The 3:1 rule

The **equidistant rule** states that you place the microphones at exactly the same distance from the sound source. This should provide a nearly perfect phase relationship. One thing to make sure of is that the actual diaphragms or ribbons of the mics (rather than the noses) are lined up. For example, on a Shure SM7 the diaphragm is set back a few inches, and if you aren't aware of this you may run into phase cancellation.

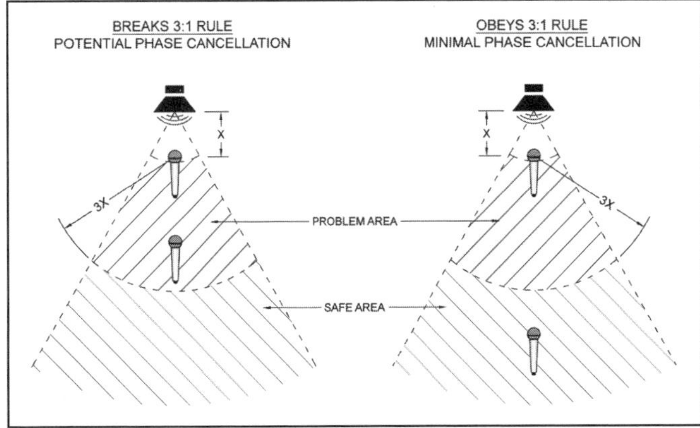

Figure 16-6

The second rule is the **3:1 rule,** and it requires that you place the second mic at least three times as far away from the first mic as the first mic is from the sound source. So, if the first mic is a foot away, then the second should be at least three feet away from the first mic. If you do this you shouldn't get any problematic cancellation, but sometimes I find that inverting the polarity of the room mic can still yield a fuller, more coherent result, so it's always smart to try that and hear.

Speaking of inverting the polarity of a waveform, let's look at *how* to check the phase. While you can correct any phase problems after your tracks have been recorded, it's definitely preferable to get it correct at the recording stage because you will make better choices if what you are listening to is in phase.

First off, when checking phase relationships, ensure your tracks are panned to the center. Then, once you're confident they are correct, you can pan as desired. Most preamps have a switch to invert, i.e., flip, the polarity. While listening to both mics, flip the polarity of one and listen. If the sound gets thinner and quieter, you don't have a problem. Un-flip the polarity and proceed as you were. If, on the other hand, the sound becomes thin, quiet and/or swirly when you flip the polarity, you likely are experiencing some phase cancellation. Inverting the polarity likely corrected the problem, and if it sounds good then you can record with the polarity flipped. Alternatively, you could correct your mic placement.

If you are recording and listening in the same room, you may need to record sections with and without the polarity flipped and A/B them as you listen back in order to determine the best setting. **A/B**'ing is the process of comparing two sources in quick succession to reveal differences.

As we noted earlier, while it's preferable to get the phase relationship correct at the recording stage, it can be corrected afterwards. Most DAWs and many third party plug-ins have polarity switches. In Pro Tools, for instance, you have the Trim plug-in, and in Logic you have the Gain plug-in. In addition, there are both hardware units and software plug-ins that are capable of variable phase, not just 180-degree polarity inversion. Little Labs makes one, for example.

Stereo Miking

Stereo miking is often preferred for many applications such as recording drums, percussion, piano, strings and horn sections, vocal ensembles, and sometimes acoustic guitar (depending on how large a role it's playing and how much space there is the arrangement). While there are a lot of different, useful techniques, here are four in particular that I use most often:

- XY
- Near XY
- Spaced pair
- Blumlein

XY, or coincident pair, is arguably the most reliable stereo miking technique for a couple of reasons. First of all, it yields excellent phase coherence; secondly, it provides a natural-sounding stereo image. With drums, I will often use XY when I want to hear the entire drum kit through the overhead mics.

If I feel like I want the stereo image to be wider, I simply spread the mics apart into a **near XY** configuration.

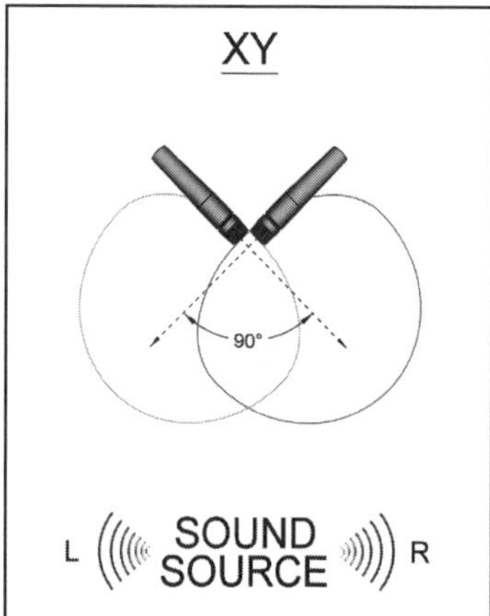

Figure 16-7

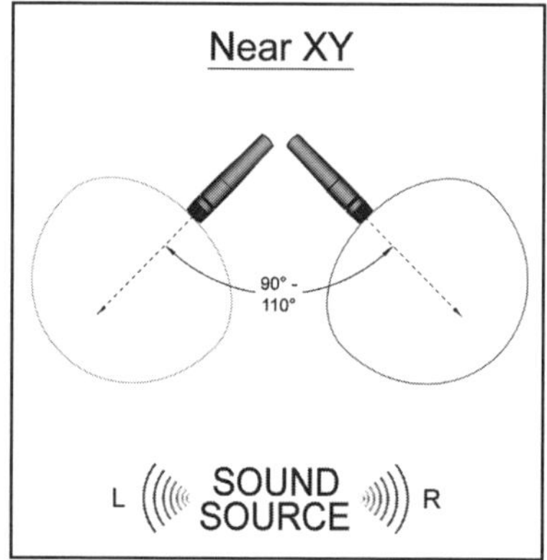

Figure 16-8

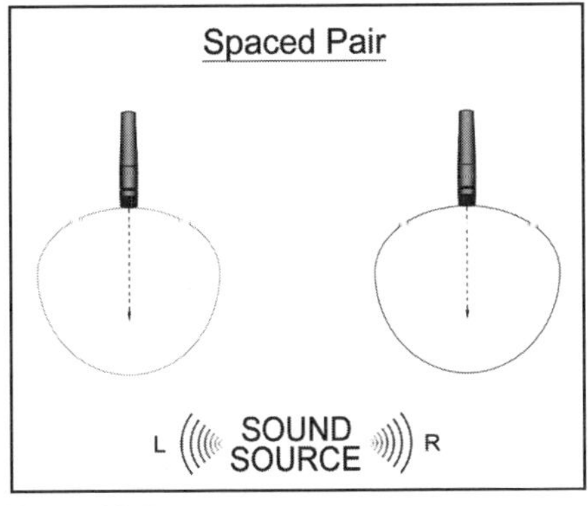

Figure 16-9

I usually elect to use a **spaced pair (A-B)** when I want to exaggerate the width of the stereo image. This can work well for room mics on a drum kit or string quartet, or for the drum overheads when I want the focus to be primarily on the cymbals. This will often be the case when recording heavy rock or mainstream pop where the sonic aesthetic has more separation and presence. In these genres I rely more on the close mics (as opposed to room mics) and use the overheads more like cymbal mics.

Sometimes a spaced pair can feel *too* wide, for example, miking a set of conga drums, which can produce a ping-ponging effect between the left and right speakers. Then again, it might be really cool for a particular effect in a particular song.

One thing to keep in mind with this technique is that when playing back in mono, the phase coherence won't be quite as good as with XY; however, I find employing the equidistant and 3:1 rules usually prevents any significant cancellation.

When I'm in a nice room, I really love **Blumlein** stereo miking, named after the British engineer who conceived of this technique, Alan Blumlein. The mics are set up exactly the same way as with XY, the difference being the figure 8 polar pattern. When you place two mics using figure 8 polar patterns in XY you get coverage of the entire room, as each mic is picking up sound (front and back) where the other is rejecting sound (the sides).

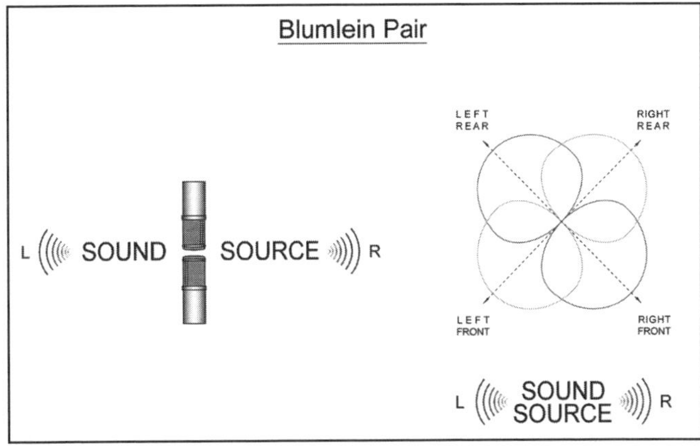

Figure 16-10

One other comment about stereo miking is that just because you recorded in stereo doesn't mean the tracks have to be panned hard (all the way) left and right. Feel free to experiment with the width of the panning, as you may want to have other mix elements panned wider than this stereo track.

Recording Different Instruments

Recording Drums

This is definitely one area of the production process that requires a more advanced skill set. That said, if it's something you have the drive to do, read on and you'll find the information you need to get started.

Here are some important factors to consider:

- Polarity check
- Drum tuning
- Drum treatment
- Mic configurations
- Drum programming

In my opinion, many of the most important factors that contribute to a great drum sound happen before I even go and listen to the microphones in the control room. The first thing we need to do is answer some key questions, like, what type of drum sound are we going for, modern or vintage, and hence what kind of drum kit? How should the drums be tuned, tighter and more high-pitched, or deep in tone? Do we want the drums to ring open with a longer decay, or would a "deader," muted sound be more suitable? And what are the important factors to consider when answering these questions?

First, do your homework, analyzing the sounds and styles you like, including the type of equipment used in these recordings. Remember, there are always less expensive options made of the same or comparable materials. You need to investigate if it's important to you. Borrowing and renting are options, as well—whatever it takes! If you have the wrong instruments you will never get the right sounds.

Polarity Check

Recording drums can be particularly tricky because there are often ten or more microphones on a drum kit, and making sure that they are all in phase takes experience.

First, if you are using multiple mics on, say, the kick (inside and outside the drumhead) or the snare (top and bottom), check the polarity/phase on each group. The snare bottom will almost always need to have its polarity flipped. This is due to the fact that the mics are pointing directly at each other, polar opposites. Once this is correct, check the overheads with the kick and snare by flipping and un-flipping the polarity of the overheads, listening for the thicker sound with the more solid center. It's also a good idea to do the same with the room mics and to check their phase against the kick and snare.

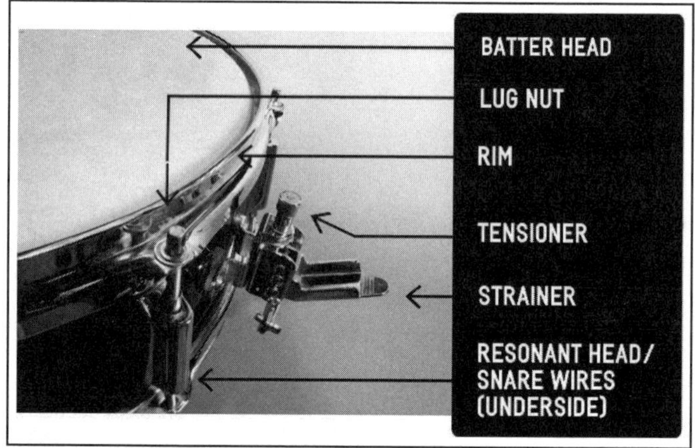

Figure 16-11

Drum Tuning

Drum tuning is another important part of a good drum sound and a very underrated skill. If you are hiring a drummer or even getting a friend to help out, make sure they know how to tune the drums or have someone come in to do it. There are also plenty of videos you can watch to learn how, and even some handy drum tuners similar to what you'd use to tune a guitar.

It'll always be a taste thing and a song-by-song consideration as to *how* you tune the drums, but one general tip is to make sure the pitch sounds consistent when you tap on the drum next to each lug nut (please see the illustration). If it doesn't, use a drum key to tighten (raise) or loosen (lower) the pitch accordingly.

Three important considerations when tuning drums are:

- The overall pitch of the drum
- Getting the drum in tune with itself (see illustration)
- The amount of resonance/decay

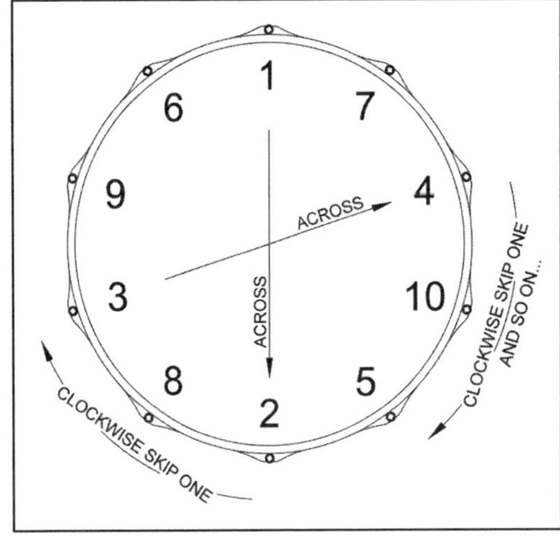

Figure 16-12

Tuning the resonant heads higher in pitch than the batter heads will generally get you more resonance. With snare drums, you have the additional variable of the snare wire tension—you want to make sure the snare is tight enough for articulation, loose enough that you don't choke the tone out of the drum, with a decay that complements the tempo and vibe of the song. For example, a spacey ballad usually calls for loose snares, and an up-tempo funk tune with lots of ghost notes usually calls for tighter snares.

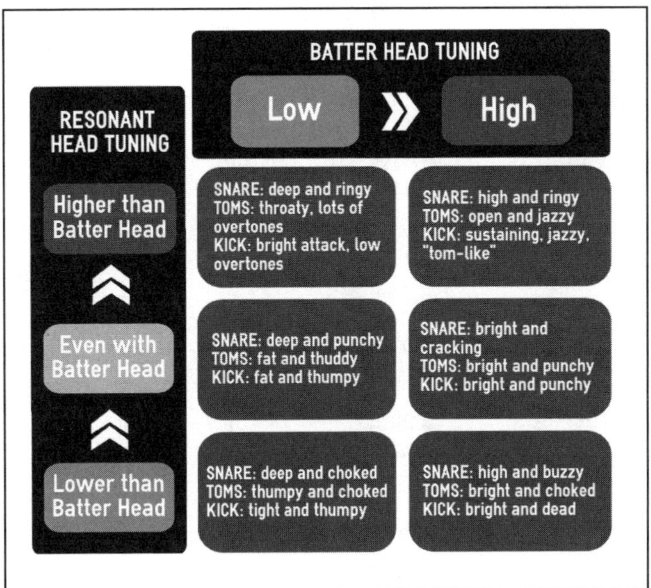

Figure 16-13

Most drums will have a tuning "sweet spot" where they really speak, which is why it's great to have several bass drums and snares of different sizes, with different shell types to choose from.

Although some professional studio drummers will show up to a session with up to fifty snare drums, a little knowledge of tuning and treatment will allow you to get wildly different sounds out of a single drum.

Drum Treatment

Drum treatment is another critical determination of your drum sound. I'm talking about how live/ringy or dead/muted to make the kit. A couple of factors to consider are the tempo and how dense the arrangement will be. If the tempo is slow and the arrangement sparse, I often like to open up the drums and let them ring out a little more to take advantage of the extra space.

In more up-tempo songs with denser arrangements, there just isn't room for this type of long decay with the drums. It ends up just muddying the overall sound and diminishing clarity and distinction between sounds/instruments. As a result, I will work with the drummer to dampen or mute the decay of the drums using moon gels, gaffer tape, tea towels, blankets, pillows, and/or sand bags. I can also use noise gates to achieve this at the mix stage, but it's preferable to get it right at the recording stage, as we can't gate overhead and room mics. (Please see "Noise Gates" on p. 200.)

Taping the bottom heads of toms will shorten the decay without drastically changing the overall tone of the drum. For more extreme dampening, treat both the top and bottom heads. Keep in mind double-ply heads will be punchier than single-ply heads.

Removing the front head of a bass drum will give you a very dry and articulate 1970s-style bass drum sound, as will a hard plastic or wood bass drum beater, as opposed to a soft felt beater.

Mic Configuration

Mic configuration, or where you place the microphones, can also have a significant effect on the overall drum sound. Since we've already gone over the basics of mic placement, let's focus on some different miking approaches based on the number of mics/channels available.

Most modern recordings include ten to fifteen mics on the kit, resulting in a crisp, punchy, detailed sound. Let's begin with a look at some useful minimal mic setups made famous in the 1960s and still being utilized by some great bands and artists today, like the White Stripes and early Black Keys, for example.

If you only have two mics, I'd suggest using one for the kick (probably a foot or so back) and one as a mono overhead to get the snare, toms, and cymbals. For a punchier kick sound, with more attack, place the kick mic inside the drumhead.

If you have a third mic, you could put it on the snare or use a pair of overheads in combination with a kick mic. Alternatively, you could try what's known as the **Glyn Johns method** (the Beatles, the Stones, Led Zeppelin, the Who). It includes one mic on the kick drum as before, one as an overhead in the middle of the kit above the tom, and a third mic just outside the floor tom, peeking across the top of it, pointing towards the snare drum.

Minimal miking works best when you have a drummer who understands how to dynamically balance the various elements of the kit—mixing him- or herself, so to speak.

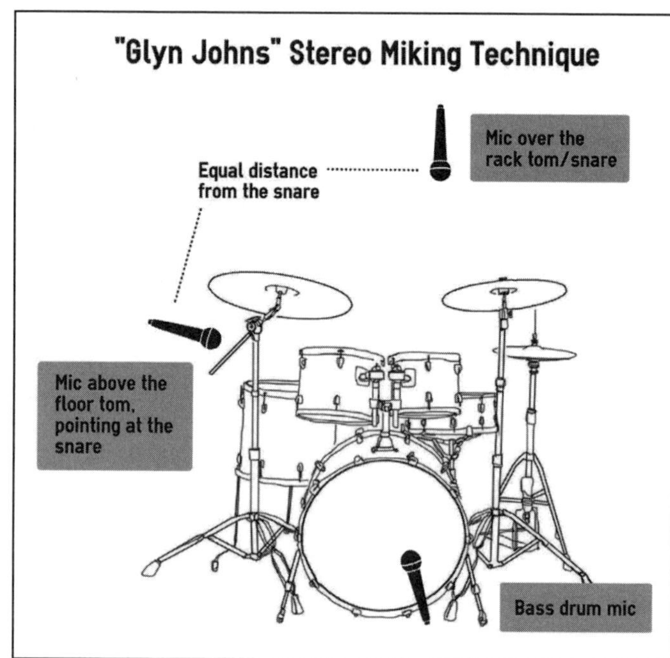

Figure 16-14

With a fourth mic I'd either use two stereo overheads *or* one mono overhead and one mono room mic along with mics on both the kick and snare. This would depend on whether or not I wanted mono or stereo drums.

Depending on how many mics or channels you have, you can keep adding mics to include each individual tom, hi-hats, ride cymbal, snare top and bottom (with the polarity flipped), inside and outside kick, mono room, stereo rooms, and more.

When miking the kick drum, you place the microphone inside the drumhead for more beater attack and isolation or outside for a warmer more vintage, thuddy sound, with less attack and more natural bleed from the rest of the kit.

Miking the snare, I usually place the mic at a 45-degree angle, pointed at the center of the snare, about three to six inches above the top of the rim. I'll point a little more straight down if I want more lows, or come across the top more horizontally for fewer lows. Another tip for miking the snare is to point the rejection point of the mic toward the hi-hat as much as possible. There is often a lot of hi-hat bleed in the snare mic, and while we will discuss some mix tips to deal with this, it's smart to do as much as possible at the recording stage.

Try compressing your room mics as a way to create some extra ambience and excitement. Keep in mind, if you're in a smaller room, there may be some unpleasant reflections that you may want to minimize utilizing some of the tips noted earlier on p. 167.

Also remember, because you are recording with more than one mic on the drums, you'll need to check for any phase cancellation.

In an effort to avoid redundancy, let's leave any specifics about EQ and compression for the mixing chapter, since this type of processing can be done at *either* the recording or mixing stages.

Drum Programming

Whether you are using drum programming as a writing or preproduction tool or as a core element of your production, it's an essential skill for a producer. The first step is identifying the right tools for the job. If you just plan to use a drum machine as a writing or preproduction tool, you can likely suffice with the native one in your DAW. If you are using programmed drums in your productions, do your homework much the way we discussed above, with respect to recording live drums. Whether it's an Akai MPC 2000, an 808 drum machine, Maschine, or Ableton Live, you should research what the artists you most admire are using and begin to learn how to use those tools.

The second step is learning how to count in different subdivisions, the main ones being sixteenth notes, triplets, and dotted feels. This will help with your programming, as well as your communication with drummers and other musicians.

Recording Vocals

I usually favor a large-diaphragm condenser mic for a bigger, more open sound, or a dynamic mic for a grittier, tighter sound. A vintage ribbon can be gorgeous in some applications but may be a little too dark for most modern recordings. I usually place the mic just above the singer's upper lip, pointing down at it. This helps reduce **sibilance** and **plosives**.

Sibilance describes the harsh S's or T's that can occur with some vocals. In the mixing chapter, we'll learn how to use a de-esser to reduce sibilance. Choosing the right microphone and singing with good technique will also help reduce sibilance.

Plosives occur when a vocalist pops a P or B, producing a burst of low-frequency wind that causes a popping sound when it hits the diaphragm of the microphone. Plosives can be reduced with wind screens/pop filters (try taping a pencil across the diaphragm, if you don't have one . . . but you should have one). A high-pass filter (used to cut the low frequencies) will also help reduce plosives, as will good mic technique—softening P's, B's, S's, and T's, or quickly and subtly turning your head away from the microphone.

Another part of mic technique involves controlling your dynamics by gently moving in on quiet lines and slightly pulling back when belting. Just watch out that you don't hear the tone change too much. Listen closely and practice it and you'll be amazed at the results.

When a vocal isn't too sibilant, it be can be brightened more, and when singers control their own dynamics, less compression is needed, which is generally a good thing. Having said this, however, vocals are one instrument that I feel almost always benefits from some compression. We will cover this in the mixing chapter, but, if you are a serious singer recording your own vocals, I would strongly consider getting a good compressor. Yes, you can compress at the mix stage, but by compressing a little at *each* stage you will get a more transparent result.

If you are having any problems with your pitch, try taking one earphone off. This works for some singers better than others. Also, watch that the overall volume isn't too loud and you aren't using too much reverb, as these can mask pitch problems and obscure what you're hearing. In general, create a headphone mix that will facilitate good phrasing and pitch by raising the volume of a key rhythm element and turning down countermelodies and instruments with pitch bending/modulation. Be smart about it.

Another overlooked area might be the environment itself. Singers often feed off their environment and feel more comfortable with soft lighting or candles and the warmth that can come from rugs, a sofa, cool pictures, or other inspiring art or memorabilia.

I typically do about five to ten takes when recording vocals, though with some singers as few as two or three takes is all that's required, while with others it can be more like fifty. Then I listen through and "comp" the vocal.

Comping is the process of compiling bits and pieces (words and lines) from different takes into one master composite track. You can do this for any track, but it's most commonly done with vocals. Next, I'll listen to the comp and find anything that needs to be fixed.

When I'm done, I document the settings on the equipment I used in case I ever need to recall that sound in order to fix a portion of the vocal. I have always been able to find any recall sheet I've ever needed at barryrudolph.com.

A question I get asked a lot is how and when to double vocals. There are no rules, really. For me, I usually consider the lyrics and lean towards not doubling when the subject matter is very personal, intimate, or serious in nature. A single voice is just more honest and intimate.

I like to double vocals for songs that are more upbeat and fun; or sometimes just to add texture throughout; or for variation, like on a chorus; or for punctuation, accenting key words. Some great singers like John Lennon and Elliott Smith doubled their vocals almost all the time.

To be clear, when I refer to doubling vocals, I mean singing it twice, not copying and pasting. Copying and pasting to a new track is really just making it louder. Unless you change things about the tone, the timing, or the pitch of the double, you are just making it louder. I also recommend using a different mic, if possible, for variation/blending.

Then I tuck it down about 10 dBs and just use it to thicken the lead vocal, *or* only 5 dB to hear *more* of the double, sometimes panning slightly away from the center where the lead vocal is. It can also be cool to filter the double, cutting the lows and highs or processing it with other modulating or harmonic effects.

In pop and mainstream pop/rock, the vocals can be really stacked, often quadrupled. The same goes for harmonies. In more honest, organic music, I usually prefer a single voice singing the harmony. If the style lends itself to a more layered sound, each harmony part could be doubled or quadrupled and panned, or left down the middle for a solid mono thing.

Another thing I like to do when recording harmonies is have the singer stand further away from the microphone. This allows for more room sound and a supportive vocal that sits more evenly in the background, while also providing a little more depth. In addition, I find it helpful to try to make sure the harmony doesn't begin before the lead vocal or trail off after it. Finally, try to soften your consonants, especially your S's and T's. Let the lead provide most of that and just blend in the background part/s.

Recording Bass

Unlike guitar, bass usually sounds great plugging directly into a preamp. Just set the input source of the preamp to "instrument" (sometimes labeled "hi-z / low impedance") rather than "mic" or "line."

If you have a good amplifier sound and a DI (direct-input box) you can record both the amp and the direct sound simultaneously. You would plug your bass into the DI with a ¼" cable, and then you would take two signals out of the DI. One would be a ¼" cable to the bass amp and the other an XLR cable to a preamp. If you do this, be sure to test the phase as explained above in the Phase Cancellation section.

Usually a dynamic mic like a Sennheiser 421 or Electro Voice RE20 will work well on the amp, or try a condenser for more detail. Another cool thing to do with bass is to put foam or felt under the strings, near the bridge. This can dampen the ring/decay of the strings nicely for a muted sound or can be positioned more loosely to allow the sound to ring out but merely cut down on the overtones that can result from a plucked string. Of course, both the player and the type of instrument will play a big role in the sound you get, as will the preamp, pickup selection, tone settings, and whether the musician is playing closer to the bridge (more percussive) or the neck (smoother) of the instrument.

When recording upright bass, I like to point a mic at the *f*-hole on the G-string side, as the E-string is louder, and sometimes I'll add a second mic on the fretboard. I don't usually like to use a DI for upright, but I sometimes record it as a safety when there's heavy drum bleed, or to process later through an amp.

It's not uncommon to add a little EQ and compression when recording bass. (More on EQ and compression in the mixing chapter.)

Recording Acoustic Guitar

There are many ways you can record an acoustic, but the one nearly surefire way to get a well-balanced sound is by pointing the mic at the guitar between the twelfth and fourteenth fret (where the neck and body of the guitar meet). I find this yields a crisp, yet full sound.

If you want a more percussive sound, try pointing the mic closer to where the pick is striking the strings, near the bridge. This will capture more of the transient, which can help cut through thick electric guitars, keyboards, and drums. You can even try miking the body for a "woodier" tone. The one area you should avoid miking directly is the sound hole, because it generally sounds too boomy or bassy.

If the acoustic is playing a major role in the production, you may want to try stereo miking it, using one of the techniques discussed above. As for microphones, I prefer condensers (large- or small-diaphragm). Ribbons are great as long as the guitarist isn't playing too quietly (ribbons have a low output) or the arrangement isn't too dense (ribbons are a little dark sounding). I don't like to record acoustic direct unless I intend to process it with an effect in some way.

Recording Electric Guitar

When it comes to electric guitar I would always rather have a real amp over a virtual one, but I would rather use the *right* virtual amp than the *wrong* amplifier. As always, the musician, the instrument, and the amplifier are the most important factors. Assuming you've made the best choices here, you can do just fine pointing a SM57 at the cone of the speaker, a few inches back. You can get right up on the grill cloth of the amp for more presence and proximity/lows.

If I'm looking for a chunkier guitar with more lows (and often I am not), I'll use a different dynamic mic, like a Sennheiser 421. Sometimes a ribbon placed a foot or two back from the amp can capture a more dimensional, richer sound, with its figure 8 / bi-directional polar pattern. Other times I will blend the two mics/tones, adhering to the equidistant rule discussed along with phase cancellation on p. 172.

Another option would be to add a room mic. I like condensers for this because of their hotter/louder output and emphasis of high and low frequencies, two ranges that are diminished when the mics are placed further from the sound source. When using a room mic with a close mic, be sure to follow the 3:1 rule discussed along with phase cancellation. Also, remember our tips in the production chapter when deciding on sounds such as, clean vs. distorted, bright vs. dark, and dry vs. ambient.

For some kinds of music I like the sound of older, duller strings. Other times, new, brighter strings are preferable.

Finally, whether you are recording acoustic or electric guitar, take the time to tune and check it regularly. There's nothing worse than a great performance that's compromised by a pitchy instrument.

Recording Piano

I usually record grand piano in stereo using any of the stereo miking techniques covered earlier. If the track is rocking hard I lean towards an XY setup near the hammers of the piano for more transient detail. Other times, I'll back away into a near XY for a little more air. A spaced pair can be great for more distinction between the left and right hands, but be careful not to spread the mics *too* wide, where they sound disconnected from each other. You can also try adding a third mic at middle C or a room mic or two.

Dynamics, ribbons, condensers—I've had great success with them all recording piano. As always, condensers are brighter, dynamics grittier, and ribbons warmer and more dimensional.

I usually record upright piano in stereo, but sometimes I record mono for a more "Stonsey"/"Beatlesy" kind of thing. Another option is miking the soundboard from behind. This will generally work better if the piano doesn't need to be overly bright.

Recording Wind Instruments and Strings

For louder, brighter horns like trumpet and sax I often like to use ribbon mics because of the way they soften the high frequencies. When I want a more sparkly sound I opt for a condenser, but much of the time I like a dynamic for the extra grit it adds.

I usually start about a foot away from the bell and move the mic as needed. Softer wind instruments like flute or oboe usually do better with a condenser, due to its hotter output. If I am recording a horn section, I like to add a pair of stereo room mics.

For violin or viola I usually use a small-diaphragm condenser or ribbon mic about a foot above the instrument, closer and more direct to capture more attack, and further away and off axis for a warmer sound. For cello, I prefer a large-diaphragm condenser pointed at the *f*-hole on the G-string side, but other mics can work, too. Experiment with how closely to mic it and consider adding room mics, as that's how we are accustomed to hearing strings.

Now that we've gone over the basics of setting up a home studio and many of the tools, techniques, and strategies involved in producing and recording your songs, it's time to turn our attention to mixing.

17 Mixing

During the mixing stage, all of the various instruments and voices will be balanced, in terms of volume, tone, and stereo imaging. In addition, effects will be applied. When the mix is finished, all of the tracks and effects will be combined together and bounced or printed (recorded) onto one stereo track, containing all of the information on the left and right sides. Then you'll be ready to master all of your stereo mixes.

Mixing is arguably the most challenging part of the production process, but if you have an aptitude and a passion for it and put in the time, you can be successful at it. And, whether or not you go on to mix your own demos, your own records, or those of third party clients, you should at the very least come away from reading this chapter a more savvy musician with a greater hand in shaping the sound and style of your productions. It is especially important to have this confidence when working with other studio professionals.

In this chapter we will look at some fundamentals of mixing, as well as some more advanced techniques and tools, including:

1. Understanding signal flow (routing, gain structure, headroom)
2. Defining your approach
3. Balancing your levels
4. Applying panning
5. Applying EQ
6. Applying compression/limiting
7. Applying advanced dynamic techniques (serial, parallel, mix bus, side chain)
8. Applying advanced dynamic effects (noise gates, transient designers, de-essers)
9. Applying timed-based effects (delay, reverb, other modulating effects)
10. Automating (volume, sends, effects)
11. How do you know when the mix is done?

Regarding the tasks and tools above, while I have tried sequencing them in a sensible, organic way, I wouldn't typically mix in any predetermined sequence in practice. Instead, as I turn up a fader, I go with my instincts. If I think right away that this or that instrument could benefit from being panned, EQ'd, compressed or having reverb added to it, I will do it right then. If I'm not sure, I take a wait-and-see approach, since once the instrument is interacting with the other instruments, it may benefit from certain processing that is not yet apparent. So I wait and revisit it at that time.

Understanding Signal Flow

Signal flow is the path the audio takes from its input source (microphone or instrument) to your mixer's outputs (headphones or speakers). Three important subtopics of signal flow are signal routing, gain structure, and headroom.

Routing

When it comes to signal flow, I think it helps to differentiate between signal routed inside your DAW and signal routed between your DAW and external devices like preamps and compressors. The **I/O** (inputs/outputs) controls how we get signal from the interface into the DAW and signal from the DAW out through the interface to your speakers or headphones. **Buses**, on the other hand, are used to route signal within the DAW. Examples might include a drum sub mix (routing all the drum mics to one auxiliary/effects channel) or time-based effects, like reverb or delay.

Time-based effects are routed differently than EQs and compressors, which are inserted directly onto the channel you want to add them to. Instead, time-based effects are placed on auxiliary channels (sometimes called returns) and we use auxiliary sends to *bus* tracks *to* the effect (please see illustration).

So, for example, let's say you want to add reverb to a vocal. Instead of putting a reverb plug-in on the vocal channel, you'd create an aux channel (probably stereo), insert the reverb on it, and assign it a bus input. Make sure the input you choose is not being used anywhere else. If any two effects have the same bus input, you won't be able to increase or decrease one without the other.

Next, create a send from your vocal channel using the same bus number or bus name you assigned to the input of the reverb aux channel. So, if you assigned bus 1 as the input of your reverb aux channel, you would use bus 1 on the vocal channel to send vocal signal to the reverb. Now, you can send as many tracks to that one reverb as you like, and if you want a different type of reverb, you simply create another aux channel and follow the same steps.

There are a few reasons why it's better to put time-based effects on aux.

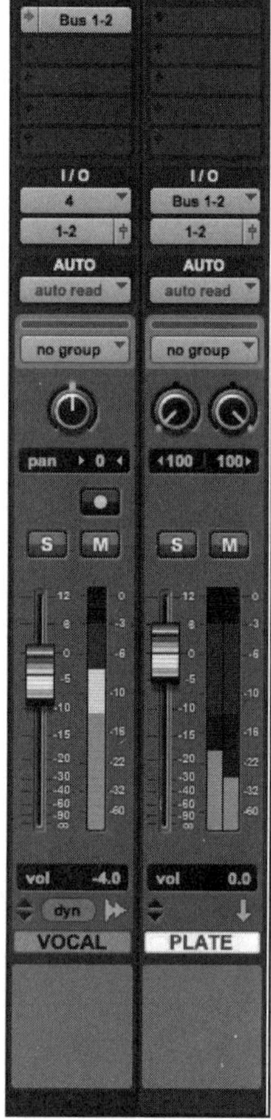

Figure 17-1

- Efficiency
- Panning
- Independent processing

I've seen sessions where people have twenty vocal tracks, and each one has the same five identical plugins inserted on them. That's one hundred plugins eating up your computer's CPU power for a job that could have been done with, you guessed it, five plugins! If instead you created five aux channels, one for each plug-in, then you could use sends to bus all twenty vocal tracks to the effects. This is a much more efficient use of system resources

Can you imagine someone mixing with analog equipment having twenty plate reverbs? They'd be extremely lucky to have two to make go around.

Another reason to put time-based effects on aux channels is the ability to pan the track and the effect independently of one another. This can provide for some cool stereo imaging. Examples include sending a vocal to a short delay and panning the effect slightly off-center, or panning a guitar to one side and sending it to a short delay or reverb panned to the opposite side.

A third reason would be to process the effect independently of the main signal, for example, EQ'ing a reverb bright or dark for effect. Finally, I just think it's more natural for an engineer to work with a send where units are measured in dBs rather than altering the wet/dry blend of a plug-in.

Gain Structure

Gain structure refers to how you set your levels throughout your recording and mixing chain. In order to maximize the clean level (without noise or clipping) we need to properly balance the levels in and out of any piece of equipment, hardware or software.

An example of poor gain structure would be a mixer with its mix bus –10 or –20 dBs below unity/0 dBs and the individual channel faders far above unity. **Unity** refers to when the input and output of two devices are equal. Your **mix bus**, sometimes referred to as the stereo bus, output, or master fader, is the channel where all of your other channels are summed together. From there the sound goes to your speakers or headphones.

Your software has been designed to operate with the mix bus fader at or near unity. If you start pulling it down, it will force you to compensate by turning your channel faders up past unity, which can reduce clarity and cause distortion. Eventually, you may run out of headroom on those tracks. (More about gain structure below, under "Compression.")

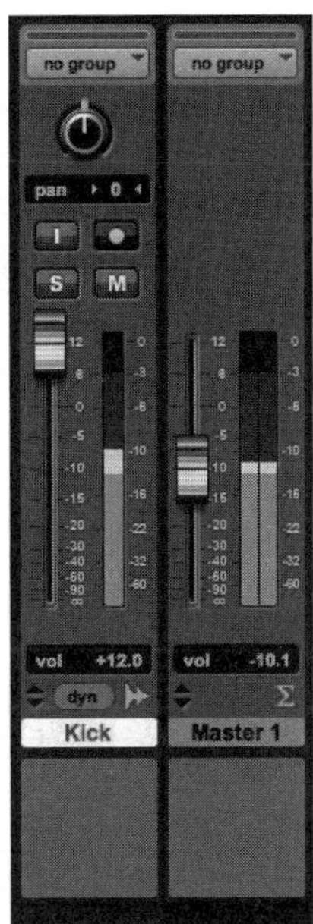

Figure 17-2

Headroom

Headroom is the amount of volume available before clipping. On analog equipment, a signal reaching and even exceeding unity is usually fine. In fact there is usually about +18 dB of headroom in most analog equipment. In digital recording, however, it's preferable to leave some headroom and shoot for a level of –15 dBFS to –3 dBFS. This is because 0 dBvu in the analog world is the equivalent of –18 dBFS in the digital world.

In general, pushing the level too much or not enough anywhere in the signal path can result in distortion or poor signal-to-noise ratio. A good rule of thumb is to check that you're not clipping the input *or* the output of any channel *or* plug-in/effects unit. The most important channel not to clip is the mix bus/master fader. If you apply good gain structure fundamentals you will maximize the headroom of your mix.

Another thing that can help increase headroom is high-pass filtering at 40–80Hz on most tracks, other than the kick and bass. Low frequencies eat up a lot of headroom. Eliminating them will free up headroom.

Defining Your Approach

In the mixing stage, you will build upon the overall production vision established in the preproduction and recording stages. And, much like we discussed in the production chapter, mixing can also benefit from a clearly defined approach, e.g., punchy or ambient, raw or refined, vintage or modern.

One of the things I enjoy most about mixing is altering my approach for different songs or albums. For example, let's say I'm mixing some wild electro rock record. I might go for a modern, refined, punchy mix, using a lot of aggressive processing—heavily compressing, distorting and EQing stuff, triggering lots of modulating and time-based effects, wild panning.

If, on the other hand, I was mixing a more chill, jazzy pop album, for example, I could never get away with half of the things I did on the electro rock record. On the chill record I might take a more ambient, live, vintage approach, relaxing the settings on compressors, EQ'ing less, and taking a much more natural approach to time-based effects, bringing the listener into the room with the band. I might mix the voice more up front (louder) if it's a solo artist, or back (quieter) if it's a band, especially a heavier/louder band, to make them sound bigger.

Even if you are primarily mixing your own music, and it's of a consistent style, it's helpful to define your approach. And don't be afraid to mix things up, like using vintage sounds with modern processing or making the drums raw and the vocals more refined. Explore, experiment, be creative.

I think the two elements that will most profoundly affect the overall sound of a mix are how you treat the lead melody (usually the vocals) and the rhythm section (which would include drums, bass, rhythm guitar and/or keys).

I like to characterize the emotion in the vocal or lead melodic instrument and think about what I can do to enhance that emotion. So, if it's anger, for example, I'll keep the vocal dry (no reverb) and compress it to pull it forward in the mix. If it's loneliness, I may add some echo.

With respect to the rhythm instruments, I'll consider how I want them to hit the listener—hard and punchy, gentle and ambient, or a combination of the two.

As you read on about the various processing tools below, notice how I connect different techniques to different approaches. Think about which will work best for you, as you begin to use these tools.

Balancing Your Levels

Once I have an approach in mind I'll start getting static levels (volumes) on all of the various tracks. Sometimes I like to do this while listening to the whole mix; other times I like to start with the drums or maybe the vocal and build up or down from there.

If you're just beginning, I think it can be beneficial to solo out instruments like the drums, for example. It's a good way to do some ear training as you add processing—and there are actually reasons, which we'll get to in a moment, why it's smart to set the drum levels first. Just remember that when you un-solo these tracks and begin to hear how they interact with the other elements of the mix, you'll likely need to refine things to work *together* better.

Let's say you want to start with drums. That's a sensible option, as the drums are akin to the frame of the house. In addition, since the drums produce arguably the heaviest transients, they are the element that is most likely to cause clipping on your mix bus. As a result, it can be helpful to set their levels first. I recommend doing this in the loudest section of the song, where clipping is most likely to occur.

Now, you have a choice whether to begin with the close-miked tracks (often kick, snare, and toms) or the room mics and overheads. I usually start with my rooms and overheads. I just find that it gives me a better overview of how the kit sounded in the room, and then I can add in the close mics to bring particular elements of the kit more into focus.

If, however I'm mixing a song where I intend to rely much more heavily on the close mics, I may begin with those. For example, in heavy rock, where the drums need to cut through thick, distorted guitars, the close mics will have much more transient detail, providing the attack and presence necessary for them to be heard clearly in a denser mix. If you are mixing programmed drums, then there probably aren't any room mics, so you'd probably just start with your kick, snare, and hi-hat.

One thing that really helps with mixing, in general, is identifying key relationships between tracks, for example, the kick and the bass, or the snare and a rhythm guitar—elements that share a frequency range.

On the drum kit itself, I will balance the four main elements, kick, snare, toms and cymbals. Try to get the kick, snare, and toms to feel equal in energy, and watch that the cymbals aren't too loud. Because they are so bright and decay for so long, the cymbals can really eat up a mix, especially the high frequencies, where you need space for the vocals. Again, setting levels in the loudest parts of the song can help manage this potential pitfall.

Once the four elements of the drums sound balanced, start adding in other elements. Bring up the bass until it sounds like it locks in with the kick drum, and then begin to turn up the harmonic rhythm instruments like guitars and keyboards and try to balance them with the snare. It's a bit of a taste thing, but I've found that this is a good way to start getting initial balances.

Now let's move on to panning.

Applying Panning

I think panning is one of the most underrated parts of mixing. This is where conversations are created and conflicts are resolved! Panning refers to the stereo image and where you place things in that left/right spectrum: in the center (mono), hard left, hard right, or somewhere in between.

If you have two competing elements, playing a similar rhythm or in a similar register/octave range, try panning them apart. If you have two instruments doing call-and-response, try panning them apart so that it feels like they are facing each other, having a conversation.

Let's first look at panning anything recorded using both close mics and room mics, like drums or a string quartet. What is fundamentally important is to have the panning of your close mics reflect the panning of your room mics. What you need to know about the room mics is whether they were recorded from the audience or the players' perspective.

So, if you were looking at a drummer like the one in the illustration from the "audience" perspective, there would be more hi-hat in the room/overhead right channels and more floor tom in the left. As a result, you would pan your hi-hat slightly to the right and your floor tom slightly to the left. If you recorded your rooms/overheads from the drummer's (player's) perspective, your panning would be reversed. It doesn't matter which perspective the recording engineer used, but the mixing engineer needs to know this and conform to it.

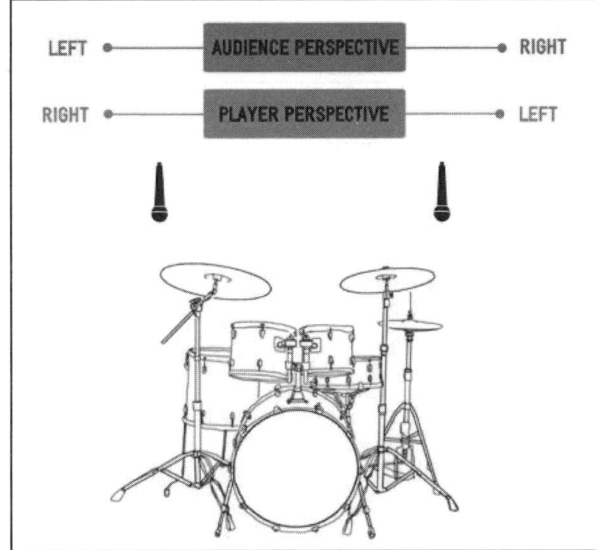

Figure 17-3

The biggest challenge with panning, in my opinion, is how to pan the harmonic mid-range instruments like guitars and keyboards, especially when you have a lot of stereo tracks like strings, or horns, or harmonies. Sometimes what I'll do is solo these instruments without the drums, bass, and lead vocal (since they are all centered most of the time). Then, I logically begin to pan apart elements that are either masking one another or talking to one another. I'd usually take a similar approach to things like percussion. For example, if the hi-hat is on the right, I'd likely pan the tambourine to the left, though there are exceptions and you should do what *feels* the best.

Regarding stereo tracks, especially keyboard patches, remember that you don't always need to pan them all 100 percent left and right. You can lose the sense of width if everything is panned wide, so experiment with it and try processing the left and right sides differently sometimes. You can also try tilting them to the left or right with more of a ten and five o'clock panning.

Another cool thing to do is to take a mono track and pan it to one side. Then, send it to a short delay panned to the other side. (For more on this topic please see "Stereoizing" on p. 203.)

Finally, sometimes it can be interesting to have an instrument sweep across the stereo spectrum, panning from one side to the other. Try it at different rates locking to the tempo, like every quarter note or every measure, or simply as a one-time effect.

Applying EQ

EQ is short for equalization, or balancing, of the sound frequencies. In short, it's a way to alter the tone of a voice or instrument.

Unlike the volume fader, which controls the overall volume, EQ's boost or cut the gain/volume of specific frequency ranges. With a good EQ, sometimes 1 dB or even less can be enough. All EQ's are designed a little differently and therefore sound a little different. As you gain more experience you will start to gravitate more toward certain EQ's, depending on your goal at the time.

I'll EQ something if I want to accentuate its sweet spot or make it "pop" more, or to diminish something displeasing in the sound. Other times I'll EQ just to make elements fit together better, say if the sound of one instrument is masking another. Finally, EQ can be a cool way to manipulate the sound in more extreme ways, more like a special effect. For example, filtering out lows and highs to create a vintage telephone/transistor radio sound.

Parametric EQ's have the ability to alter the frequency, gain, and bandwidth of a signal, using a variety of different EQ shapes.

EQ Parameters

- Frequency—Measured in Hertz (Hz). Most EQ's range from 20 Hz to 20 kHz, which is the approximate range of human hearing.
- Gain (Boost/Cut)—Measured in decibels (dBs).
- Q/Bandwidth—Determines the width of the frequency band being altered. A higher Q value will boost/cut a narrower frequency range.
- Shape/Type

- *High-Pass Filter*: Cuts the lows and allows the highs to pass. It will cut all the frequencies below the chosen frequency.
- *Low-Pass Filter*: Cuts the highs and allows the lows to pass. It will cut all the frequencies above the chosen frequency.
- *Bell/Peak*: Boosts/cuts near and around a particular frequency.
- *Low Shelf*: Boosts/cuts from a particular frequency and all the frequencies below it.
- *High Shelf*: Boosts/cuts from a particular frequency and all the frequencies above it.

Figure 17-4

How to EQ

I think one has to be careful with EQ not to rush in without having a goal in mind. Instead of just doing what you've heard or read, listen, diagnose the issue, formulate a goal, and then EQ. For example, consider this: if the guitar sounds a little muddy, try cutting the low mid frequencies around 200 Hz. Or, say the vocal lacks air, boost in the high frequencies around 16 kHz.

The problem with just following steps you've read is that it doesn't take into account two critical factors: the source recording you're working with (is it thin or muddy? dull or bright?) and the other variables of the mix (is it dense or sparse, for example?). That's why you have to learn to listen deeply with your "mixer's ears."

I think it's particularly helpful to do so in order to "get your ears on" before you start mixing and again when you feel your mix is getting close. By listening to a top mix in your genre you get attuned to how deep the lows should be, how punchy the mids are, where the vocal is sitting, and how much air there is on top. While some mixers may prefer not to do so, I do find it helps to lend some perspective by providing a point of reference. It's almost like calibrating your ears.

Here are some basic variables to listen for:

Kick

The kick can usually benefit from some extra lows. If you want a deep modern sub to it, try boosting between 30 and 70 Hz. For more of a vintage thud (a harder sound), try boosting between 100 and 125 Hz. Another key with the kick is the amount of beater attack. I personally like just enough to hear the attack, but I prefer to feel the bottom-end weight of the kick. A "clicky" kick drum with too much beater sound can take focus away from the low end. I find boosting/cutting around 3 kHz can adjust the amount of attack the kick has. If needed, I'll do another boost/cut above 10 kHz. In addition, sometimes cutting between 300 and 500 Hz can add a little extra punch, by putting a little extra focus on the lows and highs.

Snare

If I want to beef up the snare I usually look to boost between 100 and 250 Hz. Cutting between 500 Hz and 1 kHz can reduce any "boxy" or "nasal" characteristics. Stick attack can be found between 2 and 4 kHz; boost/cut to taste. Finally, sometimes I'll boost closer to 10 kHz to further brighten. As I mentioned earlier when talking about miking the snare, hi-hat bleed is often a concern, and boosting in the upper mid and high frequencies of a snare will bring out more hi-hat. I have a good solution for this, however, using a noise gate that I'll explain below in the Dynamics section.

Bass

Try boosting between 60 and 90 Hz for a deeper bass sound and up around 100–125 Hz for a little more articulate low end. If things get muddy, try cutting around 300 Hz, or down around 150 Hz if it's a bit boomy. I often boost around 700 Hz to 1 kHz to bring some mid-range clarity to the bass notes and up at 2 or 3 kHz for some sizzle. I don't usually boost much higher than this and sometimes will roll off the highs with a low-pass filter, if the bass is too trebly or metallic-sounding.

Guitars/Keys

If I don't need the lows on the guitar, I routinely high-pass filter them somewhere between 40 and 80 Hz (sometimes even higher depending on the needs of the bass/low end). This is true for most vocals and instruments, though if the track feels at all thin or cold I don't filter it or I offset the filter with a low mid boost.

Muddy guitars usually get cut around 200 Hz. Try boosting near 200 Hz to beef up guitars. A little extra body/nasal sound can be found around 500 Hz – 1 kHz. I'll cut here to reduce that "tin can" sound, which can often also have the effect of adding clarity. The crisp bite of the guitar is usually around 2–4 kHz with the presence a little higher around 4–6 kHz. I often cut here on distorted electrics that have too much of that "white noise" sound, causing a glare in upper mids that reduces definition. Boosting above 10 kHz can bring out more sparkle and air or, with an acoustic, more of the percussiveness of the pick.

Vocals

I'll often high-pass filter unless the vocal sounds thin or cold. If it does, I'll try boosting between 150 and 300 Hz, depending on the range of the vocalist (soprano, alto, tenor, baritone) and the other elements in the arrangement. Sometimes a vocal can be a little too nasal-sounding and I'll cut near 1 kHz. Boosting between 1.5 and 3 kHz will bring out more of the vocal's crispness. Boosts in the highs, above 10 kHz, will add brightness, and 16 kHz will add "air." Be careful boosting too much between 4 and 10 kHz, because, while it can add clarity and brilliance, it can also exacerbate sibilance.

Boost and Search Technique

This is a great way to do some ear training and pinpoint the exact sound you are seeking to enhance or reduce. Here's how you do it.

1. With a bell shape EQ, make an extreme boost of 10–12 dBs.
2. Create a fairly narrow Q/bandwidth.
3. Scroll around the frequency range where you are looking.
4. Once you've found the spot, remove the boost and listen for a minute to recalibrate your ears.
5. Begin to gradually boost/cut the chosen frequency and possibly widen out the Q.

I find that wider bandwidths generally sound more musical when boosting, but often a narrow bandwidth can work to notch out a problem frequency.

Applying Compression/Limiting

Dynamic effects are used to control the volume of a track by detecting peaks in the audio and turning them down. There are several different tools and techniques to highlight, including noise gates, de-essers, and more, but let's begin with the most essential dynamic processing tool, the compressor.

Compression is one of the most essential tools in mixing. It can help add an element of cohesion and consistency essential to a great mix. Here's an example of how compression works.

Have you ever listened to playback of a vocal performance and found that some words are too quiet and others are too loud? Well, a compressor can detect this and automatically turn down the loud words while leaving alone quiet ones. You can control which ones get turned down and which don't. Then you can take the whole track (the words that were too quiet and the loud ones that got turned down) and turn it all back up. The end result is a vocal that is more even and dynamically consistent, allowing it to sit in the track better and giving your production a more cohesive, consistent, and professional sound.

So, essentially, compressors control the dynamic range of a track, any track. The **dynamic range** is the volume difference between its loudest and quietest moments. Dynamics are essential, but dynamic inconsistencies are distracting, especially in a vocal. Compressors even out these unwanted volume fluctuations and more.

Compression Parameters

While all compressors are set up a little differently, most of them have the following parameters listed and explained below:

- **Threshold** controls the volume at which the compressor begins turning down the signal. The user sets the volume (measured in decibels) at which the compressor will kick in. So, if you set the threshold at, say, –15 dB, and there is a peak in the audio that is –14 dB, the compressor kicks in and turns the volume of that word down. If the next word is –16 dB, it doesn't get turned down because it is not louder than the volume at which you set the threshold.

- **Ratio** controls how much the audio above the threshold is turned down. The higher the ratio, the more you are going to turn down the signal. A compressor set to a ratio of 3:1, for example, will reduce the level of a signal that is 3 dB over the threshold to just 1 dB over the threshold, for a "gain reduction" of 2 dB. Hence, **gain reduction** is the amount the signal is turned down. Compressors have a gain reduction window/meter to help you gauge the amount of compression being applied.
- **Attack** controls how quickly the compressor turns down the signal after it goes above the threshold. If no audio is louder than the threshold, then the attack time is not in play. The attack time is set in milliseconds. The lower the number, the faster the attack time. Generally, if you want to compress more of the transient—the beginning of the sound—you set the attack faster. If the compressor seems to be dulling the attack of the instrument, try slowing it down.
- **Release** controls how quickly the compressor stops turning down the signal once its volume has gone below the threshold. The compressor won't begin to release the audio (stop compressing) until the signal's volume goes below the threshold. The length of the sound and the tempo of the track are considerations here. Instruments with a lot of sustain, bass, strings, and other pads, for example, often benefit from longer release times. Otherwise, they may swell or balloon back up in a distracting way.
- **(Makeup) Gain** controls how much volume is added back into the signal on the way out of the compressor. A good rule of thumb, and one that adheres to our gain structure guidelines discussed on p. 187, is to offset the average gain reduction with the makeup gain. For example, if we see an average gain reduction of -6 dBs, we would set the makeup gain for +6 dBs. On some compressors the gain is simply called the "output."
- **Knee** controls how quickly the compressor gets to the selected ratio. So, if, for example, you've chosen a ratio of 8:1, the knee controls whether the compressor begins compressing immediately at 8:1 (this would be known as a **"hard" knee**) or gradually eases its way up to the 8:1 ratio (**"soft" knee**). As you can probably guess, a hard knee is more aggressive; a soft knee, more conservative. Many compressors have a nonadjustable fixed knee.

Figure 17-5

When and How Much?

There are many different philosophies about compression. Two of the greatest records of all time were made with little or no compression: Michael Jackson's *Thriller* and Neil Young's *Harvest.* Beatles and Led Zeppelin records, on the other hand, are heavily colored by compression. Let's look at some factors to help you decide when and how much to compress.

The quality of the player is a factor. Weaker musicians are going to require more compression than highly skilled musicians, because they are less in control of their dynamics.

Another consideration is the style of the music. Most rock and other types of punchy, aggressive music use heavy amounts of compression. If, on the other hand, the music has a more chill or relaxed vibe, it may want to breathe more, requiring a more open, less compressed sound.

In addition, if you're working with samples, keep in mind that they have likely already been processed and therefore will require less compression or none at all.

So, you see, it's not always simply a question of *when* but often more a question of *how hard* you push it.

Another thing you may be wondering is whether to compress at the recording stage or wait until the mixing stage. Here's how I like to look at it. Most of the time with compression, as with other effects, I think it works best for the effects to be transparent to the listener. It's more the exception than the norm that I'll want to exaggerate a compressor for a colorful effect. As a result, when I want to heavily compress a track, I often split that compression up over multiple stages, compressing a little at the recording, mixing, and mastering stages, respectively.

In fact, I can even perform multiple layers of compression at the mix stage alone (more on that later in "Applying Advanced Dynamics" below). A good analogy is painting a wall. Three light coats will look rich and even, whereas one thick coat will appear blotchy.

Too much compression can stifle or smother a track, making it sound dull and lifeless.

Another negative artifact of compression is an unintended "pumping effect" that can occur from aggressive compression with problematic attack and release times. One thing that can help you avoid these undesirable results is being conscious of how much gain reduction you're applying.

Average gain reduction would be in the range of 5–10 dBs. Once you see the gain reduction meter getting near 10 dBs, you should proceed with caution. This is getting excessive and, if you lack experience, could lead to some negative artifacts. In many instances, as little as 1 dB of gain reduction might be enough. You definitely want to keep a close eye on the gain reduction meter while you are learning how to use compression.

Another thing that can get you into trouble with compression is a high ratio. An average ratio would be between 4:1 and 10:1. Once a compressor's ratio gets to 10:1 or greater, we give it a new name, a **limiter**. Be careful using ratios over 10:1, as they leave a bigger footprint.

How much compression you use will be determined by the goal you have in mind. Different goals can be achieved using different settings on the compressor's parameters. Let's take a look at how to set them up differently to achieve different results/goals.

Compression Goals

There are several different reasons to employ a compressor, and by modifying the way you set up its parameters you can achieve a variety of goals.

Dynamic consistency: This approach is good for light compression/dynamic control. Use a low to medium ratio (3:1 to 6:1), moderate attack/release times (15–50 ms), and moderate gain reduction (1–5 dbs).

Loud and aggressive: This is a good approach for rock drums and vocals, especially. Use a high ratio (10:1 or greater) and fast attack and release (1–15 ms), and adjust the threshold so you see constant gain reduction in the range of -10 dBs. Use your makeup gain to offset the gain reduction.

Adding punch: For a punchier sound with more emphasis on the transient attack of an instrument, try a slower attack time with a faster release.

Peak limiting: If you need to reduce some excessive peaks, use a high ratio (10:1 or greater) and fast attack and release (1–15 ms), and adjust the threshold so you only see gain reduction on the loud peaks.

Create ambience: Try heavy compression settings on room mics to enhance their decay and create extra ambience. Be careful with loud cymbals, as this can amplify them and make them unruly. Slower release times can help counteract this.

Compressor Circuit Types

The circuit affects the sonic characteristics of the compressor, and different types of circuits are best suited for different jobs. Having said that, I still like to try out a few compressors before settling on one for the task at hand. There are four main compressor circuits.

FET: Fast, clean, and aggressive. Good for dealing with fast transients. Example: Universal Audio 1176.

Figure 17-6

Opto: Slow and smooth. Good for adding rich color and softening highs. Examples: Teletronix LA2A, Avalon 737.

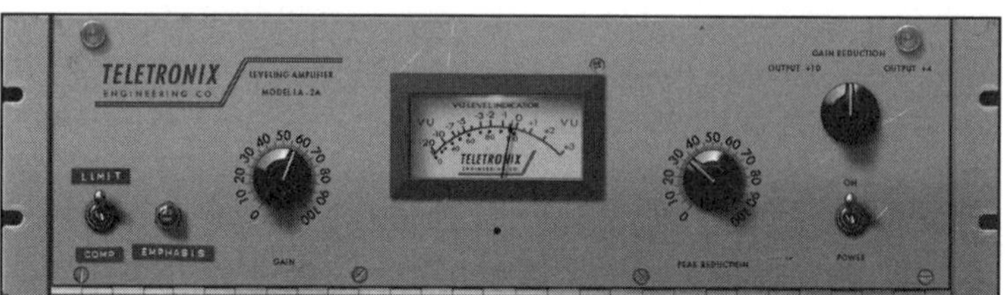

Figure 17-7

VCA: In between FET and Opto. Good for surgical and transparent compression. Examples: SSL 4000 G, DBX 160.

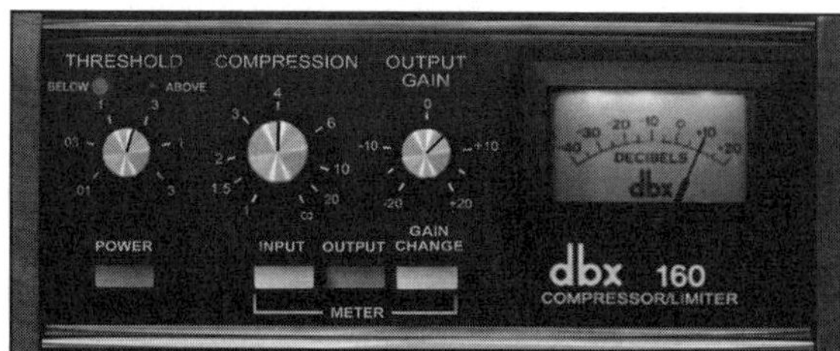

Figure 17-8

Variable-Mu: Closer to an opto. Adds density and cohesion, but still deals well with transients. Examples: Fairchild 670, Manley Vari Mu.

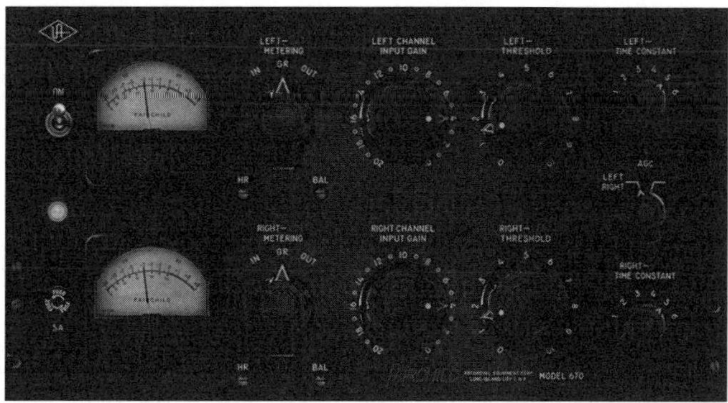

Figure 17-9

Many software designers are making excellent plugins of the above-mentioned hardware examples. This should help provide some insight into how to choose when to use which ones. Try to think more in terms of the type of sound you are trying to achieve than in terms of the specific instrument. For example, for aggressive staccato vocals I'd start with a FET compressor, whereas for a more legato jazz vocal I'd lean toward an opto.

Applying Advanced Dynamic Techniques

Once you've got a handle on how compressors work, you'll be ready to tackle some more advanced dynamic techniques such as serial compression, parallel compression, side chain compression/gating and mix bus processing.

Serial Compression

Serial compression is a technique that uses two or more compressors on one track. The advantage of serial compression is that you can do a lot of compression/gain reduction without hearing it in any hypey, intrusive way. It's more transparent, with less unintended pumping or smothering of the track. This is because you're spitting the workload up over 2 or 3 compressor/limiters, so none of them have to work *too* hard.

I especially like to use serial compression on vocals because they often have a lot of dynamic inconsistencies and I usually want the vocals fairly up front. Serial compression is a great way to add intimacy by bringing the vocal closer but without the edgy, aggressive feel you get from doing heavy gain reduction with a single compressor.

Parallel Compression

Traditionally, compressors are inserted into the signal path of a track and, as such, process 100 percent of the sound. Parallel compression is a technique that inserts the compressor on an auxiliary channel, allowing you to blend in as much or as little of the compression bus (explained earlier in "Routing" on p. 186).

This works particularly great with a heavily compressed sound. If it represented 100 percent of the sound, the track might lack punch and transient detail. However, since a parallel compressor is on a bus, you simply blend it in like a spice and season to taste! I especially love parallel compression on drums, but you can use it on any track.

It can also work great for a mellower compressed sound by relaxing the parameters on your compressor, for example using a lower ratio, slower attack with less gain reduction. This may work better for tracks with a more chill, laid-back vibe.

Side-Chain Compression

Side chaining uses a different track in the session to trigger a dynamic effect, like a compressor or gate. For example, you might put a compressor on the bass but have it controlled by the kick drum via a side chain. Then, every time the kick drum hits, it triggers compression on the bass. The idea is that you want the bass loud but it's drowning out the kick drum, so by having the bass compressor's threshold controlled by the kick drum, every time the kick drum hits, the volume of the bass is ducked slightly and extremely quickly. The key is that you don't hear the bass duck but rather hear more of the transient attack of the kick drum.

A similar approach could be taken with the snare and your rhythm guitars. I find this type of side-chain compression particularly helpful with heavy music or power pop, anything with loud guitars or keys that are making it difficult for the drums to punch through.

Or sometimes I'll use side-chain compression to keep a vocal or other solo instrument on top of loud rhythm instruments by turning the rhythm instruments down with a compressor, controlled by the vocal/solo instrument.

Another side-chain compression technique is to make the entire mix pulse in time with a four-on-the-floor kick drum (quarter notes). This is an effect that Daft Punk helped popularize and it's especially common in dance music.

To do this:

1. Send all your tracks and effects *except the kick* to a stereo aux channel.
2. Insert a compressor and use compression settings suggested below.
3. Assign the side chain to the kick drum.

Now, every time the kick drum hits, the entire mix ducks slightly.

Side-chain compression works best with VCA circuits, due to their transparency, very fast attack and release times and no make-up gain.

While side-chain compression can be a very useful technique, if you do too much it can be very detrimental, possibly doing more harm than good. Be sure to master the more basic compression techniques before trying to tackle the more advanced ones covered in this chapter.

Side-Chain Gating

There are also some cool things you can do with side-chain gating, such as creating a sub kick with a low tone from a signal generator or oscillator, or making a pad (synth, strings, organ) pulse in time with drums.

Sub Kick

1. Create an auxiliary channel.
2. Insert a signal generator or test oscillator set to 40–50 Hz.
3. Insert a noise gate.
4. Assign its side chain to the kick drum.
5. Lower the threshold so that only the kick triggers it to open.
6. Adjust hold and release times to taste.
7. Blend in with regular kick drum.

Pulsing Pad

1. Create a pad.
2. Insert a noise gate.
3. Create a send using a bus on the kick and snare channels.
4. Turn both sends up to 0 dB.
5. Assign the bus as the side chain of the noise gate.
6. Adjust the threshold so only the kick and snare trigger the gate to open.
7. Adjust the hold and release to taste (try locking to the track's BPM).

Mix Bus Processing

Mix bus processing refers to effects inserted across the mix bus channel. This of course means you will be processing the entire mix at once, and so it calls for a more conservative approach. The most common effects to use are a compressor and EQ. Some engineers may do a little light limiting (1–2 dBs of gain reduction) at the mixing stage, but anything more than that could lead to problems at the mastering stage, where you *should* be applying a limiter. I often like to add some tape saturation or other harmonic effects, and, once in a while, a reverb or a triggered delay or modulation effect, like a flanger (covered below in "Other Modulating Effects").

Now, some engineers like mix bus compression and some don't, but the important thing to remember is not to do too much, because you are processing the entire mix. I don't recommend ratios of more than 4:1 or more than 4 dB of gain reduction, and I also don't recommend EQ boosts or cuts of more than 2 or 3 dBs. 1 dB or less is often enough. The mix bus processing should just add a little extra cohesion, excitement, and proximity, pulling the mix forward slightly.

Some engineers like to add this toward the end of the mix, but I personally prefer to build my mix through the processing from the beginning. That way, there are fewer surprises and I end up doing less compression on the individual channels—and I think that's usually a good thing.

Applying Advanced Dynamic Effects

Now it's time to take a look at some other, more advanced dynamic tools, including noise gates, to help reduce instrument bleed; transient designers, to manipulate the attack and decay of a sound; and narrow band limiters like de-essers, to deal with intermittent frequency-specific problems like vocal sibilance.

Noise Gates

Gates are used to get rid of unwanted noise or bleed. **Bleed** is the leakage of one instrument into the mic of another. On drums, for example, it's common to put gates on the kick, snare, and toms.

Gates work similarly to compressors in that they have a threshold. When the audio is louder than the threshold the gate opens and allows the sound through. When the volume drops below the threshold the gate closes, shutting off the sound. If you put a gate on the kick drum, for example, the idea would be to set the threshold so that the kick triggers the gate to open, but then the gate closes and shuts out the bleed. You can control how quickly the gate opens with the attack time and how long it stays open with the hold and release parameters.

By cutting out the bleed you essentially make each drum sound more like a sample. This can be really cool if you want to combine a live feel with more of a hip-hop aesthetic; for metal or loud rock, where you need the drums to have a lot of presence in order to cut through loud distorted guitars; or just for a more refined or produced sound.

Gates are a useful tool in many styles of mixing; however, there are many records where I don't use a single one. Bleed (or leakage) was an important part of the sound on many classic records from Motown and Bob Marley to the Rolling Stones and the Beach Boys. The extra natural ambience is a big part of the vibe and often hard to duplicate with artificial reverb. So, in some styles of music, bleed can be an asset.

Gates can serve other purposes, too. For example, let's say you had a bass drum with a long decay, muddying up a track. You could use the gate to shorten the decay by shortening the hold and release times on the gate. Or, let's say you wanted to reduce, but not eliminate, the hi-hat leaking into the snare mic. Most gates have a parameter called "reduction" or "range" that allows you to simply turn down the leakage rather than get rid of it entirely.

One thing to be careful of when using gates is a **false trigger**. For example, if you put a gate on the kick, a loud snare hit may *unintentionally* cause the gate to open, *or* a couple of very quiet kicks may not get above the threshold, *preventing* the gate from opening. Neither of these scenarios is acceptable, as it would alter the sound of the kick or snare for those few hits, which would sound distracting and unprofessional.

While most gates have a side chain filter that can prevent false triggers by controlling which frequencies trigger the gate, I think it's more bulletproof to simply automate the threshold of the gate in your DAWs automation parameters.

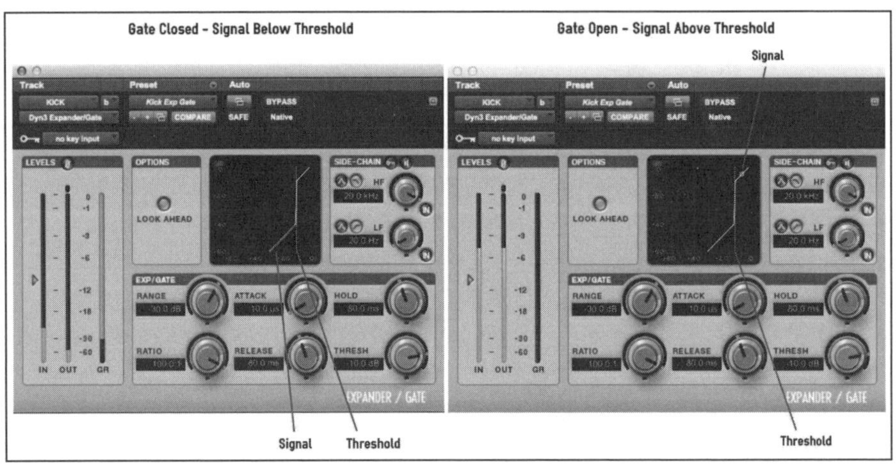

Figure 17-10

Transient Designers

Transient designers, sometimes referred to as transient modulators, envelopers, envelope shapers, and signal modelers, manipulate the attack and/or release of a signal. As a result, you can use it to make a transient sharper or duller, or to make an instrument's sustain longer or shorter. For example, you could reduce the stick attack on a snare drum, or exaggerate the room sound/sustain. Or you could reduce the amount of reverb, room sound, or distortion on a guitar or increase the transient attack on a piano.

Figure 17-11

De-Essers

A de-esser is a frequency-specific compressor most commonly used to reduce vocal sibilance, those harsh "S" and "T" sounds. Unlike an EQ, which would be on the whole time (unless it was automated), a de-esser is a dynamic effect with a frequency-based threshold and, as such, is better suited to deal with *intermittent* high frequency problems such as vocal sibilance.

Sibilance usually occurs between 4 kHz and 10 kHz. The idea would be to locate where the sibilance is most pronounced and then set the volume of the threshold so that gain reduction occurs only on the harsh "S" and "T" sounds. Be careful not to be too aggressive, or you may give the vocal a lisp.

Once you understand the concept of the de-esser and how it works, you can use it to deal with any intermittent high frequency issues from brighter instruments like cymbals, and higher-voiced guitar, violin, trumpet, and others.

I think de-essing is even more important with digital recordings. When recording to analog tape, transients get compressed naturally. This is called **tape compression**. In addition, when recording with analog equipment, the high frequencies are softened. In digital recording we don't get this, and so we have to work a little harder to achieve this type of smoothing using de-essers, multiband compressor/limiters (discussed in "Using Advanced Mastering Tools" on p. 213), and tape/tube saturation emulation plugins.

Tape/tube saturators add extra harmonic content to a track, giving it more depth or "analog warmth." Analog warmth comes from a lot of sources, tape saturation being just one, but I think it can have a positive effect on most tracks. Too much, however, can make tracks overly dense or distorted.

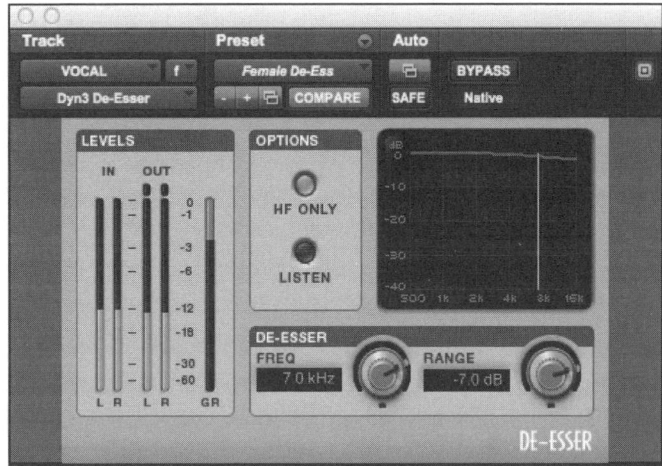

Figure 17-12

Applying Time-Based Effects

Time-based effects are effects that get added to the original signal as a delay or a modulated copy. These ambient effects, like reverb, delay, flanger, phaser, chorus, and others, add an extra sense of space, depth, and dimension to your mixes. Much of the time these effects work best when used quite subliminally. This is an important point to understand. Other times they can be exaggerated for fun effects.

Let's look at some primary time-based effects.

Delay

Delay is different from reverb in that it's a single repeating echo of a signal, often a vocal. You can control the timing of the echoes and how long they repeat for. Often, the timing of the echo is locked to the tempo/BPM of the song, say as an eighth note or quarter note, for example. These echoes gradually become quieter until they disappear.

Short delays can be a great way to thicken or add dimension to a track, while longer delays add depth and vibe or an extra layer to the rhythm, depending on how you set them up. A little goes a long way. Pick and choose the spots where you want to feature the delay and those where it should be a more subliminal layer, adding production value. The delay parameters are as follows:

- **Delay time**: This will usually be measured in milliseconds (ms) or note value based on the BPM of the track.
- **Feedback**: This controls how long the echoes continue repeating
- **Modulation**: Many delays come with an option for pitch modulation. This can be a cool way to add a little more separation between the main vocal and a short delay, and it generally makes longer delays sound a little more dreamy or watery. This also helps add a little of the characteristics you'd get from an analog tape delay.
- **Filters**: Most delays come with high- and low-pass filters. I find that filtering the lows can be helpful in reducing any muddiness, and filtering the highs prevents chattering consonants like a trail of S's at the end of the word "boss," for example.

Doubling

Short delays less than 50 ms can be used as a way to thicken the vocal. I usually prefer to have the singer sing it again, because there's more variation, especially if you use a different mic or change something else in the signal path or in the character of the performance. If artificially doubling using a delay, try a bit of pitch modulation and EQ/filtering or distortion on the double/delay.

Slapback

A slapback is one tight echo, usually around 60–180 ms after the vocal/instrument. Slapback is a great way to animate a vocal or instrument without making it sound wet or distant. Elvis Presley and John Lennon were both well known for their love of slapback, and it's still one of the most popular vocal effects in modern music—not just in rock or pop, but in hip-hop, too, where it's usually more appropriate than reverb. For a traditional slapback, set the feedback at zero so that it only produces one echo. Of course, you can increase it, if you think it sounds better. Again, a little modulation can help add some analog characteristics.

Stereoizing

Delays are a great way to "stereoize" a mono vocal or any instrument. Here are a few different things you can try with delays to create width with a vocal or instrument:

- You can try a mono delay in a verse and a stereo in the chorus to give some ebb and flow to the size of the vocal, for example.
- Pan a mono slapback 50–100 percent to one side.
- Pan an instrument to one side and pan a short 10–30 ms delay to the other side, perhaps processing each side differently with other effects.
- Use two short delays, both set around10–30 ms. Pan one left and the other right. Place a pitch shift plug-in on the left channel and raise the pitch 10–20 cents, then do the same to the right side but lower the pitch the same amount.
- Use different delay times on the left and right sides. Try it with a stereo slapback with sides set at 80 ms and 120 ms. This is a good way to make a vocal sound big and wide. Or use longer delays locked to the track's BPM with echo repeats for a lusher, dreamier effect. Sometimes I'll then bus the delay to a reverb for added depth and ambience. You can take this a step further with ping-pong and multi-tap delays.

Reverb

Reverb is the sound of hundreds, even thousands of tiny reflections that build up into a wash of reverberation. The bigger the space and the harder the surfaces in that space, the longer the reflections continue on, the longer the decay of the sound, and the more pronounced the ambience and reverb. So, for example, a huge parking garage full of concrete, metal, plastic, and glass is going to sound way more reverberant than a small bedroom with a bed, a rug, and curtains.

Digital convolution reverbs re-create real-world acoustic spaces and sometimes modulate the sound for otherworldly effects.

Let's go over the **five main parameters** most commonly found on a reverb plug-in.

1. **Reverb type**: This is where you would choose the type of acoustic space you want to place your vocal or instrument in.
    - Room—You will often have a variety of rooms to choose from, for example, bedroom, bathroom, studio live room, villa, drum room, guitar room, etc. I usually choose a room when I want it to sound very natural.
    - Hall—This could range from an intimate jazz club to a concert hall or a church.
    - Plate—A real plate is a large piece of sheet metal housed in a wooden box with wires connecting it to a mixing desk or console. The sound feeds into the plate, causing it to reverberate. Plates are a great way to brighten up and add sparkle to a track.

- Spring—A spring is similar to a plate, but the coiled metal adds a little bit of pitch warble dependent on the tension of the coil. These are commonly found in guitar amps but can also be stand-alone units used for mixing.
- Chamber—These acoustic spaces create reverb by placing a loud speaker and a microphone at opposite ends of the space, which can be anything from a hallway, to a staircase, to a large, acoustically engineered room. A vocal or other instrument is played back through the speaker, and the microphone captures the ambient sound and feeds it back to the board.

2. **Decay time**: This controls how long the reverb continues after the initial sound. I usually consider reverbs under 1 second to be small or short, 1 to 3 seconds medium, and over 3 seconds large or long. Small reverbs are great for adding a subtle space that sounds natural and also for thickening the sound of a vocal or instrument. Longer reverbs are good for adding air and vibe, lengthening decay, and adding distance.
3. **Pre-delay**: Without pre-delay, the reverb and the instrument would both be heard simultaneously. Pre-delay delays the point at which the sound of the reverb begins, typically by 10–150 milliseconds. This allows the dry sound to hit the listener's ears before the reverb, resulting in a clearer, punchier sound. Once you get over about 40 ms it can start to become audible, especially with instruments that have a strong transient like a snare drum. Longer, more paddy sounds like strings and horns will mask the pre-delay, as the reverb will enter while that dry note is still ringing. A pre-delayed plate reverb is a particularly classic sound that was traditionally done using a tape slap (discussed above under "Slapback"), by sending the signal to a tape machine before the plate reverb. The length of the pre-delay would then depend on the speed on the tape machine, usually 7.5, 15, or 30 ips (inches per second), or equivalently 250, 125, or 63 milliseconds. I often try to get close to one of these tape slap times but then lock into the track's tempo/BPM, if tracked on a click. These types of classic pre-delays are as common today as they were in the 1960s.
4. **EQ**: Most reverbs come with an EQ parameter that allows you to contour the sound of the reverb. It sounds a little different if you EQ the sound before or after it goes through the reverb, because when you EQ it first it hits the reverb differently. I prefer to insert EQ before the reverb. This is closer to the classic methods used at Abbey Road, for example, which EQ'd the send to the reverb.

One common approach is to apply a band pass filter, where you remove a lot of lows (try filtering up to 4-600 Hz) and highs (try filtering between 6 and 10 kHz). Other times I'll EQ the reverb brighter or darker. Just consider what the track needs and how it's sounding before you make your choice.

Figure 17-13

Other Modulating Effects

While reverb and delay are the most popular time-based effects, there are several other modulation effects that can add movement, vibe, and texture to your mixes. Chorus, flanger, and phaser are three similar effects with some subtle, but significant, differences.

Chorus

Based on the natural chorusing effects of a choir or string orchestra, **chorus** combines different-length delays with varying timbres and pitches to create a larger sound with a watery texture. A popular example would be the guitar in Nirvana's "Come as You Are."

Flanger

A **flanger** produces more of a swooshing sound akin to that of a jet plane. It was originally conceived of by synching two tape machines and periodically slowing one down by pressing against the flange of the tape reel. A popular example would be the guitar on "Walking on the Moon," by the Police.

Phaser

A **phaser** creates a swirly texture by slightly delaying different frequencies in the signal by different amounts, resulting in phase shifts in the output signal. Popular examples would be Jimi Hendrix's guitar on "Little Wing" and John Bonham's drums on "Kashmir."

Tremolo and Vibrato

Two other popular modulation effects I'd like to touch on are tremolo and vibrato. **Tremolo** varies the volume of a sound. "Money" by Pink Floyd is a classic example. Vibrato fluctuates the pitch of a signal like you might hear a vocalist do, or like you might hear from a Fender Rhodes electric piano or the Leslie cabinet of a Hammond organ. Both tremolo and vibrato are effective ways to add subtle movement and variation to a track in a mix.

Distortion

Finally, I often like to use distortion like a time-based effect, inserting it on an aux channel and busing to it. **Distortion** alters the amplitude of a signal, creating extra harmonic texture, thickness, and grit.

Once you get a feel for the possibilities and what effects you gravitate to, I recommend creating an effects template that you import at the start of each mix. Think of it like a painter getting out his or her paints to start work. I'll have maybe around twenty effects channels in a mix. I may not use them all, but I like them there just in case. That's because once I start working creatively I want to stay creative and not get bogged down in technical tasks like creating effects channels. Instead, I like to perform those tasks at the beginning of a mix, so that I don't have to break up my workflow.

Automating

Automation is an important part of the mixing process, and depending how in-depth you want to go and what the mix calls for, you can pretty much automate any volume, send, or plug-in you choose.

While a compressor may do the heavy lifting in terms of controlling volume fluctuations, with some vocals or instruments it may be necessary to do a lot of **volume automation** as well. This is really important if you want the vocal to be loud and up front but still sit in the track. I try to match the volumes of lead instruments to the lead vocal, except when they occur simultaneously; then I want to make sure to duck the instruments or ride up the vocal. I usually spend a little time listening to and automating the volume of each instrument, including toms and crash cymbals.

Send automation is another important technique in evolving the sound of a mix. For example, sometimes I will turn down the send to a delay when the singer hits a loud note so the delay isn't too pronounced and distracting. Or I may increase a send to a reverb or delay in a chorus or bridge to make those sections bigger, or even just on some key words as an accent where there's space for it. The mix itself can be dynamic and you should look for opportunities to create special moments as well as to enhance its peaks and valleys.

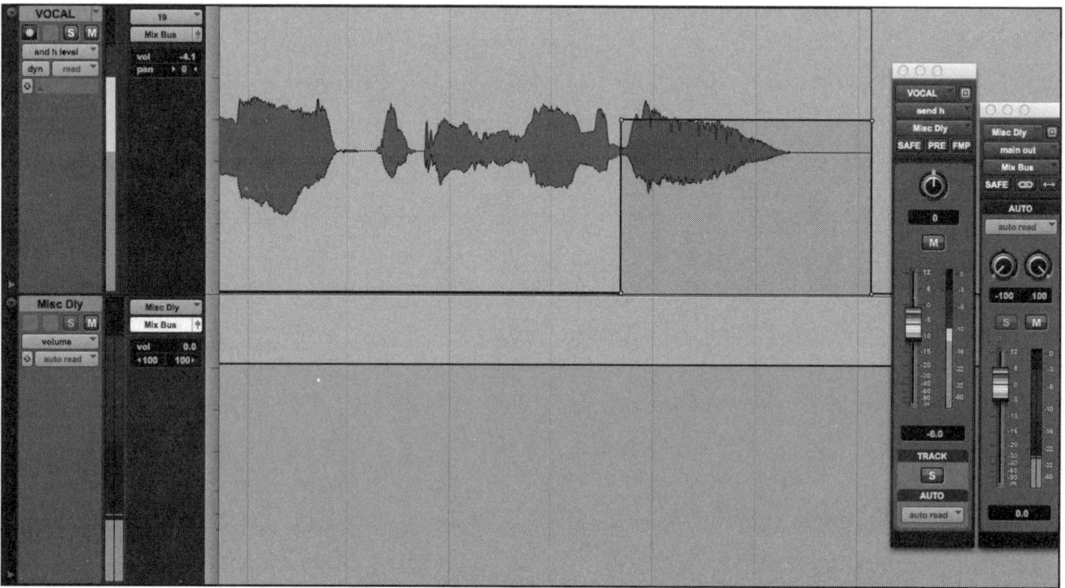

Figure 17-14

Plug-in automation refers to automating the parameters of the effects themselves. One example would be to automate the feedback of a delay, turning it up in a spot that could use a little wildness, but be careful; it can increase quickly and get really loud, not to mention, clip. Also, make sure to fade it down once the lead vocal or solo comes back in so it doesn't get in the way. You can literally automate any parameter on any plug-in.

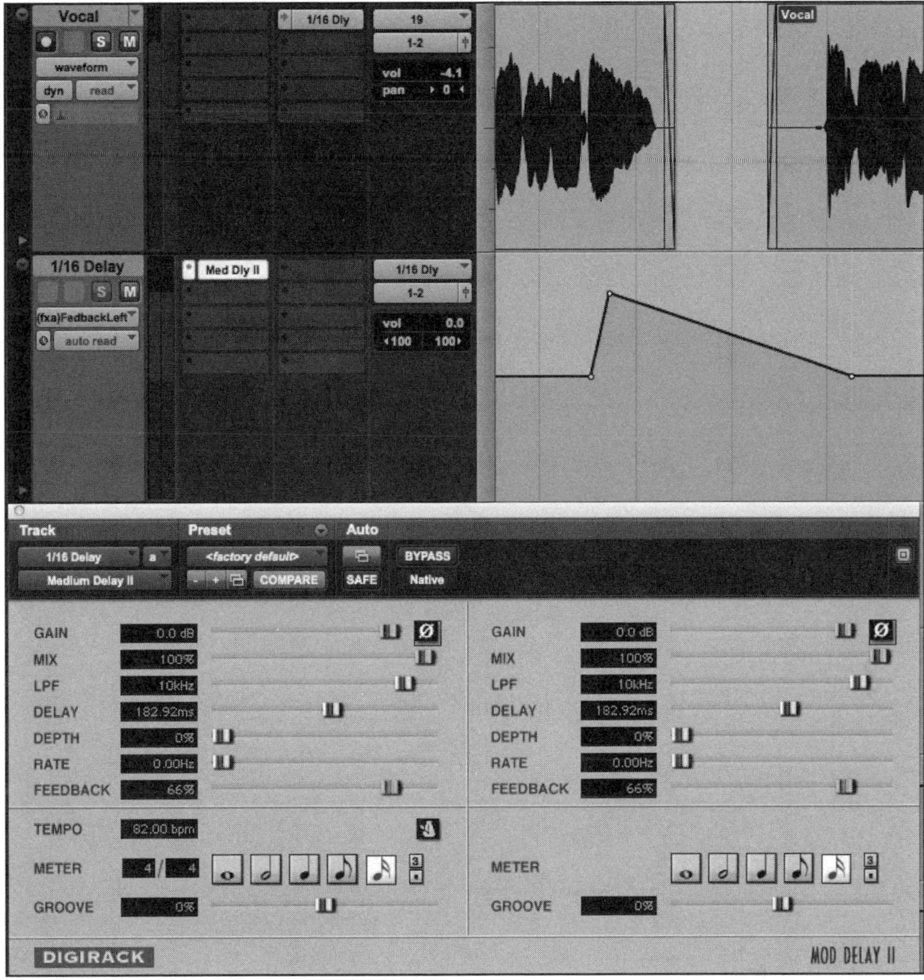

Figure 17-15

How Do You Know When the Mix Is Done?

When I feel a mix is getting close I'll reference it against some top mixes in the genre and see how my balances compare. I'll listen to the low end, the highs, and the level of the vocal, and make sure my mix is hitting with the right impact. Then I like to listen outside the studio on different speakers, in the car, in the living room, on headphones, and with ear buds. I'm looking for problems to reveal themselves.

Two tips to mention here. First, listen to a reference in each environment to calibrate your ears to it and the speakers. Second, don't be concerned about volume, because you are comparing an unmastered mix to a finished master. You won't compare in volume until after your mixes are mastered. Finally, get some feedback from the artist, band members, or other industry professionals whose ears you respect.

Once all the mixes are finished, listen to them and compare them to one another. Volume differences between the mixes will be easily corrected at mastering, but you may hear some tone or balance issues that could be fixed in the mix. For example, pay attention to things like the volume of the vocal, the bass, and the snare. Making sure they don't fluctuate too much from song to song will help ensure the project maintains an overall consistency and professionalism.

Next, it's time to master.

18 Mastering

Now, we've come to the final stage of the production process, mastering . . . the icing on the cake, in many ways. This is where the presentation of your audio is finalized. No more revisions or tweaks, this is what you will release out into the world.

In short, mastering brings the volume of your mixes up to the standard levels of modern commercial releases and evens out any discrepancies in volume and tone between songs, ensuring your album has a consistent overall sound. It's also where you do the final sequencing, editing, spacing, dithering, and bouncing of the audio, at which point it will be ready for manufacturing.

In this chapter we will discuss:

1. Mastering yourself "in the box"
2. Advanced mastering tools
3. Mastering with a professional

Mastering "In the Box"

While everyone would love to have all of their mixes mastered by a highly skilled and experienced mastering engineer in an acoustically tuned room on expensive, top-quality analog equipment, there are often situations where there simply isn't a budget to hire someone to do the mastering. In these instances it is essential to know how to master your own music; you have too much at stake to risk having your music dismissed because the audio was unmastered and, as a result, deemed unsatisfactory.

Let's look at the steps involved in mastering your own songs.

File Types

First of all, let's go back to the mixing stage. When you bounce/print your final mixes, I suggest keeping them at the same sample rate and bit-depth of your mix session. So, if your session is 48K/24-bit, this is what your mix bounces would be.

Once you have bounced all your mixes into a clearly labeled folder (called something like "48K/24-bit Mix Bounces for Mastering"), you'll need to create a new mastering session at the sample rate and resolution of your mixes. You'll then import all the mixes into this session. Be sure each mix is on a separate track, as each will require its own unique plug-in chain. This will allow you to make specific changes to each master, so that when you're finished, they all sound consistent in both volume and tone.

Now we are ready to create our plug-in chain. The three main plug-ins we will use are an EQ, compressor, and brick wall limiter. While opinions vary on whether to insert the EQ or compressor first (I generally prefer to put the EQ first), it is essential that the limiter be last in the chain. If anything is placed after the limiter, it will likely cause digital clipping.

Digital clipping occurs when peaks in the audio exceed 0 dBFS (decibels relative to full scale), or the highest signal level your DAW can handle. You will hear distortion, clicks or pops, and a general loss of clarity, so it needs to be avoided.

Let's look at why this clipping will occur, if any other effects are placed after the brick wall limiter in our plug-in chain, by explaining what a brick wall limiter is.

Brick Wall Limiting

As we learned earlier in our discussion on compression, a limiter is a compressor working at a ratio of 10:1 or greater. What makes a **brick wall limiter** distinct from other limiters is its inclusion of a parameter called the **output ceiling**. This ceiling sets a level beyond which no peaks in the audio are allowed to go. Since clipping occurs at 0 dBFS, I usually set an output ceiling of -0.3 dBFS. This ensures that my masters won't clip and leaves a buffer against any potential distortion that can occur when converting to MP3.

When we master our songs, we are adding gain. We do so when we boost with an EQ, when we add makeup gain from a compressor, and when we add gain with our limiter. As we do so, the peaks in the audio will eventually exceed 0 dBFS and result in clipping. The output ceiling of the brick wall limiter prevents this, which is why it should go last in your mastering chain. But let's talk about what the limiter does to the audio in order to prevent this clipping.

A limiter heavily compresses (limits) the peaks in your audio and, as a result, shrinks the dynamic range of your master in order to add volume and prevent clipping (two goals that are working at cross-purposes). You should be crystal clear that when you make your music louder via a brick wall limiter, there is a transaction taking place. You are purchasing that extra volume and you are paying for it with your dynamic range.

Figure 18-1

As stated on p.193 in the mixing chapter, **dynamic range** is the difference in volume between the quietest and the loudest moments in a track. Dynamics create excitement and fuel emotion in the listening experience. While we all like it when our mixes sound loud on a playlist, we should be conscious of the cost we are paying to achieve this. If you listen sensitively, you will hear a point at which, as you continue to add gain, the audio starts to sound duller, less clear and punchy, and less open overall. Your music can lose depth and can become fatiguing to listen to, as notes no longer rise and fall but rather feel like they are almost smothering the listener. To my ears, this can greatly diminish the journey and emotion in the arrangement/mix.

At this point I'd like to introduce another new tool to help us stay on target with our mastering, a **level meter**. By paying attention to the level meter on our DAW's output, we can measure our levels and easily monitor how loud we are making our masters.

Most level meters can display **peak** or **RMS** (Root Mean Square) level. At mastering, we know that our peak levels will be whatever level we set the output ceiling at, in our example, -0.3 dBFS. RMS, on the other hand, is your average volume at any given moment. I recommend trying to achieve RMS levels between -14 dBFS and -8 dBFS at the loudest points of the song. Consider the genre and feel of your music and mixes when determining how loud to push it.

The average level of masters has risen steadily through the generations, and I have my theories about how this has almost mirrored the rapid development of modern life with our shortened attention spans and task-crammed days and lives. In fact, many of you may be familiar with a term called "the loudness wars." This term describes a trend in mastering procedures that has seen the levels of masters rise steadily from -20 dBFS in the 1980s to as high as -3 dBFS in the 2000s. According to the research of mastering guru, Bob Katz, "There is a point of diminishing returns above about -14 dBFS." In addition, with the proliferation of volume normalization algorithms like iTunes Sound Check, for example, we will likely see a de-escalation in the loudness wars.

Keep in mind, this trend was driven not by mastering engineers, but rather by the egos of artists and their labels. To be honest, I think mastering engineers face a difficult dilemma in choosing whether to push the volume of a master to the point where it compromises the quality of the audio, or risk losing the gig to the guy down the street who will. Remember, the mastering engineer's name and reputation goes on the work, and if other bands, artists, or labels in the music industry are unimpressed with what they hear, those are potential new gigs they are losing, so it truly is a difficult situation they are forced to navigate. However, as new volume normalisation technologies like iTunes Sound Check continue to proliferate, we will likley see a welcome end to the loudness wars.

Now that you better understand the trade-off you engage in when making your masters louder, let's get back to the steps involved in mastering your songs.

Once you have your plug-in chain inserted across your first mix and a level meter on your output/master fader, you are ready to add gain with your limiter. But before you do so, bypass the EQ and compressor. Even though they come before the limiter in the plug-in chain, I like to bring up my master level with the limiter first. Then I will be better able to determine whether or not my mix could benefit from further compression and EQ. It is not a given that I will use an EQ or compressor, but I know I will need a limiter in order to bring my mixes up to the volume of standard commercial releases.

I recommend setting the amount of gain you add with the limiter at the loudest spot in the song. As mentioned earlier, the loudest spot in the song is where the most gain reduction will occur, and this is what we want to be careful not to overdo. Some limiters, like the Waves L series, don't have a gain parameter but rather a threshold parameter which you would simply lower to achieve this added gain. The result is the same.

Be sure to watch the RMS level on your level meter as you add gain from your limiter, and remember the recommended levels we discussed (somewhere in the range of –14 dBFS to –8 dBFS).

Once you have the level up in this range, it's a good idea to reference some other great-sounding masters in your genre. Doing so will help attune your ears to the speakers and room you are working in, helping you compensate for any inaccuracies in what you're hearing. For example, if your reference master sounds a little thin in the low end and your master sounds boomy, you likely have a problem.

Obviously, it's not ideal to work in rooms that have sonic problems, but let's be honest, most rooms do. If you've ever seen pictures of the control room at Abbey Road in the 1960s, you'll notice it was full of hard surfaces, yet the Beatles' records turned out pretty good! There are some smart, simple things you can do to improve the sound of your room and how well mixes/masters will translate in other environments on other speakers. (Please see "Optimizing Your Recording Space" on p. 165–167.)

Compressing

Next, we will un-bypass our compressor and set it up. Remember, you are compressing your entire mix, so you don't want to do too much. Here are some recommended ranges to stay within:

- **Gain reduction**: 1–2 dBs is usually enough.
- **Ratio**: 1.5:1– 3:1
- **Attack time**: 10–50 ms
- **Release time**: 50–300 ms
- **Soft knee**
- **Circuit types**: Any can work. Please refer to "Compressor Circuit Types" on p. 196.

I don't always like what the compressor adds and therefore don't always use one when I master. My hope is it can add some cohesion and excitement to the mix and pull it forward slightly; however, if I feel that the music sounds less open, I may forgo using the compressor.

EQ'ing

Next, we will take a look at using mastering EQ. EQ'ing your mix is tricky, and depending on how developed your ears and skills are, you could easily do more harm than good, so proceed cautiously with EQ at the mastering stage. Most mastering engineers rarely use boosts or cuts of more than a few dBs. To be honest, it's rare that I even do more than 1 dB. If a mix requires such radical tonal adjustments, you might consider refining it before mastering it.

Sometimes this becomes clearer when you hear all of your mixes together and begin referencing other commercial releases during the mastering session. One advantage of mastering your own mixes is being able to recall and adjust the mix so easily.

Let's outline a few practical goals when applying mastering EQ.

- Set a high-pass filter at 20 or 25 Hz. There really isn't anything useful that low, and it's taking away headroom from how loud you can make your masters before clipping.
- Use EQ to alter the overall frequency balance or tone of the master.
- Use EQ to help make all the songs in your project sound consistent in tone.
- Accentuate or de-accentuate a particular instrument.

Let's look at these goals one at a time.

As you A/B with your reference mixes you may, for example, hear that your mix lacks a little bottom end. If so, try adding some lows by boosting about 1 dB near 90 Hz. This would change the frequency balance slightly, placing a little more focus on the lows (and, as a result, less on the highs). Another example of using EQ to alter the frequency balance might be using a high shelf to boost from around 16K and above, opening up the top end and adding some air to the master.

Another reason I'll use mastering EQ is to get certain instruments to pop or jump out more. For example, let's say you wanted some guitars to bite a bit more. You might try boosting around 2 kHz. As you do so, however, listen closely to how this affects other instruments that also live in this frequency range.

The mid range is very tricky in that *so* many instruments and voices live there, struggling to be heard. So, as you boost at 2 kHz and hear the guitars become more pronounced, listen also to how this affects the vocals, snare, and keyboards. Search for the frequency that works best, and consider the bigger picture.

As you progress with the mastering you may notice that there are some tonal inconsistencies between songs. If, for example, one of the songs sounds a little more brittle or strident, we might use EQ to bring it more in line with the others by cutting slightly in the upper mids, say, between 3 kHz and 7 kHz. Or perhaps the source is coming from higher up, around 10 kHz. Again, using the boost-and-search technique will help you determine this and ensure that you don't make the sound too dull.

In addition to the high cut, you may try adding some low mids between 150 and 450 kHz. This will help warm up and fill out the sound, reducing brittleness. Just be careful that the sound doesn't become too murky or boxy as you boost in the low mids. Periodically bypassing the EQ or even just the particular EQ band will help you avoid this.

Final Mastering Steps

Double-check that the tone and volume of all of the masters is consistent. Also, listen to the volume of the vocal from song to song and ensure that it is fairly consistent throughout the project. Once you have the sound and level balanced on all the songs, there are still a few more tasks to perform, such as:

- Cleaning up silence at the beginning and end of the mix
- Sequencing the track list
- Doing fade-outs
- Inserting transition gaps between the songs
- Bouncing/printing and dithering each song

When you bounce or print your final masters, you will need to convert the files to 44.1K/16-bit to be compatible with most playback devices. Since you are converting the bit rate from 24-bit to 16-bit, you need to apply **dithering**. Dithering is the introduction of low-level white noise applied during the conversion process to cancel out the distortion that results from waveforms being truncated when you reduce the bit depth. It's essentially a good trade-off, and it preserves as much dynamic range as possible. Dithering helps compensate for the loss of dynamic range that occurs when you reduce the bit-depth from 24-bit to 16-bit. Every bit has six dB of dynamic range, so 24-bit files have 144 dB of dynamic range:

24-bit × 6 dBs = 144 dBs
16-bit files have 96 dB of dynamic range:
16-bit × 6 dBs = 96 dBs

Once all your masters are bounced/printed you are ready to make CDs, upload for digital streaming or download, or even make vinyl LPs, or cassettes.

Using Advanced Mastering Tools

We've now taken a look at the three main mastering tools, the EQ, the compressor, and the limiter. We went over how to use these tools to bring your masters up to the level of other commercial releases, add cohesion and excitement, and ensure that they have good frequency balance, consistent in tone and volume from one song to the next. Now there are some more advanced mastering tools I'd like to touch on, such as de-essers, multi-band compressors, harmonic exciters, stereo-wideners, and even reverbs.

Most of the time I prefer not to use these types of effects, but sometimes they can be helpful. I suggest mastering first just with EQ, compression, and limiting, and not moving on to these more advanced tools until you are ready.

De-Essers

We discussed **de-essers** earlier in this section in the mixing chapter. Remember, the de-esser is a high frequency compressor. Sometimes if a mix has either a sibilant vocal, brittle cymbals, or even general mid-range harshness, I will try using a de-esser to reduce this. Like with vocals, a de-esser may be preferable to EQ in dealing with an intermittent high frequency problem in that it has a threshold and will only turn down the highs when they become excessive and exceed the threshold you select on the de-esser.

Multi-Band Compressors

Another more advanced tool is a **multi-band compressor/limiter.** You can think of a multi-band compressor like multiple (often four) compressors in one unit. Each frequency band—the lows (approx. 20 Hz–100 Hz), the low-mids (approx. 100 Hz – 1 kHz), the upper-mids (approximately 1 kHz–10 kHz) and the highs (10 kHz–20 kHz)—has separate controls for the threshold, attack, release, ratio, and makeup gain. As a result, it can be used as a very surgical and precise tool to deal with intermittent, frequency-specific problems like boomy lows, strident lead guitar, sibilant vocals, or harsh cymbals.

Figure 18-2

As with regular compression, be careful not to boost or cut more than a few dBs. Often, less than 1 dB of gain reduction will do. For this type of process I don't use makeup gain, because my goal is only to reduce the problem area. Finally, be wary of using auto gain functions. Sometimes they can push things too hard. That's why we discussed how to set up your makeup gain manually, instead.

Stereo-Wideners

Stereo-wideners are another tool I will occasionally employ when mastering. The goal, as you might expect, will be to create more width and distinction between instruments in the middle of the stereo image and those panned toward the sides. It can also be a good way to make more room for the lead vocal or snare, as these instruments usually occupy the middle and can be competing with guitars and keyboards.

However, I find that these tools can be overused and periodically bypass them to ensure I am not compromising the sound of the vocal or the bass, which can often feel reduced when using stereo-wideners. When I use stereo-wideners at all, it's usually fairly subtle.

Harmonic Exciters and Dynamic Equalization

Harmonic exciters come in different forms and functionality depending on the manufacturing principles applied. As a result, it's difficult to generalize when explaining how they work, but two areas where they can be helpful are as dynamic equalizers or in generating harmonic detail that is absent in the original program material.

For example, let's say you want to brighten drums or guitars but only when there is a transient attack, not all the time, because it could add hiss or other problems. You could try using **dynamic equalization** that operates with a volume threshold to control the spots you are brightening.

Other times, our goal is to bring out a frequency that doesn't really exist in the source recording. In this scenario, a harmonic exciter may prove helpful. Using psychoacoustic processes like harmonic synthesis and phase manipulation, **harmonic exciters** are able to create perceived high and low frequency enhancements to the material, often resulting in mixes that sound clearer, louder, more detailed, present, and transparent. Be discerning, though. If your mix is already too bright, a harmonic exciter will only make it worse. Again, if I use this type of tool at all, it is very subtly.

Time-Based Effects

Finally, it's pretty rare that I will add **time-based effects** like reverb when mastering, as mastering just isn't usually the place to be overly adventurous. In the rare instances when I do use reverb, I usually use a very low wet/dry mix ratio so the effect is quite subtle. Some practical goals might be to increase the cohesion of the instruments or to add a little space and depth to the mix. The thing to watch out for is that your mix doesn't lose too much clarity or punch. These are the trade-offs when adding reverb.

Finally, once in a blue moon, I may automate other time-based effects like a delay, phaser, or flanger, for example, to create an interesting moment during a short section of a song.

Mastering with a Professional

If you have the budget to work with a professional mastering engineer, there are several good reasons to do so, but choose your candidate carefully. Mastering is an art, and it's subjective in many ways.

Professional mastering engineers have skilled, acute, experienced ears. They work in a studio environment that has been designed and built by architects who specialize in studio design and acoustics, creating a very accurate listening environment that will help produce results that will translate well to other speakers and listening environments. Additionally, they have high-end analog signal processing equipment that can add a great deal of depth, width, detail, accuracy, cohesion, character, and excitement to your masters. That's what you're paying for: the ears, the room and the equipment.

So, if you can afford it, and you've developed your career to the point where it deserves this level of professionalism and quality, you should hire a top professional. If you can't afford it, or your craft/career is still in the early stages of development, you really will benefit from learning this skill and doing it yourself.

If you do decide that you want to hire a professional mastering engineer, here are a few tips to optimize the experience and results.

Revisions

Inquire whether the mastering price includes any revisions in case you aren't entirely happy with the mastering. Many mastering engineers will charge an hourly rate for revisions, and some will charge their entire mastering fee again. Since it is not uncommon for top-drawer mastering engineers to charge $2,000–$3,000 or more to master an album, this is something you'll want to know in advance.

Reference Tracks

Bringing reference tracks to the session is another suggestion that can help ensure you understand what you're hearing. It's important to understand that a mastering studio is a new environment that you've never listened in before. In addition, you will likely be listening on speakers the size of an eight year-old child… They are huge! Trust me, you've never heard your music like this before, and if you have no frame of reference, you may be very surprised with what you hear when you listen again at home or in the car.

This is why it's important to "get your ears on"; listen to reference tracks (top quality commercial releases in your genre that you're intimately familiar with) for five or ten minutes before the session begins. That way, if you hear that the bass on your reference mix is way bigger than you were used to hearing it, you can be more assured if the bass on your mixes also sounds bigger than you are used to. On the other hand, if your mix sounds considerably weaker in the low end than your reference mixes, you'll know that it likely needs to be boosted in this range.

A/B'ing

Once the engineer is happy with a master, be sure to A/B it with the unmastered mix before moving on to the next song. Most mastering facilities can compensate for the volume difference between the mastered and unmastered mixes. This is important because volume is very seductive. Our first instinct when we hear something louder is to equate this with sounding better. But, if you listen closely, you may find that some of the balances and dynamics have changed. Often this is for the better, but not always, and you need to be certain.

Make sure that no particular instrument got too loud, that the music still has good dynamics, and that the tonal balance didn't shift too much in a direction you're not happy with. I can understand that it might be a little daunting to question the results of a highly skilled professional, but there's nothing wrong with bringing up any issues you are concerned about and discussing them. The best engineers will acknowledge when you have a good point and let you know when you need to trust their expertise.

Great artists know how their art should sound. They just don't always know how to get there. Communication is key to getting there. Learning this and becoming more self-sufficient are two of the most important missions of this section of the book.

Remember, you can use this as a reference guide and return to it as you develop your craft.

Part 4
Music Publishing

With
Michael Eames

Introduction

So far you have learned how to sing better, write your songs better, and even record the songs better. Now you need to start to focus on making money with your songs! And that's where music publishing comes in, because the heart of music publishing is **licensing**. Though we have to cover some basic concepts first, some of which will inform your writing process before you begin composing your next hit, ultimately the following concepts are presented so that you can see first what you need to do to *protect* yourself while you do your business, and then what you need to do to *generate* income for yourself, from licensing your songs to films, TV shows, etc., to pitching them to be recorded by other artists.

Music publishing is one of the most lucrative areas of the music business, so it's important to understand how it works because a lot of money is at stake. As you will see, it is a pennies business, but those pennies can add up quickly, even though technology currently has us struggling to make up for record sales that are no longer happening. But in the long run, I am very excited about the future of the music publishing business, as there is more consumption of music going on now (thanks to technology, ironically!) than probably ever before. But, as with all technological advances, it's about protecting our rights during the advances and fairly monetizing them. So let's get started with some important administrative concepts that provide the foundation for music publishing, and then move on to the creative stuff that will lead to you making some hard-earned money from your songs.

19 Always Start with the Basics

When most people hear the term "music publishing" they think of printed sheet music. This is a logical assumption, as that is how the publishing business started—songwriters would write songs; publishers would get the songs transcribed, engraved, and printed; and then salesmen would take the printed sheet music to bands, ensembles, and even individual musicians around the country and pitch them the songs to be performed live and recorded. But these days, the printed sheet music business is a very minor part of the overall music publishing business. The music publishing business is one of **rights**—the rights and privileges that are granted to creators by the copyright laws of the world. So to understand the music publishing business one needs to understand what each of the basic rights is and how it operates within existing copyright laws. We will address each of the three major areas, those being mechanical rights, performance rights, and synchronization rights. But first you need to understand the basic concept of copyright, the advantages it gives you, and how the copyright is split between the writer's share and the publisher's share.

Basic Concepts of Copyright

When the United States enacted its first Copyright Act in 1790, the intent was to provide creators and authors with the ability to claim exclusive property rights in their creations and to charge money for the sale or license of those creations. This provided the incentive to create in the first place—you want to spend your time creating something that can help you pay for your living expenses. But your ability to profit from your creations was granted for a limited period of time. Afterwards, your ideas and creations would fall into what is called the **public domain**—i.e., they could be used for free by the public without any further payment to you, the creator.

The laws have changed over the years, but the protection granted to your creations by the U.S. Copyright Law currently works like this. Whether you write a song by yourself or cowrite with others, the law currently provides for you to earn royalties off your song for the lifetime of the last author to remain alive and then an additional seventy years after that person's death. So let's say you wrote a song with your band mate in 2016 and your band mate passed away in 2056 but you lived twenty years longer (a morbid thought, I know, but bear with me). Since you were the last remaining author, your cowritten song would be afforded copyright protection for the sixty years you were alive after writing the song (i.e., from 2016 to 2076) and then for another seventy years after that. So your song written in 2016 would be given 130 years of copyright protection under current laws. This allows you, your family and your heirs the ability to make money off your song for a nice chunk of time, following which that song would fall into the public domain in the year 2146. At that point, anyone could record or use that song in any way they want without having to pay your heirs any royalties. Your creations at that point are no longer your (or your heirs') exclusive property.

Copyright Protection and Registration

What is important to understand is that the great advantages you get under the U.S. Copyright Law are automatically given to you once your song is embodied in some sort of physical form. That can be handwritten sheet music, a computer hard drive, or a recording you make onto a CD or some other physical medium. Though you automatically receive the protections of the Copyright Law once your song is in a physical form, you still should look into registering your finished song with the Copyright Office of the United States. The main advantage you get by doing so is that should anyone ever steal or **infringe** your song (i.e., take some or all of your song and try to pass it off as their own without your permission or incorporate a portion of your song into their own without your permission—more on this later), you cannot sue them in a federal court until you have registered the song with the Copyright Office. And, should you be successful in pursuing someone for infringing your song, the Copyright Law provides you with the ability to be paid **damages** (which are currently $150,000 per infringement for **willful**, i.e., intentional, infringement) but you will only receive the monetary damages starting on the date you registered your song with the Copyright Office. You may have heard or read somewhere that you can also secure a "poor man's copyright" by mailing a copy of your song to yourself and keeping the envelope sealed. All this does is prove that your song existed at a certain point in time. And this can be important. But, while your copyright protection went into effect at the moment you put your song into some physical form, that protection doesn't include the ability to receive damages for infringement in a federal court unless you have registered the work with the Copyright Office.

WAS YOUR SONG STOLEN?

Hopefully you will never be in this situation ... but what if a song came out that became a hit, and you felt that it took part or all of your existing song? Having a valid copyright registration form from the Copyright Office doesn't mean that you will automatically receive any income from an infringing song. The most important thing when pursuing someone for copyright infringement is to prove that the party you are accusing of stealing your song (the defendant) had access to your song. You (the plaintiff) need to prove how and when the defendant could have come into contact with your song. If you can't prove access, then you can't win a copyright infringement action.

Registering a song with the U.S. Copyright Office is fairly easy, but there are a few things to keep in mind. For musical works, there are two different types of forms that would apply—the PA form and the SR form.

The PA Copyright Form

The PA form ("PA" stands for "performing arts") is a form that covers the intangible musical composition (i.e., music and/or lyrics and not the recording that embodies the composition—more on that shortly). You can see the forms (as well as the newer electronic way to file via the eCO system) at **www.copyright.gov/eco/**. Completing the form is relatively straightforward. The main information you need to provide is:

- The author name(s)
- The year of birth and/or death for each author
- Each author's country of nationality or residence
- Whether the author's contribution is anonymous (i.e., unnamed) or pseudonymous (i.e., using any name other than the author's legal name)
- The nature of each author's contribution (i.e., music, lyrics, or both)
- The year in which the composition was created
- The year in which the composition was **published** or offered for sale for the first time (if it has yet)
- The copyright claimants (i.e., the publisher(s) of the work)

There are some other items of information you need to provide, and the form you download includes instructions and explanations of what is required in each of the fields. We are going to talk about what being the **publisher** of a work means in the next section. But first let's address the SR form.

The SR Copyright Form

The SR form ("SR" stands for "sound recording") is a form that covers any recording of a musical composition (whether or not you wrote or own the musical composition). It doesn't matter what format the recording is in (e.g., CD or digital file, etc.), as long as you create a recording and it is embodied in physical form then you have the ability to publicly register your ownership to your recording. The SR form requires the same author information as the PA form. As a result, there is a nice option with the SR form. Should you be the sole author and claimant of your composition *and* the sole author and claimant of your recording of that composition, on the SR form you can claim copyright in *both* the composition and the recording on the one form (and then not have to file a separate PA form). To do this, under "Nature of Authorship" you would list something like "music, lyrics, producer of recording, performer on recording" and then you obtain copyright protection of all those elements on the one form. Note that this *cannot* be done on the PA form. But when you are in the unique situation where the authors of both the composition and the recording are one and the same (whether one individual or multiple ones), the SR form can be legally used to cover all, and this saves you the cost of filing two separate forms. See the sidebar for current U.S. copyright registration fees.

COPYRIGHT REGISTRATION FEES AS OF JULY 2015

$35—online registration through the eCO system for any form with one author who is also the claimant
$55—online registration through the eCO system for each form in any other scenarios
$85—registration via the pdf forms you can download and print

It is worth noting that, regardless of whether you are submitting a PA or an SR form, you are required to submit with your copyright registration what is called a **deposit copy**. This is the physical representation of your creation (even if just a digital file via the eCO system) and must accompany your registration, as the Copyright Office needs a copy of the underlying work to review it and include it in the files once your form is processed and given its unique copyright registration number. Then you receive an official acknowledgement from the Copyright Office that your registration was processed and your copyright registration officially exists as of the date you initially submitted it to them for processing. Note that as of this writing, it takes the Copyright Office eight months to process registrations submitted via the eCO system and thirteen months via the paper/pdf forms.

Now that we have established how to officially register all rights to your songs that will enable you to make money from them, let's examine what a publisher is to help us better understand the rights themselves.

Writer vs. Publisher

Of course you know who the songwriter is. But what about the publisher? That term can be used in a variety of ways and in a variety of contexts and it admittedly can get confusing at times. Ultimately, the publisher of a song is the *owner* of the song. And with that ownership comes the control of the various rights that earn the songwriter the income he or she deserves for creating the song. It must be noted that as soon as you write a song and embody it in physical form, *you* are immediately considered the publisher of the song since you own it as you created it. You are always the publisher until you sign a piece of paper that says you are assigning some or all ownership to someone else. You don't need to set up an actual publishing company to start. Creating a publishing company becomes more pressing when you initiate some sort of activity or airplay that could result in the generation of performance royalties (which we will cover in a later section when we get to the right of public performance that the Copyright Law gives us).

But for now, it's important to understand that in any music publishing copyright there is the **writer's share** and the **publisher's share**. Look at it in terms of a pie:

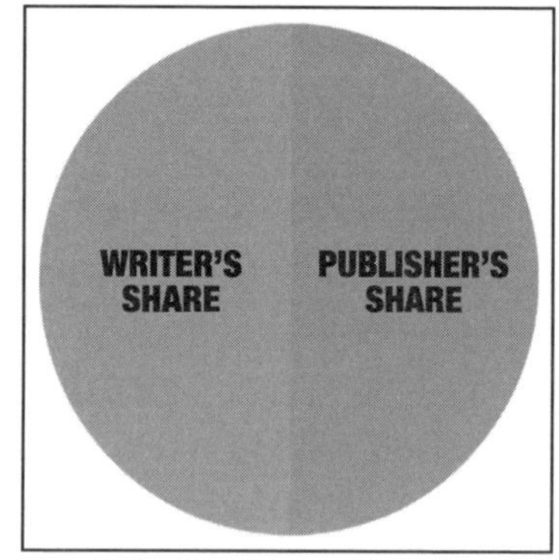

The writer's share comprises half of the copyright (or "pie"), and the publisher's share comprises the other half of the copyright (or "pie"). Remember that the ownership and control reside in the publisher's share. Realizing that these are two different halves of the copyright will become important as we talk about how money is split up when royalties are earned.

Cowriting

Many of you have cowritten or will cowrite a song with one or more people. It is important to note that the Copyright Law assumes an equal split amongst however many writers there are unless there is a signed written document that everyone has signed that states otherwise. But before you cowrite, it is a good idea to sit down with the person or people you will write with and discuss how everyone approaches dividing up songs. Some folks feel that the music is 50 percent and the lyrics are the other 50 percent. In the music business of today, where cool and "hip" instrumental tracks are a key part of commercial popular songs, the concept of **track writers** and **top-liners** has developed. As the name implies, the track writer is a writer/producer who is typically adept at beats. Whether it be in EDM, R&B, or hip-hop, their strength is creating instrumental tracks that grab the ear upon which songs can be built. The top-line writers are those who are adept at melody and/or lyrics. Some top-liners are stronger with melody and some stronger with lyric, and some are strong at both (and these latter ones are the most in demand). It is very common in today's music industry that the track writers and top-liners may never meet in person. But writing to track can be a bit of a sticky situation when one is sorting out splits between writers as the more successful track writers feel that their track alone should get 50 percent of the song ultimately created, which leaves the top line (the melody and lyric, which some consider to be 50 percent each of the song anyway) to get 50 percent. So then negotiation ensues and many times it comes down to leverage and who has the most clout or credits. It is always good practice, before you cowrite, to have a sense of how your potential cowriters approach writer splits. You would be amazed at how many songs that come out on records end up with split disputes between the writers—which only holds up any royalties that need to be paid. Then, after the song is done, it is advisable to have all writers sign a split sheet. It can be a simple document showing the split to each writer (even if they are equal) and then each writer's signature. Then there is a written document that shows that each person acknowledged—in writing—how the song is to be split amongst everyone. This can save many a headache later.

One final note on writing to track: many times a completed track will get sent to multiple top-liners. This can get dicey from a copyright perspective, because multiple top lines that were crafted to the same underlying track may end up sounding similar. I suggest that if you write to a track and it does *not* get selected as the final topline, you obtain permission in writing from the track writer(s) to take your topline and create another track around it. Obviously, the new track can't follow or sound like the original track, but you don't want your top line to be unusable if it is not selected to be paired to the original track. Again, it's all about communication, and as long as all parties involved in the cowriting process are communicating their thoughts and desires, then an agreement can usually be reached.

Now that we have covered basic copyright concepts and defined the writer and the publisher, let's start to address each of the rights granted to us in the Copyright Law that enable us to make some dough!

Mechanical Rights

The use of the term "mechanical" to describe this initial set of rights derives from the need to "mechanically reproduce" the item that stores your music for playback. When this right was first set up it was tied to piano player rolls in the early 1900s. Then came 78 rpm records, vinyl albums, cassettes, 8-tracks, CDs, and now the digital download. Every single one of these formats throughout the last hundred-plus years has had to involve "reproducing" a song in order for it to be made available for sale to the public. Everything before the digital download involved a machine that literally had to manufacture an individual unit of something onto which each song was copied. The digital download of today is still a copy—it's just made from a physical copy on a hard drive or server and then you are allowed to download the copy onto your hard drive. Whether you choose to "burn" the song onto physical media like a CD or not, you have still enabled a copy to be made and every time a copy is made a royalty must be paid. That is the **mechanical royalty**. The mechanical royalty has always been specifically stated in the U.S. Copyright Law and it is what is specifically called a **penny rate**—it is a fixed amount based on the duration of the song. Because it has always been determined by the law—i.e., by statute—you will also hear the mechanical royalty referred to as a **statutory royalty** in publishing circles. It started out in the early 1900s as 2 cents and stayed at this level until January 1, 1978, when the Copyright Law underwent a massive update that provided for continued escalation until the current mechanical rate of 9.1 cents for a song that is five minutes or less. See the sidebar for the calculation of a song that is over five minutes in length.

WHAT IF MY SONG IS A LONG SONG?

For a song over five minutes in length you calculate the mechanical royalty payable as follows:
A duration of 5:01–6:00 (min:sec) is 6 times 1.75 cents per minute or 10.5 cents.
A duration of 6:01–7:00 (min:sec) is 7 times 1.75 cents per minute or 12.25 cents.
Etc.

This 9.1 cents is the writer's share and publisher's share *combined.* So 4.55 cents is to be shared with the writer(s), and 4.55 cents is to be shared with the publisher(s). And if you are both, and the only writer and publisher, you get to keep the entire 9.1 cents! So if you had a song on a single or an album that sold 1 million copies you would gross $91,000. Not bad! This rate is specific to the U.S. (Canada's current mechanical rate, for comparison, is 8.3 Canadian cents for a song that is five minutes or less or 1.66 Canadian cents per minute (or fraction thereof) for a song that is over five minutes.)

First Use

An important thing to remember is that you as the songwriter and the publisher can control what is called the **first use** of your song. In other words, the Copyright Law gives you the ability to determine what will be the first recording of your song offered for sale to the public. So if you wrote a song and you are an artist, but someone else heard your song and wanted to record it themselves, you can deny them that and reserve the song for yourself. But the law states that once any composition is offered for sale to the public for that first time, you as the songwriter and publisher cannot stop anyone else from recording your song, as long as they adhere to certain requirements in the law (the **compulsory provisions**) that pertain to notifying you about their intended use and accounting to you on a monthly basis for units sold. But most artists and record labels do not want to have to pay on a monthly basis, so they request what is called a mechanical license to record your song.

The Mechanical License

When others want to record your song they need to request your permission to do so—and your permission comes in the form of what is called a mechanical license. The license that you issue for use of your song has to include the following information:

- Song title (of course!)
- Artist who will record the song
- Record label that release the album (or single or EP)
- Release date
- UPC (bar code) of the album (or single) being released
- ISRC of the recording of your song (see sidebar)
- Duration of the recording of your song

As we discussed earlier, the timing of the song will indicate what royalty you will be paid (e.g., if under five minutes, then 9.1 cents). And once you issue the license for the album above and both parties sign the license, then you have a binding document that gives the other party the ability to sell a recording of your song in exchange for paying you royalties. The license also stipulates that should the label *not* pay you royalties, you have the ability to terminate the license. In failing to live up to the obligations they took on, the label is infringing your song, and you can choose to sue them for copyright infringement.

WHAT IS AN ISRC CODE?

ISRC stands for International Standard Recording Code. Basically, the ISRC is the "social security number" for a master recording. It is a unique identifier that follows the master recording wherever it gets sold, and accountings for digital downloads in particular will always reference that number, as will any digital service that streams that recording (e.g., Spotify and Apple Music). More information can be obtained at www.usisrc.org.

IS A PHONE RINGTONE A MECHANICAL, TOO?

Though phone ringtones are not as popular as they once were, they still exist, and the mechanical rate payable for a ringtone is actually a fixed 24 cents compared to the 9.1 cents for a "normal" mechanical, since the ringtone is usually $2.00 or more to buy, whereas the typical single-song download costs $0.99 to $1.29. Publishing is a pennies business, but the pennies can add up quickly!

Controlled Compositions Clause

A unique concept in the world of mechanical licensing that is applicable to artists is the controlled compositions clause. It can be complex language, but in the end it is a very simple idea. That is, the record companies asked themselves back in the 1970s (in the age of the singer-songwriter) why, when they signed artists who wrote their own songs, they should pay out full royalty rates on both the publishing side (i.e., the mechanical rate) and the artist side (i.e., the artist royalty). So they created a clause in the artist's recording agreement that limits what artists who write their own songs get paid by typically doing the following:

- On a per song basis, instead of paying the full statutory mechanical rate of 9.1 cents, the record company only agrees to pay 75 percent of that full rate (or 6.825 cents) for any songs written or cowritten by the artist; and . . .
- On an aggregate basis, the record company agrees to pay that 75 percent rate on no more than ten songs, which in effect creates a static pool of money payable on mechanical royalties of 68.25 cents.

Though there can be negotiated terms different than the above, the above is the most "classic" example. So look at the math. If you are an artist who writes all your own material, whether your album has ten songs or fourteen songs, you will still only get paid a maximum of 68.25 cents for the mechanical royalties from the sale of your record. But the math can be especially cruel when you cowrite songs and your cowriters have to be paid the full mechanical rate out of your static pool that has been based on 75 percent of the full rate. Let's look at an example. Let's say you have a twelve-song album and every song on your record was cowritten fifty-fifty with another writer (i.e., a writer who is not signatory to your recording agreement and is not bound to the same controlled compositions language). Your cowriter therefore has to be paid the full 100 percent rate on his or her half of each of the twelve songs. Fifty percent of the full rate of 9.1 cents is 4.55 cents. And twelve songs times 4.55 cents is 54.6 cents. So out of your static pool of 68.25 cents, you have to pay your co-writer 54.6 cents, which leaves only 13.65 cents left over for you as a songwriter to be paid on your 50 percent of the twelve songs on your record. Crazy! But that's the danger of this kind of language in a recording agreement. For artists who are not yet known, the record label usually has the leverage in the negotiation of your recording agreement and you will likely not be able to avoid having to agree to *some* sort of controlled compositions language. This is why an experienced lawyer is a key element of your team.

Cover Songs

Let's say you decide as an artist to record someone else's song on your record (i.e., a **cover recording**). The same rules relating to mechanical licensing that apply when you are the writer and publisher also apply in the reverse. You need to find out who the publisher(s) are of the song you want to record and request a mechanical license from those publisher(s), and you have to pay the full 9.1 cents for each copy of your record sold. Assuming you are doing a smaller pressing of your record (1,000 physical copies is typical), you usually have to prepay for those 1,000 units, so when the mechanical license is issued to you by the publisher(s) of the song you covered you typically have to send them $91.00 to cover those 1,000 copies for 100 percent of the song. If there are multiple publishers and they each control a different share, then they only receive their pro-rata share of that $91.00.

Maybe you've covered someone's song on your record but don't know how to figure out who the publisher(s) are? A company called the Harry Fox Agency (or HFA at harryfox.com) handles mechanical rights for publishers, including licensing anyone who uses songs in any mechanical reproduction. Over the years they have compiled a pretty comprehensive database of song information that you can access at www.songfile.com. The website will indicate what share HFA can license to you (in many cases you will find that they could license 100 percent). You can then initiate the mechanical license request at www.songfile.com and even pay for the royalties required online and with your credit card (plus a transaction fee to HFA for providing their licensing services). Should HFA not represent 100 percent of the song, you can usually find the remaining share by searching the websites of the four performing rights societies in the U.S. (ASCAP, BMI, SESAC, and new arrival GMR) but more on that in our next section on performance rights.

Label Copy

One last important item pertaining to mechanical licenses is the concept of **label copy**. With the advent of the digital download, there are more and more records that are being offered for sale where the only artwork is the cover art. But when physical copies of records are manufactured, the artwork typically includes what is called "label copy," which is a listing of all the songs on the record along with credits to the songwriters and the publishers of each of the songs. When you are the songwriter and not the artist, the label copy is your main credit, and it is important to make sure that the information is correct. This public announcement of your accomplishment gets disseminated worldwide into many record release and copyright databases, and it is important that your songwriter and publisher information is listed and is spelled correctly!

Public Performance Rights

In addition to the mechanical right, the Copyright Law also provides us the right to control the public performance of our musical compositions. This right covers "public" uses such as:

- Performances of music (whether live or via radio) in concert venues, hotels, bars, restaurants, coffee shops, etc.
- Performances on radio stations
- Performances on TV stations or networks
- Performances on the Internet

Though the Copyright Law gives us as writers and publishers the ability to license this right ourselves, it would be pretty much impossible for all of us to negotiate licenses between ourselves and every venue, radio station, TV station, etc. using our music, so the concept of the Performing Rights Organizations (or PROs) arose. These organizations aggregate the performing rights of writers and publishers and then negotiate licenses with all the users of music, collect the income from those licenses, and distribute that income after first deducting their operating expenses. In the U.S., there are three well-known PROs, ASCAP, BMI, and SESAC, and a fourth, GMR, founded in 2013. Let's do a brief overview of each of them.

ASCAP (www.ascap.com)

ASCAP (an acronym for the nonprofit American Society of Composers, Authors and Publishers) was the first PRO to be established in the U.S. and was founded in 1914 by songwriter Victor Herbert to protect the performing rights of himself and his Tin Pan Alley contemporaries like Jerome Kern and John Philip Sousa as well as many others. But ASCAP ran into trouble in the ensuing twenty-five years due to complaints that the organization had a monopoly and was raising licensing rates too high. The Justice Department sued ASCAP for anti-trust reasons in both 1937 (in an effort that was abandoned) and 1941. As a result of the 1941 case, ASCAP signed what is referred to as a **consent decree**, stipulating that ASCAP was required to set "fair rates" and could not discriminate against any users of music. Should a user of music feel that the rate they are being asked to pay is not fair, they are able to litigate that issue with the federal court that oversees ASCAP's consent decree. (More on the consent decree later on in this section after we have covered the other PROs.)

ASCAP is owned and run by its over half a million members, who are songwriters, composers, and music publishers, and represents millions of songs. ASCAP is governed by twenty-four members of their Board of Directors, twelve of whom are songwriters or composers and the other twelve of whom are music publishers. As of this writing, songwriter Paul Williams ("We've Only Just Begun," "Rainy Days and Mondays" and "The Rainbow Connection" from 1979's *The Muppet Movie*) is the president of ASCAP and chaiman of the board of directors. In spring 2015 ASCAP announced that they were the first PRO in the world to achieve over $1 billion in revenue (for calendar year 2014) and of that amount $883 million was distributed to its members.

BMI (www.bmi.com)

BMI (an acronym for the nonprofit Broadcast Music, Inc.) was founded in 1939 by the broadcasters as a response to ASCAP trying to increase the fees they were being asked to pay—which became the subject of the Justice Department's anti-trust actions mentioned above. So in order to provide competition, the broadcasters started BMI as their own PRO and in 1941 signed their own consent decree similar to ASCAP's.

Rhythm and blues music and country music formed the initial bulk of material represented by BMI when they opened their doors, because they were genres that were not really being represented at ASCAP. BMI proudly established at their outset an open-door policy where any songwriter of any genre of music could become a BMI member. BMI now also has over a half million members and represents millions of songs. Its board of directors consists of leaders in the broadcast industry. As of this writing, BMI is run by its president and CEO, Michael O'Neill, who has risen through their ranks for the last twenty years. For its fiscal year ending June 30, 2015, BMI announced record gross revenues of $1.013 billion and distributed $877 million of this to its members.

SESAC (www.sesac.com)

SESAC (originally an acronym for Society of European Stage Authors and Composers, but the society stopped using the full name in 1940) was founded in 1930 by German immigrant Paul Heinecke in an effort to help European publishers with their American royalties. In its early years, SESAC not only represented music from Europe but also represented an extensive gospel catalogue. In 1992 SESAC was purchased by a collection of investors including Stephen Swid, Allen & Co., Freddie Gershon, and Ira Smith. In 2013 the private equity firm Rizvi Traverse Management bought a 75 percent stake in SESAC for a reported $600 million. As a privately owned, for-profit company, SESAC does not disclose its financials. SESAC controls a minority of the market compared to ASCAP and BMI but is working aggressively to change that. As of this writing, SESAC is run by its chairman and CEO, John Josephson, who has been a board member of SESAC since 1992 and was appointed to this new position in 2014. SESAC does not accept everyone who applies for membership—they must approve you or invite you to join.

GMR (www.globalmusicrights.com)

GMR (an acronym for Global Music Rights) is the fourth and newest PRO option in the U.S. It was started in 2013 by music industry mogul and legendary manager Irving Azoff and PRO executive Randy Grimmett. GMR is an invitation-only PRO that so far only represents the performing rights of superstar artists and songwriters such as Don Henley and Glenn Frey (of the Eagles), Pharrell Williams, Ryan Tedder, Shane McAnally, Bruno Mars, members of Fleetwood Mac, and the estates of John Lennon and Ira Gershwin, among others. GMR feels that through technological efficiency they will be able to extract and distribute higher royalties for their clients then the current distribution models at rivals ASCAP and BMI. GMR, like SESAC, is a private, for-profit company, and it will be interesting to see how their repertory develops over the next several years.

Which One Do I Join?

These PROs operate mainly through the issuance of what are called **blanket licenses**. They negotiate licenses with TV stations both big and small, radio stations both big and small, websites, etc., and for one blanket fee these users get the ability to perform every composition in that PRO's catalogue. The license fees in these blanket licenses are typically a percentage of that media or entity's advertising revenues for a year. So, for the most part, as long as a TV or radio station has licenses in place with all of these PROs, it can play anything from any of their catalogues.

Each PRO has its own distribution rules, and it is a subject of constant debate as to which PRO might pay better than another. Needless to say, they are all in competition with each other, and my recommendation is that, if geographically possible, you try to meet with writer/publisher representatives from each of them and determine who seems to like your music the most and who you feel "gets you," because a proactive and close relationship with advocates at your PRO can do a lot for your career. All the PROs have dedicated staffs whose job it is not only to help their writer and publisher members with anything administrative, but also in many cases to assist with collaborations and introductions to industry people who could potentially help move your career forward. Most of these PROs also sponsor various workshops and events for the benefit of their members in all aspects of the industry. Their respective websites are great sources of information both on the music publishing industry in general as well as their specific organizations.

Song Registration

The most important thing to understand with any of these PROs is that you must join whichever one you chose as two different member types—a writer member and a publisher member. They are two different agreements and thus you receive two different streams of income from the PRO when your music gets performed anywhere. If you sign up as a writer and not a publisher, you will not receive your publisher's share of income, and vice versa. Once you are both a writer and publisher member (see sidebar "What Is a Publishing Company?"), the PRO won't know what to pay you on if you don't register your songs with them! All the PROs' websites allow online registration of works, so we won't go into each PRO's procedures, which are all very similar. But I cannot stress enough that once you create a song and you put it out to the public in any fashion (even if just playing live at a local bar), you need to make sure that you register that song with your PRO. They will need all the writer names and the splits between them, and all the publishing company names and the splits between them. You can also indicate what your artist or band name is as the "performing artist" on the song registration. This information can sometimes be helpful in allowing the PRO to match your song registration to incoming performance data so that ultimately you can receive the royalties due you. All of these PROs share your song registration data with their sister PROs around the world in every country where they have reciprocal agreements, so that, should you earn royalties for performances taking place in another country, then the local PRO in that country knows where to send your royalties. We will address this situation in more detail in a later section on "International Publishing."

WHAT IS A PUBLISHING COMPANY?

When you sign up to be a publisher at a PRO you have to choose a company name. You usually have to list three choices in order of preference so that there are other names to try to secure for you should your first choice be already in use by someone else. Please know that this does not mean you must set up a real company to go with this name. The PRO publishing company names are just names—you can set one up and list yourself as the owner and use your social security number for tax purposes. Once you start earning significant money, then you can discuss with your accountant whether you would benefit tax-wise from setting up a corporation to receive your income rather than receiving it personally.

What and How You Get Paid

In the end, the PROs are doing their job when you are receiving the royalties you are rightfully owed. It is a very complex topic to address how each and every PRO tracks performances and pays out on them, but one general concept that is worth knowing about is being paid on either a **census** basis or a **survey** basis. A census basis means that a PRO pays on *every* performance that occurs. This is the case for the major TV networks like ABC, CBS, and NBC, as well as the major cable outlets like HBO and Showtime. This is also the case for the major metropolitan radio markets like New York City, Los Angeles, and others. A survey basis means that the PRO will survey a particular medium or geographical area for a limited and random period of time (or times), and if your song gets played and identified during the survey period, then you will get paid. But if your song gets performed during a time when your PRO is *not* surveying that area or medium, then you will *not* get paid. Everyone knows it's not a perfect system, but the PROs have to do what's called "follow the dollar." Where their blanket fees are large for the larger TV networks or larger radio stations in the larger cities, then it makes economic sense to spend the time and money to identify all performances from those. But the smaller the media and the smaller the city, the smaller the ad revenue is going to be, so therefore the blanket license fee will be that much smaller, and there comes a point where you can't spend more money trying to track performance data then the money a PRO is being paid for that blanket license. This makes complete sense. But it does sometimes mean that you will have performances that don't get recognized and paid. The only consolation is that the royalty you are missing would be small anyway, since that medium is being tracked on a survey basis, and the blanket license fee out of which you would be paid is small. The logic follows in reverse—the more performances you are able to get in the big TV and radio markets, then the higher your royalties will be. And they can add up to be substantial—particularly for radio. A huge commercial radio single can still generate well over $1 million in performance royalties in the U.S. alone, but those are hard to come by.

Where You Won't Get Paid

One exception where you won't get paid performance royalties that is worth mentioning is for movie theaters. You will recall the anti-trust actions against ASCAP in the 1940s that resulted in the creation of BMI. In 1942, a group of motion-picture theater owners brought a similar anti-trust action against ASCAP. The case, which was finally decided in 1948, was called *Alden Rochelle, Inc. vs. ASCAP*. The theater owners brought the action for what they felt were monopolistic practices with regard to the royalties that the theaters were at the time required to pay to show movies in their theaters. ASCAP lost this action, and as a result no PRO in the U.S. is able to collect performance royalties from theaters in the U.S. When we as publishers grant licenses to the movie studios we are also granting them the performance license to play our music in the theaters in the U.S. Though this is a bummer, it has been this way since 1948 and will likely never change. But the silver lining (which will be covered later in a bit more detail when we get to "International and Sub-publishing") is that in the remaining countries in the majority of the world, songwriters and music publishers do receive royalties from the gross box office receipts of movies shown in these countries. And when your song is used in a very successful movie, this can add up significantly.

Synchronization Rights

The third most important right that the Copyright Law gives us is the right of synchronization—or the right to be able to control the synchronizing of our music with a visual image. And, given our previous discussion about the musical composition and the sound recording embodying that composition as being two separate copyrights and therefore permissions, you should always know that you are in control of where and when your music can be synchronized and to what. This might include, just for starters,

- Theatrical films
- Made-for-TV films
- TV series
- Trailers for movies
- Promos for TV series
- TV commercials
- Radio commercials
- Internet commercials
- Video games
- Mobile phone games

You get the idea. Anywhere you can think of a visual image playing with music accompanying it, that is a synchronization right and you get to control it. How you get paid for that right is a bit more complex than the two previous rights of mechanical and performance.

What Do I Charge?

Depending on how you look at it, the fact that the synchronization world is essentially the "wild, wild west" could be a good thing or a bad thing. I personally feel it is a good thing. Let me explain. In the world of mechanical rights, there is very little negotiation necessary—if you want to record a song, then as long as the song has already had its first use, you can apply for a mechanical license (with no fear of rejection). And you know that you just have to pay 9.1 cents for every copy you sell, because that is the set rate by Copyright Law. What's involved is just more administrative paperwork and payment than anything else. In the world of performance rights, though the behind-the-scenes workings can get complex, once you have the necessary blanket licenses you can perform whatever you want (without fear of rejection), and the PRO takes care of paying the writer and publisher. The main responsibility of the writer and publisher is to just register their song with the PRO. But in the world of synchronization, we as the writer and the publisher have essentially complete control. We can say yes or no to the use of our music—and no means no, it won't happen. Some songwriters and artists don't want their music to be synchronized with anything, especially commercials (they don't want to endorse any products). And that's a personal choice. But for the purposes of this explanation, I'm going to assume that you *do* want your music synchronized and to make money off these kinds of uses. So when someone is interested in using a song of yours in any of these types of projects, there is important information you need to be provided:

- What is the context of the use? (E.g., is it in a scene with drug use or violence or sex? Or in any context that might be objectionable to you or that you feel denigrates the song in any way? If so, you can always deny the potential use as a result.)
- What is the timing of the use? (E.g., five or ten seconds? Two minutes? The longer your song is played, the bigger the fee that should be paid.)
- How prominently is the song used? (E.g., is it being used as background in a bar scene, or is it the sole focus of attention in a montage? The more featured the use, the bigger the fee that should be paid.)
- What media does the project need to license your song for? (E.g., TV only? DVD? Movie theaters? Internet? The more media they need rights for, the bigger the fee that should be paid.)
- What territory does the project need to license your song for? (Most films and TV shows these days require worldwide rights, but commercials in particular typically will limit the territory to whatever they need so as to not pay for more than they need to.)
- What period of time does the project need the license of your song for? (Most film and TV projects will want rights **in perpetuity**, which means forever, but commercials in particular will likely only require however long their commercial will run, which could be from one day up to one year or anywhere in between.)

TYPICAL INDIE SYNCH/MASTER USE FEES

TV FEES: Most TV projects these days will ask for all media excluding theatrical rights (since most TV shows will never be shown in movie theaters), for the territory of the world in perpetuity. And most indie music is licensed **one-stop**, meaning that the publishing and the master are licensed together as one whole. Typical TV fees then for indie artists will fall into the range of $1,000–$5,000 all-in (meaning half the fee is publishing and half is master).

FILM FEES: Most films will want all media *including* theatrical, worldwide in perpetuity, and are also typically licensed as one-stop. Film fees can range more broadly depending on how the song is used and the budget of the project, so I would put the range at $1,000–$10,000 all-in.

TYPICAL MAJOR LABEL SYNCH/MASTER USE FEES

TV FEES: For the same rights mentioned above in the indie fees box (all media excluding theatrical rights, worldwide in perpetuity), major label artists and well-known songs will generally be paid $10,000–$22,000 just for 100 percent of the publishing and then the same for the master recording.

FILM FEES: For the same rights described in the indie fees box, the range for major label artists can be much broader given the budget of the film and the way the song is used. I would put the film range for major label artists and well-known songs into the $15,000–$125,000 range just for 100 percent of the publishing, and then the master would receive a similar fee. Obviously, the high end of that range would be merited by a very popular artist or very well-known song in a more featured spot.

Everyone Is Looking to Synch

As record sales have been going down in recent years thanks to streaming (more on that in the next section), the industry has been relying on synchronization to help make up for income that they used to be able to count on from mechanical royalties in particular. So the synchronization world has become *very* competitive, and the indie artist's song can be vying for the same spot as a major label artist.

One of the things I love about a synchronization use is that it can tie together all of our main rights under the Copyright Law. For example:

- The initial use in a film or TV show, for example, covers the synchronization right;
- Once that project airs on TV anywhere in the world or in theaters outside the U.S., then performance royalties are generated and paid; and
- If the licensed project decides to release a soundtrack album to go along with the project and your song is included, then you can generate mechanical royalties.

So successful synchronization uses can tap into all potential sources of income and pay off in a big way. The best example I can think of is the late film composer James Horner, who composed the original score to the highest-grossing film of all time, James Cameron's *Titanic* (starring Leonardo DiCaprio and Kate Winslet). Horner composed a melody that he decided to turn into a song, so he enlisted lyricist Will Jennings and the song "My Heart Will Go On" was created. Celine Dion was brought in to sing the song, which not only appeared over the end titles of the movie but was also included on the soundtrack album to the film, and on Dion's solo album released around the same time. The song went number one on record airplay charts all over the world and is considered one of the best-selling singles of all time. The *Titanic* soundtrack album and Celine Dion's solo album *Let's Talk About Love* sold over thirty million copies *each* worldwide. I have been told that James Horner's representatives at the time asked the film studios Fox and Paramount, who jointly coproduced the film, to provide an estimate of what Horner's earnings might end up being from the music from the film . . . and the estimate was $40 million! For *one* film! It's a beautiful thing when the stars align and you can tap into every single income type that exists in the music business and maximize earnings from all of them. It is unlikely ever to happen again at the level of *Titanic*, but one never knows . . .

THE PBS EXCEPTION

Notwithstanding all the synch license factors already mentioned, it's worth pointing out that our government-subsidized Public Broadcasting Service (or PBS, as we all refer to it) is technically granted synch rights and has set fees per the Copyright Law. So a program that is only ever going to air on PBS doesn't need to seek permission to use any music—they can just use the music, and then they reach out to publishers and inform them of the use and pay per the set fee schedule. However, these days, most programs that anyone would produce for PBS would also be intended for other media, like home video or maybe even limited theatrical runs. For this reason, the music used in those programs still needs to be cleared with the publishers.

ONE FINAL LICENSING TERM—MOST FAVORED NATION

One final licensing-related concept you should know is **MOST FAVORED NATION**. Let's say you control the publishing on a song but you don't control the master. You get a request in and you decide you want to quote $10,000 for use of the song in a film. When you provide this quote to whomever is asking for the license, you tell them your quote is $10,000 *but on a most-favored-nation basis with the master recording.* What the most-favored-nation (or, in common parlance, MFN) clause requires is that you be treated just as favorably as anyone else. So, in this example, if the master recording owner of your song quoted $15,000, then your quote of $10,000 would be bumped to the same $15,000 because you have required that you get paid just as favorably as the "most favored nation" in the agreement. If the master had quoted less than the $10,000 you quoted, your fee would not go down. It would stay at $10,000. When any of us use MFN it is our protection ensuring that no one else can get paid more than us. You can use it in relation to copublishers and the master owners of your one song, or you can try to invoke MFN on every song used in a project to make sure that absolutely no one will get paid more than you; but this is harder to do, since there may be a better-known song than yours used, and the project won't want to pay you the same fee.

Print Rights

At the beginning of this section of the book I mentioned that the music publishing business started out as a sheet music business, but now the tables have turned such that the income from this area of the business is probably the smallest source of revenue. However, it is still an important source and worth paying respect to and discussing. Over the years, the sheet music companies in the U.S. have for the most part consolidated into three major players, listed here in alphabetical order: Alfred Music, Hal Leonard Corporation (the publisher of this book, in fact), and Music Sales Group. Though no longer the dominant income type in our business, a successful song (especially ballads) can still sell lots of sheet music, as people want to learn how to play their favorite songs on their respective instruments. These are the main types of printed sheet music generally available:

- Single-song sheet music (i.e., piano/vocal or guitar/vocal)
- Folios of mixed songs (usually grouped by a common theme such as "love songs" or "wedding songs" or "summer songs" or any theme you can think of)
- Matching folios (songbooks whose cover art matches that of an artist's album and the songs included in the folio are all the songs contained on that particular album—or perhaps a folio of all songs by a particular artist, etc.)

The royalties payable to the writer and publisher from these sales vary based on whether the sale is in printed, paper form or consists of a digital download where no engraving or printing has taken place. In the former category, the royalty rates are based on the retail selling price and can vary from 12 percent to 20 percent (with the higher rate being that paid to the single-song sheet music); and the latter is typically 50 percent, given that no physical costs have been incurred. Companies such as MusicNotes.com have built their entire business on the digital download of sheet music, and of course this clearly is the wave of the future for this income stream.

Custom Arrangements and the Derivative Right

One element of this area worth discussing (which also addresses an additional right given to us by the Copyright Law) is the issue of custom arrangements. Many of you may have been singers in your high school or university choir or show choir, or instrumentalists in your school's orchestra, band, or even marching band. When anyone wants to make an arrangement of a popular song to be performed by their ensemble, they must request permission to do so from the publisher(s) of the musical composition. This is referred to as the **derivative right**. Any copyright holder has the right to allow or not allow what are called **derivative works**, or works that are technically new works but draw substantially from the **original work**. Custom arrangements are an example of derivative works, as are songs whose lyrics get translated into a new language to be performed by someone else from a different country. The derivative work receives the same sort of protections granted the original work and can be yet another source of income for the writers and publishers of the original work, since all three main sources of copyright protection and income we've discussed so far (i.e., mechanicals, performance, and synchronization) apply to the derivative work as well. The concept of a derivative work is often misunderstood, and custom arrangements are frequently made by schools across the country without obtaining legal permission and paying the nominal fee. A company called Tresóna Music (www.tresonamusic.com) has been helping publishers and schools alike nationwide by making permissions and licensing a seamless and easy process for all. The majority of publishers now look to Tresóna to handle their catalogue's custom arrangement needs. This area also involves the other rights we have discussed in that many schools release CDs that include their recordings on them or sell DVDs with videos of their ensembles performing their routines, and in each of these cases both mechanical licenses and synchronization licenses are required.

20 The Future—and Don't Forget the Rest of the World

The Digital Revolution and New Media

We are in the middle of a digital revolution. And the laws are trying to catch up with technology, with limited success at the moment. But with the foundation of the basic rights granted to us by the Copyright Law now under our belts, we can now start to apply them to this new world we are all trying to make a living in. Technology has been both enabling and disruptive: now anyone with the right education (from the classroom and/or the real world) can use readily available electronic equipment and computer software to make an amazing record in their bedroom that sounds like it was recorded in the most expensive recording studio in the world (with the right training from fellow author of this book Eric Corne!). They can then upload it to YouTube and be discovered, jump to the top of the charts worldwide, and launch a huge music career. Those stories have happened and will continue to happen as technology has leveled the playing field for all. Furthermore, with companies like CDBaby, Tunecore, and other digital aggregators, independent artists have access to worldwide distribution of their music that years ago was possible only for the lucky few artists that got signed to record labels who had access to either the major labels' distribution system or the largest independent distributors. So this technological revolution has empowered artists like never before. But as a result there are more artists now than ever before, and the challenge is getting the exposure and promotion that, depending on the genre of music you do, might still be best orchestrated by the major record labels' promotional staff. But needless to say this technological revolution has disrupted what used to be a business dominated by the majors. Now everyone has a chance! That is the whole reason we wrote this book. But at the same time, these technological advances, most notably streaming services, are also blurring the lines between what have been fairly distinct and separate income types historically. And this brings up new challenges for the copyright laws and all of us who work in the business. Let's take a closer look at streaming and how everyone is impacted.

Noninteractive Streaming

Noninteractive streaming services like Pandora or Sirius XM are generally viewed as providing an experience akin to a radio broadcast, where you have no way of choosing which songs are played, and you don't know what songs will be played next. Someone else is determining the order, or the order is semi-random, but you as the listener cannot choose to listen to a particular song. On the publishing side, these services need only a license for the right of public performance from any of the four PROs we have mentioned previously. However, it is worth noting, relating to master recordings only, that prior to 1995 no exclusive performance right existed for master recordings in any medium. But the Digital Performance Right in Sound Recordings Act of 1995 and the Digital Millennium Copyright Act of 1998 together created the right of public performance in master recordings in certain types of digital transmissions, but especially noninteractive streaming. The organization SoundExchange (www.soundexchange.com) was founded in 2003 as a wholly independent nonprofit organization and is still the only organization appointed by the U.S. Copyright Law to collect these kinds of public performances for featured artists and sound recording copyright owners. Look at Soundexchange as the PRO equivalent for master owners and recording artists. *All* royalties earned by master recordings in these noninteractive digital transmissions are sent to Soundexchange, and it is free to join, so if you are a recording artist and/or master owner you should make sure you sign up and register your recordings at soundexchange.com

Interactive Streaming

Interactive streaming is when a digital audio file is transmitted electronically to a computer or some other digital device at the specific request of a user who wishes to listen to a particular recording or playlist of recordings. These are also called on-demand streams. The most popular example of an interactive streaming service is Spotify, and the newest entry into the space is Apple Music though there are others like Rdio, Deezer, and more. This kind of streaming involves a blended right that is both a public performance right and a mechanical right. There are many types of interactive streaming, and the calculations are very complex. However, the basic rate is that songwriters and publishers are entitled to 10.5 percent of the music service's revenue, split between the performance right and the mechanical right. The performance right can of course be handled by the PROs, but ASCAP and BMI, which have the majority of the performance right market, cannot handle the mechanical right due to their consent decrees. (That is, the consent decrees don't address mechanicals, so therefore ASCAP and BMI can only handle performances.) Therefore, to complete the licensing picture a potential interactive streaming service typically outsources this function and uses the Harry Fox Agency (HFA) or another third party like Music Reports, Inc. (MRI) or Medianet to acquire the mechanical rights they need to combine with the performance right. It is worth noting that this 10.5 percent rate is similar to the traditional mechanical rate of 9.1 cents in that it is set by law and there is no negotiation between the writers or publishers and the streaming service. However, master recording owners have no set rate by law (i.e., a statutory rate), so they are able to negotiate in a free market, and we will address that shortly.

Video Streaming

The most popular example of video streaming is YouTube, which is owned by Google. Millions of hours of video are uploaded to YouTube on a daily basis. The phenomenon is unprecedented. It has also wreaked havoc on copyright laws, as some of the most popular content on YouTube is what is called UGC or **user-generated content**. As its name implies, this is video content created by anyone. Many of these creators are incorporating songs into their videos, and most are not asking permission to do so, which is the right granted us in our synchronization right. So YouTube has been involved in many a copyright infringement suit, as it has been argued that YouTube is encouraging widespread infringement of copyrighted material and has done nothing to stem the tide. A number of things have resulted from this. First, YouTube does indeed have blanket licenses with the PROs, but the income being paid is incredibly minimal given the number of plays involved. These rates will continue to be negotiated. Then there's the very topical subject of "YouTube monetization," which every digital aggregator and distributor is promoting to everyone, and there are many third party services not connected to digital distributors who are promoting the same. What YouTube has offered to the music community is the opportunity to share in Google's revenue from ads that either run before the videos or appear as banner ads during their play. In return, when we as publishers participate in the ad revenue we are indemnifying YouTube from any potential infringement of our works, so they cannot be sued by us. Litigation can be expensive, so many copyright owners have opted into this scenario. The income these copyright holders can earn from YouTube is substantial, but it is a very complex world. For now, the simplest explanation of how the income is split is as follows:

- When a user uploads a video covering a song (in other words, the video does not use an existing master recording but essentially creates a new master), then, once the publisher makes a claim to that video, any ad revenue will be split 50 percent to Google and 50 percent to the writer and publisher; or
- When a user uploads a video that makes use of an existing master recording, then once the publisher and the master owner have made claims to the video, the ad revenue is split 50 percent to Google, 35 percent to the master owner and 15 percent to the publisher.

We as copyright holders also have the ability to request a "takedown" of any video that contains our copyrights and for which we do not wish to participate in any ad revenue (for whatever reason). We also as copyright holders have the option to allow the video to stay up but to request that no advertising be put against the video.

Fun stuff, huh? Well, wait for this . . .

The Future of PROs and Where Do We Go from Here?

You will recall from our earlier discussion of the public performance right that ASCAP and BMI operate off consent decrees that were established back in the 1940s. Now think about the unbelievable technological advances that have taken place in the basically seventy-five years since then. Well, those consent decrees are still in place. When they were established, they may have been enacted for good reason, but now those same consent decrees:

- don't let ASCAP and BMI say *no* to a proposed use on behalf of their writer and publisher members. Because the intent of the consent decrees at the time was such that they didn't want any music user to be discriminated against, they were set up so that ASCAP and BMI could never deny someone a license. This took away our ability to deny the public performance of our music (as long as we allowed ASCAP and BMI to continue to license that performance right on our behalf). As a result, we have our lost our leverage to negotiate in this current competitive market, whereas the synchronization market, for example, is a free market where we as the owners of our intellectual property can set the rate we want to be paid and say whether we want our works used at all.
- in preventing ASCAP and BMI from saying *no* to a possible licensee, allows the licensee to immediately start to use our music even if that licensee doesn't agree with the rate that ASCAP and BMI are proposing. The only option in that case is to go to a federal court to work out the rate with the licensee, and that is a long and expensive process. In the meantime, the music users can build up their business using our music and not having to pay a thing until a final license is agreed to.

As a result of this situation, throughout 2014 and 2015 there have been extensive investigations and reviews by the U.S. government of how the music business is operating (or not able to operate) in the current market. The Department of Justice (DOJ) has been holding hearings on the consent decrees and is considering making changes to the consent decrees that ASCAP and BMI operate under. Some parties such as the National Music Publishers Association (www.nmpa.org), have advocated that the DOJ get rid of the consent decrees altogether and have ASCAP and BMI operate and negotiate in a free market as SESAC is able to do (and as we currently do with our synch rights). Alternatively, many are arguing that SESAC, a private, for-profit company with no consent decree, should be subject to a consent decree similar to those which bind ASCAP and BMI. On that note, as this book was being written, SESAC actually bought the Harry Fox Agency, which handles mechanical rights for lots of publishers. It will be interesting to see what SESAC tries to do when they can put the performance right and mechanical right under the same roof and issue licenses for both in a package deal. Interesting times ahead!

International and Sub-Publishing

As you can tell, there are lots of facets to music publishing, and it can get complex with lots of nuances. Keep in mind that everything we have covered so far is from a U.S.-centric perspective. But many publishers these days are earning more than 50 percent of their income from *outside* the United States, so it is important to take what we have learned so far and expand our world view—which brings us to the subject of **sub-publishing**.

If I may make a general statement, you can essentially divide the publishing world into two groupings—the "major" multinational publishers and then the "independents." The independents can be further divided up by size, but one of the reasons that majors are considered "major" is that most of them have their own offices in most of the major territories outside the U.S. For example, there are four major publishers—and in alphabetical order they are BMG Rights, Sony/ATV Music Publishing, Universal Music Publishing Group and Warner/Chappell Music, Inc. Each of these companies has offices in countries like the United Kingdom, Germany, France, Italy, Japan, and Australia. And these offices are all part of the parent company. This is an expensive structure to maintain, what with overhead costs like rent, salaries for employees, etc., so these companies' catalogues are deep and throw off a lot of cash flow to support their infrastructure. Most independents, even the largest ones, may have an office in a few of these larger territories but usually not all of them (with the possible exception of peermusic, one of the largest and oldest independent publishers in the world). And when you don't have an office, you still need someone local to perform all the registration requirements that we have to do here in the U.S. in order for you to receive the income you're due from that territory. So most independent publishers "sub"-license their rights to a local publisher in each territory to look after on their behalf. It then becomes the responsibility of that local publisher (whether a fellow independent or possibly even the local office of one of the majors) to do all the work necessary to collect any income due from their client's catalogue in that local territory. These folks are called someone's "sub-publishers."

Now, some of you may recall that ASCAP, BMI, and SESAC have reciprocal agreements in place with fellow performance rights societies all over the world. So why would a sub-publisher be necessary if that international performance income could come back to you via your U.S. PRO? Well, in theory it can. But there's one very important distinction and that is that ASCAP and BMI are not permitted to handle mechanical royalties per the consent decrees. Overseas, the various societies that exist in each territory usually handle *both* performance rights *and* mechanical rights. So ASCAP and BMI would not be able to collect and pass along your foreign mechanical income. The only way for you to claim this income is via a local publisher who makes a registration and claim to your song and the resulting income. But when local publishers make registrations and claim the songs, they can't request that they be paid the mechanical income only—they have to be paid all income earned by a song. So typically once you enter a sub-publishing deal your publisher's share of performance will no longer come back via ASCAP or BMI but instead via the local sub-publishing deal that you enter into.

The international marketplace encompasses all the income types we discussed earlier (mechanicals, performance, synchronization, and print). While some territories may have other income types that the U.S. doesn't have, that's digging down to a layer that we don't need to get into for our purposes here. But one thing that is worth noting on the mechanical side is that most mechanical royalties outside the U.S. and Canada are calculated differently. They are *not* a penny rate as we have in the U.S. and Canada (i.e., the fixed 9.1 cents in the U.S. for a song five minutes or less). Most countries outside the U.S. use a concept of **PPD**, or "published price to dealer," which is their equivalent to our "wholesale" price concept here in the U.S. So in the United Kingdom, for example, the basic mechanical rate for the sale of music to the public is 8.5 percent of PPD. Then the resulting figure is divided up amongst all songs on a record based on their length—the longer the song, the more royalties you receive. Depending on the price the PPD is set for, the sale of one record in the UK may generate more mechanical royalties on a per song basis then the same sale of one record would generate in the U.S. at 9.1 cents per song. In this way foreign royalties can sometimes result in greater royalties than in the U.S.

There are further differences and idiosyncracies that exist in the international marketplace that don't exist here in the U.S. To go over all of them would involve yet another large section of a book that we will not be able to cover here. But I think you get the idea that there's a huge market outside the U.S., which you should never ignore when thinking about your plans for music publishing domination. There are some U.S. songwriters who make most if not all of their income from other countries. That's the great thing about the music publishing business—each individual country is its own music market. So, if you can gear your songwriting to not only your own artistic goals but those of artists in different countries all over the world, then you exponentially increase your chances of success.

21 Types of Publishing Deals

Now that you have the basic building blocks of music publishing, you may be asking, how will they help me pursue my dreams of songwriting success? Well, there are many types of agreements you can enter into, each with its own pros and cons. So let's take them one at a time. There are generally four different kinds of agreement types:

1. The exclusive songwriting agreement
2. The copublishing agreement
3. The administration agreement
4. The work-for-hire agreement

Exclusive Songwriting Agreement

You may have heard or read about the legendary Brill Building days in New York City when all anyone did in that building was write songs. These songwriters for the most part were considered "staff writers." They received a salary from their publishers and their job was to come to the office every day and write songs that they thought other artists would want to record. Some wonderful and classic songs came out of this time period. The concept of "staff writer" continues to this day, but it is more typically found in Nashville than in New York or Los Angeles. As the name "exclusive" implies, you can sign a deal with a publisher where they agree to give you a weekly or monthly "draw" (or salary to write songs for them). In exchange, they become your exclusive publisher, which means that you assign 100 percent of your ownership to all the songs you write over to this publisher and you split everything fifty/fifty. The publisher who pays you keeps 100 percent of the publisher's share, and you, the writer, keep 100 percent of the writer's share. This deal is no longer as prevalent as it used to be, but you can still find it available. And it could be a great opportunity for you. The idea is that someone is giving you enough of a salary that it covers your basic necessities of life and you can focus 100 percent of your time on your songwriting. Even though you are giving up a lot for the opportunity (i.e., all the ownership in your songs), many songwriters will tell you how their first publisher who had them as a staff writer helped them hone their craft and/or set up "cowrites" with other songwriters that resulted in big songs. So it is a more common scenario to see this deal with a new up-and-coming songwriter. Once you start to get songs recorded and you achieve some success, the path usually takes you to the next level, which is the copublishing deal.

Copublishing Deal

As you probably realize, *co-* implies "share"—so a **copublishing** deal is one in which you "share" your publishing. In the typical scenario, a publisher agrees to give you an advance of money (maybe all in one up-front advance, or in monthly or quarterly payments), and in return you assign them 50 percent of your publishing of any song you write during the period of time you mutually agree to. But the advance that you have been given is basically a loan—you have to pay it back. And the way you pay it back is via the income you have retained as yours in the deal: the 50 percent of the publisher's share you have left over after having assigned away the other 50 percent to the publisher who is paying you, and you have 100 percent of your writer's share as well. Now, the publisher typically cannot touch the writer's share of public performance income that is paid to you directly from that PRO—but with all other types of income other than performance, the writer's share travels with the publisher's share. So the publisher who gives you an advance for a copublishing deal recoups your advance by collecting all of your income (other than the writer's share of performance) and applying your share of it against what they paid you; and you won't receive any more royalties until your advance is paid back to the publisher. For example, let's say a song that you wrote by yourself—so you have 100 percent—got used in a TV show for $1,000. Technically, $500 of this fee is your writer's share and $500 of it is your publisher's share. But in your copublishing deal your new publisher got assigned 50 percent of your publishing for paying you the advance. So they get to keep $250 (or half of the $500 that is your publisher's share) for their own benefit, and then they take the $250 that is your 50 percent of the publisher's share *and* the $500 that is your full writer's share, and apply the entire $750 against the advance they have paid you. Let's then say that that same TV use generated $1,000 in performance royalties, of which $500 was the writer's share that went straight to you from your PRO and $500 was collected by the publisher. You have split your publishing 50/50 with them, so they keep $250 for their own benefit and apply the remaining $250 against your advance. Make sense? They keep doing this on all types of income until your advance is paid back in full. Only then will you receive further checks from them along with your royalty statements that they render to you. So, as you can see, the advance you get paid is really just your own royalties, which you are being given up front. But in the meantime, the publisher is getting their income from the publisher's share that you gave them as part of the deal. In some ways you could look at this deal as a very expensive bank loan, because you are getting money up front that you have to pay back, but it's costing you 25 percent interest, essentially, as 25 cents on the dollar goes into the pocket of the publisher you did the deal with. However, a typical bank would not have given you a loan when you had no income as a songwriter. But this publisher you did the deal with believed in your talent enough to give you money up front. Then, hopefully, if you picked the right publisher, they will work hard to pitch your songs and connect you with important songwriters and/or artists you can cowrite with. The right copublishing deal is one that is a partnership. And you should only do the co-publishing deal if you feel it is the right balance of what you need—both financially and otherwise. If it is not, you might consider an administration deal instead.

Administration Deal

In the administration deal, you, the songwriter, do not assign any ownership over to the publisher you are making the deal with. You will retain 100 percent ownership, but you want the help—either administrative only or both administrative and creative—that the publisher and their infrastructure can provide. Maybe you got a song recorded by a big artist who sells records all over the world or you are getting so many synch placements on your own that you need help keeping things straight and collecting your royalties worldwide. Then you could do an administration deal in which the publisher agrees to take care of all the things you need taken care of, and in exchange they withhold a commission from the royalties that they collect for you. Typically the fees that get charged range from 10 to 20 percent, but, depending on how much income you make and how many services you need, these percentages can go up or down accordingly. A typical administration deal does not involve an advance up front, but if you have significant income "in the pipeline" (i.e., it's coming for sure but hasn't arrived yet) then sometimes you can arrange to receive some sort of advance as an incentive to sign the deal. But, as is often the case when money changes hands, many times the administrative commission you have to give up increases when you get an advance up front. I always tell songwriters that if you don't *need* the money up front, the administration deal is always the best option, as your costs are kept lower and in the end you own everything 100 percent. Some folks feel that they won't get the attention of the publisher's creative staff if they do an admin deal and not a copublishing deal. That might be true in some cases, which is why *any* deal you do needs to be considered a partnership and you must only go with whom you feel loves what you do and will work hard to help you move to the next level and/or increase the income from your songs.

Work-for-Hire Agreements

A specific type of agreement that is worth mentioning, as it can be a valuable option, is the work-for-hire agreement. The term **work for hire** is a specific concept in the Copyright Law that permits an "employer" to hire you, the "employee," to create something specifically for the employer. These situations happen especially when the employer is going to use your work as part of a collective work or a work that has had multiple types of contributions made to it from multiple creative sources. Typically the employer wants to ensure that it owns everything and can remain in control of all the work, and that no one part of the work can be removed or considered separate from the whole. This applies mainly to films, television shows, video games, etc., where multiple creative people work their own aspect to create a piece of the whole. When film and television studios need music for their projects, they have two options—they can license in works from outside third parties (i.e., the synchronization and master use rights we discussed earlier), or they can commission someone to write something specifically for the film or TV show. Taking TV shows first, the studios usually want to own the theme of a given show, since this music becomes the show's signature sound and musical identity. It is rare that TV studios will license in third party themes, but it is not without precedent, as all the CSI franchise shows licensed in songs by the Who for their themes. Film studios also like to own songs that are written specifically for their films, especially in animation. And composers of the original instrumental background score for a film or TV show almost never own that music; it is considered a work for hire for the studio that hired them.

So there are a lot of songwriters and composers who make almost all of their income doing works for hire. What typically happens is that you negotiate an up-front creative fee for your time in creating the work. The more leverage you have, the higher the fee you can command. The studio that hired you is typically the 100 percent publisher of the work, and you are able to retain 100 percent of your writer's share *only*. But if you are part of a successful project that achieves a high level of commercial success, you can still make a crazy amount of money from just your writer's share. (Remember all the income types we discussed before!)

It is important to realize in the case of works for hire that the author cannot ever terminate the grant of rights and get back the ownership of his or her work. Works for hire by design can never be terminated, as the employer wants and needs for business reasons to retain control of the collective work that was created.

So you must bear that in mind when you decide whether or not to write songs as a work for hire. Under the right circumstances, however, these deals can be a source of significant income.

So here ends our discussion of "important administrative stuff." I know some of these topics can be a bit "dry" or even boring, but I cannot stress enough how important it is that songwriters and composers know how their business works, as it's the only way to make informed decisions. Even if you have representatives and lawyers who work for you and watch out for you (and a good and trusted attorney is a *must* when exploring and negotiating any of the above types of publishing deals), it is still better to know how your business works, even if you won't be doing the work on a day-to-day basis. So, with the administrative fundamentals in place, let's get to the fun stuff of pitching your songs!

22 Prepare to Pitch!

As you have seen so far in this book, a successful career in music requires the mastering of multiple skills. Some of these—writing, practicing, recording—can be honed in solitude. But the business of music is so strongly based on relationships that you *must* learn how to sell your songs. Pitching songs is not something everyone can do well—sales takes a certain personality trait (that not all people have) and you must be a good "people person." Some aspects of this you can learn with experience and from trial and error, but at some level you have to be equipped with the "social gene" in order to really succeed in any type of sales. If you are an artist, you presumably have the talent to "sell," because you have to sell your songs and your persona every time you go out to perform for an audience. In the end, though, of all the tools you need at your disposal for pitching, no tool is more important than a great recording of a great song.

The Art of the Demo/Master

Eric Corne covers the specifics of how to make a great recording in Part 3 of this book, but for our purposes I want to stress the difference between a **demo** and a **master**. Traditionally, when someone finished writing a song he or she would record a "demo" of it, short for "demonstration recording." It was intended to capture the essence of the song, to give listeners an idea of how it sounded and might be arranged. There was a whole class of A&R folks (A&R is short for Artists & Repertoire) who could hear a rough recording of a song and envision how it could sound with a whole band or even orchestra, and what vocalists would sound good on the song. These were music people, mainly, and not business people, so they had the talent and the background to support their ideas of what would work for a song. This was the typical process for the 1960s, 1970s, and even into the 1980s.

But then technology advanced to allow musicians to make high-quality recordings in their garages and there are examples galore of great records that were recorded in a bedroom. This development in my opinion pretty much killed the demo. Especially with the increased demand for music in television, film, and other media (which we will cover more in depth shortly), the need for master-quality recordings (i.e., recordings that sound like they could be records played on the radio as is) became increasingly important. Now the goal when you record a new song is to make a recording that sounds as much as possible like the final record of that song. Even if you don't aspire to be an artist who releases a record and tours, a great-sounding recording of your song can help you pitch it to artists who are looking for songs at the same time that you pitch it for Film & TV projects. So, if you don't have the skills to make a professional-sounding recording, connect with someone who does, even if that means you pay them for their time. It's an investment that could bring rewards. So let's say you have a great-sounding recording of a song you want your favorite artist to record. Let's explore the different ways you can do that!

A&R

I'm sure you've written more than one song where you've thought, "Hey, I think this is a good song for so-and-so to record." We all have done that. It's natural. But the issue is getting to that artist, or, more importantly, getting to the person or persons who are ultimately the decision maker(s) on what songs that artist is going to record. An artist typically has a number of different team members who might have a say in what songs they record. They are:

- **Manager:** Some artists are managed by powerful industry figures who have a proven track record of guiding their artists to successful careers. Those kinds of managers will have a big say in what their artists record. But up-and-coming artists don't typically get the attention of these kinds of managers, so maybe a family member, a friend, or a fan is managing them to start. You must find out who the manager is and assess his or her place in that artist's decision-making tree. Some artists list their managers on their websites; in addition, Pollstar (www.pollstarpro.com) is a good paid reference for who manages whom.
- **A&R person:** If the artist in question is signed to an established record label (whether a major label or an independent label), it is likely that someone in the A&R department at the record label is assigned to that artist to help choose songs for his or her record. Or, if it's a bigger artist, there may be multiple levels of A&R people at a label scouting for songs. Again, the stature of the artist is going to determine whether or not the A&R person has been given true song decision power, but you absolutely must find out who is in charge of A&R for an artist, as that person is always a voice in the process. A good paid resource of A&R people is the *A&R Directory* at www.musicregistry.com. But this is where the Internet can be your best friend, as most labels will have websites that list their artists on a roster, and you can track down a name or contact e-mail for the label and ask who at the label is handling A&R for the artist you're interested in. Another great source, if the artist has put out a record previously, is to get that record and look for any credits in the packaging of that record, as the A&R person will always get a credit (at least, the A&R person who has a true say in what gets recorded will get a credit!).
- **Producer:** Every record must be produced by someone. Some artists produce themselves, but that is tough to do and remain objective, so even artists who feel they are producers usually bring in a coproducer. Sometimes a producer will be brought in to produce an entire record. Sometimes multiple producers will be brought in to work on an artist's record. It's somewhat genre driven (e.g., country artists tend to have the same producer for a whole record, whereas pop and R&B can tend to have multiple producers on one record) but it's also driven by the other team members like the manager and A&R person already mentioned. All will have a say in what happens. But finding out who is producing an artist is key, as you can reach out to the producer to find out the direction of a record and ask whether the team might be open to "outside songs." (More on that in a moment.) But while it's relatively simple to find a manager or A&R directory, there is no easy reference that tells you who is producing an artist. Sometimes you can find this information on the Internet, but it's more than likely something you can only find out from the management office or the A&R department at the record label.

So let's say you've figured out who the major players are on an artist's record. The next thing you want to try to figure out is who likely has the most influence to decide what songs will get recorded. This is hard to figure out. When it is all people you have never met, you just have to go with your gut and then judge by the reactions you get who seems to be the main decision maker. You also need to get a sense of whether the players involved are open to "outside songs." A song is considered "outside" when it isn't already tied to one of the players in the game. For example, does the artist write? If you know from a previous record that the artist is a writer on every song on the record, then it's likely that your song may not get considered. But so many new artists have vaulted to stardom on TV shows like *American Idol* and *The Voice*, without necessarily being writers themselves, that when they make their records they often need to have someone writing for them.

Then look at the producer(s) who may be involved. Some producers are not writers, but many are. And if the projects they typically work on involve songs that they are cowriters on, then the chance of them considering an outside song is low, since cowriting opens up another income stream for them. Then look at the A&R person. Consider the other projects they have worked on, as many A&R people like to use the same people they have used on other projects if they have come to trust their judgment and how well they work with an artist. Do these A&R people tend to record songs on their projects written by certain songwriters? If so, you can make a mental note to try to reach out to whichever publisher represents that writer and explore a cowrite. Then look at the manager—does he or she manage songwriters? If so, then he or she is likely trying to cross-pollinate artist and writer clients and get them to work with each other. As you can tell, it's very much of a people game and therefore a relationship game. If you have no relationship to speak of with any of the people on an artist's team, then start to develop one. At some point you may get lucky enough to have someone be receptive to hearing your song, and you have to be ready when that moment arrives.

So let's say that moment has arrived. The door has been opened and someone wants to hear your song for the artist. What do you send and how do you send it? These days, most everyone will much prefer and appreciate a link that you send that allows them to stream the song. This is where many folks tend to use SoundCloud (www.soundcloud.com) these days. But there are many other services out there as well—like Box (www.box.com), Dropbox (www.dropbox.com), SongSpace (www.songspace.com), and others—and it's best to find one that allows both streaming and downloading of the song in the same place. And, in a perfect world, it should be a situation or service where the lyrics can be included so that listeners can read along. The constant theme you will hear from me in this pitching section is *"make it easy."* It's all about making the pitching process as seamless and effortless as possible for the potential user of your music. Many folks these days don't like being sent MP3 attachments. So never assume that is OK. If you send a streaming link and the recipient likes your song and wants an MP3, let that person ask for it, because then you know there's interest in the song. Each time you get to be in contact with someone can be an opportunity to learn yet another nugget of information about that contact and his or her process. But the flip side of that is, if you ask people to jump through many hoops (e.g., click this, then download this, then go to this browser window, etc.) they are likely going to lose interest before they even start to listen!

Then judge the reaction you get to the song. What do your contacts like or not like? If they like the song but don't feel it's right for this artist's record, ask what other projects and artists they may be working with that it might be appropriate for. If you know their artist writes and likes the song, explore whether you could arrange a cowrite sometime, perhaps for the next record if it's too late for the current one. Explore ways to capitalize on whatever element(s) the potential users said they liked. But, if you don't feel you are getting anywhere with them as you talk or exchange e-mails, then don't keep pushing. Keep up the relationship rapport and ask if you can reach out to them again to pitch for other projects. *Develop the relationship!*

If they like your song, they may ask to put it "on hold." This means that they don't want you pitching it to any other artists. And that can be great news. But first find out how long you'll have to keep the song off the market—if it's longer than three to six months, then you may not want this, as there's no guarantee that a song that's on hold will definitely get cut (especially if production in the genre your song is in changes quickly, such that if you wait while the song is on hold your song might end up sounding dated and hasn't been recorded either). There might also be other artists for whom the song would work who are recording their albums during the hold period, so you have to try to judge that as well.

You should also be aware that if there is interest in your song, depending on the artist and/or producer involved, you may get asked to cut in either the artist or the producer, or both, as writers on your song. And maybe at some point something will legitimately be rewritten such that the credit is deserved, because a true contribution was made, but sometimes you are asked to cut someone in just to give them an added incentive to record the song. It doesn't always happen, but you have to be prepared for the possibility that you might get asked, and then you'll have to decide how you want to handle that. You can always say no. But how you and they handle this kind of situation can really test the relationship. Handling it politely and respectfully can go a long way towards building that relationship and building a future. You need to trust your gut. If what you're being asked for doesn't feel right, and it would bother you forever to give something up, then say no. Depending on what you are being asked for, decide whether it's too high a price to pay for getting on a record. A known artist who has a sales history you can verify can provide you with some data on what you might actually earn on a record with that artist if you agreed to give something away. Other times, with an unknown artist, it may not be worth it. Everything is case by case. And again, this may not happen at all—I'm just saying you should be prepared for it, as it will come up at some point.

In our previous section touching on sub-publishing, we talked about how the international marketplace cannot be ignored, and that is particularly relevant in this world of A&R. Think about it—though the U.S. is its own market and it's a big one, each country around the world is its own market. And there are *lots* of artists in all of these countries looking to cut songs written by American writers. This ties back into our initial discussion about cowriting and track writing. There is a big market for tracks that are being produced in countries throughout Europe where dance and EDM music are so strong; but artists and labels want to combine those tracks with top lines written by American top-liners, since English is their first language. And not only are *American Idol* and *The Voice* syndicated around the world, but many countries have their own version of each of these shows. Each of those local productions are creating artists from their contestants, the winners (and even runners-up!) all need to make records, and they often need songs for their records. K-pop music out of South Korea is now in huge demand thanks to the worldwide success of Psy a number of years ago. There are lots of girl groups and boy groups throughout Asia in general who are constantly looking for songs. And even though you have to give up a percentage of the song to someone local who writes lyrics in that local language, that's fine, because your song can still be cut in English somewhere else. Even if your song that gets cut and released in South Korea with Korean lyrics will likely only ever be heard in South Korea and maybe in some other Asian countries where K-pop music does well, like Japan, be aware that there are songwriters who make more of a living on their songs that get cut in other countries than they do with their music in the U.S.! It's all about relationships and finding out who is looking for what songs by what artist. There are lots of ways to get this information as long as you're networking with A&R people and publishers from around the world.

Some folks wonder whether there are paid resources for leads on who is looking for songs. There are certainly some, but I have generally found that the best way to get songs cut is not from these pitch sheets (which can often be outdated anyway once you get them) but from doing the work the old-fashioned way—develop the relationships and be in constant communication with the folks who are involved with an artist. This is obviously another good reason to work with an established music publisher who already has these relationships. As long as you have good songs to back your sales efforts up, you will gain traction and get the cuts.

23 Synch It, Baby!

The process of getting songs cut by artists is very political, and it can take years to develop the relationships that are effective in getting your songs recorded on a regular basis. What I have always loved about the synchronization world is that, though it is *very* relationship driven as well, the end result is very black-and-white—if they like your song for a scene they will ask to use it, you negotiate a fee, and you're done. The mechanics of the pitching process are actually not much different from those of the A&R world. But the canvas upon which one has to pitch has become vast, and each area can have its own unique aspects. Let's start exploring.

Film & TV

When you look at the staffs of the various publishing companies, you might see titles such as Vice President, Film & TV or Manager, Film & TV. The term "Film & TV" in the music publishing world has taken on an identity beyond what it at first appears to represent, and one should not take the term literally. It involves *much* more than just film or just TV. More and more, in fact, you might see a position called "Synch Creative" to acknowledge the breadth of the exploding media landscape. But each area under the general term Film & TV deserves to be treated individually here, to point out issues specific to each.

It's worth first reminding you that the key to success in the Film & TV or synch world is well-produced, master-quality recordings that sound as if they could be on the radio right now. The bar is high—a song or record that is not well produced sticks out like a sore thumb and if the production quality is not up to certain standards, an experienced music supervisor will turn off the song within the first ten seconds and you may never have another opportunity to pitch that person again. What is a music supervisor, you may ask? He or she is the gatekeeper that you need to get your song through. Music supervisors are brought onto a project for a variety of reasons:

- Their extensive musical knowledge and taste in both historical and current music
- Their experience in knowing all the various aspects that are vitally important to delivering a project's music components on time and on budget, from dealing with hiring and managing composers and music editors, to licensing in third party music, etc.
- Their relationships with all the music publishers, record labels and music licensing sources.

Whether they are third-party, independent music supervisors who get brought into projects, or in-house staffers at the big studios and larger independent production companies, they all perform the same role. It is worth noting that in almost all cases the music supervisor is *not* the one who has final decision-making authority over what music gets used in the project. The music supervisor has a boss or bosses on the production, and they are the ones who decide what ultimately gets used. And the boss with decision-making power on each project can change. For example, in film, the director generally has the most power and say over what goes on with music for the project. And some directors are more musically savvy than others. The TV world tends to be more of a producer-driven world, where the director can have input but is more someone who executes the vision of the producer and/or show runner of the TV show. Let's look at each of the areas in the synch world and see how you might pitch differently to each.

TV

The world of TV probably offers the greatest number of shows and opportunities, at least from a volume perspective. There are the main networks, like ABC, CBS, and NBC; all the cable networks, like HBO and Showtime; and now the alternative outlets and models that are gaining traction, like Netflix, Amazon, and Hulu. Some shows are more music-driven, and hopefully their budgets reflect that. But, generally speaking, the dramas tend to be more music heavy than the comedies.

The key to successful pitching in the synch world is doing your research. Busy music supervisors don't have time to answer questions like "What are you working on?" You should already know when you reach out to them what they are working on, and there are many resources where you can get this information.

The first is the credits on the TV shows. Any music supervisor typically gets a credit, sometimes at the front of the show but most times in what are called the end title credits. In TV, these end title credits can move by quickly or get scrunched up into a small space while the network promotes the show that is on next or next week's episode of the show you just watched. Use your pause button and reverse and fast forward buttons to move frame by frame if you have to so that you can read the credit.

Another resource is the Internet Movie Database (www.imdb.com). There is also a pro version at pro-labs.imdb.com, where for an annual fee you can get deeper and more detailed access to all the available data. This is a great resource because it lists both past and current projects, and sometimes even upcoming ones. Two more great resources are TV Show Music (www.tvshowmusic.com) and TuneFind (www.tunefind.com). These websites not only may list the music supervisor of a show, but more importantly they list all the music used in each previously aired episode of music-intensive shows. So you can see not only what someone works on but also the list of songs actually chosen for the project. This can give you a sense of the musical sound of a show and help you to see where your music fits (or whether it does at all). There's nothing that turns a music supervisor off more than an inappropriate pitch. If you haven't done your research, you'll likely blow your first shot and may never get another opportunity to pitch that person. So be thorough.

Another great resource is the *Film & Television Music Guide*, published annually by www.musicregistry.com. Here you'll find contact information of both independent and in-house music supervisors along with a list of the publishers and record labels that pitch music all day to music supervisors. Definitely worth every penny if you are starting from scratch.

So let's say you have done your research. You know what supervisors are working on and what their shows sound like. Now you have to reach out to them—and you do that generally these days via e-mail or phone. If you chose the old-fashioned way (i.e., the phone), be prepared to be articulate but straight to the point. Most times an assistant answers the phone, but developing a relationship with the assistant can be one of the best investments you ever make. Quickly introduce yourself and get straight to the point of why you are calling. Be respectful. If it sounds like the person is going crazy and you can hear the phone ringing off the hook in the background, offer to call back at another time when things are less busy. Or ask when would be a better time. Let the person know that you feel you have music that is appropriate for his or her current project and you're requesting permission to submit some material. Keep it simple and to the point. If you call and get voice mail, *do not* leave a long, rambling message that will turn the recipient off and destroy your chance of a return call. Leave your name and reason for calling in a brief yet friendly message, and request a call back at your number to discuss the project further.

Same thing if you choose to reach out the first time via e-mail. These music supervisors are getting barraged at all times with music from all over—they get ridiculous amounts of e-mail. So be smart about it—don't write a long e-mail, as they won't have time to read it. Be straight and to the point and mention who you are, what you do, and what you have that is appropriate to what they are working on, and include a link where they can stream some music. *Do not send MP3 attachments!* This is almost "rude" these days, because these people are being sent so much music. The last thing they want to do initially is to have to download something in order to listen to it, because their time (and their hard drive space!) is too valuable. I would not send more than three to five songs *at most* the first time out. Don't overwhelm. Present things in small bites—this just increases their chances of committing to listen to something. And that's all you want them to do—listen. If you've done your job by writing a great song and getting a great-sounding recording produced, then once they listen and like what you do, you have their attention. That's the most important thing. Gain their respect by showing you know how to pitch and what to pitch and are respectful of their time. This will buy you the ability to pitch again.

Keeping on top of the music that is needed for TV shows is not an easy task. For a show that is already on the air, the musical identity of the show is figured out already. If you're not part of the library of music that the music supervisor has already gathered for the show, it may be too late for you to get considered. The trick is to develop a relationship with the music supervisor that will allow you to reach out on a regular basis and find out what new projects have been taken on and what music they will involve. Gone are the days when the television year revolved around the launch of new shows in the fall. Summer used to be the dumping ground for shows that didn't gain enough attention to be put on in fall or for reality TV. But some networks (e.g., USA Network) have built their entire brand around summer programming and then expanded into launching shows at other times of the year. And now, with series created for streaming on Netflix and Amazon, there can be new shows launched at almost any time of the year. This means that at any time an important music supervisor might send out an e-mail announcement to trusted music sources about the kind of music he or she needs for a new project. Ultimately, you want to be on those e-mail lists.

You also need to get to know the market and typical fees for the use of music (some fees are mentioned earlier in the chapter covering "Synchronization Rights"). But you will need to be flexible. There are some shows for which a budget for music is practically non-existent and other shows for which the budget is much larger to license in music. Knowing which area each show falls into is part of the research process. And many times a music supervisor will come to you and say, "Hey, I love your song and I'd like to use it in this project, but I only have $2,000 to give you for a license fee." Always work with supervisors to give them what they need if you can—the most experienced and respected supervisors will cut to the chase and tell you what they can do and what they can't do. Always try to accommodate what they are asking for, as this is all part of developing that relationship. In any relationship there is give and take. Help someone out when they need it, and they will remember that and want to help you out in return.

As you can see, this world of synchronization is a very people-oriented world. And it is very much a community. The people who pitch music and the people who license music tend to hang out together. There are events throughout the year like the Billboard / The Hollywood Reporter Film & TV Music Conference,

Sync Summit, the ASCAP Expo, MusExpo, and others. Attend and develop those relationships! Much of what I have mentioned applies not only to pitching to TV but to any other media we will cover. A lot of this may seem like common sense, but until you get into it and do it, you'll see that pitching is a muscle that needs constant working out. It is an art—it takes finesse.

Film

The world of film generally follows a similar path as TV but happens on a different timeline. TV is quick—with thirteen or twenty-two episodes in a typical TV show season, each episode is almost its own "film." In actual film, with release dates set way in advance, there is more time for things to happen. But along with more time, there also tend to be more people in the decision-making mix. Since TV works so quickly and with so much volume, musical decisions occur speedily and often. In film, you will find more committees. If it is a big studio film, you will frequently have the director, the music staff of the studio producing the film, the producer(s) of the film, *and* the music supervisor that was hired all have input into what music gets used. And be aware that generally speaking the people who are involved in music supervision for film are different from those who music supervise for TV. Some of the independent supervisors who work for themselves can get hired on both film and TV projects. But at the bigger studios, there is generally a film music division with its own staff and then a TV music division with its own staff. You'll need to do the same kind of research for film projects as for TV—find out what the movie is about, what time period is it set in, what geographical area, etc.—before you pitch. And the two pitching process are very similar (e.g., pitching with streaming links, etc.). The time-consuming part is developing and maintaining relationships with a whole additional set of people who work in the field.

DON'T FORGET THE INSTRUMENTALS!

One very crucial element in pitching music for synch is the availability of instrumentals for all of your songs. Music editors love having access to the instrumentals, because if there is a scene in which there is a lot of dialogue, the ability to cut the music into the scene alternating between the vocal and instrumental versions of the song means the music needn't interfere with any dialogue. So when you are recording your songs and/or album, always make sure to run a version of the final mastered song without any vocals at all so that you have high-quality mastered instrumentals ready to be pitched!

Ads

One of the most lucrative areas where you can pitch your music is advertising. But this is a tougher area to pitch in, because the brands and the ad agencies are always very secretive about what their campaigns are going to be. They don't want to openly discuss what direction their ads will take for fear of the competition getting a sense of what is going on and potentially copying it. In film and television, you generally will find lots of information on the Internet, as the producers of these projects always want to generate as much publicity as possible *before* they are released so that they open or premiere to great numbers. With ads it's the opposite in that the campaigns are kept under wraps prior to their unveiling. *Then* they want as much publicity as possible, as that's how the brands judge whether a campaign has been successful or not. This can inform the pitching process in interesting ways. Generally speaking, there are two ad areas one can pitch to: commercials, and promos or trailers.

Commercials

These of course are what you typically think of when you think of "ads." Commercials advertise products, and all commercials (for the most part) need music. The music they use generally falls into three categories: they license in music library music (more on that when we end this section), license in third party songs, or get someone to compose original music for a campaign. Some ad music supervisors do send out briefs for folks to pitch music to them, but these almost never specify who the client is. They talk in general terms about the kind of business the client is in and then lay out their music needs and you pitch accordingly. But many agencies do not send out briefs, as they feel that they are the ones best suited to come up with musical ideas for their clients' campaigns. So in those cases all we can do is keep those folks apprised of what new releases we have and at least make sure they are current.

Generally, ads like to use known songs because those songs already demonstrate familiarity and bring an equity and a history to the campaign. And, if the demographic of that song or artist lines up with the demographic of the target audience of the brand, then they know there is a fit. But many times there are opportunities for lesser-known and up-and-coming artists via the lyrics of their songs, which might fit a campaign's tagline or brand name in some way. Brands also like to tie themselves to artists who have generated some buzz and are "on the rise," and because they can often "get credit" for having helped break that artist —and at a much lower cost than that of licensing in a big, known song. Campaigns that don't necessarily need or want that known song or artist tie-in may very well license in existing instrumental library music or ask a music production house to compose original music for a campaign.

And, for the most part, the people who work as music supervisors for ads are yet another completely different set of contacts than those for film and television. There might be the occasional known Film/TV music supervisor who gets hired to music-supervise ads, but this is more the exception than the rule, so you must spend the time developing relationships with even more new people, and ad music people tend to move from one agency to another.

On the subject of the money that can be made from licensing music in commercials, it can vary widely, as now with the increasing value and validity of online-only ads, you can be asked to quote on music used in ads on TV, in theaters, on radio, and online—or maybe all at once! As with most things, the better-known the song, the higher the fee that can be commanded. For indie artists, this generally falls in the \$10,000–\$60,000 range. And with a large brand and a large song, depending on the territory and term of the use, we're talking hundreds of thousands of dollars, even, in rare cases, seven figures. For well-known artists and well-known songs, the sky's the limit.

Promos and Trailers

Another format that you might not think of right away as advertising is film trailers and TV promos. Of course, these are commercials, for films and television shows—but they generally have their own set of people who oversee the music used in these media, so this is yet another subset of contacts to develop and maintain.

Trailers are a unique animal. When a film studio decides to explore a campaign for an upcoming film, they solicit trailers from various companies. So it is common that we as publishers might receive briefs or requests for music for the same film from multiple trailer companies. Then all the different trailer companies submit their proposed ideas and the studio makes its choice and pays the negotiated fees (including whatever quote was negotiated for use of the music).

Trailers generally follow a story arc where there is an Act 1, Act 2, and final Act 3. While each "act" gets its own piece of music, it is crucial in ads that the music build steadily from its starting point towards a climax of some sort. This runs differently from most songs, which are in the verse/chorus/verse/chorus format (and maybe with a bridge and/or pre-chorus thrown in). So, in the more traditional song, the chorus is the focal point and the verses ebb and flow around it. Many times this structure won't work for trailers—that steady build is essential. As a result, there are companies that develop and maintain trailer libraries which contain music that is specifically created to fit the trailer format.

There are also different stages of a trailer campaign. The first trailer is usually the "teaser" that first introduces the upcoming movie to the world. These can be one to three minutes in length. Then you will see other trailers that expand upon the story and give you more of what the film is about. Trailers at each of these stages will typically appear both online and in theaters. As you get closer to the release, there will be trailers made for airing on TV only (shorter lengths, like thirty to sixty seconds) as the film's campaign heats up leading to the release date. The trailers released previously typically remain online as well throughout the campaign.

The fees for music used in trailers can vary significantly. Strictly instrumental pieces can be licensed starting in the $7,500–$10,000 range on up depending on whether it is part of a trailer library or is a known cue from a well-known movie (this is a one-time fee for a use usually in perpetuity). The more traditional song use might start at around $30,000–$40,000 and then again go up as high as the negotiation will allow. I've known of songs being paid $500,000 for use in a trailer. It is also more than possible, if a song were to be used both in a film and then also in a film's trailer, that the fee for use in the trailer would be more than the use in the film. This is because you are dealing with two entirely different budgets. The use in the film is the production budget, whereas the use in the trailer is in the marketing budget.

Whereas film trailers tend to license music in perpetuity (so trailers can live on DVDs released in the future, for example), TV promos tend to license music on a per-week basis. The majority of TV promos tend to use more library music than anything else because the cost (a one-time fee of $100–$250 per use and not per week) is so much cheaper. But a major network promo utilizing a well-known song can command $3,000–$5,000 per week for publishing only, and a similar amount for use of the master recording. Songs used in TV promos are usually known songs that will grab the attention of the viewer, or are selected on the basis of a direct connection to a story line or a character in the show that the promo is designed to highlight.

Pitching to trailers and promos is fun, as it involves trying to figure out what kind of story your song hook could connect to. And trailers are always interesting to pitch, given their need for those steady builds—so when you have a song that's structured that way, let your contacts know! Of course, the same pitching techniques we've talked about apply—links that allow streaming and downloading are best, and always try to avoid sending MP3 attachments.

KEEP YOUR LYRICS UNIVERSAL!

Pay attention to the songs that get used in commercials, trailers, and TV promos. Songs that are upbeat and positive with what might seem like universal or dare I even say generic lyrics are the ones that tend to get the most use—"Let's Get This Party Started," by the Black Eyed Peas, for example. "Raise Your Glass," by Pink. The list can go on. The more specific names you use in songs, the less likely your song might get used in commercials, trailers, or promos. The more general and universal the sentiment and the lyric (so that the lyrics can apply to the broadest of circumstances), the more likely your song will get used!

Video Games

No one ever makes lots of money from video games. The appeal of video games is the potentially massive exposure that one can get for your song because the most popular video games are selling millions of copies. Fees generally range from $1,000 to $5,000 for 100 percent publishing, and a similar amount for the master. And these fees are buyout fees—it's incredibly difficult to negotiate getting paid a per-unit royalty for every copy sold. Plus, for the most part there is no performance income when it comes to video games, as most folks are playing at home on their consoles instead of online. Music intensive games à la *Guitar Hero* and *Rock Band* used to pay royalties, but even then the typical royalty was one penny per copy that then had to be shared amongst all the publishers. Most everyone pitches to video games for the promotional value, because the serious gamers who do nothing but gameplay all day are potentially going to hear your song constantly and likely end up buying it somewhere. And many of these games, like the John Madden series or the Grand Theft Auto franchise, have become known for the music they include in their games, and the press releases regarding each new release and what music is included in the release can get a lot of press and exposure. Many of these games and gaming environments connect back to a central online store for ancillary purchases, so you can also end up selling singles and records. Video games also produce trailers to promote their upcoming releases, and these trailers all need music, so there can be opportunity there as well.

Writing for Music Libraries

As you can see, pitching music to the synch world can be quite a substantial endeavor. There are lots of relationships to develop and maintain. And it takes time to maintain them! And perhaps that is time that you could put to better use writing new songs. It's a personal choice. Regardless of whether you are a people person or not, there is only so much time in a day. And when you're creative and compose music, one thing that is worth considering is pitching yourself to be hired by a music library to compose and provide music to them.

Music libraries have become a core part of the synch world. There are lots of projects, and they all need music. And though I'm sure the producers of these projects would like to have unlimited budgets when it comes to music, they just don't. Music libraries receive the lowest fees generally of any music used in the licensing world. And that's not necessarily a reflection on the quality of the music—to the contrary, some music libraries have incredibly high-quality music. But the music is intended to be licensed in volume. And small fees in volume can lead to big income.

Due to the insatiable need in the licensing world for new music, composers and songwriters have the option to write for music libraries. These are typically work-for-hire agreements where you are provided an up-front fee or budget to cover your time and production costs, and in return the music library becomes the 100 percent publisher of the music you write and you retain 100 percent of the writer's share. Yes, you are giving up all the ownership in the music and half your income stream, but you are also gaining the sales force of the music library not only domestically but all over the world. The resulting income may not be large on a per-composition basis, but if you write music that is well received and you start to get a lot of uses, the income can add up quite quickly. Some people make an incredible living just writing music for libraries. Then you can still write your own projects that you retain ownership of—and you can fund them by getting paid to write music!

Working with Music Licensing Companies

Perhaps you have a lot of music that you've written but you don't yet have enough steady activity to warrant a full-on publishing deal or even an administration deal. You can of course buy the resources, do the research, and create, develop, and maintain the necessary relationships to succeed in the synch world. But sometimes it makes sense to work with a licensing company instead of doing all the work yourself.

Licensing companies are an interesting alternative to a full-on publishing deal. As their name implies, their only source of activity is synch licensing, so their work is very focused. If a licensing company likes your material, they can take it on for representation (either exclusively or non-exclusively, as we will see in a moment), pitch it to any and all synch opportunities that they feel it is appropriate for; and then, when they are successful in placing something, they will take a percentage of the up-front fee they negotiate for you. These percentages can range from 25 percent to 50 percent, so it is important to explore your options. Much like searching for any publishing deal, find folks who have good reputations and who you can see are getting music licensed. Sure, you have to give up a percentage, but in theory you are immediately tapping into their industry relationships that you don't have to develop yourself. It can be a good tradeoff to spending all of your time doing your own pitching.

Now let's look at exclusive and non-exclusive representation. If someone were to represent your music non-exclusively, it would mean that you are able to give that same music to someone else to pitch. And many do. One thing you will find with this type of deal is that many non-exclusive licensing companies will ask to retitle your song when they get a placement. Let's use an example. You have a song called "My Life Is a Party" that you wrote yourself and you own the publishing 100 percent. A non-exclusive licensing company that wants to represent your song tells you that you can still pitch it under the original title, but they will pitch it under the new title "Life's Party." When they register "Life's Party," part of their deal is that they will want to list their publishing company as either the sole publisher (à la a music library) or as a 50 percent publisher with your company listed as the other 50 percent publisher. Their idea is that any placements they do will be under their unique name, "Life's Party," so the income stream will always be clear on who generated the use.

But let's say that either you either pitch "My Life Is a Party" yourself, or your manager or someone else happens to pitch "My Life Is a Party" to the same music supervisor that got pitched "Life's Party." They will realize that they are the exact same song, being pitched to them under slightly different titles and by different companies. This will be a big red flag, as they are then not sure which party is the most appropriate and legal one to license the song from. They will most likely choose to not license the song at all, and your name and/or band name will now potentially forever be branded in that music supervisor's head as music that had an issue attached to it. That is definitely not what you want!

Many studios and prominent music supervisors have been vocal of late to say that they will not do business with any companies that are built on the non-exclusive representation of music, especially those that retitle. So, if you feel exploring a licensing company is the way to go, I would suggest meeting as many as you can and going with whomever you feel the most comfortable with and who you feel gets you as an artist. Then give them the exclusive for a year and see how they do. If it doesn't work out, you can always leave after the year and explore going to a different licensing company, or maybe at that point explore a publishing deal of some sort. A year may seem like a long time, but given the volume of music out there and the length of time it can take some time to get new music heard, a year will usually fly by.

I hope this has been a helpful overview of music publishing. It can be a complex area, especially when you take a worldwide view of all the opportunities you can pursue. But it is all time well spent, because the most valuable thing that you own is your own music. When it is handled properly and promoted properly, there is no limit to your income. So let's move on to Bobby Borg's "Promotion" section.

Part 5
Promotion

With
Bobby Borg

Introduction

After reading the first four sections of this book, you should now be more confident about writing, recording, performing, and licensing your products and services in the marketplace.

However, when it comes to promoting music and executing a successful promotion campaign, musicians will admit that they need as much help as they can get. In fact, many musicians will admit they're not even sure how to define the term "promotion."

Simply put, promotion is the process of communicating to your target audience what your product or service is and why they should care about it. By using the right words, images, prices, places, and media outlets that all appeal strongly to your audience, you can do the following:

- Get your target fans' *attention.*
- Hold their *interest.*
- Help them to *decide* that they really need your products and services.
- Get them to *act* (i.e., come to your shows, buy your recordings, and more).

Just remember that simply creating products or services and expecting people to come magically to you is unrealistic. You must seed the marketplace continually with your marketing messages, attract a loyal audience, and generate sales. Be clear that without sales, you have no business, you only have a hobby. This is why promotion is so important to your career.

Yes, I know—promoting your career takes a significant amount of time and energy. But by embracing a do-it-yourself (DIY) attitude and getting help from your friends and fans, you'll eventually get on the radar of industry persons who will be more interested in taking your career to that next level. And the best part is: a significant number of the things that I'm about to discuss can be done on a budget, or on none at all. I bet you're really happy about that!

The following five chapters cover important topics on promotion, from preparing to promote to creating promotional content that sells. Each chapter is short and sweet and provides a solid foundation on which to create a winning promotion campaign. And should you want to learn even more about music marketing and business, they make great introductory pieces to my other books, *Music Marketing for the DIY Musician* and *Business Basics for Musicians.*

Oh, and don't worry if you find one or two points in the following chapters that briefly repeat information from previous sections of this book. Promotion is not an isolated process from other aspects of your career—everything is connected.

So what are you waiting for? Turn the page and get started!

24 Preparing to Promote

You already know that promotion is the process of communicating to your target audience what your product or service is and why people should care about it. Now, to ensure that you communicate the right messages, some preliminary work is needed. This includes:

1. Segmenting and targeting your audience
2. Interpreting and defining your brand identity
3. Considering your products and services
4. Naming your price, and . . .
5. Knowing your place strategy

Step #1: Segment and Target Your Audience

The first step in preparing to promote involves considering all of the people who could potentially be fans of your music, segmenting them down into a variety of groups based on shared characteristics, and then promoting to the largest and potentially most profitable group first.

For instance, after conducting a little research, you may discover that your largest and most profitable audience consists uniquely of Irish-American metalcore rockers in Boston, ages eighteen to twenty-eight, who are into getting tattoos and piercings, skateboarding, and living a straight-edge lifestyle.

OUR MOST LIKELY FAN

With this information, you might then focus on getting airplay and interviews on Boston college radio stations, arranging sponsorships with local skateboard and tattoo shops, and creating catchy slogans for cool T-shirts that promote abstinence from drugs and alcohol.

The more you know about your target fans and their deeper preferences, the more targeted your promotion will be. You'll spend your time and money where it matters most.

Now, to segment and target your audience, and describe your most likely fan, consider these questions:

- Are your fans best described as hip-hoppers, metalheads, electronica fans, or other?
- What is their age range, gender, ethnicity, yearly income, education level, or religion?
- What are some of their lifestyle activities (e.g., going to concerts, skateboarding, going to car shows, attending yoga retreats, or reading literature)?
- What are they passionate about (e.g., politics, LGBT rights, racism, animal rights, saving the planet, playing video games, or technology)?

- What are the various websites and social networks they frequent?
- What clubs do they frequent?
- What magazines do they read?
- What radio stations do they listen to?
- What slang words or phrases do they use regularly?
- What brands (clothing, cars, alcohol, etc.) do they like?
- Can you define the geographic areas where they mostly live and where you'll most likely be performing and promoting your music (e.g., Los Angeles, Nashville, or New York City)?

To answer these questions, you can make logical assumptions based on your own observations of the world and society, examine the analytical tools provided in most social network platforms, and interview people who may already be your fans. You might also study the fans of artists who are most similar to you by examining their social networks or attending their shows, or you can use certain Web services like Quantcast (www.quantcast.com) and Alexa (www.alexa.com) that analyze customer demographics for your favorite bands and websites.

Whatever research methods you use, just be sure to seek answers to questions that make the most sense to you. In other words, focus on information that can help you to uncover what companies (clothing, alcohol, and energy drinks) are best to approach for sponsorships, what places (clubs, colleges, and military bases) are best to spread the word of mouth about your career, and what content (pictures, jokes, lyric videos, etc.) are most effective in attracting fans.

For our purposes, defining and targeting your audience should not be rocket science. Keep the process simple. Okay? Good!

Now, to illustrate the benefits of targeting your market, and to demonstrate just how easy conducting your own research can be, please see the story in the box below.

ANYTHING WORTHWHILE REQUIRES SOME WORK

Conducting research can yield some very important information about your fans, but the data is not just going to just fall into your lap. You don't have to kill yourself, but you must get out there and do a little work—oh, and have some fun, too.

One independent artist in Los Angeles (Loren Barnese of the female-fronted alternative/folk rock band Kids on McCadden) spent a weekend on several Los Angeles college campuses to uncover information about her most likely fans.

Accompanied by three volunteers who carried samples of the band's music and short questionnaires, Loren stopped students on campus who looked like they might be into alternative folk rock music.

After getting feedback on her songs, Loren and her volunteers asked the students their age, what they did for fun, what clubs they frequented, what their favorite pastimes were, what blogs they read, what internet sites they preferred, and more. Loren then considered this information when deciding on what to say in her promotional posters, what social networks to hit the hardest, and where to place promotional advertisements. In short, Loren's research helped her to focus her promotional efforts and ultimately save time and money. Good job, Loren and crew!

As you can see, anything worthwhile usually requires some work. So get busy!

Now let's move on to interpreting your brand identity.

Step #2: Interpret and Define Your Brand Identity

The next important step in preparing to promote is the process of interpreting and defining your brand identity.

Interpreting and defining your brand identity involves thinking about the image that best resonates with your target fans, deciding on important elements (like your genre, name, logo, personality, looks, and product packaging), and then making sure to convey one consistent, honest, and believable message in all of your marketing communications.

To interpret and define your brand identity, be sure to consider the following questions and make necessary adjustments:

STAND OUT FROM THE HERD

- Do your songs all have one cohesive style, and can you describe that style clearly (e.g., world, rap, country, pop, reggae, or some unique combination of styles)?
- Do your lyrics communicate a coherent message, and can you summarize that message in a few words (world peace, civil rights, life in the hood, having fun, etc.)?
- Does your band name project the vibe of your music and lyrics, and can you explain the meaning behind that name concisely (e.g., Marilyn Manson is composed of the names Marilyn Monroe [a beautiful movie star] and Charles Manson [a jailed murderer] to reinforce the artist's glam/metal sound)?
- Do the typefaces, colors, and images associated with your logo set a consistent mood, and can that mood be easily described (e.g., Pink uses a bold typeface and pink colors in her logo to convey her femininity and strong personality, and Mariah Carey displays her name in an elegant typeface with a small butterfly to convey her soft, feminine vibe)?
- Do you have a fashion style that matches your music and can it be described distinctly (e.g., Nicki Minaj's "colorful" costumes and wigs match her over-the-top alter ego personality and animated rap style, and Tony Bennett's well-pressed suits and ties match his classy behavior and his elegant jazz style)?
- Are your stage designs for your live performances intended to offer fans a certain experience, and can that experience be summed up clearly (e.g., "visually amazing" like Pretty Lights, or "intimate and stripped down" like Arthur Lee Land)?
- Do the organizations (charities, fund-raisers, foundations, etc.) with which you are associated with reinforce your overall values in life and song, and can these values be expressed easily in interviews (e.g., Ani DiFranco sang about contemporary social issues and supported certain political campaigns and human rights groups)? And finally . . .
- Is the brand identity you communicate to your audience overall cohesive in all aspects of your career, and is it something that will appear to be honest, believable, unique, interesting, and consistent compared to your musical competitors?

The above elements should help you to understand more about who you are and what you'd like to project, while also helping you better align your identity with that of your fans. To be sure, whether you're a "country/

pop rocker with Christian/family values" or a "metal madman with a passion for mayhem," interpreting and defining your brand will help you choose the right words and graphics in your advertisements, feature the right colors on your website pages, use appropriate font families on your promotional flyers, arrange sponsorships with the right product brands, and "look the part" in publicity photos and videos. Overall, you'll be more relatable. You'll stand for something clear that the fans can come to depend on time and time again.

So quit saying that "no image is your image." If you need help with deciding what your brand is all about, you can always look at other artists in your genre to see what they are doing or ask people who fit your target audience what they think. You can also consult with professionals, like graphic designers and stylists that come highly recommended. Sound good? Cool!

Now, before moving on to the next section, be sure to check out the box below.

BRAND IN A NUTSHELL: SINGER/SONGWRITER GABY MORENO

Gaby Moreno's core audience consists of Guatemalan-American music fans who appreciate quality music, meaningful lyrics, family values, art, and travel.

Her genre is "world," a blend of Latin, blues, pop, soul, and jazz music. Her lyrics are about everyday life, sung in both Spanish and English. Her look is classy and retro—she wears vintage flapper dresses, beaded headbands, and fancy hats. Her personality is friendly, warm, and gentle.

Gaby posts pictures of her travels around the globe on social networks, seeks interviews in a variety of cultural magazines, and performs on radio stations with world music formats (such as the National Public Radio station KCRW in Santa Monica).

Additionally, Gaby performs in art galleries and at world music festivals, her album artwork features scenic paintings and photographs, and her performances feature a variety of musicians and instruments. What's more, Gaby supports charities for needy kids in Guatemala.

Bottom line: Gaby's brand is seamless. From her products to her promotion—she conveys a consistent, clear, relevant, believable, and endearing brand identity to her audience in everything that she does. She is a worldly, sophisticated, bilingual artist. Her fans are extremely loyal and view her as one of their "tribe."

So what's your brand all about? Whatever it is, be sure to define it today!

Step #3: Consider Your Products and Services

So now that you've examined your target audience and interpreted your brand identity, you must thoroughly consider your products and services as yet another step in preparing to promote.

This step involves three important considerations: making sure that your products and services fit seamlessly with the overall brand image you desire, ensuring that the products you manufacture are what your target fans truly want, and identifying the characteristics that make your products unique and special.

Here are just a few specific questions to get you really thinking about your offerings:

- Have you considered all the configurations in which you can promote and sell your recordings (CD, vinyl, flash drive, download, download card, or stream), and are these choices in tune with the purchasing/listening/sharing habits of your fans?
- Have you thought about all of the different versions of just one song you can create (e.g., instrumental, acoustic, live, EDM remixes, translation versions, or sheet music) to thoroughly promote your music to your target fans and increase revenues?
- Do you have the appropriate T-shirt designs (e.g., printed with song lyrics, your album cover, or tour dates), hoodies, beanies, baseball caps, and other apparel to appeal to fans?
- Have you extended your line of merch into other interesting areas that fit with your fans' lifestyles (e.g., rolling papers, condoms, cinch bags, beer koozies, lighters, etc.)?
- Have you considered packaging a variety of items together (e.g., CDs, buttons, T-shirts, signed tour or comic books) into an attractive, limited-edition gift box set you can promote to collectors?
- Could you create additional products out of scraps (e.g., can you frame a broken drum head and drumstick that your drummer used to record your album, or make bracelets out of the broken guitar strings that your guitarist used in the studio)? Seriously! Fans love this kind of stuff.
- Have you considered creating a variety of different live performance sets (e.g., the full band set, the unplugged acoustic set, or the electronic DJ set) to increase the variety of ways you can promote to your fans and generate income?
- Do you have a "making of" video of your album, or a live concert video of a tour that you can package as a dual CD-DVD album, or just sell individually as another product?
- Have you thought about the unique selling points of each of your products and services so that you can better pitch them to your fans (perhaps it's the way your products make the audience feel, the statement they help the audience make among peers, the quality of materials they embody, the money they help save, or the customer service they guarantee)?
- Do all of your products work seamlessly with the desired image of your band? In other words, does the name of your band, the attitude you'd like to project, and the line of merch and recordings you offer all make one clear and consistent statement? Finally . . . .
- Do you have reliable companies in place to manufacture your products at the level of quality you desire and at a cost you can afford, and do you have enough units (of merch, CDs, etc.) manufactured to meet the demand of your audience in the first two months? After all, if you're going to work hard to promote yourself, you want to have enough high quality products available to sell.

I know I'm giving you a lot to think about, but I promise it will pay off. Remember, your products and services are the "stars of the show." They are at the center of your entire promotional campaign and what ultimately generates revenue and keeps your business afloat. Without quality products that meet the expectations of your audience, and without being able to clearly express why your fans should buy, you have nothing! Okay? Good!

PROMOTE THE BENEFITS!

While on the topic of your products and services, it's a good idea to further think about how they'll benefit your customers.

Be clear that at the beginning of your career, when no one knows who you are and what you do, it's going to take much more than just your name to get people interested. Understand that people buy because of how you make them feel about themselves, the problems you help them solve, and/or the fact you'll help them save time and money. In short, customers care mostly about "what's in it for them."

To illustrate my points, when creating promotional materials, the smart DJ/promoter does more than just print postcards that simply say:

DJ Bobby Vinyl, spinning tonight at Club Rave at 9:00 P.M.,
618 South Spring St., Los Angeles, CA. 90014. Be there!

Rather, the smart DJ also includes catchy information about:

1. The unique style of the music to be performed that night and how the event will be worth every penny of your money
2. The ambience of the club and the mood it will put you in
3. The hotness or coolness of the people expected to attend the event and the possibility you'll hook up with them
4. The special contest prizes you can win, and . . .
5. The special drink and food offers you'll get if you arrive before 10:00 P.M.

As you can see, these are all benefits that spell out why the customer should buy.

So don't just rely on the fact that you are God's gift to music and people will naturally come to your live performances or buy your merchandising products. Create a list that outlines the unique selling points of each of your products and services and be sure to include them in the appropriate promotional messages that you create. Okay?

Now, if this all sounds cool, then our work is done here. Let's move on to naming your price. Hang in there, we're almost done.

Step #4: Name Your Price

Determining the prices of your products and services (even if that means pricing them for "free") is yet another important preparatory step to an effective promotion campaign. Let's face it, the prices you advertise on your website, concert posters, and merch booths can affect directly whether your target audience purchases your recordings, attends your concerts, or takes home your T-shirts. In fact, your prices can even help shape the way your target audience thinks about you (i.e., low or high quality, inexperienced or experienced, etc.). Yup, that's right, folks—pricing, branding, and promoting all go hand in hand. I bet you never saw it that way!

Now, to ensure you establish the best pricing strategies for your products and services, consider the following questions:

- What are the age, social status, and income level of your target audience, and how might this information affect the prices that you'll charge?
- What is the image you hope to impress upon your audience (e.g., one of high quality for people with money, or of mid quality for people on a budget)?
- What are the prices that your target fans are used to paying for the product or services you offer, and what are the prices that you are willing to charge?
- What did, or will, it cost to bring your products and services to market?
- What are your goals (to build awareness, break even, or make a profit), and how will you set your prices to ensure that you meet these goals (e.g., price for free, price to cover your bottom-line costs, or price above your bottom-line costs to make a profit)?
- What are the prices your competition charges, and how will they affect your pricing decisions (will you match your prices with competitors and go head to head, or will you raise your prices and focus on the quality of the products you offer)?
- Do you intend to sell items separately or bundle two or three together in a package (e.g., you might sell your recording for $10, a T-shirt for $15, and a patch for $5, and then bundle them all together for $20)?
- Do you intend to offer a special holiday or event discount to entice customers? And . . .
- Will you have control over all of your pricing strategies (note that since iTunes and other services dictate pricing, you may not have a choice in deciding what to charge)?

Just be sure to consider the prices of all of your products and services including your recordings, T-shirts, buttons, hats, bandanas, patches, rolling papers, live performances, and anything else you offer. Then consider including these prices in all of your marketing communications (your Internet sites, postcards, press releases, and everywhere else that's appropriate).

Also, remember that pricing is not just about setting amounts, posting them on your websites, and forgetting about them. Pricing is an ongoing process that can be adjusted regularly utilizing short-term sales promotions and other strategies to entice customers to buy.

Finally, remember that your pricing decisions must eventually lead to company profitability, or you won't be in business for long. So be sure to monitor your strategies to make sure that they are really working. Or, to paraphrase rapper Snoop Dogg, "Keep your mind on your money and your money on your mind." Ha ha. I know that was silly, but you get the point. Right? Good! Now check out the box below.

PRICING AND PROMOTION GO HAND IN HAND

For many young artists, pricing a product amounts to arbitrarily coming up with a number and forgetting about it. However, as I am about to illustrate below, you'll see that creative and thoughtful pricing can help promote your career and create a buzz. While some of these strategies may not be something you can execute when starting out, I am sharing them with you to inspire your own innovations!

- **KID ROCK:** Just when concerts were costing from $75 to $125, and as much as $300 to $1,250 on the secondary market, Kid Rock charged a low $20 for his "$20 Best Night Ever" tour. By taking the exact opposite approach from what other artists were doing, Kid Rock created quite the buzz among fans and media folk. In fact, the strategy was so successful, Kid Rock repeated the move on his next tour in support of his album *First Kiss*.

- **WU-TANG CLAN**: Upon release of their new double album *Once Upon a Time in Shaolin*, Wu-Tang Clan announced that they'd release only one album (i.e., 1 unit) that fans could pay to hear in art galleries, museums, and festivals. Since people love exclusivity and the idea of having something no one else has, the group received bids for the album for as high as $5 million. The concept was that music should be treated as a valuable and respected piece of art, and not something people download from the Internet at no cost. Clever!
- **NIPSEY HUSSLE:** Unsigned rapper Nipsey Hussle pressed 1,000 units of his album Crenshaw and sold them at a price of $100 each. Under a campaign he entitled Proud2Pay, customers were also rewarded with concerts, priority access to new material, and one-of-a-kind gifts, like an old rap notebook or signed photo. Nipsey's intention was not necessarily to sell out the units to his target audience, but to attract the attention of a few bigwigs in the music business. It worked! Rap legend Jay-Z swooped up 100 copies of the Hussle's music.

So, as you can see, pricing and promotion really do go hand in hand. Now, let's move on to the last preparatory step in the chapter: "knowing your place."

Step #5: Know Your Place

Determining where your target audience will potentially find, purchase, and enjoy your products and services, and then including these places in your promotion campaign and marketing communications, are additional preparatory steps that cannot be overlooked. In short: Whether it's your recordings, merch, or live performances sets, you must first try to get your offerings in all of the right places, and then remind people continually where they can find and buy them. Building awareness and making sales is the essence of promotion.

Now, to determine the best places to distribute and promote your products and services, consider this:

- What type of fans do you serve (alternative rockers, ravers, hip-hoppers, etc.), and where will these fans most likely want to see, hear, and find your music?
- What is the geographic region where you and your fans live, and what are the opportunities to sell, perform, and promote music in this territory?
- What schools are your target fans enrolled in, and can you perform in these institutions and/or sell music and merch in these schools' bookstores?
- What are some of the concert venues and hangouts your target fans frequent, and can you perform and/or promote and network at any of these establishments?
- Do your fans congregate in a specific part of your town (a promenade, shopping mall, flea market), and can you busk and sell your music at these locations?
- What does your target fan do for fun (sports and other lifestyles) and do these activities offer any ideas about where (surfing competitions, tattoo festivals, weed conventions) you can place and promote your recorded music, merch, and live sets?

- Where does your target audience shop for music and merch (both online and off), and does this offer any smart ideas that you can use in your place and promotion plan?
- What distributors do your competitors use for placing their recorded music (e.g., CDBaby, Tunecore, the Orchard, MondoTunes, Ditto Music), and can any of these companies fit into your place and promotion campaign as well?
- What methods do your competitors use to plug and promote their songs in film and T.V (e.g., joining services like Taxi Music, speaking with college film departments, networking at Sundance Film festival, etc.), and are any of these methods right for you? And . . .
- Are your competitors using any local talent agents in your area to help them book shows and sell merch, and might these folks be willing to work for you as well?

A hard rock band might discover that it can play a variety of special venues (such as tattoo conventions, skateboard parks, and independent record/comic shops), license its individual songs in different media (video games, extreme sports broadcasts, and documentary ski films), and sell its recordings and merch in a variety of places (via sponsorships with athletic apparel brands, surf and skate shops, and college campus bookstores. It can then inform its target audience about where to find and buy these offerings by including specific addresses, URLs, and phone numbers in e-mails, magazine adverts, and even on the back of T-shirts. I know one band on Los Angeles that included the slogan "Find us on iTunes" on the back of their T-shirts.

Yeah, yeah—I'm aware you'll have to make some phone calls and convince some intermediary distributors (agents, retail stores, Internet sites, etc.) to let you place your offerings. And yes, I'm aware you'll often have to give these folks a percentage of the profits for helping you out. But as long as you can show there's a demand for your products and services, you're in business. And when all else fails, remember that you can often bypass certain intermediaries altogether and go directly to your fans by selling from your own website and producing your own events and raves. Okay?

Now check out the story in the box below for a real-world example of how promoting in all the right places really works. Enjoy!

PROMOTE IN ALL THE BEST PLACES

To illustrate the importance of knowing where your target audience will potentially find, purchase, and enjoy your products and services, and then including these places in your promotion campaign and marketing communications, let's take a look at an "out of the box" idea by indie artist Joe Rothe.

After considering the types of fans that he served (largely, the Jewish community), and where these people spend a great deal of time (synagogues), Joe began to craft his promotion campaign around a religious theme. Rather than just promoting his music in local bars and Internet sites (like most artists would do), Joe met face-to-face with synagogue directors, expressed how his music could be a positive influence on the younger Jewish community, and convinced the directors to hire him as a live performer.

Soon enough, Joe was able to build a live performance schedule that had him touring synagogues across the country, selling his music and T-shirts bearing positive religious messages in synagogue gift shops, and earning significant money. The best part is that the synagogues helped promote both where Joe was performing and where his music and merch were on sale via their weekly newsletters, e-mail lists, and other announcements that reached thousands of followers.

You see, it really does pay to thoroughly investigate where your target audience will potentially find, purchase, and enjoy your products and services, and then include these places in your promotion campaign and marketing communications. Bottom line: Put your stuff where your fans are most likely to find it, and then tell them where and how they can buy it.

So, that's about it on place and promotion, and for this entire chapter. Congratulations, you made it. Next up: "Choosing Your Promotion Strategies." Read on.

25 Choosing Your Promotion Strategies

Now that you've conducted some preliminary research and you're more prepared to promote, you must consider a mix of promotion strategies.

While many young musicians focus only on using the Internet, there are at least ten promotion strategies that can be used to communicate what your product is and why your audience should care. These include:

1. Stimulating publicity and building public relations
2. Utilizing paid advertising
3. Using the Internet
4. Helping to spread the word of mouth
5. Going apeshit with guerrilla marketing
6. Getting your music on the radio
7. Affiliating with sponsors
8. Using direct marketing
9. Selling your audience face-to-face, and . . .
10. Utilizing sales promotions

What follows is a tremendous amount of information and ideas. So take a deep breathe and let's get to work.

Tactic #1: Stimulate Publicity and Build Public Relations

Publicity refers to articles, reviews, and comments that journalists write about you because they want to write about you. In other words, because you "earned" their interest and respect.

PR refers to what happens in the minds of your target audience as a result of great publicity. Overall, fans are left with a much stronger image of you, your offerings, and your brand.

So how should you start stimulating publicity and building good PR? Consider the following:

- Be sure to have an interesting hook/story/position on which to launch your publicity campaign (e.g., you're an "all military" metal band, an all-girl samba group, or a band that's composed of former members of successful groups).
- Create an informative press kit (physically and digitally) that includes a biography, professional photograph, current news release (a.k.a. press release), a business card, and a sample of your music. (I'll be discussing all of these items in detail in subsequent chapters, so hang in there.)
- Create a contact list of local magazines, newspapers, and blogs read by your target audience, and jot down the names of the writers and editors you'd like to contact.

- Cultivate close relationships with the people on your contact list by first reaching out to them and complimenting them on their work.
- Send local journalists (after getting permission) your press materials and be clear about what it is you want from them: A record review, a live performance review, or an interview.
- Become part of the local news by being part of your local scene: Attend other artists' shows, go to award ceremonies, and attend parties where local press people hang out.
- Participate in community activities you strongly believe in (such as a 5k run for cancer, or a food drive for the homeless), and then inform the local press of the good deeds you do.
- Start your own magazine/blog and write about local bands (including your own).
- Capitalize on your school's paper, newsletter, etc. (where you already have an "in") by asking them to do a story or review about your band.
- Ask important people for quotes and testimonials and then include them in your biographies, press releases, and anywhere else that you can.
- Devise a "publicity stunt" (a sneaky/crazy/daring activity) that gets press people to take notice and write about you. Whether you perform on the back of a flatbed truck as it drives down Main Street, or attend a ceremony half naked with a political statement written across your chest, just don't do anything too illegal. Okay? And . . .
- Engage passionate fans to handle your publicity campaign for you, or, if you can afford it, hire a talented communications student at a local college.

As you can see, there are a variety of different ways to generate publicity and strengthen your public's perception of you. But don't be misled: publicity and PR are not as easy as 1-2-3. They require follow-up (over long periods of time) just to get one magazine or blog review. But if you are pleasant, charming, and have a great product, all the hard work will all pay off. I'm rooting for you!

Now, before moving on to the next section, let's take a more detailed look at the box below and an important question that is frequently asked: when should you hire a publicist?

TO HIRE OR NOT TO HIRE, THAT'S THE QUESTION

An important issue that always seems to come up in all discussions about publicity is when to hire a professional music publicist. Here are a few thoughts:

First, be clear that an experienced publicist can be very expensive (as much as several thousands of dollars a month) and will need several months of working with you to truly make anything happen. Therefore, if you don't have a significant amount of money in your budget, hiring an experienced publicist may not be the right move for you.

Second, while the most seasoned and expensive professionals can help to brand you and create a strong image in the minds of the fans, publicists are usually hired to promote your pre-existing and well-defined "story" (i.e., the record you've already recorded, the overall "cause" that you believe in, the tour dates that you have coming up, etc.). If you don't have any of these things in place, remember that you may not be ready for a professional publicist.

Third, while many seasoned professionals do have close relationships with top media people (at major blogs, established news networks, popular television stations, etc.), remember that unless you have some success on a national scale, you're not yet ready for these connections.

So, what's the best course of action for a young artist just starting out? Good question. How about just rolling up your sleeves and taking a DIY approach first?

Doing it yourself does take organization and persistence, but it can definitely be done by delegating the workload among band members, or by getting superfans to volunteer their help. Then, when you start making money, you can hire a talented communications student part-time or an experienced music business consultant for a few sessions to offer some helpful advice. From there, you might eventually move on to hiring an established publicity firm. Got it? Awesome! Let's move on to advertising.

Tactic #2: Utilize Paid Advertising

You already learned that publicity refers to the articles, reviews, and comments in magazines and newspapers that journalists write about you because you have earned their respect. Now, in contrast, let's take a look at paid advertising.

Paid advertising refers to the advertisements that magazines, newspapers, broadcasters, and Internet sites publish about you because you paid them. While paid advertising is not as credible as earned publicity, a well-written ad can still be quite effective when placed in the right media over an extended period of time.

Here are a few paid advertising methods you might consider:

- Use Internet search engine advertising (i.e., small text ads placed on results pages of a specific keyword search made by target consumers) to ensure that people can find your personal website. Check out Google Adwords for starters.
- Consider social media advertising with the major platforms (like Facebook, Twitter, and YouTube) to better expose your videos and text posts, and to help you build more followers/subscribers.
- Consider mobile advertising and texting banner ads, "quick response" (QR) codes, and "text-to-win" codes. Search for mobile marketing companies online to get started.
- Place print ads in local music mags, newspapers, yellow pages, and music-business-related directories that appeal to your fans.
- Look into buying local "spot ads" on radio stations that cater to your target audience (the ads may not be as expensive as you think).
- Contact local cable TV stations and buy spot ads to air before or during the shows that attract your target audience.
- Find a local company that specializes in outdoor advertising and consider getting a wrap (a large decal) for your car, band van, or business vehicle.
- Contact a manufacturer of specialty advertising items (lighters, pens, calendars, USB flash drives, etc.) that include your brand name and logo and then give them away to your target fans for free.

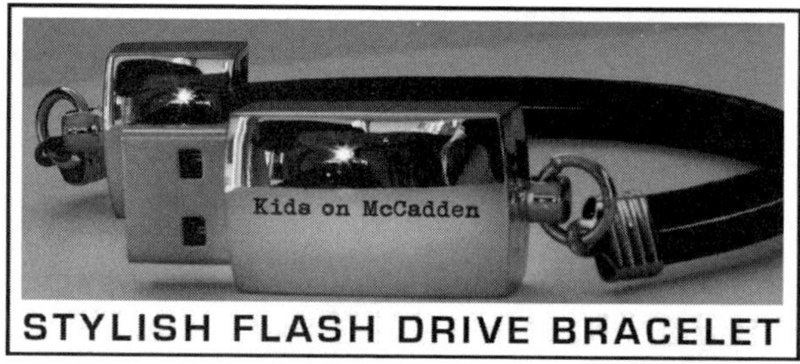

STYLISH FLASH DRIVE BRACELET

Whichever of the methods above you use, just remember that your success will depend greatly on how you craft your ads. A well crafted Web ad, for instance, will typically contain an attention-grabbing "header" (title/intro) focusing on your uniqueness, an informative "body" (middle point) selling the benefits of your products and services, and an action-packed "close" (ending) getting your target fans to take action. When appropriate, ads often contain attractive graphics that show off the product or service, or use some other photo that engages your audience.

Just be realistic and patient with paid advertising; it often takes repeated views of an advertisement over extended periods of time for it to be successful. Results won't come overnight—so you must be careful not to overextend your budget. Speak with representatives at the advertising companies you're considering and ask for media kits that outline important information about the audience, the number of people who might see the ad, and more. That's pretty much all I have to say for paid advertising.

And now, ladies and gentlemen, let's move on to the third and most popular strategy: internet promotion.

Tactic #3: Use the Internet

Internet promotion is the process of leveraging new technologies. Just like other promotion strategies, the goal should be to attract your target fans' attention, hold their interest, and get them to "take a buying action" (whether that be signing up for your newsletter or buying a T-shirt).

The Internet is one of the most popular promotion strategies these days because people believe it to be the most convenient and low-cost method.

While most of you are already savvy on the Internet, what follows are a few online promotion ideas that you might consider using for your music career:

- Create a personal website where you direct and attract potential customers. You can use services like Virb (www.virb.com) and Wix (www.wix.com).
- Maintain your own blog on platforms like Tumblr (www.tumblr.com) and WordPress (www.wordpress.com) where you post up-to-the-minute news and pictures.
- Create profiles on popular social networks like Snapchat (www.snapchat.com) to engage fans in a casual and nonintrusive way.
- Post video clips on sites like Vimeo (www.vimeo.com) and YouTube (www.youtube.com). Use concert footage, humorous videos, shocking clips, cover videos, and/or videos that feature your lyrics. (I'll discuss how to create video content in detail later.)
- Stream your performances in real-time from sites like Ustream (www.ustream.com) and other services like Periscope (www.peroscope.tv).
- Post interesting photographs on photo-sharing sites like Instagram (www.instagram.com).
- Use an e-mail service like MailChimp (www.mailchimp.com) or Constant Contact (www.constantcontact.com) to help you send personalized and targeted e-mails and newsletters.
- Create a podcast that provides news about both your local scene and your band. You can use platforms like BlogTalkRadio (www.blogtalkradio.com) for starters.

- Post your live performance events on message boards like Craigslist (www.craigslist.org) and on services like Eventbrite (www.eventbrite.com).
- Contact music blogs and fan sites that review independent artists' recordings. You can try Pitchfork (www.pitchfork.com), Stereogum (www.stereogum.com), and Rap Radar (www.rapradar.com).
- Use Web directories like DMOZ (www.dmoz.org) to list your band's website and link.
- Send your music to Web radio stations that feature independent artists just like you. Browse sites like Live365 (www.live365.com) to find the right stations for you. And . . .
- Build your own Web radio station and feature yourself and other local artists. Use software like Shoutcast (www.shoutcast.com) to help you get started today.

Just remember not to fall back exclusively on promoting yourself on the Web. To be an effective marketer you must create an integrated system of marketing communications where you are using a variety of different methods to achieve the desired results. Think of this as cooking. Would you just use salt for flavoring? Or would you use a variety of different spices? Hopefully, you answered with the latter—a variety of spices.

Let's finish off with a few more words about social networking. Check out the box below.

BUILDING YOUR NUMBERS ON SOCIAL NETWORKS

While on the topic of the Internet, it's a good idea to focus on your social networks. Having a high number of friends, followers, and subscribers on your social networks makes you appear successful in the minds of the public, which then attracts even more fans who want to be part of your tribe. But striving for "quality" numbers should always come first.

Some artists build their numbers by paying "online marketing services" to immediately add hundreds of thousands fans to their networks. While this may sound like a good idea, some companies (not all) use fake fan accounts, and/or load you up with people outside of your target market. Since "fake" fans won't engage with your postings, they can reduce the relevancy of your messages on some networks and lower your odds for reaching real fans. Even worse, did you know these fake friends are just a click away from getting deleted by the networks? Yup! According to some profiles, you can go from hero to zero over night.

Other artists build their numbers by reaching out directly to their target audience with interesting content (music, videos, pictures, and more), tagging their content with the right keywords so that fans can more easily find them, posting content at the most opportune times of the day and on a consistent schedule, and using the targeted advertising services of social networks to gain one new fan at a time.

While this approach may sound daunting and "easier said than done," your continual commitment to engaging with your fans will pay off in the long run. Most of the fans with whom you connect will be more likely to remain loyal followers for life—in part, because they are "real" fans, not fake. Furthermore, industry professionals who initially take notice of your career will see that your social success is genuine, and that it leads to conversions (i.e., real record sales, merch sales, and concert ticket sales).

Be clear that building your numbers on social networks is important and can give you the appearance of success. But "quality" numbers is what ultimately matters most. Okay? Good!

Now let's move on to spreading the word of mouth.

Tactic #4: Help Spread the Word of Mouth

Word-of-mouth marketing is the process of getting your target audience to naturally talk about your products and services and recommend your offerings to friends and fellow tribe members. The buzz created by all this chatter is one of the key reasons why people decide to check you out.

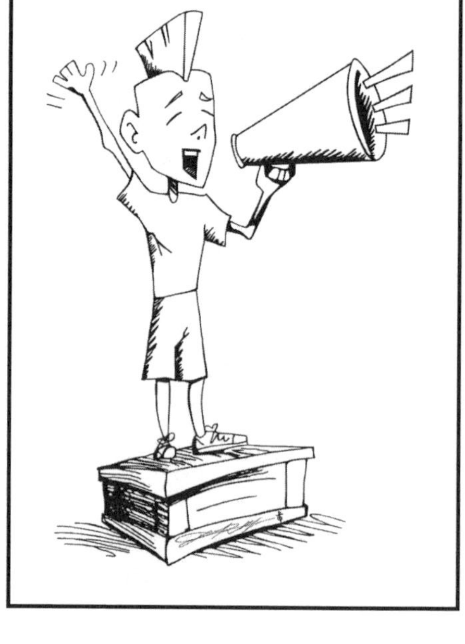

But how can you get people to start talking naturally about your products and services? Good question. Here are a few brief tips to consider:

- Create amazing products and services first and foremost. Strive for the highest quality possible in everything that you do, and the results just may surprise you.
- Offer excellent customer service (shake hands with fans after every show, send out birthday wishes, and respond to social media posts as often as you can).
- Give out samples of your work and ask people to "tell a friend" if they like it.
- Make sure to get your product in the hands of that hip journalist and social networker who has a large network of followers.
- Create "teaser ads" that leak small doses of information about your releases over time (e.g., start with a poster that includes your URL and logo and says no more than "coming January 1," and then follow up one week later by adding your name, image, and detailed info).
- Use intriguing words like "exclusive" or "never before seen" in the titles of your videos, social media posts, and more.
- Use sex, humor, and shock appeal in your videos, photographs, and postcards.
- Hold a special contest that offers a cool and valued prize.
- Create scavenger hunts where, for instance, fans must find items you place around town and post photographs of these items on the web. And . . .
- Leak information to the "cool kids" in your town that everyone trusts and wants to emulate.

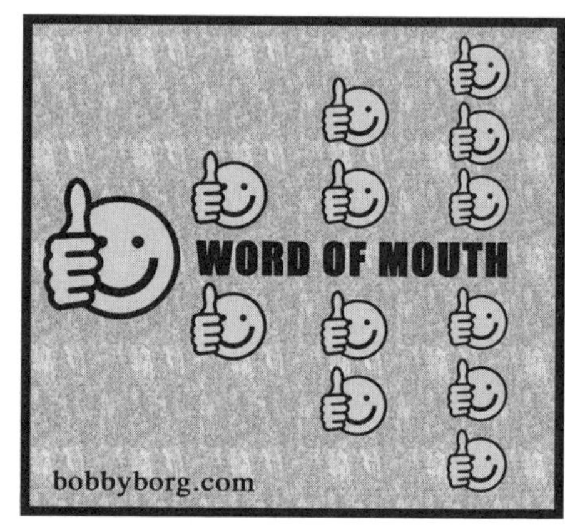

Given the development of new technologies that can help spread your marketing messages online with viral efficiency, word-of-mouth marketing is expected to evolve quickly over the coming years.

To learn more about it, check out WOMMA (The Word-of-Mouth Marketing Association), which provides webinars, conferences, and articles for its members and sets ethical guidelines (you can see them at http://womma.org). Also be sure to check out *The Tipping Point*, by Malcolm Gladwell, who focuses on word-of-mouth marketing and how news can "go viral."

Now be sure to check out the box below and read how shock appeal can get people talking.

WORD OF SHOCK

To illustrate how shock appeal can help spread the word of mouth and get people talking about your brand, let's look at Hell on Earth.

Hell on Earth is a Florida heavy metal band that claimed to support assisted suicides. The group announced that it was throwing a concert in a local club where a terminally ill fan was going to end his life on stage. As a result, the city council of St. Petersburg pressured the theater to shut down the show. This created great controversy and brought national attention to the band in magazine articles, blog postings, radio programs, television news reports, and public forums. Soon everyone was talking about the band and helping to spread the news around the country.

While the above example is certainly not something I would advocate for every band to do, it does illustrate how shock appeal can help a message spreadlike wildfire. If you can create something that fits your brand, that is within legal limits, and that is well thought out and planned, then why not create a little shock in your target audience's lives? Of course you should always rely on your talents and music first and foremost, but in the crowded marketplace in which we all live, sometimes a little shock is just what's needed to cut through all the clutter and get people to start the conversation.

So, that's all I have to say about this topic. What do you say we move on to another form of promotion that is both low-budget and easy to execute? At number 5, introducing guerrilla marketing. Read on, my friends.

Tactic #5: Go Apeshit with Guerrilla Marketing

Guerrilla marketing is akin to guerrilla warfare—anti-establishment attacks in small and menacing doses followed by a quick retreat into the thickly grown jungles.

Okay, so promoting your career isn't quite like going to war, but the principle is similar: you have a fraction of the money that the big record labels have, you're on your own despite your business partners and a few loyal fans, and you must resort to low-budget street techniques executed in the dark of night to make your mark. Dramatic, isn't it?

Here are some guerrilla marketing strategies you might use to promote your career:

- Stand in front of nightclubs that play your kind of music and hand out postcards or flyers to fans.
- Create cardboard stencils of your name and "spray chalk" your brand on city sidewalks.
- Make intriguing flyers announcing your gigs and tack them up around your town.
- Burn CDs of your music that includes information about your next gig on the disc and give them away for free.

- Manufacture stickers including your URL and stick them everywhere you can (e.g., in the bathroom stalls of cool clubs, tattoo shops, etc.). And . . .
- Perform in an unauthorized place (a crowded mall or city street) and split before the cops get there to tell you the act was illegal.

All jokes aside, I should really say (as a disclaimer) that you should never promote your products and services in a way that can get you in trouble. Examine and respect the laws of your town, city, state, country, etc., and always trust your better judgment. Speak with a public official such as your local police department if you have any questions. Would you believe that the police department once phoned and asked me to remove all the flyers I had hung up on telephone poles? (It was either that or receive a $250 littering fine. At sixteen years of age, I was scared out of my pants!) So behave.

Next up, radio promotion at number 6. Hang in there, we're more than halfway done.

Tactic #6: Get Your Music on the Radio

Radio is a powerful medium that allows artists to reach several hundred—or even several thousand—potential fans in just one play. While commercial radio stations in major cities (like New York, Los Angeles, and Nashville) are a tough nut to crack, most artists can use a number of other radio media. These include: college radio stations, National Public Radio stations (NPR), commercial specialty shows (the "locals only" shows you hear on the weekends on major stations), satellite radio stations (like Sirius XM Radio), Web radio stations, and smaller market commercial stations.

Obtaining station contact information and submission policies is not difficult to do. For starters, you can use Radio-Locator (www.radio-locator.com), Indie Bible (www.indiebible.com), and Live365 (www.live365.com). Next, you can follow the directions listed on the station's website about what to send (e.g., CD or digital file) and to whom to send it (e.g., the disc jockey or music director).

After sending the station your music, you are now ready to promote it. Consider this:

- Call and/or e-mail the station and politely ask for feedback.
- If the station likes your music, ask them to add it to their playlists.
- Send a personable "thank you" card immediately after they play your music.
- Ask for a testimonial about your music to use on your website and in promo kits.
- Try to schedule station interviews and live station performances.
- Provide the station's personnel with records, merchandise, and concert tickets they can give away on their shows.
- Send in prerecorded "station identifications" (e.g., "This is John Doe and you're listening to KXLU").
- Provide pre-recorded "station drops" to the DJ (where you remix a song to include a specific station's call letters or DJ's name).
- Invite the DJ to your shows as a guest.
- Ask the DJ to MC your live performance (i.e., introduce you before you perform).
- Ask your fans to listen to the station and to call and inquire about your music when they hear your songs played. And . . .

- Ask the DJs for references to college bookers, other radio DJs, and publicists (note that radio people are usually well connected and willing to help you spread the word).

While the above strategies may sound like a lot of work, you should know that radio promotion is not that difficult to do on your own. To be successful, you just need to be organized, persistent, and pleasant.

And who knows, if you're able to get your music added to several college stations in the same week, you just might chart with College Music Journal (CMJ), an organization that charts college radio play. Note that CMJ's charts are viewed by a wide array of music industry folk (from A&R to music publishers), and charting can open some doors for you. Sounds pretty darn good to me! You can check out more about CMJ by visiting their website (www.cmj.com).

But wait! What about hiring an independent radio promoter to do all of the work for you? Well, if you've a few thousand dollars for a short campaign, go for it. But I'd suggest that you check out the story in the box below to confirm just how it easy it can be to do it yourself.

GETTING PLAYED IS EASIER THAN YOU THINK

To illustrate the ease of getting broadcast on college radio stations, allow me to share a story about the first time I got played.

As the member of a progressive rock band in Princeton, N.J., I become a fan of a local progressive rock show on Princeton University's college radio (WPRB).

Upon the release of my band's first record, I visited the station on campus—just as the DJ was finishing his show—and told him face-to-face that I loved his music and would give anything to get his opinion of our album. I handed him an attractive envelope that included our album and an informational "one-sheet" (one sheet of paper that included our name, picture, key accomplishments, brief history, and contact number) and thanked him for his time. It was as simple as that.

Within one week, the DJ played our song. I was so excited when I heard it that I literally knocked the radio off of my desk at home. To add to the excitement, in the following weeks the DJ provided flattering testimonials that we used in promotional pieces, interviewed me on-air, and referred us to other college DJs that were interested in broadcasting our music. Cool!

Today, getting played on college radio can be as easy as sending an e-mail. Just make a list of your local college radio stations by searching online, visit the stations' websites for submission guidelines, and fire away. Just be sure to follow up and always be extremely pleasant and patient. Remember, in this crazy business of music, no one owes you anything!

Tactic #7: Affiliate with Sponsors

Moving to yet another promotion strategy, sponsorships are mutually beneficial relationships in which artists can receive assistance in promoting their records and performances, and branded companies can advertise their products and services.

To arrange sponsorships, you can begin by making a list of all the products and services associated with your target fans. If you're a pop punk band, for instance, you might list Doc Marten boots, Flowlab skateboards, Ray-Ban glasses, Zippo lighters, and Rockstar energy drinks.

Next, make a detailed list of the local businesses and national corporations associated with the products and services on your list, visit these companies' websites, and jot down the name of the store owner, corporate brand manager, or company event coordinator.

When contacting these companies (by phone, e-mail, etc.), be prepared to show that you've already created a strong buzz in your community, and that you can help expose their brand.

Once sponsors are in place, you can do the following to maximize your relationships:

- Ask sponsors to hang your flyers (for local live performances, etc.) in their retail stores.
- Ask retail sponsors to broadcast your music over their PA systems during store hours.
- Ask local sponsors if you can perform live in their retail stores.
- Ask retail sponsors if you can sell your physical product (CDs, merch, etc.) in their stores.
- Ask sponsors to include your name and image on their websites and in their advertising (print ads, television spots, etc.).
- Build credibility by including your sponsors' logos on your flyers, websites, and more.
- Participate in any special events (battle of the bands, etc.) held by your sponsors.
- Inquire about getting on music compilations or special mixes that branded companies often produce (e.g., Saturn put together a music compilation of unsigned singer/songwriters and distributed it with all of its cars). And . . .
- Arrange cross-branding opportunities (e.g., I arranged the Dean Markley / Bobby Borg Model Drum stick, which helped spread the word about my band and generate income for me).

For more information, please refer to the global authority on sponsorships, IEG, and its two books: *The IEG Source Book* and *The IEG Complete Guide to Sponsorships* (www.sponsorship.com). These resources list strategies for obtaining sponsorships and are incredibly helpful to developing artists like you. Note that IEG even holds a regular convention that could be a good networking opportunity.

For a great example of how sponsorships can help you to creatively promote your products and services, check out the box below.

SPONSORSHIPS IN ACTION

For an annual charity concert I organized in Los Angeles, my UCLA marketing students approached a local hip clothing store on Melrose Avenue called Golf Punk. The store provided the students with free clothing to wear on stage and T-shirts to give-away to fans, it played the students' music in its retail store, and it hung large posters in its store windows to promote the event. All the class had to do was include the store's logo on posters and mention the store's name when on stage.

In another example, the local Hollywood metal band Kings of Carnage joined forces with the alcohol brand Cold Cock Whiskey. The company provides the band with free product (such as alcohol, T-shirts, and stickers), it promotes the band on its company website and advertising collateral, and it is willing to show up to their concerts to provide free taste tests. All the band has to do is hang a Cold Cock Whiskey banner on stage when it performs and mention the whiskey in blog interviews and social network posts.

The above examples, while not groundbreaking, illustrate how easily sponsorships can be arranged. In the overcrowded music marketplace, where hundreds of thousands of bands are trying to get noticed, you must always think of new ways to spread the word about your music. Just pick up the phone, contact the store owner or corporate brand manager of products/services that fit your audience, and tell them how both you and they can benefit. The rest will lead to increased exposure, sales, and success! So be proactive and start making deals happen today. You'll be glad you did.

Tactic #8: Use Direct Marketing

Getting close to the end of this chapter, allow me to introduce one of the oldest—yet still relevant—promotional tactics today: direct marketing.

Direct marketing is a promotional strategy whereby you bypass middle persons and directly contact customers. Using a contact database, it involves communicating marketing messages via snail mail, e-mail, telephone, text message, mobile apps, and more.

Here are a few ways that you might use direct marketing to promote your music:

- Create an attractive postcard that announces your next gig and send it in the mail.
- Design a small poster on 8.5" x 11" paper folded in thirds and send it in an envelope.
- Hire a fan with an attractive voice to telephone your fans and invite them to your events. Since no one does this anymore, the message may really stick with your fans.
- Set up a toll-free hotline where customers can call in to receive information (you can search the Web for info on doing this).
- Send a concise text message and inform fans about your record release.
- E-mail offers to your fans using concise subject lines and to-the-point messages.
- Invite your social network contacts to click on links to your website store. And . . .
- Search online for companies that build customized mobile apps complete with links to your store, and then distribute the app to potential customers.

No matter what direct marketing method you use, just remember that "content is king." Hence, it is crucial that you craft an effective message that earns your customers' attention, explains what's in it for them (i.e., why they should care), and gets them to take action (i.e., gets them to come to your gig or click on your link). Your messages must be short, sweet, and respectful of peoples' time. If needed, test your messages out on a few fans before soliciting your entire list.

When executing your direct marketing strategy, be sure to use multiple direct marketing methods with optimum timing. For instance, send an e-mail to your list two weeks before a show, send out postcards one week before the show, and call each fan one night before the show. Since the recipients are hearing about your gig through a number of different sources, one after the other, your message is more likely to stick.

Finally, always be sure to keep your database of fans and industry professionals up to date. Delete old addresses immediately and remove the names of people who no longer want to receive your information.

While direct marketing techniques are often frowned upon and considered spam or junk mail, they can be quite effective when targeting your contacts in a polite and friendly manner.

Now let's discuss our next-to-last strategy, face-to-face selling.

Tactic #9: Sell Your Audience Face-to-Face

Face-to-face selling is an extremely effective promotional strategy where you meet with contacts, inform them about your products and services, and get them to take action.

Contacts can be "pitched" casually during lunch, a coffee break, or even a relaxing cocktail.

The best part about face-to-face selling is that you can adjust your marketing messages according to each receiver's response, body language, or overall personality. Your good looks, manners, smile, and humor can also be used professionally to persuade your contacts.

While it usually takes a lot of persistence, charm, and personal referrals to get a meeting, here are a few of the people and conversations you might consider:

- Meet with event promoters to discuss bookings.
- Visit with retail store managers to get them to carry your recordings.
- Go see radio station music directors to get them to play your music.
- Talk with brand managers to propose sponsorship ideas.
- Have lunch with equipment manufacturers to ask them to consider you for endorsements.
- Converse with personal managers to discuss management or auditions.
- Talk with music producers to ask them to consider recording your next batch of songs.
- Meet with music library personnel to talk about licensing your music.
- Visit bank managers to discuss personal loans to finance your projects.
- Have dinner with investors to get them to fund your project. And . . .
- Approach music industry panelists at conventions and offer your business card.

No matter what it is that you are trying to communicate face-to-face, just remember to have a solid pitch that gets your intended recipient's attention (this is often called a "thirty-second elevator pitch," discussed more later). Be able to describe what you want and explain how the other party will benefit.

Second, you must be ready to present more detailed information to interested persons. Just saying, "I think doing business together will be great" is not enough. You must stress why.

Third, you must be prepared to overcome your contact's objections (i.e., reasons for not doing business together) and respond with logical explanations.

Fourth, once you overcome these objections, you must ask for the sale (often referred to as the close).

Finally, you must understand that face-to-face selling is all about following up, checking in with your contacts, and building long-term relationships from which both parties can benefit time and time again.

For more information about face-to-face sales, negotiations, and interpersonal skills, be sure to read books like Gerald Manning's *Selling Today*, Tom Hopkins's *How to Master the Art of Selling*, and Gerard Nierenberg's *How to Read a Person Like a Book*.

Now, before moving on to sales promotions, be sure to read the story in the box below.

KEEP IT BUSINESS FIRST

When communicating face-to-face with influential people who can help you to achieve your professional goals, you must never cross the fine line between selling and flirting. As they say, "sex sells," but if you push the "tease" in business, you could easily mislead people, cause drama you won't know how to handle, and gain nothing.

When I first moved to New York City, I believed that by getting female journalists to like me, I could also get them to publish major stories about my band. When meeting these journalists, I would compliment them on their looks, look in their eyes with a big smile, and suggest they meet me in charming restaurants for late-night drinks. Funny, right? But when I didn't follow through romantically, I attracted a lot more anger than good press. My band never got those big stories, but I did make a few enemies.

I'm not alone in having run into difficulty with this approach. One of my female clients admits that she "played along" with the advances of one very important record producer because she "desperately needed to get her tracks recorded." But, when the producer wanted more than her voice one night after a recording session and she rejected him, the project came to a halt. Even worse, he refused to give her the master recordings of the work that was already completed, and he badmouthed and labeled her as a "user" and "social climber" within important circles.

To be sure, face-to-face selling is a powerful promotional tool, but it can also work against you if you are not extremely mindful. Remember that if it's business you're really interested in, then it's best to be businesslike at all times. Enough said!

Tactic #10: Utilize Sales Promotions

The last but not least strategy I'll discuss in this chapter deals with sales promotions, which are short-term incentives intended to stimulate an immediate buying response in your customers. They include discount coupons, loyalty cards, and one-time exclusive deals.

Sales promotions can be communicated using the Internet (via e-mail and personal websites), guerrilla marketing (via postcards and flyers), and direct marketing (via posters you mail).

While you may have to give away your music for free early in your career to build awareness and start a buzz, discount sales promotions can be applied to everything, including your merchandise, studio time, music lessons, concert tickets, and more.

Here are a few different sales promotions strategies you might consider:

- Post discount coupons on your website that fans can download and use at your merch booth.
- Enter fans who buy your recordings into a drawing to win a special gift.
- Offer free specialty products (such as shot glasses, key chains, and beer koozies) to customers who make a purchase from your merch booth or website.
- Offer raffle tickets to fans who make purchases, giving them the chance to win special prizes donated by your sponsors.
- Create a customer loyalty card that rewards fans for the number of purchases they make (e.g., come to four shows and get a free T-shirt and a CD).
- Offer a reduced price or a "two for the price of one" deal on a special holiday or at your record release party. And . . .
- Design an exclusive, limited-run product (e.g., a boxed set containing your record, merch, and buttons) and make it available to the first 100 people at a special price.

While sales promotions can be very effective, remember that too much of a good thing is a bad thing. For instance, sending out e-mails every other week telling people that they can rent your studio to record "at a one-time specially reduced price" just looks bad.

Also, remember that sales promotions must have a clearly defined beginning and an end. While it might be tempting to bend the rules for a specific fan, you must stick to the rules of your own promotion or risk compromising your brand's integrity.

Finally, remember that you must always stay in synch with your brand image. For instance, an anti-capitalistic punk band must use sales promotions very subtly (or not at all), or they might otherwise come across as being phony. Got it? Good!

SALES PROMOTIONS IN ACTION

As you've already learned, sales promotions are an extremely useful strategy used to stimulate an immediate buying response in your fans. Below are a few simple examples of sales promotions that have been largely successful.

- **BARGAIN BINS:** The metal band Kaustik had a "five dollar bargain bin" next to their merch table at their live performances that included older merchandising items (albums, T-shirts designs, stickers, etc.) that fans could sift through.
- **SPIN AND WIN:** Behind their merch booth at their live performances, the metal band Rattlehead had a large game wheel that all paying customers could spin to win a second merchandising item for free.
- **HAGGLE AT THE SHOW:** The punk/metal band Clepto offered a special promotion immediately after their live performances where fans could "haggle for the best price" on merchandise with a band member—note that this also reinforced the band's Saudi Arabian roots and desire to brand their merch booth after an Arabic Souq (i.e., market).
- **WIN A CHAT:** For a limited time, Levi Strauss and Sears teamed up with pop artist Christina Aguilera and offered consumers (who bought $35 in Levi's merchandise) an opportunity to buy one of Christina's hit songs and get a promotional code to an online chat with the artist.

- **BUNDLE PACKAGE:** Country artist Dean Kalogris created a bundle package available only at select live performances where fans could buy his CD, T-shirt, and sticker as a set for $20 (normally valued at $32 when sold separately).
- **LIMITED-RUN GIFT SETS:** For a limited time, alt rocker Trent Reznor charged a hefty $300 on the release of his recording, but this was specifically for a limited-edition box set that included the songs on high-quality vinyl together with attractive print images—all personally signed by Reznor. As there were only 2,500 copies manufactured as part of a special sales promotion, the sets sold out quickly.
- **SPECIAL PERKS:** Finally, the author of this book—yup, me—offered customers who bought my book *Music Marketing for the DIY Musician* the opportunity to get a free music business DVD and audio CD for a limited time. Additionally, when artists took a picture of themselves holding the book and e-mailed me a link to their band's music, I provided them with free promotion.

So, what are your sales promotion ideas? Be sure to write them into your plan and make some sales! Good luck.

26 Setting Your Promotion in Motion

Now that you've done some preliminary research and you know a little bit more about promotion strategies, you're nearly ready to set your promotion in motion. But first you must consider the following five topics:

1. Defining your promotion goals
2. Executing your goals effectively
3. Tracking and measuring your promotion success
4. Continuing to learn about promotion, and . . .
5. Utilizing useful promotion resources

What do you say we get this show on the road?

Step #1: Define Your Promotion Goals

Your promotion campaign is not complete until you've set your goals and written them down. Goals help you to focus on a specific outcome and implement the actions that can get you the results that you desire.

This brings us to a very useful goal setting strategy known as SMART Goals. SMART is an acronym that stands for specific, measurable, attainable, roadmapped, and time-based goals.

To help you apply this technique, consider the following list of key questions:

- What are the "specific" products and/or services that you will be promoting over the next year? Are you promoting an album, merch line, concert tour, production studio, or single songs?
- What are your "measurable" sales forecasts and/or the desired fan awareness for your individual products/services? For instance, how many units of your recording or merch would you like to sell as a result of your promotion?
- Given your manpower and financial resources, is your goal truly "attainable" or doable? In other words, do you have a reasonable budget to accomplish your goals? Do you have the manpower to implement the strategies necessary to accomplish your goals?
- What is the "roadmap" you'll use to accomplish your goals? Said another way, what promotion strategies (publicity, advertising, Internet, word of mouth, guerrilla street marketing, direct marketing, sales promotions, etc.) will you use to promote your products and services? If you're unsure about what strategies to use, refer to the research you conducted earlier on your fans, and/or study what other artists of your genre are doing to promote themselves. And . . .
- Within what "time" frame will your promotion strategies be executed? Note that many promotional plans are scheduled to start a few months prior to the release of the products and services and end several months (or even years) after the launch. Once you've thoroughly considered all of your answers to the above questions, be sure to write them down on paper

(computer tablet, note application, or whatever) and keep them in a place where you can refer to them regularly.

The SMART model was created by management strategists several decades ago, and it continues to be used today by highly successful companies of all types and sizes. Now you can use it, too.

To sum things up in the words of Vince Lombardi, the legendary coach for the Green Bay Packers, "Results come only from knowing what you are achieving today and having a clear, specific strategy for closing the gap between today's reality and your vision for tomorrow." I couldn't agree more!

Now check out the box below to get a better idea of how your goals might be formed.

SCORE POINTS WITH SMART GOALS

To illustrate goals that are specific, measurable, attainable, road-mapped, and time based, here is what the goals of a solo artist releasing his next EP might look like for the year:

With the release of my debut EP recording entitled *Jon Doe Sings*, my goal is to:

1. Give 24 local live performances in alternative venues (clubs, colleges, festivals) that draw an average crowd of 50 people per performance
2. Net $20,000 in merchandising items (T-shirts, hats, stickers, and patches)
3. Sell 500 CDs and 300 USB flash drives, and get 30,000 streams of our record
4. Get 3 placements in a cool documentary film or current television show

This goal will be accomplished primarily by:

1. Utilizing film and TV licensing services like Taxi.com and working directly with local college film departments
2. Enticing local sponsors like Golf Punk to create an engaging line of co-branded merchandising that both parties help sell/promote
3. Creating an engaging website/webstore that draws traffic from our social networks.
4. Creating a highly visual live performance show that partners with other local acts and supports important local charities like Heal the Bay and Toys for Tots.
5. Posting 12 high quality lifestyle/humorous/shocking music videos monthly on YouTube and utilizing YouTube's ad services
6. Networking at important local events (like magazine-sponsored parties, local awards shows, and other bands' shows) and collecting e-mails for our database
7. Servicing local college radio stations and specialty shows, conducting interviews, and creating giveaways/contests for our record and concert tickets
8. Hiring a talented communications student three days a week to help inform and engage fans on social networks, and to pitch blogs for reviews nationwide

The timeline for this goal will commence 3 months before the release of the record and continue for another 9 months. The campaign will last a total of one year.

So that's about it! Just remember that it's okay for your goals to evolve as new information, opportunities, and challenges in the marketplace are uncovered. Okay? Cool! Let's move on.

Step #2: Execute Your Goals Effectively

DIY OR DIE! SAVE YOURSELF

Now that you've learned about setting goals, it's a perfect time for me to talk about execution.

Execution is the art of getting things done. It involves adopting the right "policies" to help you close the gap between your promotion goals and your promotion results.

But many musicians fail to get to that next level of their careers. They have no problem creating master plans to "rule the world," but they fall short with seeing these promotion plans through effectively. What an unfortunate waste!

As Ralph S. Larsen, CEO of Johnson & Johnson, said, "The best-thought-out plans in the world are worthless if you can't pull them off."

So, to help you execute your promotion goals effectively, be sure to do the following:

- **Stay proactive**! Attract the attention of those who can help you by first promoting yourself. Remember that no one (not a personal manager, agent, or A&R rep) is going to come save you and whisk you from garage to superstardom until you've accomplished some things on your own. Light as many fires as you can and people will see the smoke. My motto is "do it yourself (DIY) or die."
- **Secure your campaign funds.** Plan wisely so that you don't run out of money. You might use your own funds, get fans to invest in you via crowd funding services like Kickstarter, get interested parties (such as family members and friends) to front the cash, or arrange "barter" deals where you pay for services with your special skills.
- **Schedule efficiently.** This means that you prioritize your tasks and schedule the most important things first, find ways to accomplish tasks simultaneously to maximize your resources, and allocate enough time to complete each task on time and on budget.
- **Delegate the workload.** Assess your team's special talents and capitalize on them. The drummer can be in charge of booking, the bass player might do all the social media, and the guitarist can be the one that seeks out music placements. If you're a solo artist and don't have other members to depend on, then you can enlist a talented fan to help you.
- **Follow up diligently.** After sending off your initial correspondence (e-mails, tweets, or whatever), follow up in a week if the intended recipient has not replied. Repeat this technique for several weeks or attempt to use another means of communication (phone, letter, etc.) if necessary. And remember to always be nice in all of your correspondences.
- **Don't spread yourself too thin online**. It makes no sense to have ten social profiles with only a few hundred followers when you can have one or two with several thousand.
- **Be social on your social media.** Practice the same etiquette that exists offline, online. Address people by their first names, have an attractive profile picture, and don't be overly pushy with trying to get people to "check you out" or "click on your link."

- **Work smart.** Keep informed on changing technologies and how they might affect your promotion. For instance, due to computer "algorithms" (sets of rules programmed by certain companies), there are more advantageous times (e.g., weekends and early mornings) to post on your social networks, and more advantageous methods (e.g., social media advertisements) to increase the number of people who see your posts.
- **Use helpful tools.** Stay current with the most popular online tools that can increase the effectiveness of your marketing. Two that I use all of the time are Hootsuite and Bitly.
- **Never be shy and afraid to sell yourself**. When you're selling merch at your live performances, make sure that people know about it! Ask them politely for their business. Always remember that if you ask for the sale, people are more likely to buy.
- **Reward yourself.** Don't just wait for the big payoff when you reach your ultimate goal. Celebrate the small successes too and show thanks to all who have offered their help. And . . .
- **Be ready to go the distance.** Remember that promotion is a process—it's not something you do on the weekend and then stop. Keep the promotion in motion, people!

I know that promoting yourself is not easy, especially when you have to write and record your own music, and deal with everyday life, your job, your family and friends. But perhaps these famous quotes will offer some inspiration: "Success is 10 percent inspiration and 90 percent perspiration" (Thomas Edison); "Impossible is a word only to be found in the dictionary of fools" (Napoleon Bonaparte); and "Riches do not respond to wishes, only to definitive plans and constant persistence" (Napoleon Hill). In other words, folks, there is no escaping the hard work. So roll up those sleeves and get going one way or another.

DEVELOP A "WHATEVER IT TAKES" ATTITUDE!

While there are many wonderful tips on executing your goals effectively, like the ones discussed above, one can't forget about simply developing a "whatever it takes" attitude.

Clepto, a high-energy punk band that's slowly gaining traction in the indie world, is one band that is willing to sacrifice it all. The band has been literally living in their rehearsal room for years so that they can keep their expenses to a minimum and dedicate 100 percent of their time to writing and promoting music.

Even more extreme, after totaling their van on route to a gig in Las Vegas, the band immediately called U-Haul rental centers from the side of the road—rather than going to the hospital and tending to their bruises—so that they could make it their show on time. Call them inhuman or call them insane, but you gotta love Clepto's fighting spirit.

I once heard someone say that the key to success is just doing what you say you are going to do, no matter what it takes! This is not always an easy thing to do, since "life" often gets in the way. But, by making a few sacrifices, you just might get further than you've ever imagined. "Fight the good fight," my friends.

Now let's move on to creating a measuring strategy.

Step #3: Track and Measure Your Promotion Success

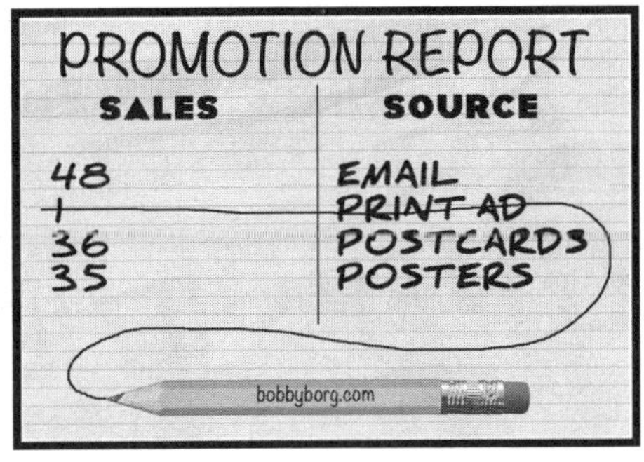

Measuring is the process of collecting, analyzing, and acting on information that is relevant to the goals of your promotion plan. Or, in plain English, measuring is identifying what is and what is not working. After all, there's no reason to repeat the same promotion strategies over and over again if you're not getting the desired results. That would be a complete waste of your time and money.

What follows are a few easy-to-execute measuring strategies to informally "keep score" of your promotional efforts and help you to be more efficient.

- Examine your sales records at the end of each night. Do you notice any spikes in sales that can be directly tied to a recent promotional effort? For instance, did the sales promotion coupon that you uploaded on your website generate new sales?
- Count your inventory before and after each show. How many shirts did you sell on the night of your last concert and how does that match up with other nights? To what can you attribute your success or failure?
- What is your search engine ranking for keywords related to your products this month as compared to last month? For instance, when using the keywords "studios in LA," is your business showing up on the first page of the search results, or is it still on the third page? If it's still on the third page, than what can you adjust to improve your ranking?
- How many new friends and followers do your have on your social networks this week as compared to last week? Is the social networking you're doing really working? How can you improve?
- How many comments are you getting on the content you're posting on your social networks? If you're getting several comments, what can you repeat? If you're getting few comments, what should you avoid?
- How many fans are opening the e-mail messages that you're sending out? Did you know that there are useful analytics built into e-mail services like MailChimp and Constant Contact that can help you to uncover this important data? What can you do to craft better e-mails and subject lines to attract more attention?
- How many fans visited your website this month, and which pages did they visit the most? Did you know that embedding Google Analytics into your website can help you to answer all of these questions? And . . .
- Of the people who came to your gig, how many came because of a specific marketing strategy you executed? By asking, "How did you hear about us?," you can find out.

Look, gang, whatever strategies you decide to use, remember that measuring is all about keeping your eyes and ears open for ways to continually improve your business and yourself. If something is not working, you must decide why it's not working and figure out what to do about it. As they say, the definition of insanity is doing the same things over and over and expecting different results.

Now check out the box below for a perfect example of how measuring can help make you a more efficient promoter.

THE BENEFITS OF MEASURING

A student at Musicians Institute in Hollywood confided in me that he was very disappointed with the number of people (5 in total) who had shown up to his live performance. He was completely at a loss about what he was doing wrong, and he was ready to throw in the towel and call it quits.

Being that a major part of his promotion campaign consisted of an e-mail correspondence he sent out to a list of 500 people, I directed him to the analytics page of the e-mail service he was using. Upon closer investigation, we discovered that only 2 out of the 500 people he solicited had read his e-mail. I knew immediately that this was the result of a poorly composed e-mail.

Together the student and I crafted a new e-mail for his next gig that contained an attention-getting subject line, a clear body that expressed why people should care about the event, and an enticing "call to action" that asked people to RSVP for the gig.

Several weeks later, the student had much better news to report. Fifty-eight people had attended his latest live performance and 127 people had read his new e-mail—much better than the initial 5 people who showed up to his first event and the 2 people who had read his first e-mail!

You see, if the student had not taken the time to speak with me, investigate why his promotion was not working, and use easy-to-access analytics, he would have continued to make the same mistakes over and over again while hoping for different results—but without ever knowing what was wrong.

Remember, folks, your time and money are precious. So be sure to measure all of your promotional strategies today. You'll learn to work much smarter, and not harder.

Step #4: Continue to Learn About Promotion

Getting close to the end of this chapter, I want to be sure to stress the importance of continuing to learn as much as you can about promotion. While the basic methodologies and theories behind promotion have remained constant for several decades, new interpretations and useful examples pop up every day.

What follows are just a few methods to help you stay up-to-date on this fascinating topic:

- Analyze the careers of artists who have succeeded. Consider the promotion strategies they used and whether you can emulate any of these strategies for your own campaign.
- Analyze the careers of artists who have failed. Learning what not to do is just as important as learning what to do.
- Take an online class in promotion at the University of California Los Angeles, Berklee College of Music in Boston, or some other fine school that offers distance learning.
- Subscribe to blogs that feature articles on promotion like Harvard Business Review, Mashable, Wired, Hypebot, Fast Company, and TedTalks.

- Follow a variety of marketing experts on their social networks and discover amazing articles, promotion tips, and inspirational quotes you can use.
- Take advantage of "open course" materials from major institutions like Yale University (oyc.yale.edu), Berklee College of Music (www.berkleeshares.com), and University of California at Berkeley (webcast.berkeley.edu).
- Become a member of a popular business organization like the American Marketing Association, the Word-of-Mouth Marketing Association, and the American Association of Advertising Agencies (4A's). All of these organizations provide useful webinars and networking opportunities.
- Read the greatest and latest books on promotion such as *Ogilvy on Advertising*, by David Ogilvy; *Tested Advertising Methods*, by John Caples, and my own book *Music Marketing for the DIY Musician*. You should also check out anything from Seth Goodwin, Malcolm Gladwell, and Guy Kawasaki.
- Get an internship in a marketing company and see how experienced promotion professionals make important decisions in the real world. Check out MyMusicJob (www.mymusicjob.com), ShowBizJobs (www.showbizjobs.com), and Monster (www.monsterjobs.com) for opportunities. Good luck!

There are countless more methods you can use to continue learning about promotion. Just conduct a search on the Internet using key words like "music promotion" and you'll be surprised at how many hits you get. Read everything you can!

If you have a few of your own ideas about how to continue learning about promotion, please be sure to share them with me and my other readers at (www.bobbyborg.com).

Now, to close out this chapter, let's move on to examining a few helpful promotion resources that you can use to execute your promotion plan.

Step #5: Utilize Useful Promotion Resources

Thanks to advances in technology, the tools that are available to musicians to promote their careers are plentiful. It can get quite confusing to try to figure out what sites to use and what sites to avoid. Generally I like to stick with companies that have been around for several years, rather than with newbie companies that can go out of business as fast as they started.

What follows are just a few of my favorite promotional resources that you can use to further your own career—some of which I'm sure you are already familiar with. Here they are:

- **Funding:** To fund your promotional campaigns, you might consider raising money using the following resources: Small Business Administration (www.sba.gov), Kickstarter (www.kickstarter.com), PledgeMusic (http://www.pledgemusic.com), Indiegogo (www.indiegogo.com), and GoFundMe (www.gofundme.com).
- **Booking:** To book your live performances and promote your music, you can use the Musician's Atlas (www.musiciansatlas.com), the National Association for Campus Activities (www.naca.org), the Booking Agency Directory (www.pollstar.com), and SonicBids (www.sonicbids.com).

- **Music distribution:** To place and promote your records, you might use CD Baby (www.cdbaby.com), the Orchard (www.theorchard.com), TuneCore (www.tunecore.com), and Distrokid (www.distrokid.com).
- **Song placements:** To place and promote your songs to film and television, you might use TAXI (www.taxi.com), Pump Audio (www.pumpaudio.com), RipTide Music (www.riptidemusic.com), Killer Tracks (www.killertracks.com), and Opus1 Music Library (www.opus1musiclibrary.com).
- **Paid advertising:** To advertise your music online, you might consider Google AdWords (www.adwords.google.com), Twitterads (https://ads.twitter.com), and YouTube (ads.youtube.com).
- **Direct marketing:** To send direct marketing messages online, try MailChimp (www.mailchimp.com), Constant Contact (www.constantcontact.com), Bronto (www.bronto.com), FanBridge (www.fanbridge.com), and Campaigner (www.campaignercrm.com).
- **Personal website:** To create a personal website to promote yourself, consider Flavors.me (www.flavors.me), Virb (www.virb.com), Bandzoogle (www.bandzoogle.com), WordPress (www.wordpress.org), and Adobe Dreamweaver (www.adobe.com/products/dreamweaver).
- **Branding:** To create logos, business cards, and more, check out Fiverr (www.fiverr.com), Vistaprint (www.vistaprint.com), and PlasticPrinters.com (www.plasticprinters.com).
- **Radio promotion:** To create lists of radio stations that will play your music, use Radio-Locator (www.radio-locator.com), Indie Bible (www.indiebible.com), and Live365 (www.live365.com).
- **Social media platforms:** To create social media profiles to spread the word of mouth, try the following: Facebook (www.facebook.com), Twitter (www.twitter.com), LinkedIn (www.linkedin.com), YouTube (www.youtube.com), Google+ (www.plus.google.com), and Instagram (www.instagram.com).
- **Video:** To stream videos, use Vimeo (vimeo.com), DailyMotion (http://www.dailymotion.com/us), StageIt (http://www.stageit.com), Ustream (www.ustream.tv), Vine (www.vine.co), Periscope (www.periscope.com), and Youtube (www.youtube.com).
- **Conventions/networking:** To network at conferences, check out South by Southwest (www.sxsw.com), West Coast Songwriters (www.westcoastsongwriters.org/Conference), Durango Songwriters Expo (www.durango-songwriters-expo.com), ASCAP "I Create Music" Expo (www.ascap.com), and NAMM Convention (www.namm.org).
- **Social networking tools:** For useful social networking tools, use Bitly (www.Bitly.com), TweetDeck (www.tweetdeck.com), and HootSuite (www.hootsuite.com).
- **Mobile:** To build a mobile app or website, try GoDaddy's Goodnight and dotMobi Feature (www.godaddy.com), mobiSiteGalore (www.mobisitegalore.com), and Mobileroadie (www.mobileroadie.com).
- **Blogging:** To create a blog, I like Tumblr (www.tumblr.com), TypePad (www.typepad.com), and WordPress (www.wordpress.com).
- **Specialty advertising products:** For creating specialty products that bear your name and logo, try CaféPress (www.cafepress.com), Spreadshirt (www.spreadshirt.com), Vistaprint (www.vistaprint.com), StickerJunkie.com (www.stickerjunkie.com), and Branders.com (www.branders.com).

- **Marketing plans:** To create a more detailed marketing plan of attack, I'll say it again: check out my book *Music Marketing for the DIY Musician* (www.bobbyborg.com/store). Hey, if I'm going to teach you about promotion, I better practice it myself.

There are literally hundreds of sites that I could list, but what I posted above should be enough to keep you busy for a very long time. While the above companies have been around for several years, the URLs may change, so I apologize if any links have suddenly gone dead.

Also remember that while the websites, magazines, and resources suggested are recommended highly, the authors cannot be held responsible for the materials, business practices, and viewpoints of these sources—so please exercise caution.

Lastly, Bobby Borg and his publishers cannot be held accountable for any third party licenses or agreements that you enter into—so please, always seek the advice of a personal consultant or attorney in any business matter about which you are unclear. Got it? Cool!

Now let's move on to two bonus chapters on creating winning content. We're almost done!

27 Creating Promotion Content That Sells: Part 1

Congratulations! You've made it through several chapters on the basics of music promotion.

Now, as promised in previous chapters, I'd like to offer further information about creating some of the most important content you'll need for getting your promotion campaign off the ground, and for getting the five-star promotion results that you deserve.

The focus in this chapter, "Creating Promotion Content That Sells: Part 1," will be on the following:

1. Writing an effective introduction (cover letter or e-mail)
2. Writing an informational bio
3. Writing a newsworthy press release
4. Capturing great photographs
5. Creating an easy–to-scan one-sheet, and . . .
6. Creating an attractive business card

Part 2, Chapter 28, covers these methods:

7. Preparing your elevator pitch
8. Designing an effective flyer or postcard
9. Preparing a great interview
10. Creating merch items that help spread the word
11. Producing videos that get attention, and . . .
12. Developing and maintaining a personal website

All of this content can be useful in one or all of the following situations:

- When seeking interviews, stories, and reviews in newspapers, magazines, and Internet blogs
- When trying to book gigs and entice industry professionals into doing deals with you
- When compiling the information into physical or electronic press kits with services like SonicBids or Presskit to send out to your contacts
- When posting content on your personal websites and social networks, and . . .
- When networking at music industry events and trying to make new connections

Now let's get started with Part 1 and learning to create some amazing content. The information is all fairly straightforward and you may have heard it all before, but now it's time to put it to use so you can get out there and accomplish your goals.

Are you already to rock 'n' roll? Cool. Check out the box below and then let's get this party started.

SUBMITTING PROMOTION MATERIALS

You already know that biographies, one-sheets, photographs, videos, and press releases are all tools that can be used to help get gigs, reviews, radio play, sponsorships, and so much more.

However, if you're like many artists, you're slightly confused about the format to use when submiting these materials to your contacts. Let's take a look at the most common options:

- **PHYSICAL PRESS KIT:** This involves gathering your bio, press release, cover letter, and business card into an attractive folder (such as one you customized using services like Vistaprint), deciding whether to send your music in CD or flash drive format, and mailing all of these materials in a padded envelope via FedEx or the United States Postal Service.
- **PERSONAL WEBSITE LINK(S):** This involves creating a customized destination on the Web that includes music, videos, pictures, and bios, and then e-mailing a link (or a number of direct links to different pages on your site) to your professional contacts.
- **ZIP FILE OR DROPBOX INVITE:** This involves gathering your music files, video files, and picture files, compressing them into one zip file, and e-mailing your contact the file for him or her to download. Alternatively, it involves uploading your files via a service like Dropbox, and then e-mailing your contact an invitation to download the files from a folder on Dropbox.
- **ELECTRONIC PRESS KIT (EPK):** This involves subscribing to an online press kit service, creating a streamedlined digital press kit intended for industry professionals, and then 1) e-mailing it to your interested contacts, 2) e-mailing a link to the service that is hosting your EPK, and/or 3) submitting the EPK for exclusive opportunities provided on your service's site. SonicBids (www.sonicbids.com), ReverbNation (www.reverbnation.com) and PressKit.to (www.presskit.to) all specialize in EPKs.

So then, which format is right for you? The short answer is: all of them! It depends on the personal preferences of your contacts. Therefore, speak with your network before sending anything and be prepared for all situations. Yeah, I know this requires more time and hard work, but who ever said that being a successful musician was going to be easy?

Method #1: Write an Effective Introduction (Cover Letter or E-mail)

There is no better way to begin a chapter on creating promotional content than by explaining how to write an effective introduction. Simply put, a cover letter or e-mail introduction provides an opener to more detailed communication between two or more parties.

A cover letter or e-mail introduction tells the reader who you are and what you want and causes him or her to want to find out more about you and your career. It is usually written in the first person (i.e., from your perspective, referring to yourself as "I," "me," etc.) and is no longer than 350 words in length.

While there are many methods you can use to write an introduction, what follows are a few helpful tips that have worked incredibly well for me when reaching out to professional contacts. Enjoy:

- **Company name/contact info:** Include your name, address, phone number, e-mail address, and/or website URL at the top center of the correspondence. If you have a logo, consider using it here if applicable.
- **Address of contact:** Include the name, address, phone number, e-mail address, and website of the company or person you are trying to contact.
- **Greeting:** Greet your contact formally (e.g., Dear Mr. Borg) or informally (e.g., Hello, Bobby). The approach you use should depend on the company and whether you know the person you are addressing. Some entertainment-based companies such as consumer rock magazines are fine with the informal approach.
- **Subject line:** When e-mailing your contact, be sure to use a clear and concise headline that gets the attention of your intended party. For instance, when writing a booker, you might write: Booking Inquiry / Experienced Band with Draw / Thanks.
- **Purpose:** State briefly in the body of your introduction why you are writing and what you intend to gain. Is it "to submit a press package with the hopes of getting booked for the battle of the bands event," or "to interview for the job with hopes of starting immediately?"
- **Reminder:** Briefly remind the contact where and when you received permission to contact him or her. Was there an address on a website? Did you see an ad in a paper? Or did you meet the contact at a convention?
- **Credibility:** Show your contact that you have some credibility by listing a few of your accomplishments (e.g., number of college radio stations playing you), and/or quotes from important industry persons (e.g., testimonials from club owners). Just don't overdo it and be sure to tell the truth—do not exaggerate.
- **Benefit to the contact:** Stress how your contact will benefit and profit by responding to you. For instance, you might tell the booker of a club that you have an e-mail list of over 5,000 people and are confident that you can draw at least 200 people into his club. Just be sure that whatever you say, you can live up to it.
- **Return contact:** Tell your contact that you'll check back with him or her at a specific date and time. This is a polite method for putting the control of the situation in your hands and provides your contact with some notice that you are on top of your game.
- **Thank-you note:** Thank your contact in advance for taking the time to review your materials. This is to show you're respectful of their time.
- **Signature**: Close the letter "sincerely" or "enthusiastically" and sign your name. The idea is to end on a professional, polite, and positive note.
- **Contact information:** Include your contact information (address, phone, e-mail address, and/or website URL) once again at the end of your cover letter or e-mail. And . . .
- **Design:** Format your cover letter using an easy-to-read, standard typeface (such as Times New Roman, Helvetica or Cambria), a type size that is either 11 or 12 point, and a line spacing that is set to either 1 or 1.5.

That's about all. Now be sure to check out the sample introduction letter below.

SAMPLE COVER LETTER

What follows is a brief, 178-word e-mail between an artist's production company—which builds catalogues of music for licensing purposes—and a music library—which places music in film, television, and games.

CMH Productions
1831 Pontius Ave.
Los Angeles, CA 90029
Ph: (888) 888 8888. www.nritdraska.com

Trust Music Library
Sharal Coinski
4234 Broadway
New York, NY 10001
March 18

Dear Sharal,

This is to introduce my company, CMH Productions®, with hopes you'll consider licensing our tracks in your upcoming documentary film. If you recall, we met at the ASCAP Expo in Hollywood on March 24 and you asked me to contact you.

CMH® is a production company that specializes in harder-edged music for commercials and television shows, including theme and bumper packages for series and game shows. Additionally, we have worked on a number of small films and documentaries including *Occupy World*, nominated by PBS for best new documentary, and the history of Harley Davidson motorcycles. We have an excellent reputation for meeting our clients' deadlines.

Samples on our website at www.cmh.com are intended to demonstrate both the diversity and marketability of our catalog. If you're interested in licensing our material, please indicate the titles you find most suitable and I shall contact you with licensing information.

I am confident you'll enjoy our music and find a relationship with CMH® beneficial to all parties involved. I will check back with you by March 28 to be sure that you received my package.

Sincerely,
Britt Draska
Licensing & Royalties Manager, CMH Productions®
1831 Pontius Ave
Los Angeles, CA 90024
Ph: (888) 888 8888. www.nritdraska.com

Method #2: Write an Informative Bio

A biography (or "bio") provides readers with a detailed description of your career and helps strengthen their interest in you.

While there are many formats for writing an effective bio, the "informational bio format" is quite effective for young artists—it is concise and without flowery adjectives. Bottom line: until you're a big star, industry professionals and fans may not be interested in the details about how "your music represents a cacophony of colors similar to a rainbow on a bright spring day."

An informational bio should contain your career name, the date you started, and most importantly your accomplishments and future goals. It is usually written in the third person (e.g., John Doe is a country singer) and not in the first person (e.g., I am a country singer).

It's a good idea to have both a 500-word bio and a short-form, 75-word version in order to meet any need. Now let's look at a few specific tips to help you get started with your biography:

- **Company name/title:** List your name or logo at the top and center of your page, followed by the title "Biography" (e.g., Bobby Borg Biography).
- **Date formed:** Start your bio with the date that your band formed, the date you started writing music for your latest solo project, or the date you started working professionally. This helps people gauge your level of experience.
- **Territory:** Include the territory (city, state, country) in which your business resides. If you started your business in another territory and recently relocated, briefly state where and when as well.
- **Name:** State your business name (band name, solo artist name, etc.) and be sure to include the phonetic spelling if you have a name that is difficult to pronounce.
- **Genre:** Describe your general format in one or two words (e.g., pop, hip-hop, country, etc.). If you're having trouble with this, think about the radio stations that would most likely broadcast your music.
- **List your like bands:** Indicate the names and artists that you sound the most like. While you may think that you are totally unique, there are at least a few comparable bands that you could open for on tour. List these bands to give your reader an idea of your target audience.
- **Members' names/instruments/age range:** List your members' professional names along with the instruments they play. Additionally, list the age range from the youngest to the oldest musician in order to give your reader some idea of your target audience and your long-term career potential as a musical act.
- **Brief history:** Tell the story of how your career or band came together. For instance, you might say that the members have known each other since kindergarten, are the children of famous parents, have been part of other famous groups, have had success in other fields such as acting, or formed the band as a result of some tragedy (9/11, etc.). If it fits your brand, you can even invent a story and be humorous. For instance, you might say that the members met in outer space on a mission to Mars. Look, whatever you say, just be concise (about one to two sentences in length is all you need).

- **Accomplishments:** List your recent successes that show off your work ethic. Include things like record sales, social media numbers, video plays, college radio play, sold-out shows, bands you opened for, or placements in film and TV. If you are just starting out and don't have any accomplishments, then focus on your future plans (discussed later).
- **Quotes to back up accomplishments:** Include any flattering quotes that you might have received from industry professionals, particularly any quotes that support your accomplishments mentioned above.
- **Future plans:** Show your reader that you're unstoppable and that you already have a plan of attack to move ahead to the next level of your career. Talk about future tours or record releases. This will really impress your readers.
- **Links to further information:** Include links where interested parties can listen to your music, view and download your pictures, and watch videos.
- **Contact information:** Conclude your bio with an e-mail or number where you can be contacted.
- **Picture:** Post an attractive picture of you or your band in the proximity of your bio (when using your bio online) or drag a JPEG file into the top left or right corner of a Microsoft Word document (when using your bio in physical form). And . . .
- **Design:** Format your bio using an easy-to-read, standard typeface (such as Helvetica, Cambria, or Times New Roman), a type size that is either 11 or 12 point, and a line spacing that is set to either 1 or 1.5.

That's about it for writing an effective informational bio. Now take a look at the sample provided in the box below.

SAMPLE LONG-FORM AND SHORT-FORM BIOGRAPHY

What follows is the heart of what should be included in a long-form and short-form bio. I've purposely left out the name and title, since that should already be perfectly clear.

Let's start with a long-form bio for artist Chas Castell:

> Hooked by the Britpop sound as a teenager in the early 1990s, English-born Chas Castell is a Los Angeles-based singer/songwriter in the style of Oasis, Damien Rice, and Ed Sheeran.

After graduating from Boston University, Chas founded his own digital media company, started a blog for the British Broadcasting Corporation, and designed the first mobile network for Warner Brothers. Notwithstanding these impressive accomplishments, Chaz decided to leave the corporate world behind him and pursue his true calling—music—full-time.

His first solo recording—mixed by Grammy-nominated Nels Jensen (Sigur Ros) was released in 2015 on his own label. In the same year, he released three more consecutive solo EPs, as well as an EP with his side project, Mellott—featuring Berklee College of Music grad Jessica Mellott. With Mellott, and with his one-man band show using loop pedals, Chas performed throughout LA and the UK and placed several songs on Sony PlayStation and Tiscali.

Today, Chas is writing material for his next solo recording, performing regularly in LA, and volunteering for a number of charities for children and young adults, including Create Now, Education Through Music LA, and the "I Can Change the World" Project.

To view further materials or download pictures, go to www.chascastell.com. To contact Chas, e-mail Chas@chascastell.com or call: 310 890 9859.

Now here's a short-form bio for Chas:

Hooked by the Britpop sound as a teenager in the early 1990s, Chas Castell is an LA-based singer/songwriter in the style of Oasis and Ed Sheeran. He recorded with notable producer/engineer Nels Jensen (Sigur Ros), toured extensively with his one-man band show, and placed several songs with Sony Playstation and Tiscali. His next release is due out in March 2016. www.chascastell.com or Chas@chascastell.com

Method #3: Write a Newsworthy Press Release

A press release, which contains current and newsworthy bits of information presented in a very specific format, is yet another important promotional tool.

When released to press persons and press organizations (such as editors of magazines, blogs, or newswires—like the well-known PR Newswire at www.prnewswire.com)—a press release can be a very effective promotional tool that leads to significant exposure for your career.

Just be sure to eliminate unneeded words, use short sentences, and be concise.

Here are a few more specific tips on how to write a quality press release that sells:

- **Contact info:** Include your name, address, phone number, e-mail address, and/or website URL at the top center of the correspondence. If you have a logo, consider using it here if applicable.
- **Immediate release:** Write the phrase "For Immediate Release" at the top of your press release. This indicates to press persons that it's okay to immediately use the information.
- **Caption:** Write a strong headline that sums up your news and gets your readers' attention. Answer "the five W's" (who, what, where, when, and why), use active verbs and keywords that your target customer may use when conducting an online search for you, and format your headline using capital letters. A terrific caption might say: "LOCAL ARTIST RAISES $100,000 FOR THE AMERICAN CANCER SOCIETY AND GETS BOOKED TO PLAY THIS YEAR'S WARP TOUR."
- **Date/time/place:** Start the body of your press release with the city and date from which the news is being distributed (e.g., Sep. 1, 2015: Los Angeles, CA). Note that the city is usually the same one as the address you listed at the top of the release.
- **Inverted triangle style:** Write the main body of your press release starting with the most important information (this might mean repeating the caption) and continuing with the less important information. This style of writing is often referred to as an "inverted pyramid style,"

since the information gets less and less important as the press release continues. The inverted pyramid style makes it easy for editors to cut your press release if they are short on space in their publication.

- **Call-outs:** Highlight key information about an event or a product's or service's specifications. This might mean using bullet points to emphasize information such as your album title, track names and lengths, and ordering information. Or it could mean mentioning the date and time of an event, the address, and how to RSVP.
- **Company information:** Provide a few lines about your company, such as when it formed and what you do.
- **Design**: Format your press release using an easy-to-read, standard typeface (such as Helvetica, Cambria, or Times New Roman), a type size that is either 11 or 12 point, and a line spacing that is set to either 1 or 1.5.
- **The end:** Use the symbol -###- at the bottom of the press release. This indicates the end of the release.

So, that's about all, folks.

For further information on writing presss releases, check out *The Associated Press Guide to News Writing*, by René J. Cappon. Also see the sample press release in the box below.

PRESS RELEASE SAMPLE

What follows is a press release sample written for one of my other books available from Hal Leonard Performing Arts Publishing Group.

Bobby Borg
PO Box 18564
Beverly Hills, CA 90209
Contact: Bobby Borg Consulting (bborg@bobbyborg.com)
Contact: Hal Leonard Corporation, Publicity and Marketing (973) 337-5034 x208

For Immediate Release:

DISRUPTIVE TIMES IN THE MUSIC INDUSTRY DRIVE FORMER MAJOR LABEL ROCK DRUMMER TO RELEASE NEW BOOK FOR MUSICIANS THAT NAVIGATES THE MINE FIELDS.

Sep. 1, 2015: Beverly Hills, CA: Former major label recording artist Bobby Borg has released his new book, *Business Basics for Musicians*, which delivers a powerful message that's loud and clear: *music is an art, but making money from it is a serious business!*

Written in a conversational tone and an easy-to-scan format, the book simplifies five vital areas that musicians need to succeed in today's unpredictable and ever-changing music industry: Career Execution, Business Relationships, Pro Teams, Deals and Dollars, and Future Predictions.

The book covers everything from copyright, to record deals, to managers, to merchandising, to doing it yourself. With pro interviews, anecdotes, and review quizzes, it's "the complete handbook from start to success."

When emerging technologies make it possible for artists to act as their own record labels, and new contracts are structured to grab the greatest share of an artist's revenue pie, there has never been a greater need for musicians to understand the business of music than now.

Business Basics for Musicians is the layperson's guide to the music industry. It will help musicians master business basics quickly, so that they can get back to doing what they love best—creating music!

Title: *Business Basics for Musicians: The Complete Handbook from Start to Success*
Price: $29.99 (US)
Inventory #HL00139915 / ISBN: 9781495007767 / UPS: 888680039820
Width: 8.0" / Length: 10.0" / 304 Pages
Contact: Bobby Borg Consulting (bborg@bobbyborg.com or Wes Seely (wseeley@halleonard.com).
Bobby Borg Consulting is a Los Angeles–based company that has been helping musicians turn their art into a more successful business since 1988. Hal Leonard Corporation is a US music publishing company founded in Winona, Minnesota, in 1947.
-###-

Method #4: Capture Great Photographs

Moving along in our discussion about creating promotional content that sells, let me stress that photographs are extremely important tools in communicating to your target audience what you and your products are all about. As they say, a picture is worth a thousand words.

A great photograph captures the genuine personality of your brand and tells a unique story. Photographs can be used to complement bios, one-sheets, websites, social profiles, postcards, business cards, and so much more.

To ensure you capture the best photos for any need, check out the following tips:

- **Fashion/style:** Consider the genre of your music and your personality, and then find a style of dress that genuinely matches. As discussed in the section on branding in a previous chapter, consistency is key. If you're a good ol' boy who plays country music, then perhaps you should dress like a country artist and not a Starbucks barista. Find photos of artists that you admire, emulate their fashion strengths, and look for ways to express your own true uniqueness. Just be sure to be stylish down to the very last detail—whether it's the jewelry, a pair of sunglasses, or a stylish hat or cool scarf, your attention to the finer details can really make all of the difference.
- **Type of shot:** Consider the various shots that will best capture the mood for your brand and fit with your promotional campaign. Will you shoot in a more controlled setting like a studio with a plain background, will you shoot in some really cool locations around your city to capture more of a lifestyle vibe, or will you shoot during one of your live performances to catch

you in action? Studio profile shots work great for press persons because they tend to be clearly shot and show your face close up, while fans tend to love lifestyle and concert shots since they tend to be more raw and real.

- **Pose:** Practice various poses before your shoot and know what works well for you and your brand. Will you stand, sit in a chair, kneel down, fold your arms, smile, grin, look directly into the camera, look off to the side, point your guitar at the camera, or hold your mic at your side while looking down? Remember that great shots usually don't happen by accident. The more prepared you are, the more successful you'll be at capturing great photographs that you can use for your promotional campaign. Check out cool magazines for inspiration if needed. Get a friend to take a few practice shots or try taking some selfies to see what really works and does not work.

SABRINA PETRINI

- **Shopping:** Locate cool and affordable shops in advance so that you're not running around trying to put together outfits the night before your shoot, and, more importantly, so that you're not stressing out about spending a lot of money. There are vintage clothing stores, bargain basements, and Goodwill stores in most major cities. You can even hire consultants who will help you shop for clothes or just put together outfits from the clothes that you already own. (Check out websites like www.modelmayhem.com.)
- **Efficiency:** Lay out all your clothes in advance and plan out what you want to wear so that you can shed your clothing accordingly as the shoot progresses. For instance, you might start with a certain jacket, hat, and pair of shades, and then shed these items to expose a cool T-shirt, belt, and that new hair style. And so on. The less changing you have to do on set, the more smoothly the session will run.
- **Tanning beds, hair coloring, and more:** Be careful about taking drastic measures the night before your photo shoot. Remember that getting a haircut, coloring your hair, or hitting the tanning beds can have unpredictable results. One of my guitarists fell asleep in a tanning bed with protective eyewear and ended up with a red face and what looked like raccoon eyes. Yikes!
- **Food:** Don't eat greasy foods the night before your shoot to avoid unwanted pimples. While blemishes can be covered up with makeup, they can affect your confidence and mood.
- **Water:** Drink plenty of water before and during the shoot. Remember that water makes your skin look well nourished and vibrant.
- **Rest:** Get plenty of rest the night before your shoot to avoid bags under your eyes—unless of course bags under your eyes genuinely fit your style of music and lifestyle.
- **Mood/music:** Play recordings of your music during the shoot to inspire everyone (photographer included) to create the photos needed to capture your brand.
- **Presentation:** Make sure your clothing isn't dirty or wrinkled. Nothing says "budget photo shoot" like clothing that looks like it was just picked up off the floor.

- **Composure:** Breathe deeply, chill, and just have fun. Relax and be in control of your body, mind, and surroundings. Just be careful about self-medicating. I've found that alcohol and marijuana, even a little, can make you look a bit lazy-eyed and droopy-jawed on camera. But, of course, if that's your look, then all is cool!
- **Professional photographers:** While your best friend with a camera phone can capture a great photo, it's best to invest in an experienced music photographer. A pro understands proper lighting, knows how to frame a picture to make it look well-balanced, and knows where to find hair/makeup/wardrobe persons. Get referrals from other local artists for photographers who are reasonably priced, make contact with these persons, and view their portfolios carefully. If the images fit your brand, and if the photographer is confident he or she can deliver what you're looking for, then discuss price and other business matters. Remember that you can always hunt down a talented art student at a local college to do the job if you're on a really tight budget. But just be careful—you often get what you pay for.
- **Business issues:** Discuss specific terms of your session and get them in writing. Establish price, how many shots (or how many hours or different outfit changes he or she will shoot), and copyright issues. Typically, the photographer maintains the copyrights, but he or she will indicate how you'll be able to use the shots, and will quote a price for any other additional uses. If you want to own the copyrights to the photos, note that the session will typically cost you a lot more.
- **Deliverables:** Be sure that your photographer provides you with high-resolution digital files in a few different sizes of the shots that you desire. For instance, on a recent photo session that I did, the photographer provided me with 8" x 10", 4" x 6", and 1" x 1" digital files at 300 pixels per inch. This was perfect for what I needed (i.e., for printing on the back covers of my books, and posting on Internet blogs). And finally . . .
- **Feedback:** Take your time when going through your photos and deciding which ones you'll use for your campaign. If you are part of a group, consider the look and pose of all members, and not just your own. Be sure to get some feedback from your photographer, industry professionals, and your target fans. Once again, your photos should immediately help to convey the image you desire in the minds of your fans. Have fun and good luck.

Be sure to check out the graphic of Sabrina Petrini I included on the previous page. It contains a few examples of the types of photographs you can take: profile, lifestyle, and live shots. Note that your photographs will come in handy when creating your one-sheet, which is what I discuss next.

Method #5: Create an Easy-to-Scan One-Sheet

A one-sheet (or "artist one-sheet") is yet another important promotional tool for artists. It can be used when promoting your music to radio stations, club promoters, distributors, and others.

A one-sheet contains brief information about your career on one sheet of paper (8.5" x 11") and is formatted so that it can be viewed quickly in one glance.

Here are a few quick tips for creating your very own artist one-sheet.

- **Name/logo:** Include your artist name centered at the top of the page. If you write your name using a particular font, or if you have a logo that includes both your name and a graphic (known as a combinedmark), then be sure to use it here.
- **Photograph**: Insert your picture at the top left corner of the page just below your name. It's okay to use one of a variety of shots—a studio profile shot, a lifestyle shot, or a live performance shot. But note that because a one-sheet only allows for a photgraph that's about 4" x 6" in size, the larger your image in the shot, and the clearer your face is shown in the picture without a lot of background noise, the better.
- **Key accomplishments and information:** Insert specific and measurable accomplishments about your band, and format it so that the information wraps around your photograph (i.e., insert the text to the right of the picture). The information should be short and sweet and be phrased in a way so that the most powerful words come at the front of the phrase. For instance, instead of writing: "Played a showcase at SXSW music conference in 2016," you might write: "SXSW Showcase Performance, 2016." Or, instead of writing: "Charted on the CMJ Top 200 College Music Charts in August 2016", you might write, "CMJ Top 200 Charts, Aug 2016."
- **Biographical information:** Include a brief bio about your career directly below your picture. Include the date your band formed (or the date you started writing for your solo record), the city in which you reside, and a short description of your sound (genre and like bands). You can also include the names of the musicians and the instruments they play. For instance, a band might write: "Formed in 2015 in Los Angeles, California, Rally the Tribes is a rock/rave band in the style of Tupac, meets Skrillex, meets Rage Against the Machine. Founding members include Kennedy Robert Jr. on vocals, K. Luther Martin on turntables, Ace Lincoln on guitar, Robbie Roosevelt on electric drums, and Churchill Preston on electric cello and bass guitar."
- **Contact:** Include a place where the reader can find more information about you. A Web URL, an e-mail address, and/or a phone number is all you need. Keep it simple.
- **Design:** Use the colors, typeface, and layout that conveys your desired image.

While the style described above is rather standard, be clear that one-sheets can come in all types of designs.

Sometimes one-sheets (or "distributor one-sheets") are used to publicize an artist's recording. In this case, a photograph of the recording's artwork is also included together with the track listings, song lengths, and the album's identification code (called a barcode).

Be sure to search the Web for a variety of one-sheets and decide on the style that works best for you. Also be sure to study the artist one-sheet I've included as a sample on the previous page.

Method #6: Create a Practical Business Card

To complete this chapter on creating promotional content, now I'll discuss the physical business card, which is something every artist should have in his or her pocket when networking.

A business card provides your contact information and helps to convey your brand image. It can be used when networking with professionals face-to-face at conferences, and when sending materials to press persons and sponsors via the mail.

While there are hundreds of design and print options available online, you'll find the following 15 brief tips helpful in creating a business card that's just right for you.

- **Name/title:** Feature your professional business name and professional role where it is easy to see and read. If you're a singer-songwriter, use your stage name followed by "singer-songwriter" (e.g., Jane Doe, Singer-Songwriter). If you're a band, include the band name as well as the name of the person responsible for handling the business (e.g., Zombie Zone, Business Contact: John Doe). You get the idea.
- **Logo:** Use your logo to help convey the image you'd like to project in the minds of your target audience. This can simply mean using a specific typeface for your business name, including the right graphic merged with your company name in a specific typeface, or including a graphic that helps convey your image. If you have not yet designed a logo, contact a graphic designer today or consider fast and affordable options found on sites like Fiverr (www.fiverr.com).
- **Slogan or tag line:** Include a short phrase that provides more information about who you are and what you do. A slogan is not for everyone, but you'd be surprised at the number of people who use them. The Los Angeles indie metal band Clepto, which has Saudi Arabian roots, uses the slogan "Thrash Punk Gypsies," which totally sums up the band's sound and spirit.
- **E-mail:** Use a reliable e-mail address that, in the best case, helps brand your business. For instance, rather than use something abstract like 123@gmail.com, use something more personalized and professional like janedoe@janedoemusic.com. To learn how to get your personalized e-mail, go to GoDaddy (www.godaddy.com) or just search online using keywords like "personalized e-mail address."
- **Website/social media URLs:** Add your personal website URL and/or one or two key social media sites. Just be careful not to include too many URLs or your card will look cluttered and confuse people.
- **Quick response (QR) code:** Consider generating your own QR code (utilizing one of a number of services you can find online, such as www.qr-code-generator.com) and including it on your business card. When a person scans your QR code with his or her smartphone, he or she will be taken immediately to your website or some other Web page you desire. Note: While QR codes were once all the rage, their popularity has died down a bit.
- **Phone number:** Include a phone number where people can get ahold of you. If possible, provide a line that you use exclusively for business. The last thing you want is to answer your phone in a silly voice thinking it's a friend, when it's an important business contact calling to offer you a gig.
- **Business address:** Consider adding a business mailing address, since it is quite possible that you will still have to use snail mail to receive signed copies of contracts and other items. However, think twice about including your home mailing address. You never really know who you're trading business cards with at networking events, and the last thing you want to do is let some nut know where you live. As an alternative to all of the above, you can at least list the city

and state you live in to give people a general sense of where you are located, and offer your full address later.

- **Photograph:** Consider including a photograph that clearly shows your face. This is a great way to ensure that people will remember you long after you've given them your card. If you're afraid that a picture will make your card look too cluttered, consider putting it on the back of your card. Note that double-sided cards are the rage these days.
- **Design:** Keep your design simple, spacious, and easy to read. As previously stated, you can choose a single-sided or double-sided card. You can use a variety of predesigned templates with a variety of different colors, font families, and layouts at print shops like Vistaprint (www.vistaprint.com), Moo (www.moo.com) or Tiny Prints (www.tinyprints.com), or upload your own design you create using a program like Adobe Photoshop. Generally, I'd suggest customizing your own design and uploading it, but I've seen several very cool template designs at the aforementioned sites too.
- **Shape/size:** Decide on the shape and size of your card. The standard is a rectangular shape that measures 3.5" x 2", but for a more unique look, you might try a square shape that measure 2.25" x 2.25". And if you are really bold, you might customize your card in the shape of a guitar or a record, but of course, you'll end up paying a lot more per card too.

GUITAR-SHAPED CARDS FRONT / BACK

- **Paper:** Choose standard, medium, or heavy paper for your business card. While standard paper is fine, a card with medium or heavy paper can help you stand out.
- **Finish:** Consider the variety of customized finishes available for your card. You can get a raised print that appears to pop off the page, a metallic finish that sparkles, or a gloss finish that shines (my favorite). Choose the finish that works best for your brand. And finally . . .
- **3-D printing, folded cards, plastic cards, and more**: Create a totally unique business card to stand out from the pack. Choose cards with 3-D designs and printing, folded two-panel business cards, plastic cards (similar to a credit card), aluminum multipurpose cards that double as bottle-openers and combs, and pick cards (heavy-duty celluloid cards that allow you to punch out a section and use it as a guitar pick). To get your unique card, check out PlasticPrinters.com (www.plasticprinters.com).

So that's pretty much all for business cards. If you're still undecided about the type of card that is right for you, note that most printers will send you samples to help you make your final decision.

Just be sure to check out the sample business card that I've provided, and surf the Web for a number of other examples, too. Have fun and good luck.

So that's it for this chapter. Coming up in the next (and last) chapter, you'll learn about creating even more promotional content, including interviews, elevator pitches, and postcards. By the time you're done reading, you are going to be armed with a lot of tools to succeed. I bet you're happy about that!

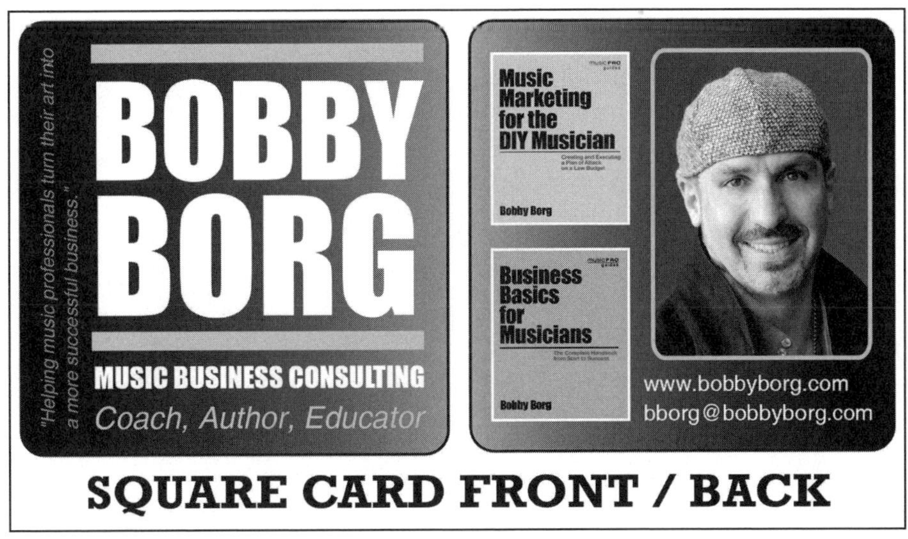

28 Creating Promotion Content That Sells: Part 2

In Part 1 you learned how to create important promotion content (methods #1–6) including introduction letters, one-sheets, and business cards. Now in Part 2, the focus will be on the following (methods #7–12):

7. Preparing your elevator pitch
8. Designing an effective flyer or postcard
9. Preparing a great interview
10. Creating merch items that help spread the word
11. Producing videos that get attention, and . . .
12. Developing and maintaining a personal website

Remember that all of this content will come in handy when networking at industry events to spread the word about your brand, compiling the information into physical or electronic press kits to send off to press persons, and posting content on your personal websites and social networks. And so much more.

So, without further delay, I say that we should get this show on the road. Let's do this.

Method #7: Prepare a Thirty-Second "Elevator Pitch"

An elevator pitch is a useful promotion tool when meeting new industry contacts face-to-face at networking events and conventions. It's called an elevator pitch because it's intended to grab a person's immediate attention and hold his or her interest within the time of a short elevator ride.

An elevator pitch must be well written and well rehearsed. While you may have to create a variety of different pitches based on who (booking agents, bloggers, sponsors, etc.) you are pitching, let's take a look at the essential elements you should include when preparing your pitch.

- **Name and a memorable twist:** Be prepared to state your personal name and title along with an interesting and memorable twist. For instance, I might say, "Hey there, my name is Bobby Borg. Borg, as in the Cyborg characters on Star Trek." While this is a little silly, it's memorable and can help break the ice and get a smile.
- **Flattery:** Consider complimenting the person that you are approaching. If at a convention, you might congratulate a person on their inspiring keynote presentation. Just don't overdo it. You don't want to sound like an overexcited fan.
- **Title and uniqueness:** State what you do and how you are unique. Are you a Native American rapper who draws awareness to indigenous rights, or a solo jazz guitarist who triggers robots to play multiple instruments on stage? Whatever makes you unique, just be sure to state it concisely.

- **Hype:** Include one or two of your most impressive accomplishments to build credibility. You might state that you are the recent winner of the John Lennon Songwriting Competition or a runner-up on the latest season of *American Idol* or *The Voice*.
- **Benefits:** State how you can help the person you are pitching. In other words, don't focus on you; focus on the recipient. For instance, you might say, "Given our upcoming tour with Band X, I'm confident that as an endorser of Pearl drums, I would get your company exposed significantly and help generate sales."
- **Appointment close:** Schedule a meeting where you can provide more information about what you have to offer. Prepare two convenient times and locations. For instance, you might say: "Can I buy you lunch in the hotel restaurant this Sunday at twelve thirty, or meet for a beverage in the lobby bar tonight at eight o'clock?"
- **Executive summary:** Have detailed information ready for your follow-up meeting. For instance, you might say more about what your long-term vision is, what your short-term goals are, how you plan to promote yourself, how much money you may need, what your biggest risks are, and how you plan to reduce these risks.
- **Objections:** Make a list of the things people may say in disagreement with what you have to offer, and create a series of wise answers. For instance, if a manager says that he or she is not currently looking for new clients, you might respond with, "I understand that you get pitched every five minutes by unknown acts at a convention like this, but we're convinced that you'll be absolutely impressed with our performance and draw. Can we send you an Uber to our show tonight and cover the tab for you and a guest? Would seven or seven thirty be best?" While this is an aggressive move on your part, many people will appreciate your salesmanship. Just be sure to always smile, don't stand too close to the person you are pitching, and be good at reading a person's body language. It's important to know when enough is enough.
- **Business card:** Offer to provide a business card to the person you are pitching, and ask for a card in return. Follow up in a week or two (or as otherwise directed).

So, that's about it for creating an elevator pitch. Check out the sample pitches below.

SAMPLE ELEVATOR PITCHES

What follows are two different elevator pitches: one for a personal manager and one for the artist relations director of a major equipment manufacturer. Note that they are not only thirty seconds long, they introduce, flatter, hype, sell a benefit, and strive to get an appointment where more information can be given.

Here's the pitch to the manager:

> Mr. Rick Sales! Excellent speech on management, sir. I'm with Kings of Carnage, an all-military metal band who recently played Knotfest with Slipknot. I'd love to have you see my band play tonight in the main ballroom at seven, or, at the least, to buy you lunch tomorrow at twelve and tell you more about my band. Might you be available, sir?

Now here's the pitch to the artist relations director:

> Hey, Christian, hope the NAMM show isn't too crazy for you. I'm Nathan Kotur of the band Kings of Carnage. We're attracting a lot of attention these days, and as a current user of Sabian, I was hoping that we might discuss how I can help promote your cymbals. Can I buy you a drink in the Hilton bar this evening, or lunch by the pool tomorrow afternoon?

Practice reading both of these pitches while changing the speed and tone of your voice. The point is to not sound like a robot. Once you get the hang of it, try writing an elevator pitch of your own and ask a friend to role-play with you.

A great elevator pitch can mean the difference between getting that manager or endorsement, or getting nowhere and feeling let down. So take this very seriously!

Now let's move on to flyers or postcards.

Method #8: Design an Effective Flyer or Postcard

Flyers and postcards are incredibly useful tools for getting the word out about your recording or live event. They can be handed out face-to-face to fans in front of venues, hung on the side of walls, and mailed via the United States Postal Service.

Besides providing basic information (like the date, time, and place of an event), a great flyer or postcard sells a benefit to the intended reader and triggers a buying action, such as purchasing your EP or coming to a record release performance.

While there are many ways to design a flyer or postcard, here are the core essentials:

- **Headline:** Create a short phrase at the top of the flyer or postcard that will grab the attention of your target audience. Consider using engaging words (like "introducing," "new," "exclusive," and "free") and crafting humorous or shocking questions or commands. For instance, you might write: "Looking to Get Laid?" or "Want to Get Paid to Play?" Just remember to feature your headline prominently in your design. The headline is the most important and most-read part of any flyer or postcard. As advertising legend David Ogilvy once said, "If the headline doesn't grab the reader, chances are that they will not read anything else."
- **Subhead:** Add a subhead that completes your headline and gets the interest of your target audience. For instance, below our clever headline "Want to Get Laid?," you might write: "Free Hawaiian-themed BBQ Bash with DJ Doe this July 4th." Keep this text slightly smaller than the headline so that it does not steal away any attention.
- **Body text:** Provide benefits that help your target audience make a decision about what you are offering. For example, tell the audience about the feel-good musical style of DJ Doe, the swimsuit contest with special prizes, the large pools and Jacuzzis on the premises, the free Hawaiian leis, and the wonderful BBQ food and drink specials. Present this information midway down the flyer or postcard (in the body or heart) and consider using smaller type size, bullet points, and short sentences.

- **Graphic:** Include an attractive high-resolution graphic that ties in nicely with the headline. You can use graphics anywhere in the design, but for a really cool effect, use them for your background with your text laid out on top (just be sure that your text is still readable). Use your own high-resolution images (such as the profile pictures you get done with a professional photographer), or search through hundreds of free stock photos on sites such as NASA (www.nasa.gov), StockSnap, (www.stocksnap.io), and Lock & Stock Photography (www.lockandstockphotos.com).
- **Call to Action:** Write a "call to action" at the bottom of your design to get your reader to take the next step. For instance, you might write, "To get leied this July 4th, RSVP at DJDoe.com." Use a medium to small type size.
- **Address/date/time:** Include important dates, addresses, phone numbers, websites, and start times. Provide this information in small type somewhere at the bottom of the flyer or card. If the date is very significant, such as a holiday, include the type at the top.
- **Logo(s):** Include your logo—and the logos of any sponsors that may be involved—anywhere on your flyer or postcard. Just be sure to keep your design clean and uncluttered.
- **Market information system code (MISC):** Use a market information system code in small print at the bottom of the flyer. An MISC helps you to monitor the effectiveness of your promotion, and adjust your promotion campaign accordingly. For example, you might write, "Use 'code beach' at the door to claim a free prize."
- **DIY vs. pro:** Use Adobe Photoshop to create your designs or just leave it up to one of your talented fans with graphic arts skills to help get the job done. If you can spring for it, hire a professional designer to create several basic templates that you can use throughout the year.
- **Design:** Be sure to use no more than three colors and typefaces per design and leave a lot of blank space (often referred to as negative space). Make sure your text is easy to read and that you leave enough room around the edges of your design to ensure that nothing cuts off in the printing process.
- **Size/paper/finish:** Make your flyers no larger than 8.5" x 11" and your postcards no larger than 4.4" x 6". Use heavy high quality paper and glossy finishes whenever applicable. And finally . . .
- **Printing:** To print your flyers and postcards, take your design to local print shops or use online companies like Vistaprint (www.vistaprint.com), Overnight Prints (www.overnightprints.com), or Zazzle (www.zazzle.com).

That's pretty much it. To learn more about creative designs and effective advertising, read books like *Kiss and Sell*, by Robert Sawyer, and *Graphic Design for Non Graphic Designers*, by Tony Seddon and Jane Waterhouse. Also check out resources like Brandweek, AdWeek, and Advertising Age.

Be sure to check out the sample postcard that I created as well. Have fun!

Method #9: Prepare a Great Interview (Oral and Written)

Getting close to the end of this chapter, and this book, it's time to discuss one of the best forms of promotion for an artist: the interview.

Whether communicated orally or in writing, interviews help to inform your target audience about who you are and why they should care. Additionally, they help to communicate your personality in a way that is unmatched by other promotion tools discussed so far.

Great interviews don't happen by accident. Both parties, the interviewer and the interviewee, typically do a great deal of preliminary research. In fact, preparing your complete interview in writing before the interview can serve as helpful research for the busy interviewer and provide additional content that can be posted on your personal websites.

Below are a few of the most common interview topics—from the meaning of your name, to how your band formed, to your closing thoughts. A good portion of these issues have already been discussed in previous chapters, so you should be ready to fire off some great commentary.

- **Name:** Be prepared to succinctly describe the purpose behind your name. Ryan Raddon, a popular American DJ, chose the stage name Kaskade after he saw a picture of a waterfall, which he felt fit perfectly with the continuous, flowing sounds and textures he creates on stage.
- **Sound/style:** Be ready to state your genre, name a few like bands, and offer a fun and descriptive phrase that perfectly sums up your sound and style. For instance, the Tikiyaki Orchestra describes itself as being an "exotica band in the style of Martin Denny and Arthur Lyman," "a broad mix of lounge, Latin, and Hawaiian music," and "a sonic adventure to a faraway South Pacific island."

- **Audience:** Use the information you gathered from my chapter on analyzing your fans and explain to whom your music appeals. For instance, Lady Gaga's audience is specifically made up of electropop fans, as well as the "the outsider culture—the freaks, the rebellious and the dispossessed." The more concise you are, the better.
- **Earliest influences:** Describe the various musicians who helped shaped your musical sound and style early on. For me, it was the drummers on the big band albums that my father played around the house (mainly Buddy Rich and Gene Krupa), and on the rock albums that my older brother blasted from his room (mainly Ginger Baker and John Bonham). By the way, this question is one of the most common interview questions asked, so be prepared to answer it succinctly.
- **Biggest inspiration:** Explain how you got started in music. Nas's exposure to his father's professional jazz instruments (mainly trumpet), and his father's large collection of books (including Sun Tzu's *The Art of War*) were huge motivators. Additionally, the struggles he witnessed in his hood of Queens, New York, and his desire for a better life motivated him to start writing raps at a very young age.
- **How the band formed:** Formulate a genuine answer that everyone in your group can agree on in advance. For instance, in 2007, Passion Pit started in one member's dorm room at Emerson College in Boston. Coldplay started after Chris Martin met Jonny Buckland during orientation week at University College London in 1996—or was it during spring break in 1993? Get what I mean? Have your story together.
- **Current record/tour/crusade:** Explain the purpose behind your current project and why people should take notice. For instance, Cypress Hill founded the Cypress Hill Smokeout "to create the ultimate music-fusion festival and advance and educate festival-goers on the medical marijuana movement." Bam! Nice and concise! SupaMan, a Native American rapper, began making music "to bring awareness to the injustices suffered by indigenous people and prove that native lives matter." Wow! Now that's what I call music with a mission.
- **Differentiators**: Explain what separates your work from others'. When jazz guitarist Pat Metheny introduced his album *Orchestrion* (which featured robots triggered by switches), he positioned it as the "first and never-to-be-done-again technological project intended to push new limits." When Nas released his album *Life Is Good*, he differentiated it as being "unlike most of the music in my genre that tends to dwell on the darker side of life."
- **Funny/crazy stories:** Be prepared to share a short tale from the studio or the stage. Ozzy Osbourne got so drunk that he snorted a line of ants. Keith Richards mixed his dead father's ashes with a line of cocaine. And Keith Moon filled his clear drums with goldfish and water, and performed a live concert dressed like a cat. Okay, so you may not be able to top these stories, but I bet you have something interesting to share.
- **Hobbies:** Reveal what you do outside of music. In the best case, you'll share something that reinforces your brand image and/or endears you to your target fan. For instance, Rivers Cuomo (of the nerd/alternative/pop band Weezer), claims he knits sweaters. A coincidence or silly joke? Weezer's biggest hit was "Sweater Song."
- **Upcoming projects:** Be prepared to fire off what's next on your agenda. Have the exact dates of performances and the release dates of your singles. Don't mess this up—the whole point of giving interviews is to ultimately sell your products and services and generate income. And finally . . .

- **Closing thoughts (anything else you want to add):** Leave your contact information, thoughtful quotes, shout-outs to people who have helped you, and reminders to buy your music. Or you might leave some important message to the world like, "Don't forget to save the whale forests, everyone." Ha ha. You get the idea.

When answering the questions in a written interview, the process is pretty straightforward (you write thoughtful, concise responses and make sure to check your grammar and spelling). However, when answering these questions in a live face-to-face interview, you must remember a number of things.

First, you must have basic interview skills together. Always repeat questions before your answer, use dynamics and various speech rates, be aware of your body movement (sit up straight, make eye contact, and speak into the microphone), make sure your clothing does not give the camera a sneak peek of what's underneath), and keep your answers short and sweet.

Second, you must also be prepared to respond to that uncomfortable question that might get thrown at you. Stay calm, breathe deeply, smile, and think before speaking. Don't be afraid to tell the interviewer that you wish to skip the question if you feel too uncomfortable to answer.

Finally, you must know something about the interviewer. I've literally started interviewing the host at a time when he left a long, uncomfortable pause. Yikes!

For more information on the things I've covered here, check out *Interview Tactics*, by Gayle Murphy, *Emotional Intelligence*, by Daniel Goldberg, and *How to Read a Person Like a Book*, by Gerard Nierenberg.

Now check out a few funny stories below that I often tell in the interviews that I give.

MY PERSONAL CRAZY/FUNNY STORIES

While on the topic of crazy or funny stories that can be used in interviews, I thought that I would share two stories of my own.

A reporter was asking my band the strangest questions during an interview (things like "If you had one week to live, what color would you be emotionally?"). So when the interview was over and the interviewer left the hotel room, we started bad-mouthing him. After about five minutes of this, he returned to our door claiming that he had forgotten something. As it turns out, it was his tape recorder, which he had left running. Yes, everything bad that we said about the interviewer was captured on tape. Yikes! Needless to say, he never ran our story.

While playing a packed house in Los Angeles at Universal Amphitheater (capacity 7,000), my singer looked at me and called what I thought was the last song of the band's set. So, naturally, on the last note of the song, I kicked over my drum set as I usually did and ran out to the front of the stage like a total maniac. My singer looked at me and at my kit smashed all over the stage with an expression of complete horror. You see, we still hadn't played the band's grand finale hit. What had I been I thinking? While my techs frantically rebuilt my kit, my singer did his best at talking to the audience. I still laugh about that moment now and again.

Now let's move away from interview techniques and discuss merchandising.

Method #10: Design Merchandising Items That Help Spread the Word

Merchandising (a.k.a merch) refers to the T-shirts, hats, and stickers that bear your name, logo or slogan. They help to increase your exposure, strengthen your brand name, and provide an ancillary form of income.

Merch is one of the best ways to stimulate word-of-mouth promotion. Just one fan wearing your T-shirt to school can stimulate interest and get people talking. Multiply that fan by ten, another ten, and then another ten, and you have a virtual army of walking billboard advertisements around your hometown.

Merch also brings your audience "closer" and makes them feel like a part of your tribe. Slipping into your uniform and flying your team's colors immediately makes them a brand representative. Their identity, in part, is formed through you—and this builds loyal fans.

Last, merch can generate a substantial amout of money for you. A young band who may still have to play for free can bring in enough money to cover road expenses and get to the next city safely. This is why creating a solid merchandising plan is important.

To ensure that you receive all the benefits from the merch that you create, here are a few tips to think about.

- **Shirt styles:** Create a variety of shirts including short-sleeved T-shirts, long-sleeved T-shirts, tank tops, baseball jerseys, and women's baby T's. If you can only afford to make one style of shirt, ask your target fans what style they prefer most.
- **Secondary merch:** Create a number of secondary merchandising items that are appropriate for your target fans. This might include hats, hoodies, patches, bandanas, stickers, buttons, lighters, condoms, dog tags, cinch bags, koozies, and more.
- **Name/logo:** Promote your name and logo on your merchandising items. Common designs include a wordmark (your full name in a unique typeface like Iron Maiden's logo), a lettermark (your name abbreviated in a cool typeface like Nine Inch Nails's logo), or a combinedmark (your name in a unique typeface merged with an image, like Wu-Tang Clan's logo).
- **Symbolism:** Stimulate intrigue by using a cool and mysterious image on your merchandising items. This might be a brandmark (an image without your name, like the Rolling Stones' tongue logo or the Misfits' skull logo).
- **Song lyrics:** Use a cool lyric from one of your songs to help promote your brand. The California metal band Atreyu had its lyric "Live, Love, Burn, and Die" from its single "Lip Gloss and Black" all over its merchandising. Beyoncé had "I sneezed on the beat and the beat got sicka" from her song "Partition" as one of her T-shirt designs.
- **Album titles:** Use album titles to promote your recording and give your fans a clean and simple merchandising design. One of the most popular examples of a band that uses its album title on T-shirts is AC/DC. To this day, the words Back in Black can be seen across the chests of rock fans everywhere.
- **Slogans:** Create merch with slogans that are so interesting and fun, people will want to wear the items just for the merch itself—regardless of whether or not they've heard of your band. The California-based smooth R&B artist Nathan Nice cleverly designed a women's baby T-shirt with the phrase "Naughty or Nice?" on the front and www.nathannice.com on the back. According to him, girls were buying several shirts at a time for themselves and their girlfriends, sisters, and mothers back home.

- **Album cover/tour dates:** Include a graphic of your album cover on the front and the dates of all your shows on the back. This is the classic T-shirt design that you've probably seen at the concerts of famous bands.
- **Colors and typefaces:** Use the colors and typefaces that represent your brand. Harley Davidson (a company regularly associated with music culture) consistently uses the colors black and orange in all of its merchandising (and its website and logo designs). When you see black and orange jackets or shirts, you almost immediately know it's Harley Davidson without even seeing the name. That's pretty powerful.
- **Do it yourself:** Create shirts using a number of available home tools. Use Adobe Photoshop to prepare your designs, buy T-shirts like Hanes or American Apparel brand, and print your designs on heat transfer paper that can be applied with a hot iron. You can also tie-dye your shirts by folding them into patterns, binding them with string or rubber bands, and applying special inks that can be found in local hardware stores. Some bands even go as far as screen printing their own shirts (a process that can be quite messy if you don't know what you are doing). Whatever methods you use, just be sure that you create the level of quality that fits your brand.
- **Merch on demand:** Check out companies that manufacture merch items as they are ordered and that cover all up-front costs. This is a convenient method when you are low on investment capital and when considering secondary merchandising items like coffee cups that are difficult to carry from gig to gig or mail to fans. Check out companies such as CafePress (www.cafepress.com), and Zazzle (www.zazzle.com).
- **Professional companies:** Use companies experienced in handling a variety of merchandising products ranging from the basics (T-shirts, hoodies, and hats) to secondary items (lighters, patches, and rolling papers). Using a pro provides many options compared to doing it yourself—you receive help with design and print preparation, you can choose from a variety of different inks, and you can receive discounts for bulk printing services. While using a pro is more expensive, the results are also guaranteed. Find reputable and experienced companies online by using key words like "screen printing" and "promotional items," or ask other local bands for recommendations.

For further ideas and guidance, examine the merchandising concepts and designs of bands who are most like you. Check out their website stores and you'll find all of the information you need. Beyoncé has quite an extensive line of shirts and secondary merch items on her site.

Also be sure to check out the sites of major merchandisers such as Bravado (www.bravado.com), Band Merch (www.bandmerch.com), and Global Merchandising Services (www.globalmerchservices.com). These companies represent some of the world's best bands.

Now, with only two topics left, let's move on to videos, which all of you should be creating and posting online.

Method #11: Produce Videos That Get Attention

Videos posted on video sharing sites, personal websites, and blogs have become an incredible method to promote your music.

Sites like YouTube (www.youtube.com), Vimeo (www.vimeo.com), DailyMotion (www.dailymotion.com/us), StupidVideos (www.stupidvideos.com), eBaums World (www.ebaumsworld.com), Break (www.break.com), and Ustream (http://www.ustream.tv) host millions of videos featuring artists just like you.

But with the vast number of videos on the Web these days, how can one expect to get noticed amid the clutter? Here are some basic tips to creating video content that gets attention.

- **Humor:** Create videos that stimulate laughter—laughter makes people feel good. Singer-songwriter Dave Carroll wrote and filmed a humorous video called "United Breaks Guitars" after the airline trashed one of his instruments during a flight. Not only did the video receive several million hits, Dave received a sponsorship from a guitar case company and wrote a book on customer service. To check out Dave's video, search online for "United Breaks Guitars."
- **Lifestyle:** Create videos that depict the lifestyles of your fans and set your music as the soundtrack. If you're an alternative, punk, or metal band, you might create a video with rad skateboard footage of kids riding in the parks of Venice Beach, kids jumping the stairs at Hollywood High school, or kids cruising down the Hollywood Walk of Fame at night—all set to your songs. To view lifestyle videos, check out Skatevideosite (www.skatevideosite.com) and other sites like it.
- **Lyric:** Develop videos that feature the written lyrics to one of your songs set over cool still photographs and video footage. While lyric videos were originally created by fans as a show of admiration to the artists they loved, bands are releasing their own lyric videos, too. To view the most popular lyric videos, search for "When I Was Your Man," by Bruno Mars, "Problem," by Ariana Grande, and "Wake Me Up," by Avicii.
- **Cover:** Film yourself covering a hit song and capitalize on that song's built-in audience. While there are millions of artists already doing this, there are new success stories unfolding seemingly every day. Chloe and Halle, an adorable teen sister duo, attracted the attention of megastar Beyoncé after posting a cover of the pop diva's song "Pretty Hurts." Subsequently, the girls signed a five-year management contract to Beyoncé's company, Parkwood Entertainment. Now that's impressive!
- **Fan-generated:** For instance, initiate a fun contest for the best lip-synched video of one of your singles. This might motivate your fans to create cool video content and help you spread the word of mouth.
- **Shock:** Use shock as another method to promote your music and get people interested in your band. Rapper Tyler the Creator released a video of him eating a Madagascar cockroach, throwing up, and then hanging himself. The video received nearly 100 million hits and still counting. Shock may not work for you if you're a Christian country artist, but it could certainly work wonders for just about everyone else. Human beings are psychologically drawn to shock and gore. Why not give this a try?
- **News/commentary/interview:** Report upcoming shows, important happenings in your career, or thoughts about world events. Film interviews about how you got started or how you are enjoying life on the road. All this shows off a more personal side of your brand and helps you to connect with fans in an entirely natural way.

- **Live streaming:** Use sites like Ustream (http://www.ustream.tv) and StageIt (www.stageit.com) to present "real-time" videos for your audience. For instance, you can invite fans to tune in with you at a set hour every night while you're recording your album and ask them for feedback. This makes fans feel like they are really invested in your cause.
- **Documentary:** Record a documentary about the making of your band. Film clips of the house you grew up in, the high school where your band members met, and any other behind-the-scenes footage you can think of. Fans really love this type of stuff because it helps them to learn more about the person behind the artist. Check out documentaries like *Time Is Illmatic* by Nas.
- **Standard video:** Record the typical music video of you performing along to one of your studio recordings. Just be sure to hire the appropriate professionals (i.e., actors, models, and/or dancers) where you might be lacking. If there is one thing that the world can do without, it's more bad actors. [Ha ha.]
- **Live performance:** Capture footage of you performing live on stage. Club bookers and equipment sponsors typically love this type of footage since it doesn't lie—what they see and hear is what they know they are going to get.
- **Slideshow:** Use amazing still photographs of you and your band to create slideshow videos. You can use several videos that fade in and out using that awesome Ken Burns effect, or you can just use one continual shot of your album cover and URL.
- **DIY production:** Get your videos produced by rolling up your sleeves and doing it yourself. Use high-def digital video cameras (like the ones by Canon or Sony), editing software (like Sony Vegas Pro or Final Cut Pro), and stock footage from sites like Videoblocks (www.videoblocks.com). You might also think about using online tools like Animoto (http://animoto.com) to produce fun videos using your photos and video clips. Just remember that producing high-quality videos yourself requires a little know-how and a lot of patience. Bottom line: you gotta have some skills. And . . .
- **Professional videographers:** Hire a senior student at a local film school who has access to great equipment (which could cost you nothing or a few hundred dollars), a videographer at a club who is set up to record your live show (which could cost $100 to $200), or an experienced professional who makes documentaries and videos for a living (which could cost you from $3,000 to more than $35,000). Keep in mind that the multiple cameras, professional lighting, sound equipment, editing expertise, sound stage, make-up artists, and fashion consultants that professionals use make a big difference in quality. Contact local colleges, ask for referrals from other bands in your area who already have great videos you've seen, or just conduct a search online for videographers to find someone who you feel can get the job done right.

Just be sure to keep up to date with the latest techniques for creating and promoting video content. Search keywords online like "video content creation" and "YouTube tutorials." You'll learn basic tips about posting consistently, titling your videos, tagging your videos with keywords so that they are easier to find, including links to get people to subscribe to your videos, responding to comments, and so much more One of my favorite tutorial pages can be found on YouTube here: https://www.youtube.com/yt/creators/tutorials.html. Enjoy!

Method #12: Develop and Maintain a Personal Website

Finally, the last promotion tool of this chapter is your personal website. I saved this for last, because a website can contain virtually all of the tools previously discussed—from bios, to press releases, to photos, to interviews.

Personal websites serve as your home base on the Web where you drive traffic from other online and offline sources. A personal website is where you want to inform your target audience about what you do, capture important data about your fans, and sell your products and services.

Since there is so much information available on the Web about developing personal websites, we'll look at just a few of the basics to get your creative juices flowing.

- **Platform/service/software:** Choose between easy-to-build software programs (such as Adobe Dreamweaver), pre-built or template sites and services (such as HostBaby or Bandzoogle), and a number of free service destinations online (such as WordPress, Flavors.Me, Virb, Wix, or Squarespace). Where the above methods may be lacking, you can use a variety of Web tools or widgets that can be embedded onto your site allowing visitors to download music, order merchandise, buy tickets, join your fan clubs, view pictures, and more (check out Bandcamp and FanBridge for starters).
- **Design:** Use a theme and layout that engages your target audience and reinforces your desired brand image. I've seen artists use a blog/news format with information in chronological order that fans can scroll, one solid background picture with menu links at the top that fans can click on, and an elaborate landing page with spinning graphics and menu links. Be sure that your design looks equally great on a number of different devices (mobile phone, desktop computer, and tablet). For examples of the aforementioned designs, check out Green Day (www.greenday.com), Beyoncé (www.beyonce.com), and Tool (www.toolband.com), but note that these sites may have changed since the time of this writing.
- **Menu items:** Create important pages such as an about page (that includes your biography and interviews), a media page (that includes music samples and videos clips), a store (that offers your merch and recordings in physical and digital formats), a mailing list (that includes fields to capture e-mails), a news page (that provides the latest reviews and gossip), a gig page (that lists upcoming gigs), and a contact page (that includes your e-mail). These are the standard menu items and pages. You don't have to use all of these ideas, just choose the one that work best for you.
- **Social media buttons:** Be sure to also include the social media buttons for your most-frequented social media sites. These might include Facebook, Instagram, YouTube, SoundCloud, and Snapchat.
- **Current content:** Create and upload new content continually. Don't leave your site stagnant or people won't come back. Upload new songs, lyrics, pictures, podcasts, videos, surveys, contests, testimonials, press releases, and tour dates. For more advice on creating promotional content for the Web, check out two classic books: *The Copywriter's Handbook*, by Robert Bly, and *The Idea Writers*, by Teressa Iezzi.

- **Optimization:** To help ensure that your target fans will find your site (a process called "optimization"), be sure to do the following: Regularly identify keywords that people might use to search for the type of things you offer (e.g., "music in L.A.," "local bands in Austin," etc.), strategically incorporate these words into the text of your site, and then make sure your web developer uses these words when creating meta tags and meta descriptions for your site. Be sure to post your website link literally everywhere (on social networks, blogs, and other relevant websites) and ask these sites to link back to you. This is just the tip of the iceberg. If all this sounds confusing, read books like *SEO: Search Engine Optimization Bible*, by Jerri Ledford, visit sites like Search Engine Watch (www.searchenginewatch.com), and contact a hosting service like GoDaddy (www.GoDaddy.com), which can tell you about the SEO services they provide.
- **Hosting:** Pick any one of a number of affordable hosting companies (such as GoDaddy) to launch your site on the Web, to register a domain (.com, .net, .org), and to provide a number of other services (like setting up your e-mail address).
- **DIY:** Build and maintain a site yourself using helpful books like *Web Design All-In-One for Dummies* by Sue Jenkins. Hey, if the results uphold your desired brand image, then why not go for it? And finally . . .
- **Professional developer:** Use a professional Web developer if you have the money needed to cover the costs (a basic site can cost anywhere from $1,500 to $5,000) and if you lack the skills and the patience to do it yourself. Seek referrals from close friends, contact art schools for competent graduates, or use a website like Freelancer (www.freelancer.com) where developers submit bids for the job.

So that's about all on creating winning content that sells. Again, while things like writing bios and one-sheets really are not rocket science, it's amazing how many people get some of the most basic elements of promotion wrong.

I hope that you've found the tips that I've provided in the last two chapters, as well as the theoretical aspects of promotion in the first three chapters, helpful in getting you started toward achieving the five-star results that you deserve.

And remember, for more information on music marketing and music business in general, please reach out to me at www.bobbyborg.com, where you'll find my other books (*Music Marketing for the DIY Musician* and *Business Basics for Musicians*), free articles, and one-on-one coaching opportunities. Cheers and all the best.

Index

Image Credits

Part 1: The Voice: p. 1—photo by Natalie Bopp; p. 15 and 16—artwork by Coreen Sheehan, Mark Thomas, and Natalie Bopp; p. 6, 9, 10, 12, 27 (keys), 53, 65, and 72—iStock; p.7, 17, 20, 21, 22, 27, 28, 32, 33, 34, 36, 37, 38, 39, 40, 43, 46, 50, 51, and 55—courtesy of Coreen Sheehan.

Part 2: The Art of Songwriting: p. 73—photo by Leanna Conley; p. 78, 95, 101, 102, 109, 110, 111, 113, 124, 133, 136 (Billie Holiday), and 138—artwork by Anika Paris; p. 81, 83, 84, 85, and 89—artwork by Anika Paris, with images from iStock; p. 134, 136, 137, 130 (LP), 139, 140, and 141—iStock.

Part 3: Recording and Production: p. 143—Triffin Constantine; p. 152, 158, 166, 173, 174, 175, 176, 177, 178, 179, 180, and 189—diagrams by Ben Loshin; p. 175, 186, 187, 191, 194, 196, 197, 200, 201, 204, 206, 207, 210, and 214—screenshots courtesy of Eric Corne; p. 177—photo by Eric Corne.

Part 4: Music Publishing: p. 217—photo by Clinton Ashton; p. 224 and 225—artwork by Mark Nubar.

Part 5: Promotion: p. 265—photo by Todd Cheney/UCLA Photography; p. 269, 271, 284, 290, and 297—Jessica Rottshafer; p. 284 (Word of Mouth) and 299—courtesy of Bobby Borg; p. 282—courtesy of Loren Barnese; p. 314 and 314—Sabrina Petrini; p. 318 and 319—courtesy of Tania Pryor of plasticprinters.com; p. 325—iStock.